THE
GREEK
POETS

THE
GREEK
POETS

EDITED, WITH AN INTRODUCTION, BY

MOSES HADAS *Associate Professor of Greek and Latin*

COLUMBIA UNIVERSITY

THE MODERN LIBRARY · NEW YORK

Library of Congress Catalog Card Number: 52-9774

Random House IS THE PUBLISHER OF *The Modern Library*

BENNETT A. CERF · DONALD S. KLOPFER · ROBERT K. HAAS

Manufactured in the United States of America

By H. Wolff

PREFACE

THE ANTHOLOGIST of Greek poetry must be haunted by the thought that his ancient colleagues were responsible for the loss of the bulk of classical Greek poetry. He may draw solace from the reflection that if what they failed to include fell into oblivion, perhaps what they did include would not otherwise have survived. Happily the power of the anthologist is no longer so absolute, for full printed texts are preserved in many libraries; nevertheless, his responsibility both to the ancients and to posterity remains great. Whatever the anthologist's intentions, for a large number of readers the Greek poets he chooses, and the versions in which he chooses to present them, come to constitute a sort of canon.

It is with this consideration in mind that the selections here presented have been made. It might be argued (as Theocritus complains his contemporaries argued) that Homer is enough: fill the book with Homer and you have the best. Or, as my friend Mark Van Doren has in fact suggested, put in a single Greek tragedy instead of selections from many. There can be no question that Homer is better read as a whole, or that any single tragedy will convey a truer notion of the whole than snippets from many. But here the assumption is made that the reader possesses Homer and knows what a Greek tragedy is. For both Homer and tragedy, therefore, the editor has preferred to present a number of characteristic passages in a studied variety of translations, so that the reader who knows these works may have a selection of significant passages and of various modes of translation. This has made possible the inclusion of more extensive selections from poets who are likely to be less familiar—Hesiod and the Homeric Hymns, Apollonius and Quintus and Musaeus, even the Battle of the Frogs and the Mice.

The criterion has been the Greek rather than the version. First a list of passages was drawn up, and then suitable translations were sought. The editor is well enough aware that some of the selections are not great poetry; their inclusion was in his judgment necessary in order to present a complete picture. Translators have of course been allowed to retain their own terminology and spelling; it is assumed that the reader will move easily from Aphrodite to Venus, from Hermes to Mercury, from "colour" to "color." The arrangement is mainly chronological, but other factors have been considered. Thus *Batrachomyomachia*, though of later date, has been put after authentic heroic poetry, the philosophical poets after Hesiod, and the Hellenistic poets more or less by genre. In lyric the order is elegy, iambic, solo lyric, and choral lyric. This arrangement follows that in my own *History of Greek Literature*, and has been found practical in teaching.

Where necessary the location of the passage in the standard Greek text is indicated at the foot of a passage. The names and dates of both authors and translators are listed in the Index. Here it remains to express grateful acknowledgement to publishers and individuals who have made materials available; the numbers in brackets refer to selections in this volume:

University of Chicago Press: Richmond Lattimore, *The Iliad of Homer*, 1951 (1, 5, 33); Frank L. Clark, *A Study of the Iliad in Translation*, 1927 (9); Richmond Lattimore, *The Odes of Pindar*, 1947 (137-38); David Grene, *Three Greek Tragedies in Translation*, 1942 (171-2).

Oxford University Press: George Ernle, *The Wrath of Achilleus*, 1922 (2, 13, 23); William Wallace and Mary Wallace, *Asklepiades of Samos*, 1941 (246-9, 251); Edwyn Bevan, *The Poems of Leonidas of Tarentum*, 1931 (260).

H. N. Couch, *Beauty and Parting*, 1945 (7, 162, 296).

Macmillan and Co., Ltd.: Andrew Lang, Walter Leaf, and Ernest Myers, *The Iliad*, 1883 (11, 20, 27).

George G. Harrap and Co., Ltd.: H. B. Cotterill, *Homer's Odyssey*, 1911 (36, 44, 50).

Estate of Lewis Parke Chamberlayne, 1880-1918 (45, 264, 282, 298, 344-5, 370, 372, 375).

Norman O. Brown and the University of Wisconsin Press: *Classics in Translation*, 1952 (66, 69).

Emily Ann Wolff: original versions (74-5).

Charles H. Kahn: original versions (76-9, 201, 213).

Open Court Publishing Co.: William Ellery Leonard, *The Fragments of Empedocles*, 1908 (80-81).

Martin Ostwald: original version (88).

Benj. H. Sanborn and Co.: Paul Shorey, *Horace: Odes and Epodes*, 1898 (91).

Richmond Lattimore, *Twelve Greek Lyrics*, Bryn Mawr, 1949 (99-101, 103, 110-111, 113, 136). See also under "University of Chicago Press."

Harvard University Press: J. M. Edmonds, *Lyra Graeca I*, 1922 (127); F. G. Allinson, *Menander*, 1921 (217-18); A. S. Way, *Quintus of Smyrna*, 1913 (337-40); W. H. D. Rouse, *Nonnos*, 1940 (351), all the above reprinted by permission of the publishers from the Loeb Classical Library; Henry Harmon Chamberlin, *Last Flowers*, 1937 (278-81).

Basil Blackwell and Mott, Ltd.: G. B. Grundy, *Ancient Gems in Modern Settings*, 1913 (132).

Barnicott's, Ltd., Taunton, England: Arthur S. Way, *The Odes of Bacchylides in English Verse* (Macmillan and Co.), 1927 (139).

Heath Cranton, Ltd.: J. C. Wordsworth, *Adventures in Literature*, 1929 (152, 178, 181, 266-9).

Dial Press: Moses Hadas and J. H. McLean, *The Plays of Euripides*, 1936 (169-70, 173, 176).

Methuen and Co., Ltd.: G. M. A. Grube, *The Drama of Euripides*, 1941 (177, 182).

John Murray: William Rann Kennedy, *The Plutus of Aristophanes*, 1912 (198).

The Richards Press, Ltd.: Walter Leaf, *Little Poems from the Greek*, 1922 (203, 244, 286-7, 299).

Ralph Gladstone: original versions (205, 324).

Bowes and Bowes, Ltd.: F. E. Garrett, *Rhymes and Renderings*, 1887 (206).

Earl of Cromer: *Paraphrases and Translations from the Greek*, 1903 (242-3, 257, 261, 292, 304-5, 307, 317, 333, 350, 361).

Routledge and Kegan Paul, Ltd.: J. A. Pott, *Greek Love Songs and Epigrams from the Anthology*, 1911 (252, 256, 343); F. A. Wright, *The Poets of the Greek Anthology* and *The Girdle of Aphrodite*, no dates (258, 301-2, 306, 309, 313, 316, 342, 346-8, 364).

Yale University Press: W. C. Lawton, *The Soul of the Anthology*, 1923 (262, 288, 310-11, 357, 359).

J. M. Dent and Sons Ltd.: A. S. Way, *The Tale of the Argonauts*, 1901 (263).

Columbia University Press: J. Hammer and M. Hadas, *Koerte's Hellenistic Poetry*, 1929 (275-7, 283).

Ernest Benn Ltd.: William Stebbing, *Greek and Latin Anthology Thought into English Verse*, 1923 (289, 358, 360).

Longmans Green and Co. Ltd.: Andrew Lang, *Grass of Parnassus*, 1892 (291, 368).

Elsie Spoerl: original versions (303, 315, 318, 354-6, 363).

For advice, encouragement, or the loan of books I should like to record my thanks to my friends and colleagues Angus Burrell, Andrew Chiappe, Gilbert Highet, Marjorie Nicolson, and Mark Van Doren.

MOSES HADAS

Columbia University
25 June, 1952

CONTENTS

		Page
Preface		v
Introduction		xiii

Selection Number

1-35	Homer: *Iliad*	3
36-55	Homer: *Odyssey*	62
56-61	Hesiod	106
62-72	*Homeric Hymns*	116
73	*Batrachomyomachia*	145
74-75	Xenophanes	154
76-79	Parmenides	155
80-81	Empedocles	158
82	Callinus	160
83-84	Tyrtaeus	161
85-86	Mimnermus	164
87-88	Solon	166
89-90	Theognis	168
91-99	Archilochus	175
100	Semonides	178
101-109	Sappho	182
110-113	Alcaeus	186
114-115	Anacreon	188
116-126	*Anacreontics*	189
127-128	Alcman	195
129	Arion	197
130	Ibycus	198
131-136	Simonides	199

137-138	Pindar	201
139-140	Bacchylides	208
141-142	*Delphian Oracle*	212
143	Hybrias	214
144	Callistratus	214
145	*Swallow Song*	215
146-155	Aeschylus	216
156-166	Sophocles	225
167-186	Euripides	236
187	Thucydides	258
188	Timotheus	258
189-198	Aristophanes	259
199	Eupolis	270
200	Metagenes	270
201	Epicharmus	271
202	Praxilla	272
203	Parrhasius	272
204-208	Plato	273
209	Aristotle	274
210	*Epitaph for Chaeroneia*	275
211	*Processional for Demetrius Poliorcetes*	276
212	Erinna	277
213-214	Antiphanes	277
215	Anaxandrides	279
216	Alexis	279
217-221	Menander	280
222-223	Philemon	284
224	Diphilus	285
225-230	Lycophron	285
231	Cleanthes	288
232-233	Aratus	290
234-241	Callimachus	292

242	Addaeus	301
243-244	Anyte	301
245	Simmias	302
246-251	Asclepiades	303
252-254	Posidippus	305
255	Metrodorus	306
256	Hedylus	307
257-260	Leonidas of Tarentum	307
261	Nossis	309
262	Moero	309
263-270	Apollonius of Rhodes	310
271-274	Theocritus	325
275-277	Herodas	343
278-282	Moschus	352
283	*Alexandrian Erotic Fragment*	363
284-286	Alcaeus of Messene	365
287	Dionysius	366
288-289	Dioscorides	366
290-293	Antipater of Sidon	367
294	Bion	369
295-300	Meleager	373
301-305	Philodemus	376
306-307	Archias	378
308-311	Crinagoras	379
312-313	Automedon	380
314-316	Marcus Argentarius	382
317-318	Antipater of Thessalonica	383
319-320	Evenus	384
321	Philip of Thessalonica	384
322-325	Lucilius	385
326	Antiphilus	386
327-331	Lucian	387

332-333	Ammianus	388
334-335	Babrius	388
336	Oppian	389
337-340	Quintus of Smyrna	393
341-348	Palladas	400
349	Aesop	402
350	Glyco	402
351	Nonnos	403
352	Tryphiodorus	405
353	Colluthus	406
354-357	Rufinus	408
358-359	Macedonius	409
360	Joannes Barbocollas	409
361-364	Paul the Silentiary	410
365-368	Agathias	411
369-374	Musaeus	412
375	Synesius	419

Index of Authors and Translators   422

INTRODUCTION

by Moses Hadas

FOR NO European people does poetry seem so natural and necessary a commodity as for the ancient Greeks. With them as with other people fashions in poetry change, according as men are proud or tired, speculative or erudite, exalted or complacent, demonic or correct; but in Greece the vogue of poetry continues undiminished. That is why Greece is dotted with ruins of capacious theaters where poetic drama was presented; that is why the history of poetry in Greece is five hundred years older than the history of prose. Obviously prose must have been known, for even Homeric heroes cannot have lived without it; but Greek taste demanded that significant utterance be clothed in artistic and memorable form. The most significant, because the most characteristically human, utterance of which man is capable belongs to the realm of the intellect, and hence not only the products of the ranging imagination and questing mind, but practical moral and political doctrine also were communicated in poetry.

Because poetry was the normal medium for literary expression, neither the poet nor his audience were constrained by an awareness of difference and distinction which must affect devotees of poetry in an age of prose. In such an age the attitude of even the sincere artist must seem to be, and to a degree must in fact be, a self-conscious posture; and there is always the danger that the posture will dominate the art. In classical Greece the poet was a craftsman, like other craftsmen purveying a necessity of civilized life; there was no need for him to emphasize his distinction by externals. Naturally an experienced public demanded superior craftsmanship of the poet, as it did of the sculptor or of the orator. But in one respect the demands upon the poet were higher: his gifts

were believed to derive from special inspiration and his calling
therefore involved a special responsibility.

As compared with antecedent and contemporary literatures
of the Near and Middle East, Greek literature is to a pe-
culiar degree anthropocentric in substance and secular in out-
look. It is the palpable humanism of Greek literature, indeed,
which makes it more sympathetic than its predecessors to
modern readers—and tempts them to apply to it the same
critical canons as are appropriate to other European litera-
tures. Hence it becomes important to notice that the Greek
poet was regarded as an instrument of inspiration and there-
fore responsible to requirements approaching those of a sacer-
dotal office. The source of the inspiration is not as exalted
and as exclusive as in the East, and no Greek poet seals a
discourse with the cachet "Thus saith the Lord"; but dedi-
cated poets like Pindar are nevertheless deeply convinced of
their mission and speak of it explicitly. Even the Homeric
minstrel holds a commission from supernatural powers; of
Demodocus, for example, it is said (*Odyssey* 8.63) that "the
Muse had greatly loved him and had given him good and ill:
she took away his eyesight but gave him delightful song."
The bard's productions are regularly characterized as "charm-
ing" or "enchanting," and we must remember that such ex-
pressions were not yet reduced to mere metaphor but in all
likelihood reflected a belief that an actual magical power had
been communicated by a divine patron. When Hesiod re-
ceived his call he was given a rod as a manifest symbol of
this magical power; the Muses, he says (*Theogony* 29-35),

> A branch of laurel gave, which they had plucked,
> To be my sceptre; and they breathed a song
> In music on my soul, and bade me set
> Things past and things to be to that high strain.
> Also they bade me sing the race of gods,
> Themselves, at first and last, ever remembering.
>   EDWIN ARNOLD

Nor is the theory of inspiration peculiar to dedicated poets
like Hesiod or Pindar; it persisted throughout the classical

period and is repeatedly set forth by Plato. "The poet," he writes (*Ion* 534b), "is a light and winged and holy thing, and there is no invention in him until he is inspired and out of his senses, and the mind is no longer in him." And again: "Whoever knocks at the door of poetry without the Muses' frenzy, persuaded that by art alone he will be a sufficient poet, fails of perfection, and the work of the sober is forthwith eclipsed by that of the frenzied" (*Phaedrus* 245a). In the *Apology* Socrates discovers that poets are least of all men able to talk intelligently about the poems they themselves write.

In such a view of the poet's office a special responsibility attaches to his work. We tend to think of Old Testament writers as being austerely devoted to their mission and of the Greek poets as blithely giving free rein to their fancy. In point of fact an equally Puritanical devotion was expected of the Greek poet. When Solon went to see Thespis act his tragedy he was shocked and remonstrated: how was Thespis not ashamed to tell so many lies before so many people? Solon was unfair because he did not make the distinction (made explicit in Aristotle) between the chronicler's truth and the poet's. The tragic poet was in fact austerely committed to the mission of apprehending truth and setting it forth.

The notion that the poet's prime function was to teach was a persistent factor in determining the course of poetry. Among ourselves even ardent advocates of pure poetry would doubtless grant the poet the *privilege* of teaching and admit the possibility that even pure poetry might be instructive; what is striking in the ancient concept is the *obligation* of the poet to teach and the consequent assumption that the principal consideration in judging a poem is its doctrinal value. In a familiar line of *Frogs* (1055) Aristophanes gives it as a truism that "boys have a master for their schooling; men have the poets," and at the end of that play Aeschylus receives a *poetic* award for *political* advice.

Whether this concept was the cause of the practice or its result, the fact is that poetry was the staple of all education.

After children have learned their letters, writes Plato (*Protagoras* 325e),

> they are furnished with works of good poets to read as
> they sit in class, and are made to learn them off by
> heart: here they meet with many admonitions, many
> descriptions and praises and eulogies of good men in
> times past, that the boys in envy may imitate them and
> yearn to become even as they.

Even the Spartans used poets like Tyrtaeus to indoctrinate
their embryo warriors. Not only the gnomic and lyric poets
but the dramatists also were continually quarried for whole-
some tags, and then not merely for tags but for wise counsel
in all the concerns of life.

This utilitarian demand on poetry came near to choking
its wellsprings. In 427 B.C. Gorgias of Leontini introduced a
new kind of artistic prose, as demanding as poetry in its elabo-
rate attention to choice and arrangement of words and to
sound. A serious prose writer like Isocrates could then claim
that artistic prose had supplanted poetry as a medium for
teaching, and after Isocrates there is indeed a marked lull in
poetic production except for the practical requirements of the
stage and of inscriptions. At the same time, because of the
partial interruption of continuity, the ancient writers more
and more took on the status of classics—but still mainly as
classics of doctrine rather than of form. People must always
have clung to Homer for the reasons that people read him
today, but now he was expected to teach all the subjects in
the curriculum, from ethics to cookery, even if some violence
was required to extract the appropriate lessons. As must al-
ways happen when ancient and revered texts no longer suit
the ethical premises of a more refined age, resort was had to
allegorical exegesis. The Stoics in particular employed the
same techniques in explaining away crudities in Homer as
Philo used in dealing with Scripture.

Even during periods of lull in creativity, therefore, poetry
occupied a central and authoritative position and made large

claims on public attention. The theaters which supply part of our evidence for the vogue of Greek poetry were mostly built during the lull. Their number and size bear witness not only to the appetite for poetry but also to the fact that the normal means of publication was by recitation. Generations of Greeks who had never looked into a text of Homer must have been familiar with *Iliad* and *Odyssey,* just as moderns to whom a printed score is meaningless may yet be intimately familiar with a Beethoven symphony. Heroic poetry continued to be recited by rhapsodes at festival occasions, elegy was chanted to the accompaniment of a flute and iambic to that of a lyre, solo lyric was sung, choral lyric was performed with elaborate music and dance, and drama was naturally acted. In epigrams the stone itself is usually thought of as addressing the reader. Even after books became common the normal method of presenting poetry was *viva voce.*

The public character of Greek poetry naturally affected both its spirit and its form. In poetry intended for presentation in bright sunlight to large audiences with serious expectations there can be no place for strained subtleties or for preciosity of any kind. This by no means implies that perceptions and their expression must be simplified for the immature; it does involve a directness, a spaciousness, an architectural quality. This is obviously true of epic, drama, and choral lyric, but it is also true of solo lyric; even Sappho's intimate reflections and petitions have a similar sharpness of outline and directness.

In the matter of form the effect is more plainly perceptible. In an art which was regarded as a public function and was accorded official recognition it was natural that received forms be observed. When any art reached its perfect form, as Aristotle noted, that form was retained. All Doric temples follow a single pattern; where one differs from another is in subtle refinements and variations. In literature canons of form are equally strict. There are worlds of differences between Aeschylus and Sophocles and Euripides, but formally, as compared with other drama, they are virtually identical.

Poetry of a certain content and mood must be written in hexameter, of another in elegiacs, and so on. The word "iambic" alone carries a connotation of outspokenness.

These distinctions are not accidental, for the various classes of poetic composition have a natural affinity for the forms Greek usage found appropriate for them. Aristotle's basic analysis of poetry as deriving not only from an instinct for imitation and recognition but also from an instinct for rhythm is applicable to all poetry, but the mechanics of rhythm are not the same in Greek as in English poetry. Where our metrical patterns depend mainly on stress accent, Greek versification depends mainly on quantity. Greek verse patterns are constructed on systems of long and short syllables, corresponding precisely to quarter-notes and half-notes in music. The additional factor of pitch (designated by acute, grave, and circumflex accents) makes Greek versification a highly refined art whose subtlety we can only imperfectly understand. The dactyls ($- \smile \smile$) or equivalent spondees ($- -$) of the hexameter roll give it a quality of high formalism, and such lines repeated in series are almost liturgical in effect. Elegiac meter consists of one hexameter line followed by another curtailed by a syllable at middle and end. Slight as it seems to be this change makes the verse less liturgical, more pliant, more like ordinary speech. Iambic poetry, written in lines of six iambs ($\smile -$) or their equivalent, proceeds further in the same direction; it is the regular meter for speech in drama.

Lyric is more subjective, and affords the poet freer choice of metrical pattern. Here, instead of one indefinite series of lines of the same pattern, we have lines of various patterns grouped into strophes, which are then repeated; and whereas the repeated-line poetry is intoned, strophic poetry is sung or sung and danced. As compared with the intricacies of choral lyric, solo lyric is relatively simple in versification, but it is still more complex than repeated-line poetry. The distinction of lyric like Sappho's lies in its combination of perception of extraordinary delicacy and truth with a meticulous adherence to form that is apparently effortless and never

forced. Such lyric never seeks out strained expression or ar-
rangement; it is ordinary speech raised to its highest poten-
tial.

In choral lyric, whether in Pindar or in the odes of
tragedy, the strophes usually have very elaborate metrical pat-
terns and are arranged architecturally in triads—strophe,
antistrophe, epode. However varied and elaborate the pattern
of the strophe, the treatment is precise and the correspond-
ence between parallel strophes exact. Pindar's elaborate metri-
cal architecture was long misunderstood, so that "Pindaric
Ode" came to signify metrical anarchy; in point of fact
Pindar's metrical art is perhaps the subtlest of all. The art
of Pindar is very different from Sappho's. Pindar is majestic.
Exalted and glittering language and exquisite rhythms are
built into grand structures in which the line of thought as of
music moves not by regular progression but by leaps from
height to height. The audience is expected to acquire some-
thing of the poet's exaltation and agility, and this the mere
reader, without the prime accessories of music and dance,
may find it difficult to do. In Aeschylus, whose odes are
formally very like Pindar's, weighty theologic and moral doc-
trine may preoccupy and direct our attention. But even in
Aeschylus a reader is too apt to be like an auditor at a Bach
chorale who would sit unmoved through the swirling gran-
deur of the orchestral music and be impatient for the soprano
to utter words whose meaning he can look up in a dictionary.
It is in choral lyric that the artistic loss to a reader is greatest.

Not choral lyric alone but all public poetry, like demo-
cratic oratory, ended with the extinction of Athenian liberty.
Expanded geographical horizons and a shift in the political
center of gravity that came with the conquests of Alexander
reduced Athens from its eminence as the intellectual capital
and dissipated the homogeneous audience which could have
a communal proprietary interest in the poet's work. The con-
glomerate metropolis of Alexandria could afford no such au-
dience; the Alexandrian poets were self-conscious professional
scholars, responsible only to the patronage of Ptolemy and to
their reputation among their colleagues. They wrote not to

satisfy the needs of a community but to parade their virtuos-
ity to each other. In such an atmosphere euphuism displaces
frenzy and form becomes an end in itself. The Homeric
Hymn to Demeter or Sappho's petition to Aphrodite have
the power of manifest sincerity; Callimachus' hymns are as
polished as they are learned, but do not, and were not meant
to, reflect or communicate conviction. Callimachus' rules
make Homer's meter faulty; Apollonius' learning and court-
liness make Homer seem naive. And yet the poetic eye, the
sense of wonder, the electric flash of true poetry, survive. Few
would deny the title poet to Apollonius, though his realm is
the scholar's study; none could deny it to Theocritus, though
he makes the natural artificial. But little more than artifice
can be discerned in men like Aratus or Nicander, who versi-
fied treatises on astronomy or on antidotes to poisons.

During the centuries when poetry was constricted first by
utilitarianism and then by erudition, true lyric which speaks
to the heart survived in short poems of the epigram form.
These were written in all parts of the Hellenistic world, but
with conspicuous success and with a new delight in the
senses and in romantic love by a group of Syrian poets, chief
among whom is Meleager of Gadara. More ambitious forms
degenerate. The mime retains vitality, though its pastoral
forms begin to cloy. There are fresh treatments of heroic saga
in forms closely imitating Homer, but Quintus of Smyrna
and Musaeus, who are the best in this kind, betray their age
by a sentimentality alien to Homer. Out of corruption comes
new life. The most decadent of Greek poets is the prodigious
Nonnos, and out of his very decadence there arises a new
strength, of a quality like that of a James Joyce. Quintus and
Nonnos and many of the poets of the *Anthology* were Chris-
tians, but the tradition of poetry continued pagan, and there
is no hint of Christianity in their works. The welding of the
two traditions, in poetry as in life, and the inception of a
new age is illustrated in the hymns of Synesius, who puts
pagan forms and imagery to the service of Christianity.

In the versions which comprise this book, unfortunately,
the qualities touched upon above cannot always be easily de-

tected. At best, viewing the translation of a great poem is like inspecting the corpse of a great man; at worst it is seeing the original darkly through an unevenly cast and wrongly (however brightly) tinted slab of glass. Of prose there have been very successful translations which combine high fidelity to both the manner and matter of their originals. If a prose version can approach adequacy for any kind of poetry, it is most apt to do so for narrative poetry. In epic the "story" itself is sufficiently absorbing so that any version not distorted by the translator's own vagaries is tolerable; no translator, provided he understands his original and the use of English, can fail to transmit some aspects of the truth of his original, and a good translator will transmit many aspects. But an epic is more than its story, and only a poetic version can transmit the poetic values of the original. Chapman, Pope, Bryant, Lattimore—each present reflections of Homer valid for their generations, and each, as it happens, is, by any absolute gauge, truer than his predecessor. Because epic (and to an even greater degree, drama) contains more than any single translator is likely to reproduce, the conscientious reader will wish to examine several interpretations in order to obtain the fullest possible appreciation of the original.

It is in lyric that translation becomes almost hopeless. No canon of translation can be satisfactory. Merely to render words and syntax makes a gem in the *Anthology* banal or the rugged brilliance of Pindar grotesque. On the other hand, the attempt to reproduce the total effect of the original leads to uncontrolled subjectivity, and the reader may justly feel that the excellence of a version is in inverse ratio to its merits as a translation. Only poets can do any sort of justice to lyric, and since poets cannot be expected to efface themselves, disparate versions of the same poem will show great diversity. Lyric utterance is often so concentrated and gemlike as to make many refractions possible, some perhaps unperceived by the author himself. Only a lyric translation can reproduce analogous refractions with the requisite conciseness and finish. The successful translator is as likely to be an Elizabethan as a modern, more likely to belong to the eight-eenth century than to the nineteenth. From the modern scholar's point of view the great defect of most translations is their diffuseness. Whether to elaborate what to them appears bald or merely to fill a line, they expand, and in so doing not only destroy both the conciseness and directness which are the virtues of the Greek, but introduce alien directions to distract the reader's fancy.

Many of the selections offered in this volume perforce suffer from this diffuseness; others may be both bare and thin. For a work of this character such diversity is necessary. In the handful of prose selections the glass through which the reader is asked to look is as even and clear as modern skill can make it; in the *Anacreontics* of Thomas Moore, for example, the glass is uneven and very richly tinted. Occasionally, as in Lattimore's *Iliad* or Matthew Prior's Callimachus, we have both substantive poetry of high excellence and extraordinary fidelity to the vitality of the original. In some of the selections the light of poesy wanes and its pulse becomes pedestrian; but frequently enough, in the span of fifteen hundred years, it quickens into a bright flame to excite and enrich the perceptions of the modern reader.

THE GREEK POETS

HOMER: ILIAD

Iliad's major theme is the wrath of Achilles, of which the issues are intertwined with the events of the Trojan war and the working out of the will of Zeus. All three themes, in their interconnection, are stated in the opening lines:

Sing, goddess, the anger of Peleus' son Achilleus   **1**
and its devastation, which put pains thousandfold upon the
    Achaians,
hurled in their multitudes to the house of Hades strong souls
of heroes, but gave their bodies to be the delicate feasting
of dogs, of all birds, and the will of Zeus was accomplished
since that time when first there stood in division of conflict
Atreus' son the lord of men and brilliant Achilleus.

   RICHMOND LATTIMORE (*Iliad* 1.1-17)

Apollo has sent a plague upon the Greeks because his priest Chryses who petitioned Agamemnon for the return of his captive daughter Chryseis had been rebuffed. When the seer Calchas, with Achilles' encouragement, explains the cause of the plague, Agamemnon agrees to surrender Chryseis but threatens to compensate himself by taking some other chieftain's prize. Achilles protests:

"Have you the face to utter such a threat, most grasping   **2**
    Atrides?
How shall a chief of Achaia rejoice hereafter to serve you,
Faring on expeditions or fighting bravely in action?
I left not my country to fight here over a private
Injury. I never had been wrong'd by people of Ilium.
They never drove *our* horses away nor spoil'd *us* of oxen,
Nor in a raid on Phthia, the deep-soiled breeder of heroes,
Harm'd any crop. Too mighty a distance keeps us asunder,
Mountains rise shadowy and wide seas thunder between us.

3

'Twas to oblige *you* only, to serve *you*, marvellous ingrate,
And Menelaos yonder,—to win *you* glory besieging
Ilium! And is it all despised and counted a trifle?
Now you propose ravishing my maiden wrongfully from me,
Won with a world of labour, a free gift of the Achaeans.
Mine is a far lesser prize than yours, sir, when the Achaeans
Plunder a rich stronghold they win from children of Ilium.
I have enough trouble on my hands—ye give me the lion's
Portion of every battle! When spoils are parted asunder,
Yours is a prize of value: but I go wearily limping
Home to the ships cherishing my own, though only a mean
    one.
I shall array the vessels and sail home unto the land of
Phthia! It is better so. I have no fancy to bide here
Heaping a King riches up when treated shamefully by him."
    His Sovereign Agamemnon Atrides spake thus in answer:
"Flee home, if you desire to. Remain no longer, we beg you,
Serving us unwilling and unwanted. Plenty remain here
Yet to uphold our glory,—the Lord God being amongst them.
I ever have least liked you of all chiefs of the Achaeans,
Since it is only quarrels and strife and slaughter delight you.
Strength is a gift given us by God,—cease boasting about it.
Flee to the land of Phthia with all your company—rule there
Over the Myrmidones, since I no longer require you,
Neither regard your fury! A word more, master Achilleus!
Since Phoebos constrains me to yield his daughter to Chryses,
Home in a swift ship of ours my folk shall speedily bear her:
I shall arise, and enter your own tent, forcing an entrance,
And carry your Briseis away thence, merely to teach you
I have a hand heavier than yours, and warn the remainder
Not to oppose their Ruler in open council as equals."
    Anguish assail'd Achilleus at these words, so that his heart
        seem'd
Cloven in his shaggy breast, two halves diversely desiring,
One to pluck out the weapon, slung sharp and mighty beside
    him,
Sunder the King's followers with a bound and slaughter
    Atrides,

One to refrain his fury, to curb and bridle his anger.
While he remained still searching his heart and doubtfully
    minded,
Fingering his sword-hilt, down grey-eyed Maiden Athene
Came to him out of Heaven, dispatch'd by ivory-shoulder'd
Hera, who loved Achilleus and likewise royal Atrides.
And the Goddess, gripping his gold hair, stood closely behind
    him,
Invisible to the people assembled, saving Achilleus.
Turning around in wonder he looked on Maiden Athene,
Knowing her. And terribly those eyes flamed, as she beheld
    him!
So the son of Peleus spake wing'd words unto the Maiden:
    "What brings thee, O Daughter of Aegis-wielder Cronion?
Is't to behold Agamemnon Atrides shamefully use me?
Hearken as I prophesy what thou shalt see me accomplish.
This bitter jest shall cost him his own life ere he believes it."
    Then she address'd Achilleus and spake thus, saying in
        answer:
"I am arrived from Heaven to refrain your fury, Achilleus,
If you will only listen—sent down by ivory-shoulder'd
Hera, who loves Achilleus and loves Agamemnon Atrides.
Nay, Achilleus, leave fighting alone, and draw not against him!
Only give him bitter words—foretell the disaster approaching.
Hearken as I prophesy what time shall shortly accomplish.
Thrice what he seizes from you, the King shall speedily give
    you
For this offense he offers. Strike not therefore, but obey me."
    Thus she besought. The gallant Achilleus spake saying in
        answer:
"I shall obey thy holy commandment, lady Athene,
Even in extremity of wrath. 'Tis seemly to do so.
Him that obeys their order, the Gods hear calling upon
    them."
    Smiting his hilt of silver with huge hand, noble Achilleus
Thrust the massive sword home and hearken'd unto Athene.
So she arose and, leaving Achilleus, flew to Olympos

Where the divine Cronides, her Sire, dwells with the Immortals.
  But the son of Peleus turn'd once more unto Atrides,
Railing on him bitterly, nowise restraining his anger.
"You with a doe's spirit and dog's eyes! Wine-bloated Atrides!
That never have the courage to put arms on when the Achaeans
Are coming out to battle nor join in laying an ambush
Like other chiefs—'twould scare you to death straight, did you attempt it!
Truly it is better far to sit over the host of Achaia,
Taking away their prizes, who durst in Council oppose you.
Ours is an abject people who let so worthless a Ruler
Eat us up, or otherwise 'twere your last infamous action.
Now therefore I swear you an oath and call you to witness.
By this sapless sceptre,—as it no longer produces
Foliage or puts forth fresh twigs, since hewn from a parent
Trunk in a mountain hollow; or grows green after the ax-edge
Has cut away both bark and boughs and made it an emblem
For Danaans to carry, watching over the laws of Achaia
Under divine governance, ('tis a great oath, awful of import).
When the Achaean people on all sides yearn for Achilleus
Vainly—when all agonized, you strive and may not avail them—
When warriors are dying in heaps and merciless Hector
Slaughtering—oh, bitter be your thoughts then—rage to remember
How you regarded lightly the bravest of the Achaeans!"
  Here the son of Peleus dashed down that sceptre before him,
Plentifully studded with gold, and seated him after.
Great was Atrides' fury! Then up rose Nestor amongst them,
Who was a wise Pylian, most smooth-tongued of the Achaeans.
Sweeter than oozing honey his words dropp'd while he address'd them.
Nestor in his lifetime had seen two whole generations
Growing up and flourishing for a while and dying around him.

It was a third generation who fill'd his goodly dominions.
Now he arose eloquent and spake out, standing amongst
    them.
    "Oh, what a black misfortune is overwhelming Achaia!
What merry news goes shortly to Priamos and to the sons of
Priamos! How citizens of Troy shall glory to hear it,
When the report shall reach them of how ye wrangle in idle
Anger, the best warriors and wisest of the Achaeans!"
    GEORGE ERNLE (*Iliad* 1.149-258)

Achilles surrenders Briseis, but grieves at the affront:

> Meanwhile Achilles, plung'd   **3**
> In bitter grief, from all the band apart,
> Upon the margin of the hoary sea
> Sat idly gazing on the dark-blue waves;
> And to his Goddess-mother long he pray'd,
> With outstretch'd hands, "Oh, mother! since thy son
> To early death by destiny is doom'd,
> I might have hoped the Thunderer on high,
> Olympian Jove, with honour would have crown'd
> My little space; but now disgrace is mine;
> Since Agamemnon, the wide-ruling King,
> Hath wrested from me, and still holds, my prize."
>   Weeping, he spoke; his Goddess-mother heard,
> Beside her aged father where she sat
> In the deep ocean-caves: ascending quick
> Through the dark waves, like to a misty cloud,
> Beside her son she stood; and as he wept,
> She gently touched him with her hand.
>   EDWARD EARL OF DERBY (*Iliad* 1.348-361)

*He asks his mother to beg Zeus to punish Agamemnon. Chry-
seis, meantime, is returned, and the plague ended.*

> Meantime the goddess-born in secret pin'd: **4**
> Nor visited the camp, nor in the council join'd;
> But, keeping close, his gnawing heart he fed

With hopes of vengeance on the tyrant's head;
And wish'd for bloody wars and mortal wounds,
And of the Greeks oppress'd in fight to hear the dying sounds.
   Now, when twelve days complete had run their race,
The gods bethought them of the cares belonging to their
      place.
Jove at their head ascending from the sea,
A shoal of puny pow'rs attend his way.
Then Thetis, not unmindful of her son,
Emerging from the deep, to beg her boon,
Pursu'd their track; and, waken'd from his rest,
Before the sovereign stood a morning guest.
Him in the circle, but apart, she found;
The rest at awful distance stood around.
She bow'd, and ere she durst her suit begin,
One hand embrac'd his knees, one propp'd his chin.
Then thus: "If I, celestial sire, in aught
Have serv'd thy will, or gratify'd thy thought,
One glimpse of glory to my issue give,
Grac'd for the little time he has to live.
Dishonor'd by the King of Men he stands;
His rightful prize is ravish'd from his hands.
But thou, O father, in my son's defense,
Assume thy pow'r, assert thy providence.
Let Troy prevail, till Greece th' affront has paid
With doubled honors, and redeem'd his aid."
      JOHN DRYDEN (*Iliad* 1.488-511)

*On Olympos Hera's jealousy of Zeus' kindness to Thetis
leads to a quarrel, which Hephaestus allays by conversation
and by serving nectar.*

5   But among the immortals uncontrollable laughter
      went up as they saw Hephaistos bustling about the palace.
         Thus thereafter the whole day long until the sun went
            under
      they feasted, nor was anyone's hunger denied a fair portion,
      nor denied the beautifully wrought lyre in the hands of Apollo

nor the antiphonal sweet sound of the Muses singing.
Afterwards when the light of the flaming sun went under
they went away each one to sleep in his home where
for each one the far-renowned strong-handed Hephaistos
had built a house by means of his craftsmanship and cunning.
Zeus the Olympian and lord of the lightning went to
his own bed, where always he lay when sweet sleep came on
    him.
Going up to the bed he slept and Hera of the gold throne
    beside him.

    RICHMOND LATTIMORE (*Iliad* 1.599-611)

At another assembly, in the second book, Thersites objects to the unfair distribution of work and pay. The reception given to Odysseus' retort shows where the sympathies of Homer's heroes and of his audience lay.

6

The rest now took their seats and kept to their own several places, but Thersites still went on wagging his unbridled tongue—a man of many words, and those unseemly; a monger of sedition, a railer against all who were in authority, who cared not what he said, so that he might set the Achaeans in a laugh. He was the ugliest man of all those that came before Troy—bandy-legged, lame of one foot, with his two shoulders rounded and hunched over his chest. His head ran up to a point, but there was little hair on the top of it. Achilles and Odysseus hated him worst of all, for it was with them that he was most wont to wrangle. Now, however, with a shrill squeaky voice he began heaping his abuse on Agamemnon. The Achaeans were angry and disgusted, yet nonetheless he kept on brawling and bawling at the son of Atreus.

"Agamemnon," he cried, "what ails you now, and what more do you want? Your tents are filled with bronze and with fair women, for whenever we take a town we give you the pick of them. Would you have yet more gold, which some Trojan is to give you as a ransom for his son, when I or another Achaean has taken him prisoner? Or is it some young girl to hide away and lie with? It is not well that you, the ruler of the Achaeans, should bring them into such misery. Weakling cowards, women rather than men, let us sail home, and leave this fellow here at Troy to stew in his own meeds of honor, and discover whether we were of any service to him or no. Achilles is a much better man than he is, and see how he has treated him—robbing him of his prize and keeping it himself. Achilles takes it meekly and shows no fight; if he did, son of Atreus, you would never again insult him."

Thus railed Thersites, but Odysseus at once went up to him and rebuked him sternly. "Check your glib tongue, Thersites," said he, "and babble not a word further. Chide not with princes when you have none to back you. There is no viler creature come before Troy with the sons of Atreus. Drop this chatter about kings, and neither revile them nor keep harping about going home. We do not yet know how things are going to be, nor whether the Achaeans are to return with good success or evil. How dare you gibe at Agamemnon because the Danaans have awarded him so many prizes? I tell you, therefore—and it shall surely be—that if I again catch you talking such nonsense, I will either forfeit my own head and be no more called father of Telemachus, or I will take you, strip you stark naked, and whip you out of the assembly till you go blubbering back to the ships."

On this he beat him with his staff about the back and shoulders till he dropped and fell a-weeping. The golden scepter raised a bloody weal on his back, so he sat down frightened and in pain, looking foolish as he wiped the tears from his eyes. The people were sorry for him, yet they laughed heartily, and one would turn to his neighbor, saying: "Odysseus has done many a good thing ere now in fight and council, but he never did the Argives a better turn than when he stopped this fellow's mouth from prating further. He will give the kings no more of his insolence."

SAMUEL BUTLER (*Iliad* 2.211-277)

Helen appears as a tragic and beautiful figure. The sense of her beauty the poet conveys not by describing it but by show-

ing its effect upon the old men, who would be least suscep-
tible to it and who had suffered most from it:

> And then came Iris as a messenger
> to Helen of the white arms,
> likening herself to her husband's sister,
> the wife of Antenor's son,
> her whom the lord Helicaon, the son of Antenor,
> had to wife, even Laodice,
> fairest in form of the daughters of Priam.

7

> Helen she found in the great hall.
> There she wove a goodly web,
> double and of sea-purple stain,
> and on it she broidered the many contests
> of the horse-taming Trojans
> and the bronze-clad Achaeans,
> which they suffered beneath the hands of Ares,
> the war god, for her sake.

> And standing near to her,
> Iris the swift-footed spake:
> "Come hither, dear lady, that thou mayst behold
> the wondrous deeds
> of the horse-taming Trojans
> and the bronze-clad Achaeans.
> Ever aforetime have they waged tearful war
> one 'gainst the other upon the plain,
> eager for the grim combat;
> but now in silence they rest,
> the battle-din has ceas'd,
> they lean upon their shields,
> and their long spears are fix'd in the ground.
> For now will Paris and Menelaus, dear to Ares,
> contend with their long spears
> for thy sake,
> and thou shalt be called the dear consort
> of him who shall prevail."

Thus spake the goddess
and infus'd into the soul of Helen
a sweet longing to behold her former lord,
and her city and the parents
whom once she knew.
Straightway she wrapp'd a gleaming veil
about her face
and forth from the chamber she sped,
letting fall a rounded tear;
not alone went she, for with her followed
two handmaidens,
even Aithre, the daughter of Pittheus,
and Clymene, the ox-eyed,
and swiftly they came to the place
where lay the Scaean Gates.

Those who were about Priam
and Panthoos and Thymoetes
and Lampos and Clytios and Hiketaon,
of the seed of Ares,
even Ucalegon and Antenor,
wise men both and elders of the people,
were seated by the Scaean Gates.
By reason of age they had ceased from war,
but orators of honied charm they were,
like unto the cicadas,
that rest within the woods upon a tree
and utter voices lily-clear—
even such were the elders of the Trojans
who sat upon the tower.

And as they look'd on Helen
drawing nigh unto the wall,
softly one to another they spake
wingèd words:
"No cause for wonder is it
that Trojans and well-greaved Achaeans
for such a woman's sake

should suffer long and grievous woe;
for like in wondrous wise is she
to the immortal goddesses
in loveliness of countenance."
          H. N. Couch (*Iliad* 3.121-158)

*At the instigation of Athena the Trojan archer Pandarus
breaks a truce by wounding Menelaus.*

He heard, and madly at the motion pleased,   **8**
His polish'd bow with hasty rashness seized.
'Twas form'd of horn, and smooth'd with artful toil:
A mountain goat resign'd the shining spoil.
Who pierced long since beneath his arrows bled;
The stately quarry on the cliffs lay dead,
And sixteen palms his brow's large honours spread:
The workmen join'd, and shaped the bended horns,
And beaten gold each taper point adorns.
This, by the Greeks unseen, the warrior bends,
Screen'd by the shields of his surrounding friends:
There meditates the mark; and couching low,
Fits the sharp arrow to the well-strung bow.
One from a hundred feather'd deaths he chose,
Fated to wound, and cause of future woes;
Then offers vows with hecatombs to crown
Apollo's altars in his native town.
   Now with full force the yielding horn he bends,
Drawn to an arch, and joins the doubling ends;
Close to his breast he strains the nerve below,
Till the barb'd points approach the circling bow;
The impatient weapon whizzes on the wing;
Sounds the tough horn, and twangs the quivering string.
   But thee, Atrides! in that dangerous hour
The gods forget not, nor thy guardian power,
Pallas assists, and (weakened in its force)
Diverts the weapon from its destined course:
So from her babe, when slumber seals his eye,
The watchful mother wafts the envenom'd fly.

Just where his belt with golden buckles join'd,
Where linen folds the double corslet lin'd,
She turn'd the shaft, which, hissing from above,
Pass'd the broad belt, and through the corslet drove;
The folds it pierced, the plaited linen tore,
And razed the skin, and drew the purple gore.
As when some stately trappings are decreed
To grace a monarch on his bounding steed,
A nymph in Caria or Mæonia bred,
Stains the pure ivory with a lively red;
With equal lustre various colours vie,
The shining whiteness, and the Tyrian dye:
So great Atrides! show'd thy sacred blood,
As down thy snowy thigh distill'd the streaming flood.
With horror seized, the king of men descried
The shaft infix'd, and saw the gushing tide:
Nor less the Spartan fear'd, before he found
The shining barb appear above the wound,
Then, with a sigh, that heaved his manly breast,
The royal brother, thus his grief express'd,
And grasp'd his hand; while all the Greeks around
With answering sighs return'd the plaintive sound.

   "Oh, dear as life! did I for this agree
The solemn truce, a fatal truce to thee!
Wert thou exposed to all the hostile train,
To fight for Greece, and conquer, to be slain!
The race of Trojans in thy ruin join,
And faith is scorn'd by all the perjured line.
Not thus our vows, confirm'd with wine and gore,
Those hands we plighted, and those oaths we swore,
Shall all be vain: when Heaven's revenge is slow,
Jove but prepares to strike the fiercer blow.
The day shall come, that great avenging day,
When Troy's proud glories in the dust shall lay,
When Priam's powers and Priam's self shall fall,
And one prodigious ruin swallow all.
     ALEXANDER POPE (*Iliad* 4.104-167)

*The magnificent prowess of Diomedes in the fifth book almost
reconciles us to the absence of Achilles. His victories, which
included wounding Aphrodite herself, are stopped by a Trojan
stand, and Hera and Athena rush to the aid of the Greeks.*

Now when the goddess, white-armed Hera,   **9**
Saw the Argives perishing in that stern combat,
Straightway she addressed Athena with winged words:
"Alas, child of aegis-bearing Zeus, thou Unwearied One,
Vain is the promise we made to Menelaus
That he should not return home till he had sacked well-walled
       Troy,
If we are to allow destructive Ares thus to play the madman.
But come, let us too bethink ourselves of impetuous valor!"
So spake she, nor did the goddess, gleaming-eyed Athena,
       disobey.
Now did she go and harness the gold-filleted horses,
Hera, revered goddess, daughter of great Kronos;
And Hebe swiftly set the curved wheels to the chariot,
Brazen wheels, eight-spoked, about the axle of iron,
About which ran a golden felloe imperishable,
And over this tires of bronze were fitted, a wonder to behold;
And the hubs were of silver, revolving on both sides.
And the body of the chariot was strung within with gold and
       silver straps,
And two rims ran about it, and the pole was of silver;
And at its end she bound a beautiful, golden yoke,
And fastened thereto breast collars all of gold;
And Hera, eager for strife and the battle-cry, brought the
       swift-footed horses beneath the yoke.
But Athena, daughter of aegis-bearing Zeus,
Let fall her pliant peplos upon her father's floor,
An embroidered robe, which she herself had made and toiled
       over with her hands;
And she put on the tunic of Zeus, the Cloud-Gatherer,
And began to array herself with weapons for tearful war.
And about her shoulders she cast her aegis fringed with tassels,
Terrible, around which on all sides was set fear like a circlet;

And on it was strife, and on it was valor, and on it was bloody
  onset;
And on it was the head of the Gorgon,
A monster dread and terrible, a portent of aegis-bearing Zeus.
And on her head she placed a two-horned, dog-skin helmet,
  four plated,
Large enough to fit the footmen of a hundred cities.
And she set foot in the resplendent chariot, and grasped her
  spear,
Heavy, great, and firm, with which she overcomes the ranks
  of heroes,
Those with whom the Daughter of a Mighty Father is wroth.
And Hera with a whip quickly urged on the horses;
And, self-moved, resounded the gates of heaven, which the
  Seasons guard,
To whom has been entrusted great heaven and Olympus,
Both to bend back the thick cloud and to replace it.
There then, straight through them, they directed their goaded
  horses,
And they found the son of Kronos sitting apart from the other
  gods
On the highest peak of many-ridged Olympus;
There the goddess, white-armed Hera, stayed her horses,
And inquired of Zeus most high, the son of Kronos, and
  addressed him:
"Father Zeus, art thou not indignant at Ares for these deeds
  of violence,
So great and so good a host of the Achaeans he hath destroyed
Wantonly, unfittingly, and to me lasting pain!
While, unopposed, Cypris and silver-bowed Apollo rejoice
Now that they have let loose this madman, who knows not
  any law or justice.
Father Zeus, wilt thou be angry with me if I
Smite Ares grievously and drive him from the field of battle?"
And cloud-gathering Zeus answered her and said:
"Quick now! set Athena the Giver of Booty upon him,
She who oftenest forces him near to bitter pains."
So spake he; nor did the goddess disobey, white-armed Hera,

But lashed the horses, and they not unwillingly flew
Betwixt earth and starry heaven.
As far as a man can see with his eyes into the misty distance,
As he sits on a cliff looking over the wine-faced deep,
So far leap the high-necked horses of the gods.
But when now they came to Troy and her flowing rivers,
Where the Simois and the Scamander join their streams,
There the goddess stayed her horses, white-armed Hera,
And loosed them from the chariot, and poured thick mist
 about them;
And the Simois caused ambrosia to spring up for them to feed
 upon.
And the two goddesses went their way with footsteps as light
 as those of trembling pigeons,
Eager to make defense for Argive men.
  F. L. CLARK (*Iliad* 5.711-779)

While Diomedes is carrying all before him Hector goes to Troy to ask the matrons' prayers and Paris' assistance. On his way back he stops to say farewell to Andromache.

Hector left in haste

10

The mansion, retraced his way between
The rows of stately dwellings, traversing
The mighty city. When at length he reached
The Scaean gates, that issue on the field,
His spouse, the nobly dowered Andromache,
Came forth to meet him—daughter of the prince
Eëtion, who, among the woody slopes
Of Placos, in the Hypoplacian town
Of Thebè, ruled Cilicia and her sons,
And gave his child to Hector, great in arms.
She came attended by a maid, who bore
A tender child—a babe too young to speak—
Upon her bosom—Hector's only son,
Beautiful as a star, whom Hector called
Scamandrius, but all else Astyanax—
The city's lord—since Hector stood the sole

Defence of Troy. The father on his child
Looked with a silent smile. Andromache
Pressed to his side meanwhile, and, all in tears,
Clung to his hand, and, thus beginning, said:
    "Too brave! thy valor yet will cause thy death.
Thou hast no pity on thy tender child,
Nor me, unhappy one, who soon must be
Thy widow. All the Greeks will rush on thee
To take thy life. A happier lot were mine,
If I must lose thee, to go down to earth,
For I shall have no hope when thou art gone,—
Nothing but sorrow. Father have I none,
And no dear mother. Great Achilles slew
My father when he sacked the populous town
Of the Cilicians,—Thebè with high gates.
'T was there he smote Eëtion, yet forbore
To make his arms a spoil; he dared not that,
But burned the dead with his bright armor on,
And raised a mound above him. Mountain-nymphs,
Daughters of Aegis-bearing Jupiter,
Came to the spot and planted it with elms.—
Seven brothers had I in my father's house,
And all went down to Hades in one day.
Achilles, the swift-footed, slew them all
Among their slow-paced bullocks and white sheep.
My mother, princess on the woody slopes
Of Placos, with his spoils he bare away,
And only for large ransom gave her back.
But her Diana, archer-queen, struck down
Within her father's palace. Hector, thou
Art father and dear mother now to me,
And brother and my youthful spouse besides.
In pity keep within the fortress here,
Nor make thy child an orphan—nor thy wife
A widow. Post thine army near the place
Of the wild fig-tree, where the city walls
Are low and may be scaled. Thrice in the war
The boldest of the foe have tried the spot—

The Ajaces and the famed Idomeneus,
The two chiefs born to Atreus, and the brave
Tydides, whether counselled by some seer,
Or prompted to the attempt by their own minds."
    Then answered Hector, great in war: "All this
I bear in mind, dear wife; but I should stand
Ashamed before the men and long-robed dames
Of Troy, were I to keep aloof and shun
The conflict, coward-like. Not thus my heart
Prompts me, for greatly have I learned to dare
And strike among the foremost sons of Troy,
Upholding my great father's fame and mine;
Yet well in my undoubting mind I know
The day shall come in which our sacred Troy,
And Priam, and the people over whom
Spear-bearing Priam rules, shall perish all.
But not the sorrows of the Trojan race,
Nor those of Hecuba herself, nor those
Of royal Priam, nor the woes that wait
My brothers many and brave—who all at last,
Slain by the pitiless foe, shall lie in dust—
Grieve me so much as thine, when some mailed Greek
Shall lead thee weeping hence, and take from thee
Thy day of freedom. Thou in Argos then
Shalt, at another's bidding, ply thy loom,
And from the fountain of Messeïs draw
Water, or from the Hypereian spring,
Constrained unwillingly by some cruel lot.
And then shall some one say that sees thee weep,
'This was the wife of Hector, most renowned
Of the horse-taming Trojans, when they fought
Around their city.' So shall some one say,
And thou shalt grieve the more, lamenting him
Who haply might have kept afar the day
Of thy captivity. O let the earth
Be heaped above my head in death before
I hear thy cries as thou art borne away!"
    So speaking, mighty Hector stretched his arms

To take the boy; the boy shrank crying back
To his fair nurse's bosom, scared to see
His father helmeted in glittering brass,
And eyeing with affright the horse-hair plume
That grimly nodded from the lofty crest.
At this both parents in their fondness laughed;
And hastily the mighty Hector took
The helmet from his brow and laid it down
Gleaming upon the ground, and, having kissed
His darling son and tossed him up in play,
Prayed thus to Jove and all the gods of heaven:
    "O Jupiter and all ye deities,
Vouchsafe that this my son may yet become
Among the Trojans eminent like me,
And nobly rule in Ilium. May they say,
'This man is greater than his father was!'
When they behold him from the battlefield
Bring back the bloody spoil of the slain foe,
That so his mother may be glad at heart."
    So speaking, to the arms of his dear spouse
He gave the boy; she on her fragrant breast
Received him, weeping as she smiled. The chief
Beheld, and, moved with tender pity, smoothed
Her forehead gently with his hand and said:
    "Sorrow not thus, beloved one, for me.
No living man can send me to the shades
Before my time; no man of woman born,
Coward or brave, can shun his destiny.
But go thou home, and tend thy labors there,—
The web, the distaff,—and command thy maids
To speed the work. The cares of war pertain
To all men born in Troy, and most to me."
    Thus speaking, mighty Hector took again
His helmet, shadowed with the horse-hair plume,
While homeward his beloved consort went,
Oft looking back, and shedding many tears.
    W. C. BRYANT (*Iliad* 6.390-502)

Hector returns to the battle and presses the Greeks hard; here is how they conclude a hard day of fighting.

The sun went down, and the work of the Achaians was **11** accomplished; and they slaughtered oxen amid the huts, and took supper. And many ships from Lemnos, bearing wine, were at hand, sent of Jason's son Euneos, whom Hypsipyle bare to Jason shepherd of the host. And specially for Atreus' sons, Agamemnon and Menelaos, Jason's son gave a freight of wine, even a thousand measures. So the flowing-haired Achaians bought them wine thence, some for bronze and some for gleaming iron, and some with hides and some with whole kine, and some with captives; and they set a rich feast before them. Then all night long feasted the flowing-haired Achaians, and in the city the Trojans and allies; and all night long Zeus the lord of counsel devised them ill with terrible thunderings. Then pale fear gat hold upon them, and they spilt wine from their cups upon the earth, neither durst any drink till he had made libation to most mighty Kronion. Then laid they them to rest and took the boon of sleep.

LANG, LEAF, AND MYERS (*Iliad* 7.465-482)

At the height of their surge forward, the Trojans bivouac on the plain.

So Hector spake; the Trojans roared applause;   **12**
Then loost their sweating horses from the yoke,
And each beside his chariot bound his own;
And oxen from the city and goodly sheep
In haste they drove and honey-hearted wine
And bread from out the houses brought and heapt
Their fire-wood, and the wind from off the plain
Rolled the rich vapour far into the heaven.
And these all night upon the bridge of war
Sat glorying; many a fire before them blazed:
As when in heaven the stars about the moon
Look beautiful, when all the winds are laid,
And every height comes out and jutting peak

And valley, and the immeasurable heavens
Break open to their highest, and all the stars
Shine, and the Shepherd gladdens in his heart:
So many a fire between the ships and stream
Of Xanthus blazed before the towers of Troy,
A thousand on the plain; and close by each
Sat fifty in the blaze of burning fire;
And eating hoary grain and pulse the steeds
Fixt by their cars, waited the golden dawn.
ALFRED TENNYSON (*Iliad* 8.542-565)

*In Book 9 Agamemnon admits his error and sends Odysseus,
Ajax, and Phoenix (Achilles' old tutor) to placate Achilles.
This is Achilles' reply:*

13 Most valiant and noble Odysseus, seeing Atrides
Sends you upon this errand, 'tis fairest plainly to tell you
My full opinion of it, my fixed intention about it,
Not to sit and listen here while you strive vainly to coax me.
Hateful as Hell's gateway is a man concealing his inward
Purposes and giving us smooth answers, noble Odysseus,
I therefore shall tell you the plain truth though it offend you.
Rest you assured that neither Atrides nor the Achaean
Army will e'er persuade me: for I am weary of always
Fighting a King's enemies—'tis far too thankless a business.
For we behold the laggard and foremost fighter rewarded
Equally, and valiant and base all treated as equals,
And death alike coming to the toil-worn as to the idle.
It profited me nothing to be worn out—weary of hardships,
Weary of imperilling my life in dangerous actions.
Just as a toilful bird, that bearing savoury morsels
Home to her own nestlings, herself goes hungry to feed them,
Often have I sat awake all night long, serving Atrides,
Fought for him in bloody fields from sunrise unto sunset,
Only to win the women my foes died stoutly defending.
Twelve cities I have wasted across seas, sailing against them;
I have attacked and taken elev'n towns under the walls of
Ilium. I carried off their spoils, I faithfully told them

Into the King's treasury, to the hands of royal Atrides,
That sitting at the vessels in comfort used to receive them
And give away a little to the chiefs and keep the remainder.
All other kings and princes who had such prizes assign'd them
Hold them on his sufferance. I only of all the Achaeans
Had to return the woman my heart loved. Let the Atrides
Lie with her—I care not! Danaans, why fight you the Trojans?
Why has Atrides brought you to die here, sons of Achaia?
Why, on account of Helen's bright hair! But do you believe
them
Singular in cherishing their wives, these children of Atreus?
Nay, any man worth calling a man, not merely a rascal,
Clings to the wife he wedded. Though mine were only a
captive,
None the less I loved her with a deep and tender affection.
After having carried off my prize let not the deceiver
Tempt me again. I know him. He shall not make me believe
him.
You, Odysseus, you princes of his, can counsel Atrides
How to protect the vessels from fierce flame, if you desire to.
Me he requires no longer—he does so bravely without me,
Building a high rampart, good Gods! and delving a deep moat
Under it and filling it with sharpen'd stakes to defend him!
And cannot all his efforts keep out victorious Hector?
There was a vast difference while I was fighting amongst you.
Hector arrayed the battles in my time under the gates of
Ilium or sallied out at most to the neighbouring oak-tree.
I sprang alone upon him one day there and he abode me
And very nearly perish'd. But now my fighting is over,
I offer up tomorrow to the Lord and all the immortal
Deities and victual all my ships and launch them in Ocean.
Look forth, if you desire to, if it concerns you to see us.
Starting about sunrise my ships sail over the teeming
Water, the crews pulling at their oars and driving us home-
wards.
'Tis but a three days' journey, if Earth-enfolder Poseidon
Favour us, and Achilleus shall come to the land of Phthia.
I've many great possessions I left in Phthia behind me

And carry home the treasures of gold, grey-glistering iron
And ruddy bronze and shapely women, my duly apportioned
Booty. But I carry not my prize home, since Agamemnon,
(Curses on his tyranny!) took back that maiden he gave me.
Go to him and tell him all I say—tell him in the assembly—
Let the Achaeans hear you. What indignation against him
Over the next Danaan, that he thinks of cheating as I was
Cheated. He can never change his spots, can shameless
    Atrides,
Though, it appears, in public he dares not face me, the das-
    tard.
Fight for him I never will, by God, nor counsel him either
After the tricks he's played me! He seeks now how to beguile
    me
By flatteries. But once is enough. We've parted asunder
Finally. I'm quit of him. God's wrath has made him a mad-
    man.
I spit upon the offers that he makes,—they move me to
    laughter.
Were he to give fivefold or tenfold all that he boasts of
Owning in his treasuries or dreams hereafter of owning;
Give me what Orchomenos contains, what children of Egypt
Garner up in Thebae, where huge hoards cumber the
    houses,—
Thebes of a hundred gates, where ten score fighters in armour
With chariots and horses abreast march out at a gateway;
Were he to lay me treasure like stars in number before me,
Numberless as sand-grains or dust, they should not appease
    me
Till the debt of bitter shame were paid back down to the last
    pang.
I never will wed daughter of his—tell that to Atrides.
Were she a maiden fairer than Ocean-born Aphrodite,
Mistress of as many arts as grey-eyed Maiden Athene,
Ne'ertheless I would not marry her. Let lord Agamemnon
Find her a mate elsewhere—I were too lowly a husband.
If we return home safely from Ilium, and the Immortals
Spare me, the king Peleus himself shall find me a maiden.

There's many maids in Hellas, many maids in Phthia to
  choose from,
Ladies of high lineage whose sires ward wealthy dominions:
And Achilleus shall find him a bride there, choosing amongst
  them.
My spirit has long moved me to sail home, look for a noble
Maiden, a fair helpmate, and dwell thereafter beside her
Peacefully on the riches my aged father bequeaths me.
Life is a far better thing than wealth is—life is a jewel
Of many times more value than all proud Ilium erewhile
Boasted of in peace time ere foes came out of Achaia,
And richer than the treasures which lie 'neath Phoebos Apol-
  lon's
Temple upon the rock of Pytho in chambers of hewn stone.
I can acquire cattle and fat sheep by seizing upon them,
And money buys me tripods and bright-maned fiery horses,
But nothing e'er can capture a man's life, after he breathes it
Out of him, and nothing in God's world can purchase it
  either.
My mother lady Thetis, long since has plainly assured me
Two different fates bear me upon my journey to Death's
  Gate;
Told me, if I tarry here and fight, God gives me eternal
Glory, but I fling away my hopes of safely returning;
And if again I fight not, if I sail home to Achaia,
I fling away my glory to gain life—life for a longer
Period instead of it—death shall not speedily seize me.
You other folk were wiser to sail home even as I do
And tarry here no longer. The hope of capturing Ilium
Has manifestly vanish'd, since Zeus extendeth his awful
Hand, covering the city, and new hope nerves the defenders.
Go your ways therefore, bear my words unto the Council
Of the Achaean princes. It is your duty as elders.
Seek for a fresh stratagem, for a plan more likely to help you
And to preserve the vessels and whole host of the Achaeans
That dwell around the vessels. Your first has proven a failure
As reckoning completely without my deadly resentment.
You, Phoenix, I bid you remain and slumber beside me.

When we set out tomorrow at day-break, you shall attend me
Home—that is, if you wish it. There's no compulsion about
    it.
    GEORGE ERNLE (*Iliad* 9.307-429)

*As the Greeks are forced back towards their ships the resist-
ance of Ajax is a tower of strength.*

14   But the eternal father throned on high
             With fear fill'd Ajax; panic-fixt he stood,
             His seven-fold shield behind his shoulder cast,
             And, hemm'd by numbers, with an eye askant,
             Watchful retreated. As a beast of prey
             Retiring, turns and looks, so he his face
             Turn'd oft, retiring slow, and step by step.
             As when the watch-dogs and assembled swains
             Have driv'n a tawny lion from the stalls,
             Then, interdicting him his wished repast,
             Watch all the night, he, famished, yet again
             Comes furious on, but speeds not, kept aloof
             By frequent spears from daring hands, but more
             By flash of torches, which, though fierce, he dreads,
             Till, at the dawn, sullen he stalks away;
             So from before the Trojans Ajax stalk'd
             Sullen, and with reluctance slow retir'd,
             His brave heart trembling for the fleet of Greece.
             As when (the boys o'erpower'd) a sluggish ass,
             Whose tough sides erst have shiver'd many a staff,
             Enters the harvest, and the spiry ears
             Crops persevering; with their rods the boys
             Still ply him hard, but all their puny might
             Scarce drives him forth when he hath browzed his fill,
             So, there, the Trojans and their foreign aids
             With glitt'ring lances keen, huge Ajax urged
             His broad shield's centre smiting. He, by turns,
             With desp'rate force the Trojan phalanx dense
             Facing, repulsed them, and by turns retired,
             But still forbad all inroad on the fleet.

Trojans and Greeks between, alone, he stood
A bulwark. Spears from daring hands dismiss'd
Some, in his shield's thick folds unwilling stay'd,
While others, in the midway falling, spent
Their disappointed fury in the ground.
    WILLIAM COWPER (*Iliad* 11.544-574)

*Sarpedon's speech to Glaucus is a fine statement of the heroic
principle of noblesse oblige.*

    Whence is it, Glaucus, that in Lycian land   **15**
We two at feasts the foremost seats may claim,
The largest portions, and the fullest cups?
Why held as Gods in honour? why endow'd
With ample heritage, by Xanthus' banks,
Of vineyard, and of wheat producing land?
Then by the Lycians should we not be seen
The foremost to affront the raging fight?
So may our well-arm'd Lycians make their boast;
'To no inglorious Kings we Lycians owe
Allegiance; they on richest viands feed;
Of luscious flavour drink the choicest wine;
But still their valour brightest shows; and they,
Where Lycians war, are foremost in the fight!'
O friend! if we, survivors of this war,
Could live, from age and death for ever free,
Thou shouldst not see me foremost in the fight,
Nor would I urge thee to the glorious field:
But since on man ten thousand forms of death
Attend, which none may 'scape, then on, that we
May glory on others gain, or they on us!
    EDWARD EARL OF DERBY (*Iliad* 12.310-328)

*To distract Zeus' attention from the battlefield Hera plans
an elaborate seduction.*

    Standing on high Olympus' topmost peak,   **16**
The golden-thronèd Juno downward look'd,

And, busied in the glory-giving strife,
Her husband's brother and her own she saw,
Saw, and rejoic'd; next, seated on the crest
Of spring-abounding Ida, Jove she saw,
Sight hateful in her eyes! then ponder'd deep
The stag-ey'd Queen, how best she might beguile
The wakeful mind of ægis-bearing Jove;
And, musing, this appear'd the readiest mode:
Herself with art adorning, to repair
To Ida; there, with fondest blandishment
And female charm, her husband to enfold
In love's embrace; and gentle, careless sleep
Around his eyelids and his senses pour.
Her chamber straight she sought, by Vulcan built,
Her son; by whom were to the door-posts hung
Close-fitting doors, with secret keys secur'd,
That, save herself, no God might enter in.
There enter'd she, and clos'd the shining doors;
And with ambrosia first her lovely skin
She purify'd, with fragrant oil anointing,
Ambrosial, breathing forth such odours sweet
That, wav'd above the brazen floor of Jove,
All earth and Heav'n were with the fragrance fill'd;
O'er her fair skin this precious oil she spread;
Comb'd out her flowing locks, and with her hand
Wreath'd the thick masses of the glossy hair,
Immortal, bright, that crown'd th' imperial head.
A robe ambrosial then, by Pallas wrought,
She donn'd, in many a curious pattern trac'd,
With golden brooch beneath her breast confin'd.
Her zone, from which a hundred tassels hung,
She girt about her; and, in three bright drops,
Her glitt'ring gems suspended from her ears;
And all around her grace and beauty shone.
Then o'er her head th' imperial Goddess threw
A beauteous veil, new-wrought, as sunlight white;
And on her well-turn'd feet her sandals bound.
Her dress completed, from her chamber forth

She issued, and from th' other Gods apart
She call'd to Venus, and address'd her thus:
"Say, wilt thou grant, dear child, the boon I ask?
Or wilt thou say me nay, in wrath that I
Espouse the Greek, as thou the Trojan cause?"
　　To whom the laughter-loving Venus thus:
"Daughter of Saturn, Juno, mighty Queen,
Tell me thy wish; to grant it if my pow'r
May aught avail, thy pleasure shall be done."
　　To whom great Juno thus, with artful speech:
"Give me the loveliness, and pow'r to charm,
Whereby thou reign'st o'er Gods and men supreme.
For to the bounteous Earth's extremest bounds
I go, to visit old Oceanus,
The sire of Gods, and Tethys, who of yore
From Rhæa took me, when all-seeing Jove
Hurl'd Saturn down below the earth and seas,
And nurs'd me in their home with tend'rest care;
I go to visit them, and reconcile
A lengthen'd feud; for since some cause of wrath
Has come between them, they from rites of love
And from the marriage-bed have long abstain'd:
Could I unite them by persuasive words,
And to their former intercourse restore,
Their love and rev'rence were for ever mine."
　　Whom answer'd thus the laughter-loving Queen:
"I ought not, and I cannot, say thee nay,
Who liest encircled by the arms of Jove."
　　Thus Venus spoke; and from her bosom loos'd
Her broider'd cestus, wrought with ev'ry charm
To win the heart; there Love, there young Desire,
There fond Discourse, and there Persuasion dwelt,
Which oft enthralls the mind of wisest men.
This in her hand she plac'd, as thus she spoke:
"Take thou from me, and in thy bosom hide,
This broider'd cestus; and, whate'er thy wish,
Thou shalt not here ungratified return."
　　Thus Venus; smil'd the stag-ey'd Queen of Heav'n,

And, smiling, in her bosom hid the gift.
Then Venus to her father's house return'd;
But Juno down from high Olympus sped;
O'er sweet Emathia, and Pieria's range,
O'er snowy mountains of horse-breeding Thrace,
Their topmost heights, she soar'd, nor touch'd the earth.
From Athos then she cross'd the swelling sea,
Until to Lemnos, godlike Thoas' seat,
She came; there met she Sleep, twin-born with Death,
Whom, as his hand she clasp'd, she thus address'd:
   "Sleep, universal King of Gods and men,
If ever thou hast listen'd to my voice,
Grant me the boon which now I ask, and win
My ceaseless favour in all time to come.
When Jove thou seest in my embraces lock'd,
Do thou his piercing eyes in slumber seal.
Rich guerdon shall be thine; a gorgeous throne,
Immortal, golden; which my skilful son,
Vulcan, shall deftly frame; beneath, a stool
Whereon at feasts thy feet may softly rest."
   Whom answer'd thus the gentle God of Sleep:
"Daughter of Saturn, Juno, mighty Queen,
On any other of th' immortal Gods
I can with ease exert my slumb'rous pow'r;
Even to the stream of old Oceanus,
Prime origin of all; but Saturn's son,
Imperial Jove, I dare not so approach,
Nor sink in sleep, save by his own desire.
Already once, obeying thy command,
A fearful warning I receiv'd, that day
When from the capture and the sack of Troy
That mighty warrior, son of Jove, set sail;
For, circumfus'd around, with sweet constraint
I bound the sense of ægis-bearing Jove,
While thou, with ill-design, rousing the force
Of winds tempestuous o'er the stormy sea,
Didst cast him forth on Coös' thriving isle,
Far from his friends; then Jove, awaking, pour'd

His wrath, promiscuous, on th' assembled Gods;
Me chief his anger sought; and from on high
Had hurl'd me, plung'd beneath th' unfathom'd sea,
But Night, the vanquisher of Gods and men,
Her fugitive received me; he his wrath
Repress'd, unwilling to invade the claims
Of holy Night; and now thou fain wouldst urge
That I another reckless deed essay."

Whom answer'd thus the stag-ey'd Queen of Heav'n:
"Why, Sleep, with thoughts like these perplex thy mind?
Think'st thou that Jove as ardently desires
To aid the men of Troy, as fiercely burn'd
His anger on his valiant son's behalf?
Grant my request; and of the Graces one,
The youngest and the fairest, have to wife,
Pasithea, whom thy love hath long pursued."

Thus promis'd Juno; Sleep, rejoicing, heard,
And answer'd thus: "Swear then the awful oath,
Inviolable, by the stream of Styx,
Thy one hand laid upon the fruitful earth,
The other resting on the sparkling sea;
That all the Gods who in the nether realms
With Saturn dwell, may of our solemn bond
Be witnesses, that of the Graces one,
The youngest, fairest, I shall have to wife,
Pasithea, whom my love hath long pursued."

He said: nor did the white-arm'd Queen refuse;
She took the oath requir'd; and call'd by name
On all the Titans, sub-Tartarean Gods:
Then, sworn and ratified the oath, they pass'd
From Lemnos, and from Imbros, veil'd in cloud,
Skimming their airy way; on Lectum first,
In spring-abounding Ida, nurse of beasts,
The sea they left, and journey'd o'er the land,
While wav'd beneath their feet the lofty woods.
There Sleep, ere yet he met the eye of Jove,
Remain'd; and, mounted on a lofty pine,
The tallest growth of Ida, that on high

Flung through the desert air its boughs to Heav'n,
Amid the pine's close branches lay ensconc'd;
Like to a mountain bird of shrillest note,
Whom Gods the Chalcis, men the night-hawk call.
Juno meanwhile to Ida's summit sped,
To Gargarus; the Cloud-compeller saw;
He saw, and sudden passion fir'd his soul,
As when, their parents' eyes eluding, first
They tasted of the secret joys of love.
He rose to meet her, and address'd her thus:
    "From high Olympus, Juno, whither bound,
And how, to Ida hast thou come in haste?
For horses here or chariot hast thou none."
    To whom thus Juno with deceitful speech
Replied: "To fertile earth's extremest bounds
I go, to visit old Oceanus,
The sire of Gods, and Tethys, who of yore
Receiv'd, and nurtur'd me with tend'rest care.
I go to visit them, and reconcile
A lengthen'd feud; for since some cause of wrath
Has come between them, they from rites of love
And from the marriage-bed have long abstain'd.
Meanwhile at spring-abounding Ida's foot
My horses wait me, that o'er land and sea
Alike my chariot bear; on thine account
From high Olympus hither have I come,
Lest it displease thee, if, to thee unknown,
I sought the Ocean's deeply-flowing stream."
    To whom the Cloud-compeller thus replied:
"Juno, thy visit yet awhile defer;
And let us now in love's delights indulge:
For never yet did such a flood of love
For Goddess or for mortal fill my soul;
Not for Ixion's beauteous wife, who bore
Pirithöus, sage in council as the Gods;
Nor the neat-footed maiden Danäe,
Acrisius' daughter, her who Perseus bore,

Th' observ'd of all; nor noble Phœnix' child,
Who bore me Minos, and the godlike might
Of Rhadamanthus; nor for Semele,
Nor for Alcmena fair, of whom was born
In Thebes the mighty warrior Hercules,
As Bacchus, joy of men, of Semele:
No, nor for Ceres, golden-tressèd Queen,
Nor for Latona bright, nor for thyself,
As now with fond desire for thee I burn."

   To whom thus Juno with deceitful speech:
"What words, dread son of Saturn, dost thou speak?
If here on Ida, in the face of day,
We celebrate the mystic rites of love,
How if some other of th' immortal Gods
Should find us sleeping, and 'mid all the Gods
Should spread the tale abroad? I could not then
Straight to thy house, for very shame, return.
But if indeed such passion fill thy soul,
Thou hast thy secret chamber, built for thee
By Vulcan, with close-fitting doors secur'd;
Thither, if such thy pleasure, go we now."

   To whom the Cloud-compeller thus replied:
"Juno, nor fear the eye of God or man;
For all around us I will throw such veil
Of golden cloud, that not the sun himself
With sharpest beam of light may pierce it through."

   Thus saying, in his arms he clasp'd his wife;
The teeming earth beneath them caus'd to spring
The tender grass, and lotus dew-besprent,
Crocus and hyacinth, a fragrant couch,
Profuse and soft, upspringing from the earth.
There lay they, all around them spread a veil
Of golden cloud, whence heav'nly dews distill'd.
There on the topmost height of Gargarus,
By sleep and love subdued, th' immortal Sire,
Clasp'd in his arms his wife, repos'd in peace.

   EDWARD EARL OF DERBY (*Iliad* 14.153-353)

*Patroclus, whom Achilles had sent for news, reports that the
chief Greeks are wounded and begs permission to join the
fight.*

17   Meanwhile Patroclus stood beside his friend
          The shepherd of the people, Peleus' son,
          And shed hot tears, as when a fountain sheds
          Dark waters streaming down a precipice.
          The great Achilles, swift of foot, beheld
          And pitied him, and spake these wingèd words:—
              "Why weepest thou, Patroclus, like a girl,—
          A little girl that by her mother's side
          Runs, importuning to be taken up,
          And plucks her by the robe, and stops her way,
          And looks at her, and cries, until at last
          She rests within her arms? Thou art like her,
          Patroclus, with thy tears. Dost thou then bring
          Sad tidings to the Myrmidons or me?
          Or hast thou news from Phthia? It is said
          That still Menœtius, son of Actor, lives,
          And Peleus also, son of Æacus,
          Among the Myrmidons. Full bitterly
          Should we lament to hear that either died.
          Or mournest thou because the Achaians fall
          Through their own folly by the roomy ships?
          Speak, and hide nothing, for I too would know."
              And thou, O knight Patroclus, with a sigh
          Deep-drawn, didst answer thus: "Be not displeased,
          Achilles, son of Peleus, bravest far
          Of all the Achaian army! for the Greeks
          Endure a bitter lot. The chiefs who late
          Were deemed their mightiest are within the ships,
          Wounded or stricken down. There Diomed,
          The gallant son of Tydeus, lies, and there
          Ulysses, the great spearman, wounded both;
          And Agamemnon; and Eurypylus,
          Driven from the field, an arrow in his thigh.

Round them the healers, skilled in remedies,
Attend and dress their painful wounds, while thou,
Achilles, sittest here implacable.
O, never be such fierce resentments mine
As thou dost cherish, who art only brave
For mischief! Whom wilt thou hereafter aid,
If now thou rescue not the perishing Greeks?
O merciless! it cannot surely be
That Peleus was thy father, or the queen
Thetis thy mother; the green sea instead
And rugged precipices brought thee forth,
For savage is thy heart. But if thou heed
The warning of some god, if thou hast heard
Aught which thy goddess-mother has received
From Jove, send me at least into the war,
And let me lead thy Myrmidons, that thus
The Greeks may have some gleam of hope. And give
The armor from thy shoulders. I will wear
Thy mail, and then the Trojans, at the sight,
May think I am Achilles, and may pause
From fighting, and the warlike sons of Greece,
Tired as they are, may breathe once more, and gain
A respite from the conflict. Our fresh troops
May easily drive back upon their town
The weary Trojans from our tents and fleet."
    W. C. Bryant (*Iliad* 16.2-45)

Achilles lends Patroclus his own armor, and sends him into battle with a prayer.

Achilles then within his tent withdrew,   **18**
And of a gorgeous coffer rais'd the lid,
Well-wrought, by silver-footed Thetis plac'd
On board his ship, and fill'd with rich attire,
With store of wind-proof cloaks, and carpets soft.
There lay a goblet, richly chas'd, whence none,
But he alone, might drink the ruddy wine,

Nor might libations thence to other Gods
Be made, save only Jove: this brought he forth,
And first with sulphur purified, and next
Wash'd with pure water; then his hands he wash'd,
And drew the ruddy wine; then standing forth
Made in the centre of the court his pray'r,
And as he pour'd the wine, look'd up to Heav'n,
Not unbeheld of Jove, the lightning's Lord:
   "Great King, Dodona's Lord, Pelasgian Jove,
Who dwell'st on high, and rul'st with sov'reign sway
Dodona's wintry heights; where dwell around
Thy Sellian priests, men of unwashen feet,
That on the bare ground sleep; thou once before
Hast heard my pray'r, and me with honour crown'd,
And on the Greeks inflicted all thy plagues;
Hear yet again, and this my boon accord.
I 'mid the throng of ships myself remain;
But with a num'rous force of Myrmidons
I send my comrade in my stead to fight:
On him, all-seeing Jove, thy favour pour;
Strengthen his heart, that Hector's self may learn
If, e'en alone, my follower knows to fight,
Or only then resistless pow'r displays,
When I myself the toil of battle share.
And from our vessels when the foe is driv'n,
Grant that with all his arms and comrades true
He may in safety to the ships return."
     EDWARD EARL OF DERBY (*Iliad* 16.220-248)

---

*Hector with his charioteer Cebriones drives to meet Patroclus,
who taunts Cebriones when his missile flings him from the
chariot.*

19   Patroclus lights, impatient for the fight;
A spear his left, a stone employs his right:
With all his nerves he drives it at the foe.
Pointed above, and rough and gross below:
The falling ruin crushed Cebrion's head,

The lawless offspring of king Priam's bed;
His front, brows, eyes, one undistinguish'd wound:
The bursting balls drop sightless to the ground.
The charioteer, while yet he held the rein,
Struck from the car, falls headlong on the plain.
To the dark shades the soul unwilling glides,
While the proud victor thus his fall derides.
    "Good heaven! what active feats yon artist shows!
What skilful divers are our Phrygian foes!
Mark with what ease they sink into the sand!
Pity that all their practice is by land!"
    ALEXANDER POPE (*Iliad* 16.733-750)

*The struggle over the body of Cebriones culminates in the
death of Patroclus; Hector's conduct falls short of the re-
quirements of the heroic code.*

Now while the sun was going about mid-heaven, so long **20**
the darts smote either side, and the host fell, but when the
sun turned to the time of the loosing of oxen, lo, then be-
yond their doom the Achaians proved the better. The hero
Kebriones drew they forth from the darts, out of the tumult
of the Trojans, and stripped the harness from his shoulders,
and with ill design against the Trojans, Patroklos rushed upon
them. Three times then rushed he on, peer of swift Ares,
shouting terribly, and thrice he slew nine men. But when the
fourth time he sped on like a god, thereon to thee, Patroklos,
did the end of life appear, for Phoebus met thee in the strong
battle, in dreadful wise. And Patroklos was not ware of him
coming through the press, for hidden in thick mist did he
meet him, and stood behind him, and smote his back and
broad shoulders with a down-stroke of his hand, and his
eyes were dazed. And from his head Phoebus Apollo smote
the helmet that rolled rattling away with a din beneath the
hooves of the horses, the helm with upright socket, and the
crests were defiled with blood and dust. Not of old was it
suffered that the helm with horsehair crest should be defiled
with dust, nay, but it kept the head and beautiful face of a

man divine, even of Achilles. But as then Zeus gave it to Hector, to bear on his head, yet was destruction near him. And all the long-shadowed spear was shattered in the hands of Patroklos, the spear great and heavy and strong, and sharp, while from his shoulders the tasselled shield with the baldric fell to the ground.

And the prince Apollo, son of Zeus, loosed his corslet, and blindness seized his heart and his shining limbs were unstrung, and he stood in amaze, and at close quarters from behind a Dardanian smote him on the back, between the shoulders, with a sharp spear, even Euphorbos, son of Panthoös, who excelled them of his age in casting the spear, and in horsemanship, and in speed of foot. Even thus, verily, had he cast down twenty men from their chariots, though then first had he come with his car to learn the lesson of war. He it was that first smote a dart into thee, knightly Patroklos, nor overcame thee, but ran back again and mingled with the throng, first drawing forth from the flesh his ashen spear, nor did he abide the onset of Patroklos, unarmed as he was, in the strife. But Patroklos, being overcome by the stroke of the god, and by the spear, gave ground, and retreated to the host of his comrades, avoiding Fate. But Hector, when he beheld great-hearted Patroklos give ground, being smitten with the keen bronze, came nigh unto him through the ranks, and wounded him with a spear, in the lowermost part of the belly, and drave the bronze clean through. And he fell with a crash, and sorely grieved the host of Achaians. And as when a lion hath overcome in battle an untiring boar, they twain fighting with high heart on the crests of a hill, about a little well, and both are desirous to drink, and the lion hath by force overcome the boar that draweth difficult breath; so after that he had slain many did Hector son of Priam take the life away from the strong son of Menoitios, smiting him at close quarters with the spear; and boasting over him he spake winged words: "Patroklos, surely thou saidst that thou wouldst sack my town, and from Trojan women take away the day of freedom, and bring them in ships to thine own dear country:

fool! nay, in front of these were the swift horses of Hector
straining their speed for the fight; and myself in wielding the
spear excel among the war-loving Trojans, even I who ward
from them the day of destiny: but thee shall vultures here
devour. Ah, wretch, surely Achilles for all his valour, availed
thee not, who straitly charged thee as thou camest, he abiding
there, saying, 'Come not to me, Patroklos lord of steeds, to
the hollow ships, till thou hast torn the gory doublet of man-
slaying Hector about his breast;' so, surely, he spake to thee,
and persuaded the wits of thee in thy witlessness."

Then faintly didst thou answer him, knightly Patroklos:
"Boast greatly, as now, Hector, for to thee have Zeus, son of
Kronos, and Apollo given the victory, who lightly have sub-
dued me; for themselves stripped my harness from my shoul-
ders. But if twenty such as thou had encountered me, here
had they all perished, subdued beneath my spear. But me
had ruinous Fate and the son of Leto slain, and of men
Euphorbos, but thou art the third in my slaying. But another
thing will I tell thee, and do thou lay it up in thy heart; verily
thou thyself art not long to live, but already doth Death stand
hard by thee, and strong Fate, that thou art to be subdued
by the hands of noble Achilles, of the seed of Aiakos."

Even as so he spake the end of death overshadowed him.
And his soul, fleeting from his limbs, went down to the house
of Hades, wailing its own doom, leaving manhood and youth.

Then renowned Hector spake to him even in his death:
"Patroklos, wherefore to me dost thou prophesy sheer destruc-
tion? who knows but that Achilles, the child of fair-tressed
Thetis, will first be smitten by my spear, and lose his life?"

So spake he, and drew the spear of bronze from the wound,
setting his foot on the dead, and cast him off on his back
from the spear. And straightway with the spear he went after
Automedon, the godlike squire of the swift-footed Aikides,
for he was eager to smite him; but his swift-footed immortal
horses bare him out of the battle, horses that the gods gave
to Peleus a splendid gift.

LANG, LEAF, AND MYERS (*Iliad* 16.823-867)

Achilles' horses weep for grief, and are comforted by Zeus.

21   Meantime, at distance from the scene of blood,
                The pensive steeds of great Achilles stood:
                Their godlike master slain before their eyes,
                They wept, and shared in human miseries.
                In vain Automedon now shakes the rein,
                Now plies the lash, and soothes and threats in vain;
                Nor to the fight nor Hellespont they go,
                Restive they stood, and obstinate in woe:
                Still as a tombstone, never to be moved,
                On some good man or woman unreproved
                Lays its eternal weight; or fix'd, as stands
                A marble courser by the sculptor's hands,
                Placed on the hero's grave. Along their face
                The big round drops coursed down with silent pace,
                Conglobing on the dust. Their manes, that late
                Circled their arched necks, and waved in state,
                Trail'd on the dust beneath the yoke were spread,
                And prone to earth was hung their languid head:
                Nor Jove disdain'd to cast a pitying look,
                While thus relenting to the steeds he spoke:
                "Unhappy coursers of immortal strain,
                Exempt from age, and deathless, now in vain;
                Did we your race on mortal man bestow,
                Only, alas! to share in mortal woe?
                For ah! what is there of inferior birth,
                That breathes or creeps upon the dust of earth;
                What wretched creature of what wretched kind,
                Than man more weak, calamitous, and blind?
                A miserable race! but cease to mourn:
                For not by you shall Priam's son be borne
                High on the splendid car: one glorious prize
                He rashly boasts: the rest our will denies.
                Ourself will swiftness to your nerves impart,
                Ourself with rising spirits swell your heart.
                Automedon your rapid flight shall bear

Safe to the navy through the storm of war.
For yet 'tis given to Troy to ravage o'er
The field, and spread her slaughters to the shore;
The sun shall see her conquer, till his fall
With sacred darkness shades the face of all."
ALEXANDER POPE (*Iliad* 17.426-455)

*If we are doomed, Ajax prays, let us have light to fight by,
and not darkness.*

"O Heav'n! the veriest child might plainly see   **22**
That Jove the Trojans' triumph has decreed:
Their weapons all, by whomsoever thrown,
Or weak, or strong, attain their mark; for Jove
Directs their course; while ours upon the plain
Innocuous fall. But take we counsel now
How from the fray to bear away our dead,
And by our own return rejoice those friends
Who look with sorrow on our plight, and deem
That we, all pow'rless to resist the might
Of Hector's arm, beside the ships must fall.
Would that some comrade were at hand, to bear
A message to Achilles; him, I ween,
As yet the mournful tidings have not reach'd,
That on the field his dearest friend lies dead.
But such I see not; for a veil of cloud
O'er men and horses all around is spread.
O Father Jove, from o'er the sons of Greece
Remove this cloudy darkness; clear the sky,
That we may see our fate, and die at least,
If such thy will, in th' open light of day."
He said, and, pitying, Jove beheld his tears;
The clouds he scatter'd, and the mist dispers'd;
The sun shone forth, and all the field was clear.
EDWARD EARL OF DERBY (*Iliad* 17.629-650)

Achilles is stunned by the news of Patroclus' death, and is
comforted by his mother Thetis, who also promises him new
weapons.

23   At the report agony like dark mist clouded his eyesight,
And with a cry he gather'd black dust and cast it in handfuls
Over him, and sullied his bright brows by heaping it on them,
Until his whole apparel was black with a coating of ash-dust.
Down Achilleus crashing into the dust lay mightily fallen,
Tearing up and scattering those locks so lovely of olden.
Slave-women, whom Patroclos had help'd his master to cap-
       ture,
Shriek'd as if in terror of their lives upon hearing his outcry,
And rushing out together beat their breasts over Achilleus
In such a deadly panic, their knees could scarcely support
       them.
Meanwhile Antilochos knelt weeping, wailing amongst them,
And with his hands held tightly the wrists of groaning Achil-
       leus,
Fearful of his plucking out his steel and cleaving his own
       throat.
His mother heard the sorrow they made, deep under the
       water,
And sitting, as she listen'd, with her aged father beside her,
Lifted up her voice there and wept. And every immortal
Nereid, whose dwelling is deep seas, came crowding about
       her,
And filling all the cavern, beat their breasts, bearing a burden
Unto the words their sister Thetis sang wailing amongst them.
   "Oh, listen, all ye daughters o' Nereus. I will acquaint you
Faithfully with the sorrows which wring me, if only you
       hearken.
Woe's me! How wretched is my fate in bearing a peerless
Champion—I who travailed with brave, with stainless Achil-
       leus,
Matchless among warriors. He shot upwards, clean as a
       sapling;

He was a brave fruit-tree, rear'd in my sheltering orchard.
I put him on the vessels, I sent him forth to the siege of
Ilium and the battle—never, ah, never after to greet him
Home from it in the dwellings of Peleus, where we await him.
While yet amongst the living, while sunlight warms him,
     affliction
Vexes him; and visiting my child I may not avail him
Ne'ertheless I'll visit him, my darling, if only to ask him
And to be told whereof he laments, though lying inactive."

   His mother left the cavern with these words, being at-
     tended
By the sobbing sea-nymphs, and waves fell foaming asunder
As the goddess footed it to the fertile kingdom of Ilium.
One following the other, they landed close to Achilleus,
Where the thronging warships lay beach'd in a cluster about
     him.
Lo, as he lay uttering deep groans, there stood she before him,
His mother; and she uttered one shriek, and tenderly clasping
Her son about the forehead spake thuswise unto Achilleus:

   "Child, what is all your weeping about? What makes you
     lament so?
Tell me the cause, I pray you. The Lord has surely accom-
     plish'd
What you desired so greatly, you sought so eagerly after!
See, the Achaean people is hemm'd in close to the ships'
     sterns
Yonder—it is suffering disgrace and danger without you."

   Then with a most bitter groan Achilleus spoke saying in
     answer:
"Yes, mother, all he promised to accomplish, Zeus hath
     accomplish'd.
True! But have I pleasure in such things when losing a com-
     rade—
Losing a friend far dearer than all friends—dearer than even
My very life—Patroclos! He lies slain: Hector who slew him,
Took from him our magic arms—that suit of marvellous
     armour,

Which was a wonder given King Peleus by the Immortals
That very day they led you to wed with a mortal of earth's
    race.
'Twere better had you tarried with sea-nymphs under the
    waters,
If Peleus in taking a bride had chosen a mortal,
Since as it is, need drives me to wring you with infinite
    anguish,
Pain for a son perishing soon, soon! Never shall you receive
    me
Safe back again in Phthia; because shame will not allow me
Still to live and look upon mankind, excepting if Hector
Is to be slain straightway and my spear only to slay him
And to avenge upon him that his hand dared slaughter
    Patroclos."
    His mother lady Thetis shed tears, thus saying in answer:
"Look for a short life, child, if this be spoken in earnest.
After the slaying of Hector, a like doom early awaits you."
    And Achilleus made answer with heartfelt noble emotion.
"No matter, let me perish. My friend died early as I do,
Neither did I succour him. Patroclos died in a distant
Country, yet I came not to his aid when he needed assistance.
Well then, as I am not to return home—so you assure me—
And have, alas, saved neither Patroclos nor the remaining
Myrmidones, who perished by scores encountering Hector,
But sat amongst the vessels as a useless burden on earth's
    breast,
I, that am of quality unlike other sons of Achaia
In bloody fight,—let others speak wiselier in the assembly!—
Oh, blot it out of Heaven, vile Strife; let nobody henceforth
Hear of it; or bitter wrath, which triumphs over the wisest,
Sweeter than oozing honey, while entering into a man's
    breast,
And spreading in the bosom like smoke, once finding an
    entrance:
Such bitter wrath as seized me against Agamemnon Atrides!
We will allow bygones to be bygones, though we deplore
    them,

Mastering our swelling hearts that fight so fiercely against us,
Now let us out to battle, where my friend's slayer awaits me,
Hector! If I fall there, I fall there. Let the Immortals
Order it, and Cronides, their Ruler, appoint me the season.
None can avoid death, lady. Not Heracles could avoid it.
He was a great warrior, King Zeus once mightily loved him,
And yet he had to perish by Fate and hatred of Hera.
I, if a like death-doom is mine, must bow me as he did
Into the dust. First let me achieve some noble achievement!
Let me afford a widow of Troy or daughter of Ilium
Cause to brush off bitter tears with both hands, wiping her
        eyelids
And pretty cheeks, and raising a wild wail over the fallen:
Make them aware Achilleus has long been lying inactive!
Hinder me not, loving as thou art—I may not obey thee."
    His mother, silver-footed sea-nymph, spake saying in an-
        swer:
"Nay, Achilleus, 'tis wisely resolved and worthily of you,
Not to allow followers and friends to be shamefully slaugh-
        tered.
Only the foe is master of all your beautiful armour,
And the flashing panoply of bronze high-helmeted Hector
Wears for his own and glories in it. Yet he glories a short
        while
Only, as I prophesy, for his own doom closes about him.
Now, Achilleus, I'm going away. Let nobody tempt you
Into the fight. Tarry here until you behold me returning.
I'll come again tomorrow at sunrise after procuring
From the divine Hephaestos a suit of marvellous armour."
    GEORGE ERNLE (*Iliad* 18.22-137)

*Before his new armor is ready Achilles helps his comrades by
terrifying the Trojans with his shouting.*

So saying, light-foot Iris past away.
Then rose Achilles dear to Zeus; and round
The warrior's puissant shoulders Pallas flung
Her fringed aegis, and around his head

24

The glorious goddess wreathed a golden cloud,
And from it lighted an all-shining flame.
As when a smoke from a city goes to heaven
Far off from out an island girt by foes,
All day the men contend in grievous war
From their own city, but with set of sun
Their fires flame thickly and aloft the glare
Flies streaming, if perchance the neighbours round
May see, and sail to help them in the war;
So from his head the splendour went to heaven.
From wall to dyke he stept, he stood, nor joined
The Achaians—honouring his wise mother's word—
There standing, shouted, and Pallas far away
Called; and a boundless panic shook the foe.
For like the clear voice when a trumpet shrills,
Blown by the fierce beleaguerers of a town;
So rang the clear voice of Aiakides;
And when the brazen cry of Aiakides
Was heard among the Trojans, all their hearts
Were troubled and the full-maned horses whirled
The chariots backward, knowing griefs at hand;
And sheer-astounded were the charioteers
To see the dread, unweariable fire,
That always o'er the great Peleion's head
Burned, for the bright-eyed goddess made it burn.
Thrice from the dyke he sent his mighty shout,
Thrice backward reeled the Trojans and allies;
And there and then twelve of their noblest died
Among their spears and chariots.
                ALFRED TENNYSON (*Iliad* 18.202-231)

*The shield which Hephaestus made for Achilles had upon it
representations of all human activities—men disputing, work-
ing, fighting, marrying, ploughing, working the vintage, and
(in the passage below) dancing.*

25   And there illustrious Vulcan also wrought
        A dance,—a maze like that which Dædalus

In the broad realms of Gnossus once contrived
For fair-haired Ariadne. Blooming youths
And lovely virgins, tripping to light airs,
Held fast each other's wrists. The maidens wore
Fine linen robes; the youths had tunics on
Lustrous as oil, and woven daintily.
The maids wore wreaths of flowers; the young men swords
Of gold in silver belts. They bounded now
In a swift circle,—as a potter whirls
With both his hands a wheel to try its speed,
Sitting before it,—then again they crossed
Each other, darting to their former place.
A multitude around that joyous dance
Gathered, and were amused, while from the crowd
Two tumblers raised their song, and flung themselves
About among the band that trod the dance.
   W. C. BRYANT (*Iliad* 18.590-606)

*After the assembly at which Achilles formally renounces his
wrath and Agamemnon apologizes we have a touching picture
of returned Briseis' grief for Patroclus:*

Briseis, fair as golden Venus, saw   **26**
Patroclus lying, pierc'd with mortal wounds,
Within the tent; and with a bitter cry,
She flung her down upon the corpse, and tore
Her breast, her delicate neck, and beauteous cheeks;
And, weeping, thus the lovely woman wailed:
   "Patroclus, dearly loved of this sad heart!
When last I left this tent, I left thee full
Of healthy life; returning now, I find
Only thy lifeless corpse, thou Prince of men!
So sorrow still, on sorrow heap'd, I bear.
The husband of my youth, to whom my sire
And honour'd mother gave me, I beheld
Slain with the sword before the city walls:
Three brothers, whom with me one mother bore,
My dearly lov'd ones, all were doom'd to death:

Nor wouldst thou, when Achilles swift of foot
My husband slew, and royal Mynes' town
In ruin laid, allow my tears to flow;
But thou wouldst make me (such was still thy speech)
The wedded wife of Peleus' godlike son:
Thou wouldst to Phthia bear me in thy ship,
And there, thyself, amid the Myrmidons,
Wouldst give my marriage feast; then, unconsol'd,
I weep thy death, my ever-gentle friend!"
   Weeping, she spoke; the women join'd her wail:
Patroclus' death the pretext for their tears,
But each in secret wept her private griefs.
         EDWARD EARL OF DERBY (*Iliad* 19.282-302)

*Newly armed and raging, Achilles drives the Trojans to the
river Xanthus.*

27   But when now they came unto the ford of the fair-flowing
river, even eddying Xanthos, whom immortal Zeus begat,
there sundering them he chased the one part to the plain
toward the city, even where the Achaians were flying in af-
fright the day before, when glorious Hector was in his fury—
thither poured some in flight, and Hera spread before them
thick mist to hinder them:—but half were pent into the
deep-flowing silver-eddied river, and fell therein with a mighty
noise, and the steep channel sounded, and the banks around
rang loudly; for with shouting they swam therein hither and
thither, whirled round the eddies. And as when at the rush of
fire locusts take wing to fly unto a river, and the unwearying
fire flameth forth on them with sudden onset, and they hud-
dle in the water; so before Achilles was the stream of deep-
eddying Xanthos filled with the roar and the throng of horses
and men.

   Then the seed of Zeus left behind him his spear upon the
bank, leant against tamarisk bushes, and leapt in, as it were
a god, keeping his sword alone, and devised grim work at
heart, and smote as he turned him every way about: and

their groaning went up ghastly as they were stricken by the
sword, and the water reddened with blood.

LANG, LEAF, AND MYERS (*Iliad* 21.1-21)

*The terrible carnage Achilles wreaks in its bed chokes the
river, who conspires with his brother rivers to discomfit
Achilles.*

Now bursting on his head with thundering sound,   **28**
The falling deluge whelms the hero round:
His loaded shield bends to the rushing tide;
His feet, upborne, scarce the strong flood divide,
Sliddering, and staggering. On the border stood
A spreading elm, that overhung the flood;
He seized a bending bough, his steps to stay;
The plant uprooted to his weight gave way,
Heaving the bank, and undermining all;
Loud flash the waters to the rushing fall
Of the thick foliage. The large trunk display'd
Bridged the rough flood across: the hero stay'd
On this his weight, and raised upon his hand,
Leap'd from the channel, and regain'd the land.
Then blacken'd the wild waves: the murmur rose.
The god pursues, a huger billow throws,
And bursts the bank, ambitious to destroy
The man whose fury is the fate of Troy.
He like the warlike eagle speeds his pace
(Swiftest and strongest of the aërial race);
Far as a spear can fly, Achilles springs;
At every bound his clanging armour rings:
Now here, now there, he turns on every side,
And winds his course before the following tide;
The waves flow after, wheresoe'er he wheels,
And gather fast, and murmur at his heels.
So when a peasant to his garden brings
Soft rills of water from the bubbling springs,
And calls the floods from high, to bless his bowers,

And feed with pregnant streams the plants and flowers:
Soon as he clears whate'er their passage stay'd,
And marks the future current with his spade,
Swift o'er the rolling pebbles, down the hills,
Louder and louder purl the falling rills;
Before him scattering, they prevent his pains,
And shine in mazy wanderings o'er the plains.
    ALEXANDER POPE (*Iliad* 21.240-262)

The Trojans are driven into their city, all except Hector, who disregards the pathetic appeals of Priam and of Hecuba to flee.

29　　　　Thus, weeping bitterly, the aged pair
Entreated their dear son, yet moved him not.
He stood and waited for his mighty foe,
Achilles, as a serpent at his den,
Fed on the poisons of the wild, awaits
The traveller, and, fierce with hate of man,
And glaring fearfully, lies coiled within.
So waited Hector with a resolute heart,
And kept his ground, and, leaning his bright shield
Against a tower that jutted from the walls,
Conferred with his great soul impatiently:—
    "Ah me! if I should pass within the walls,
Then will Polydamus be first to cast
Reproach upon me; for he counselled me
To lead the Trojans back into the town
That fatal night which saw Achilles rise
To join the war again. I yielded not
To his advice; far better if I had.
Now, since my fatal stubbornness has brought
This ruin on my people, I most dread
The censure of the men and long-robed dames
Of Ilium. Men less brave than I will say,
'Foolhardy Hector in his pride has thrown
His people's lives away.' So will they speak,

And better were it for me to return,
Achilles slain, or, slain myself by him,
To perish for my country gloriously.
But should I lay aside this bossy shield
And this stout helm, and lean against the wall
This spear, and go to meet the gallant son
Of Peleus, with a promise to restore
Helen and all the treasure brought with her
To Troy by Paris, in his roomy ships,—
All that the war was waged for,—that the sons
Of Atreus may convey it hence, besides
Wealth drawn from all the hoards within the town,
And to be shared among the Greeks; for I
Would bind the Trojans by a solemn oath
To keep back nothing, but divide the whole—
Whate'er of riches this fair town contains—
Into two parts—But why should I waste thought
On plans like these? I must not act the part
Of suppliant to a man who may not show
Regard or mercy, but may hew me down
Defenceless, with my armor laid aside
As if I were a woman. Not with him
May I hold parley from a tree or rock,
As youths and maidens with each other hold
Light converse. Better 't were to rush at once
To combat, and the sooner learn to whom
Olympian Jove decrees the victory."
    W. C. Bryant (*Iliad* 22.90-130)

But Hector cannot abide Achilles' approach.

    Thus pondering he stood; meantime approach'd   **30**
Achilles, terrible as fiery Mars,
Crest-tossing God, and brandish'd as he came
O'er his right shoulder high the Pêlian spear.
Like lightning, or like flame, or like the sun
Ascending, beam'd his armour. At that sight

Trembled the Trojan Chief, nor dared expect
His nearer step, but flying left the gates
Far distant, and Achilles swift pursued.
As in the mountains, fleetest fowl of air,
The hawk darts eager at the dove; she scuds
Aslant, he, screaming, springs and springs again
To seize her, all impatient for the prey,
So flew Achilles constant to the track
Of Hector, who with dreadful haste beneath
The Trojan bulwarks plied his agile limbs.
Passing the prospect-mount where high in air
The wild-fig waved, they rush'd along the road,
Declining never from the wall of Troy.
And now they reach'd the running rivulets clear,
Where from Scamander's dizzy flood arise
Two fountains, tepid one, from which a smoke
Issues voluminous as from a fire,
The other, even in summer heats, like hail
For cold, or snow, or chrystal-stream frost-bound.
Beside them may be seen the broad canals
Of marble scoop'd, in which the wives of Troy
And all her daughters fair were wont to lave
Their costly raiment, while the land had rest,
And ere the warlike sons of Greece arrived.
By these they ran, one fleeing, one in chase.
Valiant was he who fled, but valiant far
Beyond him He who urged the swift pursuit;
Nor ran they for a vulgar prize, a beast
For sacrifice, or for the hide of such,
The swift foot-racer's customary meed,
But for the noble Hector's life they ran.
As when two steeds, oft conquerors, trim the goal
For some illustrious prize, a tripod bright
Or beauteous virgin, at a funeral game,
So they with nimble feet the city thrice
Of Priam compass'd. All the Gods looked on.
　　WILLIAM COWPER (*Iliad* 22.131-166)

Athena assumes the guise of a Trojan ally and tricks Hector
into making a stand. He attempts to bargain with Achilles.

"No longer I avoid thee as of late,   **31**
O son of Peleus! Thrice around the walls
Of Priam's mighty city have I fled,
Nor dared to wait thy coming. Now my heart
Bids me encounter thee; my time is come
To slay or to be slain. Now let us call
The gods to witness, who attest and guard
The covenants of men. Should Jove bestow
On me the victory, and I take thy life,
Thou shalt meet no dishonor at my hands;
But, stripping off the armor, I will send
The Greeks thy body. Do the like by me."
    The swift Achilles answered with a frown:
"Accursed Hector, never talk to me
Of covenants. Men and lions plight no faith,
Nor wolves agree with lambs, but each must plan
Evil against the other. So between
Thyself and me no compact can exist,
Or understood intent. First, one of us
Must fall and yield his life-blood to the god
Of battles. Summon all thy valor now.
A skilful spearman thou hast need to be,
And a bold warrior. There is no escape,
For now doth Pallas doom thee to be slain
By my good spear. Thou shalt repay to me
The evils thou hast done my countrymen,—
My friends whom thou hast slaughtered in thy rage."
    W. C. BRYANT (*Iliad* 22.250-272)

Hector realizes that his ally was but a phantom, and addresses
himself to the inevitable.

Thus as he spoke, his sharp-edged sword he drew,   **32**
Pond'rous and vast, suspended at his side;

Collected for the spring, and forward dash'd:
As when an eagle, bird of loftiest flight,
Through the dark clouds swoops downward on the plain,
To seize some tender lamb, or cow'ring hare;
So Hector rush'd, and wav'd his sharp-edg'd sword.
Achilles' wrath was rous'd: with fury wild
His soul was fill'd: before his breast he bore
His well-wrought shield; and fiercely on his brow
Nodded the four-plum'd helm, as on the breeze
Floated the golden hairs, with which the crest
By Vulcan's hand was thickly interlac'd;
And as amid the stars' unnumber'd host,
When twilight yields to night, one star appears,
Hesper, the brightest star that shines in Heav'n,
Gleam'd the sharp-pointed lance, which in his right
Achilles pois'd, on godlike Hector's doom
Intent, and scanning eagerly to see
Where from attack his body least was fenc'd.
All else the glitt'ring armour guarded well,
Which Hector from Patroclus' corpse had stripp'd;
One chink appear'd, just where the collar-bone
The neck and shoulder parts, beside the throat,
Where lies expos'd the swiftest road of death.
There levell'd he, as Hector onward rush'd;
Right through the yielding neck the lance was driv'n,
But sever'd not the windpipe, nor destroy'd
His pow'r of speech; prone in the dust he fell;
And o'er him, vaunting, thus Achilles spoke:
   "Hector, Patroclus stripping of his arms,
Thy hope was that thyself wast safe; and I,
Not present, brought no terror to thy soul:
Fool! in the hollow ships I yet remain'd,
I, his avenger, mightier far than he;
I, who am now thy conqu'ror. By the dogs
And vultures shall thy corpse be foully torn,
While him the Greeks with fun'ral rites shall grace."
   Whom answer'd Hector of the glancing helm,
Prostrate and helpless: "By thy soul, thy knees,

Thy parents' heads, Achilles, I beseech,
Let not my corpse by Grecian dogs be torn.
Accept the ample stores of brass and gold,
Which as my ransom by my honour'd sire
And mother shall be paid thee; but my corpse
Restore, that so the men and wives of Troy
May deck with honours due my fun'ral pyre."

To whom, with fierce aspect, Achilles thus:
"Knee me no knees, vile hound! nor prate to me
Of parents! such my hatred, that almost
I could persuade myself to tear and eat
Thy mangled flesh; such wrongs I have to avenge.
He lives not, who can save thee from the dogs;
Not though with ransom ten and twenty fold
He here should stand, and yet should promise more;
No, not though Priam's royal self should sue
To be allow'd for gold to ransom thee;
No, not e'en so, thy mother shall obtain
To lay thee out upon the couch, and mourn
O'er thee, her offspring; but on all thy limbs
Shall dogs and carrion vultures make their feast."

To whom thus Hector of the glancing helm,
Dying: "I know thee well; nor did I hope
To change thy purpose; iron is thy soul.
But see that on thy head I bring not down
The wrath of Heav'n, when by the Scæan gate
The hand of Paris, with Apollo's aid,
Brave warrior as thou art, shall strike thee down."

E'en as he spoke, his eyes were clos'd in death;
And to the viewless shades his spirit fled,
Mourning his fate, his youth and vigour lost.

To him, though dead, Achilles thus replied:
"Die thou! my fate I then shall meet, whene'er
Jove and th' immortal Gods shall so decree."

He said, and from the corpse his spear withdrew,
And laid aside; then stripp'd the armour off,
With blood besmear'd; the Greeks around him throng'd,
Gazing on Hector's noble form and face,

And none approach'd that did not add a wound:
And one to other look'd, and said, "Good faith,
Hector is easier far to handle now,
Than when erewhile he wrapp'd our ships in fire."
Thus would they say, then stab the dead anew.

EDWARD EARL OF DERBY (*Iliad* 22.306-375)

*His parents Priam and Hecuba bewail the death of Hector;
his wife Andromache is the last to hear the news.*

33   So she spoke in tears but the wife of Hektor had not yet
heard: for no sure messenger had come to her and told her
how her husband had held his ground there outside the gates;
but she was weaving a web in the inner room of the high
          house,
a red folding robe, and inworking elaborate figures.
She called out through the house to her lovely-haired hand-
          maidens
to set a great cauldron over the fire, so that there would be
hot water for Hektor's bath as he came back out of the
          fighting;
poor innocent, nor knew how, far from waters for bathing,
Pallas Athene had cut him down at the hands of Achilleus.
She heard from the great bastion the noise of mourning and
          sorrow.
Her limbs spun, and the shuttle dropped from her hand to
          the ground. Then
she called aloud to her lovely-haired handmaidens: 'Come
          here.
Two of you come with me, so I can see what has happened.
I heard the voice of Hektor's honoured mother; within me
my own heart rising beats in my mouth, my limbs under me
are frozen. Surely some evil is near for the children of Priam.
May what I say come never close to my ear; yet dreadfully
I fear that great Achilleus might have cut off bold Hektor
alone, away from the city, and be driving him into the flat
          land,
might put an end to that bitter pride of courage, that always

was on him; since he would never stay back where the men
    were in numbers
but break far out in front, and give way in his fury to no man.'
    So she spoke, and ran out of the house like a raving woman
with pulsing heart, and her two handmaidens went along
    with her.
But when she came to the bastion and where the men were
    gathered
she stopped, staring, on the wall; and she saw him
being dragged in front of the city, and the running horses
dragged him at random toward the hollow ships of the
    Achaians.
The darkness of night misted over the eyes of Andromache.
She fell backward, and gasped the life breath from her, and
    far off
threw from her head the shining gear that ordered her head-
    dress,
the diadem and the cap, and the holding-band woven to-
    gether,
and the circlet, which Aphrodite the golden once had given
    her
on that day when Hektor of the shining helmet led her forth
from the house of Eëtion, and gave numberless gifts to win
    her.
And about her stood thronging her husband's sisters and the
    wives of his brothers
and these, in her despair for death, held her up among them.
But she, when she breathed again and the life was gathered
    back into her,
lifted her voice among the women of Troy in mourning:
'Hektor, I grieve for you. You and I were born to a single
destiny, you in Troy in the house of Priam, and I
in Thebe, underneath the timbered mountain of Plakos
in the house of Eëtion, who cared for me when I was little,
ill-fated he, I ill-starred. I wish he had never begotten me.
Now you go down to the house of Death in the secret places
of the earth, and left me here behind in the sorrow of
    mourning,

a widow in your house, and the boy is only a baby
who was born to you and me, the unfortunate. You cannot
  help him,
Hektor, any more, since you are dead. Nor can he help you.
Though he escape the attack of the Achaians with all its sor-
  rows,
yet all his days for your sake there will be hard work for him
and sorrows, for others will take his lands away from him.
  The day
of bereavement leaves a child with no agemates to befriend
  him.
He bows his head before every man, his cheeks are bewept, he
goes, needy, a boy among his father's companions,
and tugs at this man by the mantle, that man by the tunic,
and they pity him, and one gives him a tiny drink from a
  goblet,
enough to moisten his lips, not enough to moisten his palate.
But one whose parents are living beats him out of the banquet
hitting him with his fists and in words also abuses him:
"Get out, you! Your father is not dining among us."
And the boy goes away in tears to his widowed mother,
Astyanax, who in days before on the knees of his father
would eat only the marrow or the flesh of sheep that was
  fattest.
And when sleep would come upon him and he was done with
  his playing,
he would go to sleep in a bed, in the arms of his nurse, in a
  soft
bed, with his heart given all its fill of luxury.
Now, with his dear father gone, he has much to suffer:
he, whom the Trojans have called Astyanax, lord of the city,
since it was you alone who defended the gates and the long
  walls.
But now, beside the curving ships, far away from your parents,
the writhing worms will feed, when the dogs have had enough
  of you,
on your naked corpse, though in your house there is clothing
  laid up

that is fine-textured and pleasant, wrought by the hands of
    women.
But all of these I will burn up in the fire's blazing,
no use to you, since you will never be laid away in them;
but in your honour, from the men of Troy and the Trojan
    women.'
    So she spoke, in tears; and the women joined in her
    mourning.
    RICHMOND LATTIMORE (*Iliad* 22.437-515)

*Despite the admonitions of his family, but with the help of
Hermes, Priam makes his way to the tent of Achilles, enters
unseen, clasps the knees of Achilles, and appeals for the re-
turn of Hector's body. The following passage begins with the
end of his appeal.*

Then thou, Achilles, reverence the Gods;   **34**
And, for thy father's sake, look pitying down
On me, more needing pity; since I bear
Such grief as never man on earth hath borne,
Who stoop to kiss the hand that slew my son."
    Thus as he spoke, within Achilles' breast
Fond mem'ry of his father rose; he touch'd
The old man's hand, and gently put him by;
Then wept they both, by various mem'ries stirr'd:
One, prostrate at Achilles' feet, bewail'd
His warrior son; Achilles for his sire,
And for Patroclus wept, his comrade dear;
And through the house their weeping loud was heard.
But when Achilles had indulg'd his grief,
And eas'd the yearning of his heart and limbs,
Uprising, with his hand the aged sire,
Pitying his hoary head and hoary beard,
He rais'd, and thus with gentle words address'd:
    "Alas, what sorrows, poor old man, are thine!
How couldst thou venture to the Grecian ships
Alone, and to the presence of the man
Whose hand hath slain so many of thy sons,

Many and brave? an iron heart is thine!
But sit thou on this seat; and in our hearts,
Though filled with grief, let us that grief suppress;
For woful lamentation nought avails.
Such is the thread the Gods for mortals spin,
To live in woe, while they from cares are free.
Two coffers lie beside the door of Jove,
With gifts for man: one good, the other ill;
To whom from each the Lord of lightning gives,
Him sometimes evil, sometimes good befalls;
To whom the ill alone, him foul disgrace
And grinding mis'ry o'er the earth pursue:
By God and man alike despis'd he roams.
          EDWARD EARL OF DERBY (*Iliad* 24.503-533)

*When, after courteous exchanges, Achilles invites Priam to
rest, the old man replies:*

35   "Urge not, divine Achilles, me to sit,
While Hector lies unburied in the camp:
Loose him, and loose him now, that with these eyes
I may behold my son; accept a prize
Magnificent, which mayst thou long enjoy,
And, since my life was precious in thy sight,
Mayst thou revisit safe thy native shore!"
     To whom Achilles, lowering, and in wrath:
"Move me no more. I purpose of myself
To loose him; Thetis, daughter of the Deep,
Hath taught me that the will of Jove is such.
Priam! I understand thee well. I know
That, by some God conducted, thou hast reached
Achaia's fleet; for, without aid divine,
No mortal, even in his prime of youth
Had dared the attempt; guards vigilant as ours
He should not easily elude; such gates,
So massy, should not easily unbar.
Thou, therefore, vex me not in my distress,
Lest I abhor to see thee in my tent,

And, borne beyond all limits, set at naught
Thee and thy prayer, and the command of Jove."
  He said; the old king trembled, and obeyed.
Then sprang Pelides like a lion forth,
Not sole, but with his two attendant friends,
Alcimus and Automedon the brave;
For them (Patroclus slain) he honoured most
Of all the Myrmidons. They loosed the mules
And horses from the yoke, then introduced
And placed the herald of the hoary king.
They lightened next the litter of its charge
Inestimable, leaving yet a vest
With two rich robes, that Priam might convey
The body not uncovered back to Troy.
Then, calling forth his women, them he bade
Lave and anoint the body, but apart,
Lest haply Priam, noticing his son,
Through stress of grief should give resentment scope,
And irritate by some affront himself
To slay him in despite of Jove's commands.
They, therefore, laving and anointing first
The body, clothed it with a robe and vest;
Then, Peleus' son disposed it on the bier,
Lifting it from the ground, and his two friends
Together heaved it to the royal wain.
     WILLIAM COWPER (*Iliad* 24.553-590)

In an important sense both Achilles and Iliad *reach their*
height with the surrender of the body. The remainder of the
poem describes the mourning for Hector; the concluding line is

  Thus they held funeral for Hector tamer of horses.

HOMER: ODYSSEY

*Odyssey's theme, the trials of a resourceful hero striving to
reach his home, is stated in the opening lines.*

36   Sing, O Muse, of the man so wary and wise, who in far lands
Wander'd whenas he had wasted the sacred town of the
Trojans.
Many a people he saw and beheld their cities and customs,
Many a woe he endured in his heart as he tossed on the ocean,
Striving to win him his life and to bring home safely his
comrades.
Ah but he rescued them not, those comrades, much as he
wished it.
Ruined by their own act of infatuate madness they perished,
Fools that they were—who the cows of the sun-god, lord
Hyperion,
Slaughtered and ate; and he took from the men their day of
returning.
Sing—whence-ever the lay—sing, Zeus-born goddess, for us
too!
    H. B. COTTERILL (*Odyssey* 1.1-10)

*The first four books show how Telemachus matures from
adolescent into a man of the world. First, at the instigation
of Odysseus' patroness Athena, he summons an assembly of
the Ithacans to complain of the abuses of the suitors.*

37   "My own necessity—
The evil that has fallen on my house—
Constrains me; it is twofold. First, that I
Have lost an excellent father, who was king
Among you, and ruled o'er you with a sway

As gentle as a father's. Greater yet
Is the next evil, and will soon o'erthrow
My house and waste my substance utterly.
Suitors, the sons of those who, in our isle,
Hold the chief rank, importunately press
Round my unwilling mother. They disdain
To ask her of Icarius, that the king
Her father may endow her, and bestow
His daughter on the man who best may gain
His favor, but with every day they come
Into our palace, sacrificing here
Oxen and sheep and fatling goats, and hold
High festival, and drink the purple wine
Unstinted, with unbounded waste; for here
Is no man like Ulysses to repel
The mischief from my house. Not such are we
As he was, to resist the wrong. We pass
For weaklings, immature in valor, yet
If I had but the power, assuredly
I would resist, for by these men are done
Insufferable things, nor does my house
Perish with honor. Ye yourselves should feel
Shame at these doings; ye should dread reproach
From those who dwell around us, and should fear
The offended gods, lest they repay these crimes
With vengeance. I beseech you, O my friends,
Both by Olympian Jove, and her by whom
Councils of men are summoned and dissolved,—
The goddess Themis,—that ye all refrain,
And leave me to my grief alone, unless
Ulysses, my great father, may have done
Wrong in his anger to the gallant Greeks,
Which ye, by prompting men to acts like these,
Seek to avenge on me. Far better 't were,
Should ye yourselves destroy our goods and slay
Our herds, since, were it so, there might in time
Be some requital. We, from street to street,

Would plead continually for recompense,
Till all should be restored. But now ye heap
Upon me wrongs for which is no redress."

    Thus angrily he spake, and dashed to earth
The sceptre, shedding tears. The people felt
Compassion; all were silent for a space,
And there was none who dared with railing words
Answer Telemachus, save one alone,
Antinoüs, who arose and thus replied:—

    "Telemachus, thou youth of braggart speech
And boundless in abuse, what hast thou said
To our dishonor? Thou wouldst fix on us
A brand of shame. The blame is not with us,
The Achaian suitors; 'tis thy mother's fault,
Skilled as she is in crafty shifts. 'Tis now
Already the third year, and soon will be
The fourth, since she began to cozen us.
She gives us all to hope, and sends fair words
To each by message, yet in her own mind
Has other purposes. This shrewd device
She planned; she laid upon the loom a web,
Delicate, wide, and vast in length, and said
Thus to us all: 'Young princes, who are come
To woo me, since Ulysses is no more,—
My noble husband,—urge me not, I pray,
To marriage, till I finish in the loom—
That so my threads may not be spun in vain—
A funeral vesture for the hero-chief
Laertes, when his fatal hour shall come
With death's long sleep. Else some Achaian dame
Might blame me, should I leave without a shroud
Him who in life possessed such ample wealth!'
Such were her words, and easily they wrought
Upon our generous minds. So went she on,
Weaving that ample web, and every night
Unravelled it by torchlight."

    W. C. BRYANT (*Odyssey* 2.45-105)

Unbeknownst to his mother and to the suitors, Telemachus travels, to obtain information concerning his father, first to the court of Nestor and then to that of Menelaus and Helen. Here the arrival of Telemachus and his comrade, Nestor's son, is reported to Menelaus.

"There are stranger guests come hither, Menelaus God-bred king,   **38**
Two men that are like in fashion to the kin of mighty Zeus.
What say'st thou then? Their horses swift-footed shall we loose,
Or speed them on to another who to guest them may be fain?"
  But the yellow Menelaus in wrath thus answered again:
"Eteoneus, son of Boethous, no fool thou wert wont to be,
But now as a child mere folly thou babblest unto me.
What! have we not eaten guest-cheer of other men we twain,
Ere hither we got us home; if yet of Zeus we may gain
An end of trouble henceforward? Go, loose the guest-folks' steeds,
And bring the men in to be feasted according to their needs."
    WILLIAM MORRIS (*Odyssey* 4.26-36)

After the greetings Helen makes a majestic entry.

Lo, Helen came from her chamber fragrant, high-vaulted of old;   **39**
And like unto Artemis was she, the Dame of the Shaft of Gold.
And there with her came Adraste, who set forth the well-wrought chair;
But the carpet of soft wool woven forth did Alcippe bear,
And Phylo a silver basket, the gift of Polybus' wife
Alcandra; in Thebes of Egypt forsooth she weareth life,
Where of all the world most treasure the houses in them have.
But he to Menelaus two silver bath-vats gave,

Two caldrons withal three-footed, and of gold ten talents'
    weight.
And his wife to Helen moreover gave goodly gifts and great:
A distaff of gold and a basket fashioned on wheels to run,
Of silver wrought; but its edges about with gold were done.
And e'en this it was that was carried and set down by Phylo
    the maid,
With the wrought yarn all fulfilled, and the distaff over it
    laid,
Reached out therefrom, with its head well charged with dark-
    blue wool.
So Helen sat in the chair and under her feet was the stool.
    WILLIAM MORRIS (*Odyssey* 4.121-136)

Despite the suitors' evil intentions against him Telemachus
returns home safe. Meanwhile Hermes has been told off to
procure Odysseus' release from Calypso. This is his arrival at
her grotto.

40   And now arriving at the isle, he springs
Oblique, and landing with subsided wings
Walks to the cavern 'mid the tall green rocks,
Where dwelt the goddess with the lovely locks.
He paused; and there came on him as he stood
A smell of cedar and of citron wood,
That threw a perfume all about the isle;
And she within sat spinning all the while,
And sang a low sweet song that made him hark and smile.
A sylvan nook it was, grown round with trees,
Poplars, and elms, and odorous cypresses,
In which all birds of ample wing, the owl
And hawk had nests, and broad-tongued waterfowl.
The cave in front was spread with a green vine,
Whose dark round bunches almost burst with wine;
And from four springs, running a sprightly race,
Four fountains clear and crisp refreshed the place;
While all about a meadowy ground was seen,
Of violets mingling with the parsley green.

So that a stranger, though a god were he,
Might well admire it, and stand there to see;
And so admiring there stood Mercury.
    LEIGH HUNT (*Odyssey* 5.55-75)

Calypso heeds the order to dismiss Odysseus, who is at first
incredulous and then somewhat apologetic.

"Ulysses!" (with a sigh she thus began;)   **41**
"O sprung from gods! in wisdom more than man!
Is then thy home the passion of thy heart?
Thus wilt thou leave me, are we thus to part?
Farewell! and ever joyful mayst thou be,
Nor break the transport with one thought of me.
But, ah, Ulysses! wert thou given to know
What Fate yet dooms thee, yet, to undergo;
Thy heart might settle in this scene of ease,
And ev'n these slighted charms might learn to please.
A willing goddess, and immortal life,
Might banish from thy mind an absent wife.
Am I inferior to a mortal dame?
Less soft my feature, less august my frame?
Or shall the daughters of mankind compare
Their earth-born beauties with the heavenly fair?"
   "Alas! for this" (the prudent man replies)
"Against Ulysses shall thy anger rise?
Lov'd and ador'd, goddess, as thou art,
Forgive the weakness of a human heart.
Though well I see thy graces far above
The dear, though mortal, object of my love,
Of youth eternal well the difference know,
And the short date of fading charms below;
Yet every day while absent thus I roam,
I languish to return and die at home.
Whate'er the gods shall destine me to bear
In the black ocean, or the watery war,
'Tis mine to master with a constant mind;
Inur'd to perils, to the worst resign'd.

By seas, by wars, so many dangers run;
Still I can suffer: their high will be done!"
    Thus while he spoke the beamy sun descends,
And rising night her friendly shade extends.
To the close grot the lonely pair remove,
And slept delighted with the gifts of love.
          ALEXANDER POPE (*Odyssey* 5.203-227)

The raft which Odysseus built and sailed is terribly buffeted by the anger of Poseidon. At long last he is cast ashore at Phaeacia and sleeps. Meanwhile princess Nausicaa, urged by a dream, has gone down to the shore with her maidens to wash clothes and play ball.

42   Now when they were about to move for home
          With harnessed mules and with the shining robes
          Carefully folded, then the blue-eyed maid,
          Pallas, bethought herself of this,—to rouse
          Ulysses and to bring him to behold
          The bright-eyed maiden, that she might direct
          The stranger's way to the Phæacian town.
          The royal damsel at a handmaid cast
          The ball; it missed, and fell into the stream
          Where a deep eddy whirled. All shrieked aloud.
          The great Ulysses started from his sleep
          And sat upright, discoursing to himself:—
              "Ah me! upon what region am I thrown?
          What men are here,—wild, savage, and unjust,
          Or hospitable, and who hold the gods
          In reverence? There are voices in the air,
          Womanly voices, as of nymphs that haunt
          The mountain summits, and the river-founts,
          And the moist grassy meadows. Or perchance
          Am I near men who have the power of speech?
          Nay, let me then go forth at once and learn."
              Thus having said, the great Ulysses left
          The thicket. From the close-grown wood he rent,
          With his strong hand, a branch well set with leaves,

And wound it as a covering round his waist.
Then like a mountain lion he went forth,
That walks abroad, confiding in his strength,
In rain and wind; his eyes shoot fire; he falls
On oxen, or on sheep, or forest-deer,
For hunger prompts him even to attack
The flock within its closely guarded fold.
Such seemed Ulysses when about to meet
Those fair-haired maidens, naked as he was,
But forced by strong necessity. To them
His look was frightful, for his limbs were foul
With sea-foam yet. To right and left they fled
Along the jutting river-banks. Alone
The daughter of Alcinous kept her place,
For Pallas gave her courage and forbade
Her limbs to tremble. So she waited there.
Ulysses pondered whether to approach
The bright-eyed damsel and embrace her knees
And supplicate, or, keeping yet aloof,
Pray her with soothing words to show the way
Townward and give him garments. Musing thus,
It seemed the best to keep at distance still,
And use soft words, lest should he grasp her knees,
The maid might be displeased. With gentle words,
Skillfully ordered, thus Ulysses spake:—
   "O queen, I am thy suppliant, whether thou
Be mortal or a goddess. If perchance
Thou art of the immortal race who dwell
In the broad heaven, thou art, I deem, most like
To Dian, daughter of imperial Jove,
In shape, in stature, and in noble air.
If mortal and a dweller of the earth,
Thrice happy are thy father and his queen,
Thrice happy are thy brothers; and their hearts
Must overflow with gladness for thy sake,
Beholding such a scion of their house
Enter the choral dance. But happiest he
Beyond them all, who, bringing princely gifts,

Shall bear thee to his home a bride; for sure
I never looked on one of mortal race,
Woman or man, like thee, and as I gaze
I wonder. Like to thee I saw of late,
In Delos, a young palm-tree growing up
Beside Apollo's altar; for I sailed
To Delos, with much people following me,
On a disastrous voyage. Long I gazed
Upon it wonder-struck, as I am now,—
For never from the earth so fair a tree
Had sprung. So marvel I, and am amazed
At thee, O lady, and in awe forbear
To clasp thy knees. Yet much have I endured.
It was but yestereve that I escaped
From the black sea, upon the twentieth day,
So long the billows and the rushing gales
Farther and farther from Ogygia's isle
Had borne me. Now upon this shore some god
Casts me, perchance to meet new sufferings here;
For yet the end is not, and many things
The gods must first accomplish. But do thou,
O queen, have pity on me, since to thee
I come the first of all. I do not know
A single dweller of the land beside.
Show me, I pray, thy city; and bestow
Some poor old robe to wrap me,—if, indeed,
In coming hither, thou hast brought with thee
Aught poor or coarse. And may the gods vouchsafe
To thee whatever blessing thou canst wish,
Husband and home and wedded harmony.
There is no better, no more blessed state,
Than when the wife and husband in accord
Order their household lovingly. Then those
Repine who hate them, those who wish them well
Rejoice, and they themselves the most of all."
    And then the white-armed maid Nausicaä said:—
"Since then, O stranger, thou are not malign
Of purpose nor weak-minded,—yet, in truth,

Olympian Jupiter bestows the goods
Of fortune on the noble and the base
To each one at his pleasure; and thy griefs
Are doubtless sent by him, and it is fit
That thou submit in patience,—now that thou
Hast reached our lands, and art within our realm,
Thou shalt not lack for garments nor for aught
Due to a suppliant stranger in his need.
The city I will show thee, and will name
Its dwellers,—the Phæacians,—they possess
The city; all the region lying round
Is theirs, and I am daughter of the prince
Alcinoüs, large of soul, to whom are given
The rule of the Phæacians and their power.

  W. C. Bryant (*Odyssey* 6.110-197)

*Odysseus is well received at the palace, though he keeps his
identity hidden. During an entertainment at the court of the
Phaeacians the minstrel Demodocus sings the loves of Ares
and Aphrodite. Chapman's version, it will be remembered,
evoked Keats's famous ode.*

Then with the rich harp came Pontonous,
And in the midst took place Demodocus.
About him then stood forth the choice young men,
That on man's first youth made fresh entry then,
Had art to make their natural motion sweet,
And shook a most divine dance from their feet,
That twinkled star-like, mov'd as swift, and fine,
And beat the air so thin, they made it shine.
Ulysses wonder'd at it, but amaz'd
He stood in mind to hear the dance so phras'd.
For, as they danced, Demodocus did sing,
The bright-crown'd Venus' love with Battaile's King;
As first they closely mixt in th' house of fire.
What worlds of gifts won her to his desire,
Who then the night-and-day-bed did defile
Of good king Vulcan. But in little while

43

The Sun their mixture saw, and came and told.
The bitter news did by his ears take hold
Of Vulcan's heart. Then to his forge he went,
And in his shrewd mind deep stuff did invent.
His mighty anvil in the stock he put,
And forged a net that none could loose or cut,
That when it had them it might hold them fast.
Which having finisht he made utmost haste
Up to the dear room where his wife he woo'd,
And, madly wrath with Mars, he all bestrew'd
The bed, and bed-posts, all the beam above
That crost the chamber; and a circle strove
Of his device to wrap in all the room.
And 'twas as pure, as of a spider's loom
The woof before 'tis woven. No man nor God
Could set his eye on it, a sleight so odd
His art shew'd in it. All his craft bespent
About the bed, he feign'd as if he went
To well-built Lemnos, his most loved town
Of all towns earthly; nor left this unknown
To golden-bridle-using Mars, who kept
No blind watch over him, but, seeing stept
His rival so aside, he hasted home
With fair-wreathed Venus' love stung, who was come
New from the court of her most mighty Sire.
Mars enter'd, wrung her hand, and the retire
Her husband made to Lemnos told, and said:
"Now, love, is Vulcan gone, let us to bed,
He's for the barbarous Sintians." Well appay'd
Was Venus with it; and afresh assay'd
Their old encounter. Down they went; and straight
About them cling'd the artificial sleight
Of most wise Vulcan; and were so ensnar'd,
That neither they could sit their course prepar'd
In any limb about them, nor arise.
And then they knew, they would no more disguise
Their close conveyance, but lay, forc'd, stone-still.
Back rush'd the both-foot-crookt, but straight in skill,

From his near scout-hole turn'd, nor ever went
To any Lemnos, but the sure event
Left Phoebus to discover, who told all.
Then home hopt Vulcan, full of grief and gall,
Stood in the portal, and cried out so high,
That all the Gods heard: "Father of the sky,
And every other deathless God," said he
"Come all, and a ridiculous object see,
And yet not sufferable neither. Come,
And witness how, when still I stept from home,
Lame that I am, Jove's daughter doth profess
To do me all the shameful offices,
Indignities, despites, that can be thought;
And loves this all-things-making-come-to-nought,
Since he is fair forsooth, foot-sound, and I
Took in my brain a little, legg'd awry;
And no fault mine, but all my parents' fault,
Who should not get, if mock me, with my halt.
But see how fast they sleep, while I, in moan,
Am only made an idle looker on.
One bed their turn serves, and it must be mine;
I think yet, I have made their self-loves shine.
They shall no more wrong me, and none perceive;
Nor will they sleep together, I believe,
With too hot haste again. Thus both shall lie
In craft, and force, till the extremity
Of all the dower I gave her sire (to gain
A dogged set-fac'd girl, that will not stain
Her face with blushing, though she shame her head)
He pays me back. She's fair, but was no maid."
    While this long speech was making, all were come
To Vulcan's wholly-brazen-founded home,
Earth-shaking Neptune, useful Mercury,
And far-shot Phoebus. No She-deity,
For shame, would show there. All the give-good Gods
Stood in the portal, and past periods
Gave length to laughters, all rejoic'd to see
That which they said, that no impiety

Finds good success at th' end. "And now," said one,
"The slow outgoes the swift. Lame Vulcan, known
To be the slowest of the Gods, outgoes
Mars the most swift. And this is that which grows
To greatest justice: that adultery's sport,
Obtain'd by craft, by craft of other sort
(And lame craft too) is plagued, which grieves the more,
That sound limbs turning lame the lame restore."
    This speech amongst themselves they entertain'd,
When Phoebus thus asked Hermes: "Thus enchain'd
Wouldst thou be, Hermes, to be thus disclos'd?
Though with thee golden Venus were repos'd?"
    He soon gave that an answer: "O," said he,
"Thou king of archers, would 'twere thus with me!
Though thrice so much shame; nay, though infinite
Were pour'd about me, and that every light,
In great heaven shining, witnest all my harms,
So golden Venus slumber'd in my arms."
    GEORGE CHAPMAN (*Odyssey* 8.261-342)

Odysseus reveals his identity, and begins the tale of his adventures from the end of the Trojan war. Caught in the cave of the cannibal Cyclops, he resourcefully plans his escape.

44   This now seemed to my mind to be counsel the best and the
        wisest.
    Lying anigh to the fold was a monstrous club of the Cyclops,
    Yet unseasoned, of olive, the which he had hewn him to carry
    After 'twas dry; and we deemed it as huge as the mast of a
        vessel,
    E'en of a great black vessel of twice ten rowers the mainmast,
    Yea, of a broad-beamed trader that crosses the gulf of the
        ocean;
    Such was the length of the club to behold, and such was the
        thickness.
    Creeping anigh it I severed so much as the reach of a fathom,
    Handed it o'er to my mates and ordered them taper and plane
        it.

These then tapered it even, and standing before it I shaved it
Sharp to a point, then charring it quick in the glow of the
   embers
Stowed it for safety away in the sheep-dung carefully hidden,
Masses of which were lying around in the depths of the cav-
   ern.
Then I commanded my comrades to settle by lot and deter-
   mine
Who with myself should venture the spar to uplift and to
   twirl it
Round in the Cyclops' eye while slumber sweet was upon him.
Chosen by lot were just those men I had willingly chosen,
Four of my fellows, and I as the fifth to the number was
   added.

Now in the even, arrived with his fair-fleeced flocks from the
   pasture,
Into the spacious cavern the fat-fed beasts he admitted,
All of them; none did he leave outside in the high-walled
   courtyard,
Boding of ill—or perchance some deity bade him to do so.
Next he uplifted the boulder enormous and set it as door-
   stone.
Then by the bleating goats and the ewes down-sitting he
   milked them,
All of them duly in turn, and he put to the mothers the lamb-
   lings.
So, when awhile he had busied himself and had finished his
   labours,
Seizing again two men in his clutch he prepared them for
   supper.
Forthwith venturing nigh to the Cyclops thus I addressed
   him,
Holding between both hands dark wine in a mazer of ivy:
'Cyclops, drink of the wine—since done is thy cannibal ban-
   quet.
Take it and see what manner of drink I had stowed in my
   vessel.

Lo, as an offering this was I bringing thee, hoping for pity,
Hoping for homeward return; but thy rage exceedeth endurance.
Pitiless being!—and how might ever another approach thee,
Any of all mankind?—for thy deeds are verily lawless.'
Thus did I speak, and he took it and drank, and a wonderful pleasure
Felt he in draining the luscious draught; and he asked for another:
'Give me again, an thou wilt! and tell me thy name right quickly,
Now straightway! Thou'lt get thee a stranger's gift to delight thee.
Here too beareth the earth, rich giver of grain, for the Cyclops
Juice of the clustering grapes that the rain of the heaven doth nourish;
Ah but a wine like this is a draught of ambrosial nectar!'
Thus did he speak, and again of the fiery liquor I gave him;
Thrice did I bring it and give it, and thrice in his folly he drained it.
Now when I saw that the wine was invading the wits of the Cyclops,
Speaking with words right gentle and winning again I addressed him:
'Cyclops—lo, thou demandest my name. Well, listen! for plainly
Now will I tell it. So give me thy promise, the gift of a stranger!
Nobody—that is my name, and nothing but Nobody call me
Mother and father and all of the rest of my fellows and comrades.'
Thus did I speak, but with pitiless heart he addressed me in answer:
'Nobody then I shall eat when I've eaten his fellows and comrades—
All of the others before him; and that is my gift to the stranger.'

Speaking, he downward sank and fell on his back, and he lay
there

Bending his monstrous neck to the side, o'ermastered by
slumber,

Slumber that mastereth all; and out of his gullet there issued

Wine and the gobbets of human flesh; and he retched as a
drunkard.

Then did I thrust me the stake in the midst of the embers to
make it

Fiery hot, and with comforting words I addressed my com-
panions,

Giving them courage lest any in fear might fail and desert me.

So, when at last that stake sharp-pointed of olive was almost

Bursting to flame, though green was the wood, and was ter-
ribly glowing,

Then did I fetch it anigh from the fire, and around it my
comrades

Posted themselves, and courage immense some deity gave us.

Seizing the stake all glowing and sharp at the point, with a
strong thrust

Into the eye full deeply they drove it; and I at the top end

Twisted it round, as a man that is boring the beam of a vessel

Bores with an auger, and others below with the leather revolve
it,

Holding by both ends fast, as the auger is ceaselessly spinning.

Thus in his eye did we bore, and the stake sharp-pointed and
glowing

Twisted about, red-hot; and the blood ran spluttering round it.

Then did the breath of the flame scorch all of his eyelid and
eyebrow,

While consumed was the ball of the eye, and the roots of it
crackled.

E'en as a worker of metal who fashions an adze or a hatchet

Dips it aglow in the water to chill it, and fiercely it hisseth

(Thus it is tempered, and thus there cometh a strength to
the iron),

So did his eyeball hiss at the fiery stake as it entered.

Then with a loud and a terrible yelling the cavern re-echoed,
While in a panic we fled; and seizing the stake did the
Cyclops,
Drawing it out of his eye with the blood all smeared and
bedabbled,
Hurl it amain and afar with his hands, as if maddened by
anguish.

Then with his monstrous voice did he call to his fellows, the
Cyclops
Dwelling in caverns around on the wind-swept heights of the
mountain.
These then, hearing the cry, came flocking from this and from
that side,
Gathering nigh to the cavern and asking what was the trouble:
'What is it troubles thee, O Polyphemus, that thus thou art
calling
Through the ambrosial silence of night, and making us sleep-
less?
No one surely of mortals is trying of flocks to despoil thee?
No one surely by force or by cunning is trying to kill
thee?'
Forthwith out of the cavern addressed them the huge Poly-
phemus:
'Friends, it is Nobody trying by craft, not force, to destroy
me.'
Then did they answer and speak, and swift-winged words they
addressed him:
'Seeing that nobody trieth to harm thee or comes to disturb
thee,
Sickness none can avoid—that cometh from Zeus the Al-
mighty.
Nay now, offer a prayer to thy sire, Earth-shaking Poseidon!'
Spake it, and went; and the heart in my bosom was shaken
with laughter,
So had the Nobody name of my faultless cunning deceived
them.

Groaning and travailing sore in his agony then did the Cyclops

Grope with his hands all round and lifting the stone from the portal

Seat him adown by the door with his hands outspread in the doorway,

Any to catch who was issuing forth with the sheep from the cavern;

Such was the witless fool that, I ween, he expected to find me.

Then I revolved in my mind what best to devise, and bethought me

Whether a way of escaping from death for myself and my comrades

Were to be found; and I wove all manner of schemes and devices,

E'en as a man for his life; for a terrible danger was nigh us.

This now unto my mind of devices appeared to be wisest:

Rams with the sheep there were, well nurtured, heavily coated,

Beautiful beasts and great, and with fleeces violet-coloured.

Quietly these did I fasten with withes that I twisted together

(Bedding whereon he had slept, that impious monster, the Cyclops),

Taking them three and three—for a man to be borne by the midmost,

Each of the others on each of the sides protecting my comrades.

Thus three sheep bare each of my mates—and then for my own self

There was a ram that of all of the flock was the greatest and finest;

Him did I seize by the back and under the thick-fleeced stomach

Curled me and lay, and my hands in the shags of the wonderful sheep-wool

Tightly I twisted, and thus with a heart courageous I hung there.

So then uttering moans we awaited the sacred morning.

Now when the morning was newly arisen, the roseate-fingered,
Then did the males of the flock haste eagerly forth to the
    pasture,
While unmilked went bleating the mothers around in the
    sheepfolds,
Udders a-bursting. But he, their lord, in his terrible anguish
Travailing still, groped over the backs of the rams, as before
    him
Halting in turn each stood; nor, fool that he was, did he
    notice
How right under the breasts of the shag-fleeced sheep I had
    bound them.
Last of the flock came slowly the ram, and he paced to the
    doorway
Cumbered with all of his wool and weighted with me and my
    cunning.
Him too handled and thus accosted the huge Polyphemus:
'What is the reason, my pet, thou art issuing forth from the
    cavern
Last of the flock? Not ever before wast led by the others,
Nay but afar in the front didst graze fresh blooms of the
    meadows
Mightily striding, and first didst come to the streams of the
    rivers;
First too ever 'tis thou who at eveningtide to the homestead
Longst to return—while now thou art last! Ay, surely thou
    grievest,
Mourning the eye of thy lord, that an impious mortal hath
    blinded,
He and his fellows accurséd, my wits with his wine overcom-
    ing—
Nobody. . . . Ah but I deem he is not yet safe from destruc-
    tion!
Verily hadst thou but feeling as I and the power of speaking,
So as to tell me the place where shunning my wrath he is
    skulking,
Then all over the cavern his brains were this way and that way

Dashed on the ground as I crushed him to death, and happy
    my heart were,
Lightened of all of the woe that a worthless Nobody brought
    me.'
Thus then speaking, the ram he released, and it passed from
    the doorway.
Now when a little away we had got from the cavern and
    courtyard,
First from the ram I unfastened myself, then loosed my com-
    panions.
Hastily then those sheep high-stepping and rich in their fat-
    ness,
Ofttimes turning to look, did we drive, till at last to the vessel
Safe we arrived; and welcome we came to the rest of my com-
    rades,
We who from death had escaped. For the others they fain
    had lamented;
Yet I forbade it, and frowning and nodding in silence I bade
    them
Not to lament, but the fair-fleeced sheep, right many in num-
    ber,
Hurriedly casting aboard launch forth on the salt sea water.
Speedily then they embarked and taking their seats on the
    benches
Smote with the well-ranged oars on the grey-green brine of
    the ocean.
Now when as far I was come as the voice of a shouter will
    carry,
Then to the Cyclops I called and with words of derision ad-
    dressed him:
'Cyclops! wert not fated, it seems, those mates of a weakling
There in thy hollow cavern to eat, thou insatiable monster!
Nay, much rather 'tis thou wert fated to light on misfortune,
Pitiless one, ay truly and shameless, the guests in thy home-
    stead
E'en to devour! Lo, Zeus and the other immortals avenged it!'
So I did speak. Thereat, with a heart more maddened to fury,

Breaking a peak clean off from a huge high mountain, he
　　　hurled it.
Down on the water it fell to the front of the blue-prowed
　　　vessel,
Just to the fore, and it missed by a little the end of the rudder.
High upheaved was the sea when the crag descended upon it;
Backward the vessel was borne, for the swirl of the roller re-
　　　bounding
Swept to the shore as a surge of the ocean and lifted it land-
　　　ward.
Then on a long punt-pole did I seize, and strongly I thrust her
Off from the shore and exhorted and urgently bade my com-
　　　panions
Lay them with might on the oar and gain them escape from
　　　destruction,
Nodding command. Then forward they bent, all hastily row-
　　　ing.

Soon now over the brine we had traversed double the distance.
Then to the Cyclops anew I had willingly called, but my com-
　　　rades,
One and the other, with words of entreaty restraining ad-
　　　dressed me:
'Madman! wherefore arouse this terrible being to fury?
Even already the bolt that he seaward hurled hath the vessel
Drifted again to the shore, where truly we thought we had
　　　perished.
Ay and had any but uttered a word or a sound—had he heard
　　　it—
Straight he had shattered the heads of us all and the beams
　　　of the vessel,
Hurling a huge jagged block—such monstrous missiles he
　　　launches.'
Thus did they speak; but they pleaded in vain to my valiant
　　　spirit,
Since once more with a heart all flaming in wrath I addressed
　　　him:
'Cyclops, listen! If ever it happen that any of mortals

Wishes to learn of the cause of thine eye's disfiguring blind-
    ness,
Say that Odysseus, sacker of cities, was he that did blind thee,
Son of Laertes and having his dwelling in Ithaca's island.'
    H. B. COTTERILL (*Odyssey* 9.318-505)

In another episode Odysseus tells how Circe, in her demonic
menage, turned his men into swine.

Then in two several bands I did portion and number my   **45**
    comrades,
Giving each band of the bronze-greaved men a captain to
    lead them:
I myself was the one, and the other Eurylochus god-like.
Then in a brazen helm we threw in the lots and did shake
    them—
Straight outsprang the stone that was marked with Eury-
    lochus' symbol;
So he arose and went, with two and twenty companions.
Weeping they went on their way, and left lamentation be-
    hind them.
Hid in a deep ravine they found the palace of Circe
Builded of stones smooth wrought, in a place remote and
    sheltered.
Round that place lay the beasts of the mountain, lions and
    grey wolves,
Whom with evil drugs administered Circe had enchanted.
Nor did they rush at the men, but rather, fawning upon them,
Rose on their haunches and stood and wagged their tails as
    in greeting.
As when the master returns from the banquet his hounds
    fawn round him
Wagging their tails, for he brings them ever a sop for their
    anger:
So round them came, mighty of paw, the wolves and the lions
Fawning upon them, who were afeared beholding the mon-
    sters.

Thus as they stood in the porch of the goddess lovely of
  tresses,
Circe they heard within as she sang with her beautiful voice,
  and
Wove at her mighty immortal loom such web as a goddess
Only can weave, so fine, so fair, so exceeding in glory.
Then with these words outspake Polites, leader of heroes,
Who of my comrades all was dearest to me and most faith-
  ful:
"Listen, O friends. One sings within as she weaves at her
  great loom.
Lovely the song she sings—the whole house throbs with the
  music—
Goddess, it may be she is, or a woman. Come, let us call her."
  Thus did he speak, and they lift up their voices and shouted
  and called her.
Straightway forth did she come and opened the glittering
  portals,
Calling to them, who one and all in their folly did enter;
Only Eurylochus tarried behind suspecting some evil.
Them when they entered she bade sit down upon chairs and
  on couches,
Meanwhile mixing with Pramnian wine both barley and
  honey
Golden of hue, and cheese; but she mixed dread drugs in the
  porridge
That they might never remember again the land of their
  fathers.
This did she give, and they drank—when forthwith lifting
  her rod she
Smote them and drave them forth and shut them up in her
  hog-pens,
Swine both in face and voice and bristles: swine were they
  outward
But in their breasts were the minds of men as even aforetime.
Weeping they went to their styes and were penned. And
  Circe did bring them
Mast and threw them store of cornel-berries and acorns;

Such was their meat—the husks that the wallowing swine
do feed on.

L. P. CHAMBERLAYNE (*Odyssey* 10.222-243)

*By Circe's direction Odysseus visits the lower world; there he
hears the story of the death of Agamemnon.*

Afterward, soon as the chaste Persephone hither and thither
Now had scattered afar the slender shades of the women,
Came the sorrowing ghost of Agamemnon Atreides;
Round whom thronged, besides, the souls of the others who
also
Died, and met their fate, with him in the house of Aigisthos.
He, then, after he drank of the dark blood, instantly knew
me;
Ay, and he wailed aloud, and plenteous tears was shedding,
Toward me reaching hands and eagerly longing to touch me;
But he was shorn of strength, nor longer came at his bidding
That great force which once abode in his pliant members.
Seeing him thus, I wept, and my heart was laden with pity,
And, uplifting my voice, in winged words I addressed him:
"King of men, Agamemnon, thou glorious son of Atreus,
Say in what wise did the doom of prostrate death overcome
thee?
Was it within thy ships thou wast subdued by Poseidon
Rousing the dreadful blast of winds too hard to be mastered,
Or on the firm-set land did banded foemen destroy thee
Cutting their oxen off, and their flocks so fair, or it may be,
While in a town's defense, or in that of women, contending?"
Thus I spake, and he, replying, said to me straightway:
"Nobly-born and wise Odysseus, son of Laertes,
Neither within my ships was I subdued by Poseidon
Rousing the dreadful blast of winds too hard to be mastered,
Nor on the firm-set land did banded foemen destroy me;
Nay, but death and my doom were well contrived by Aigis-
thos,
Who, with my cursed wife, at his own house bidding me wel-
come,

Fed me, and slew me, as one might slay an ox at the manger!
So, by a death most wretched, I died; and all my companions
Round me were slain off-hand, like white-toothed swine that
　　are slaughtered
Thus, when some lordly man, abounding in power and riches,
Orders a wedding-feast, or a frolic, or mighty carousal.
Thou indeed hast witnessed the slaughter of numberless he-
　　roes
Massacred, one by one, in the battle's heat; but with pity
All thy heart had been full, if thou hadst seen what I tell
　　thee—
How in the hall we lay among the wine-jars, and under
Tables laden with food; and how the pavement, on all sides,
Swam with blood! And I heard the dolorous cry of Kassandra,
Priam's daughter, whom treacherous Klytaimnestra anear me
Slew; and upon the ground I fell in my death-throes, vainly
Reaching out hands to my sword, while the shameless woman
　　departed;
Nor did she even stay to press her hands on my eyelids,
No, nor to close my mouth, although I was passing to Hades.
Oh, there is naught more dire, more insolent than a woman
After the very thought of deeds like these has possessed her—
One who would dare to devise an act so utterly shameless,
Lying in wait to slay her wedded lord. I bethought me,
Verily, home to my children and servants giving me welcome
Safe to return; but she has wrought for herself confusion,
Plotting these grievous woes, and for other women hereafter,
Even for those, in sooth, whose thoughts are set upon good-
　　ness."
　　Thus he spake, and I, in turn replying, addressed him:
"Heavens! how from the first has Zeus the thunderer hated,
All for the women's wiles, the brood of Atreus! What num-
　　bers
Perished in quest of Helen—and Klytaimnestra, the mean-
　　while,
Wrought in her soul this guile for thee afar on thy journey."
　　Thus I spake, and he, replying, said to me straightway:

"See that thou art not, then, like me too mild to thy help-
    meet;
Nor to her ear reveal each secret matter thou knowest;
Tell her the part, forsooth, and see that the rest shall be
    hidden.
Nathless, not unto thee will come such murder, Odysseus,
Dealt by a wife; forewise indeed, and true in her purpose,
Noble Penelope is, the child of Ikarios. Truly,
She it was whom we left, a fair young bride, when we started
Off for the wars; and then an infant lay at her bosom,
One who now, methinks, in the list of men must be seated,
Blest indeed! ah, yes, for his well-loved father, returning,
Him shall behold, and the son shall clasp the sire, as is fitting.
Not unto me to feast my eyes with the sight of my offspring
Granted the wife of my bosom, but first of life she bereft me.
Therefore I say, moreover, and charge thee well to remember,
Unto thine own dear land steer thou thy vessel in secret,
Not in the light; since faith can be placed in woman no
    longer."

    EDMUND C. STEDMAN (*Odyssey* 11.385-456)

This is the encounter with the shade of Achilles:

He spake, to whom I, answ'ring, thus replied: **47**
"O Peleus' son! Achilles! bravest far
Of all Achaia's race! I here arrived
Seeking Tiresias, from his lips to learn,
Perchance, how I might safe regain the coast
Of craggy Ithaca; for tempest-toss'd
Perpetual, I have neither yet approach'd
Achaia's shore, or landed on my own.
But as for thee, Achilles! never man
Hath known felicity like thine, or shall,
Whom living we all honour'd as a God,
And who maintain'st, here resident, supreme
Control among the dead; indulge not then,
Achilles, causeless grief that thou hast died."
    I ceased, and answer thus instant received:

"Renown'd Ulysses! think not death a theme
Of consolation; I had rather live
The servile hind for hire, and eat the bread
Of some man scantily himself sustain'd,
Than sov'reign empire hold o'er all the shades."
           WILLIAM COWPER (*Odyssey* 11.477-491)

*After Odysseus concludes the story of his adventures the
Phaeacians give him rich presents and take him to Ithaca,
where they leave him asleep. Athena, in the guise of a young
shepherd, accosts him, and is indulgent when he attempts to
dissemble his identity.*

48 So he spake; but the Grey-eyed, the Goddess Athene, smiled
              and now
       She stroked him down with her hand and like to a woman
              did grow
       Comely and great of body, and deft fine things to make;
       So she sent her voice out toward him, and wingèd words
              she spake:
       "Ah, cunning were he and shifty, who thee should overbear
       In guilefulness of all kinds, yea e'en if a god he were!
       Thou hard one, shifty of rede, guile-greedy, nought wouldst
              thou
       From thy guilefulness refrain thee, nay not in thine own
              land now,
       And thy words of sly devising which thou lov'st from the
              root of thine heart.
       But speak we no more of such things; for we twain know
              each for our part
       All guile; since thou amidst menfolk art far the best of all
       In counsel and in speech-words; and on me mid the Gods
              doth fall
       The glory of redes and of sleight.—And thou knewest not me,
              the Maid,
       The Daughter of Zeus, e'en Pallas Athene, ever thine aid,
       Who stand beside thee and ward thee in all toil through
              which ye wear?

Who unto all Phaeacians have made me lief and dear?
And hither to thee am I come, that we may devise, we twain,
How to hide away thy treasure, the Phaeacians' gift and gain,
Which they gave thee on thy homefare by my counsel and
    device.
And now of the fateful troubles would I tell thee in like wise
In thy builded house that abide thee: now forbear, and bear
    thou the doom,
Nor unto any tell it how thou comest wandering home,
Neither of men nor of women, but in silence suffer all
Thy many griefs, and the mastery that from men shall thee
    befall."
Then the many-wiled Odysseus, he answered presently:
"O Goddess, 'tis hard for a mortal, though wise of wit he be,
To know thee when he meets thee, for shapes many dost thou
    on.
But this I know full surely, thou wert kind a while agone
While we sons of the Achaeans by Troy-town fought the
    fight."
    WILLIAM MORRIS (*Odyssey* 13.287-315)

He is entertained by his own swineherd, who refuses to be-
lieve that Odysseus is still alive.

So he spake, and fell to cleaving the logs with the ruthless **49**
    brass,
And a boar they brought withinward, a five-year-old full fat,
And on the hearth they stood him, and the swineherd nought
    forgat
The Deathless Gods, for his heart in righteous ways was fast.
So he fell to, and into the fire the forelock first he cast
Of the white-toothed boar, and fell praying to the Godfolk
    one and all
For the wise Odysseus' homefare in the end to his house and
    his hall.
Then with an oak-log that lay there, once cleft by his hand,
    he smote

The boar, and life went from him; and therewith they sheared
    his throat,
And singed, and cut him piece-meal; and the swineherd laid
    the raw
On the rich fat, which in gobbets from each limb did he draw;
And some they cast into the fire besprent with barley-meal,
And the rest they sheared into gobbets and spitted every deal,
And roasted it very deftly, and then they drew off all,
And cast it heaped on the trenchers. Then rose up the swine-
    herd withal
To carve the meat, for he wotted in his heart what was fair
    and fit,
And into seven portions he dealt the whole of it,
And one thereof to the Nymphs and to Hermes, Maia's Son,
He set by with a prayer, and the others he dealt to every one.
But the long-drawn chine of the boar white-toothed for the
    worshipful part
He gave unto Odysseus, and the King grew glad at heart,
And the many-wiled Odysseus he spake, and thus said he:
"Eumaeus, to Zeus the Father mayst thou be e'en as dear as
    to me,
Since with goodly cheer dost thou honour e'en such as I am
    today!"
Then thou, O Swineherd Eumaeus, thereto didst answer and
    say:
"Eat then, O hapless of strangers! in such as is here delight!
For God to one man giveth, and another gainsayeth outright,
In such wise as he will have it; for all things he doth and he
    may."

    WILLIAM MORRIS (*Odyssey* 14.418-445)

*Telemachus on his return, to escape the suitors' ambush, goes
to Eumaeus' hut, and shows Odysseus kindness without rec-
ognizing him. Finally Athena bids Odysseus make himself
known to his son.*

50   "Zeus-born son of Laertes, thou wise and wileful Odysseus,
    Now is the moment to speak to thy son and reveal him thy
      story;

So shall ye forge you a plot for the doom and the death of
    the suitors.

Then to the far famed city descend; nor fear ye that I too

Long shall delay to be nigh you—so fiercely I yearn for the
    combat."

Spake, and her golden wand she extended, and lo, as it
    touched him,

Firstly a fair fresh mantle around him was cast, and a doublet

Covered his breast, and renewed was his body in stature and
    manhood;

Dark once more was the tint of his skin, and in face he was
    fuller;

Blue-black bristled the beard once more on his chin as afore-
    time.

This when the goddess had wrought she departed again, and
    Odysseus

Back to the cottage returned; and his well-loved son with
    amazement

Stared—and averted his eyes in his dread to behold an im-
    mortal.

Then did he open his lips and with swift-winged words he
    addressed him:

"Wholly another a moment agone, O stranger, thou seemedst.

Other the clothes thou art wearing and other is also thy per-
    son;

Sure thou art one of the gods who inhabit the infinite heaven.

Nay then, grant us thy grace! We will offer thee grateful obla-
    tions—

Vessels of gold, well wrought, will we give. Have mercy and
    spare us!"

Him then in answer addressed long-suffering godlike Odys-
    seus:

"Sooth, I am none of the gods. Why deemst thou me like an
    immortal?

Nay, I am nought but thy father—the father for whom thou
    lamentest,

Suffering many a woe and many an insult enduring."

These words uttered, his son he embraced, and he kissed him,
    and teardrops

Fell from his cheek to the earth. (Till now he had ever re-
    strained them.)
Telemachus natheless, still doubting the man was his father,
Once more opened his lips, and in answer he spake to him
    saying:
 'No, thou art never Odysseus my sire, but a spirit from
    heaven
Come to beguile me, that ever the more I shall mourn in my
    sorrow.
Ne'er might wonders as these be devised by the wit of a
    mortal,
Never at least by himself; but a god that was present to aid
    him
Easily, just as he willed, might make one youthful or agéd.
'Twas but a moment agone thou wast old and in pitiful rai-
    ment;
Now thou art like to the gods who inhabit the infinite
    heaven."
Him then in answer addressed these words deep-plotting
    Odysseus:
"Telemachus, no need to be filled with exceeding amazement
Only for this—that thy father is here once more in his home-
    stead.
Ne'er will another Odysseus return but the man that thou
    seest here,
Even myself, as I am. Long, long have I suffered and wan-
    dered;
Now in the twentieth year I am come to the land of my
    fathers.
Touching this marvel, Athena the driver of spoil hath per-
    formed it,
Making me such as she pleased (to the gods are possible all
    things),
Changing me now to a beggar in semblance—a moment
    thereafter
Turning me into a youth that is clad in a beautiful garment.
Easy is all for the gods who inhabit the infinite heaven,
Either to grant a man great glory or else to abase him."

These words spoken he sat him adown. Then bursting in
    tears fell
Telemachus on the neck of his valiant father and kissed him.
    H. B. COTTERILL (*Odyssey* 16.167-214)

*When Odysseus approaches his own house his old dog rec-
ognizes him and dies.*

A dog lying near lifted his head and ears. Argos it was, the **51**
dog of hardy Odysseus, whom long ago he reared but never
used. Before the dog was grown, Odysseus went to sacred
Ilios. In the times past young men would take him on the
chase, for wild goats, deer, and hares; but now he lay neg-
lected, his master gone away, upon a pile of dung which had
been dropped before the door by mules and oxen, and which
lay there in a heap for slaves to carry off and dung the broad
lands of Odysseus. Here lay the dog, this Argos, full of fleas.
Yet even now, seeing Odysseus near, he wagged his tail and
dropped both ears, but toward his master he had not strength
to move. Odysseus turned aside and wiped away a tear, swiftly
concealing from Eumaeus what he did; then straightway thus
he questioned:

"Eumaeus, it is strange this dog lies on the dunghill. His
form is good; but I am not sure if he has speed of foot to
match his beauty, or if he is merely what the table-dogs be-
come which masters keep for show."

And, swineherd Eumaeus, you answered him and said:
"Aye truly, that is the dog of one who died afar. If he were
as good in form and action as when Odysseus left him and
went away to Troy, you would be much surprised to see his
speed and strength. For nothing could escape him in the
forest-depths, no creature that he started; he was keen upon
the scent. Now he has come to ill. In a strange land his mas-
ter perished, and the slack women give him no more care; for
slaves, when masters lose control, will not attend to duties.
Ah, half the value of a man far-seeing Zeus destroys when the
slave's lot befalls him!"

So saying, he entered the stately house and went straight

down the hall among the lordly suitors. But upon Argos fell
the doom of darksome death when he beheld Odysseus,
twenty years away.

GEORGE H. PALMER (*Odyssey* 17.290-327)

*As a beggar in his own house, Odysseus asks Antinous, one
of the suitors, for food.*

52   Then answered him Antinoüs and said: "What god has
brought to us this pest, this mar-feast here? Stand off there
in the middle, back from my table, or you shall find a bitter
Egypt and a bitter Cyprus too, brazen and shameless beggar
that you are! You go to all in turn, and they give lavishly. No
scruple or compunction do they feel at being generous with
others' goods, while there remains abundance for themselves."

Then stepping back said wise Odysseus: "Indeed! In you
then wisdom does not go with beauty. From your own house
you would not give a suppliant salt, if sitting at another's
table you will not take and give me bread. Yet here there is
abundance."

As he thus spoke, Antinoüs was angered in his heart the
more, and looking sternly on him said in winged words:
"Now you shall never leave the hall in peace, I think, now
you have taunted me."

So saying, he seized his footstool, flung it and struck Odys-
seus on the back of the right shoulder, near the spine. Firm
as a rock he stood; the missile of Antinoüs did not move him.
Silent he shook his head, brooding on evil.

GEORGE H. PALMER (*Odyssey* 17.445-465)

*Still without revealing himself Odysseus persuades Penelope
that her husband is yet alive. The maid Euryclea sympathizes
with him, and while bathing him recognizes him by a scar.
Odysseus frightens her into silence.*

53   "Perhaps, like thee, poor guest! in wanton pride
                The rich insult him, and the young deride!
                Conscious of worth revil'd, thy generous mind

The friendly rite of purity declin'd;
My will concurring with my queen's command,
Accept the bath from this obsequious hand.
A strong emotion shakes my anguish'd breast:
In thy whole form Ulysses seems express'd:
Of all the wretched harbour'd on our coast,
None imag'd e'er like thee my master lost."
Thus half discover'd through the dark disguise,
With cool composure feign'd, the chief replies:
"You join your suffrage to the public vote;
The same you think have all beholders thought."
He said: replenish'd from the purest springs,
The laver straight with busy care she brings:
In the deep vase, that shone like burnish'd gold,
The boiling fluid temperates the cold.
Meantime revolving in his thoughtful mind
The scar with which his manly knee was sign'd;
His face averting from the crackling blaze,
His shoulders intercept th' unfriendly rays:
Thus cautious in th' obscure he hop'd to fly
The curious search of Euryclea's eye.
Cautious in vain! nor ceas'd the dame to find
The scar with which his manly knee was sign'd.

Which noted token of the woodland war
When Euryclea found, th' ablution ceas'd;
Down dropp'd the leg, from her slack hand releas'd;
The mingled fluids from the vase redound;
The vase reclining floats the floor around!
Smiles dew'd with tears the pleasing strife express'd
Of grief and joy, alternate in her breast.
Her fluttering words in melting murmurs died;
At length abrupt—"My son!—my king!"—she cried.
His neck with fond embrace infolding fast,
Full on the queen her raptur'd eye she cast,
Ardent to speak the monarch safe restor'd:
But, studious to conceal her royal lord,

Minerva fix'd her mind on views remote,
And from the present bliss abstracts her thought.
His hand to Euryclea's mouth applied,
"Art thou foredoom'd my pest?" (the hero cried:)
"Thy milky founts my infant lips have drain'd:
And have the Fates thy babbling age ordain'd
To violate the life thy youth sustain'd?
An exile have I told, with weeping eyes,
Full twenty annual suns in distant skies:
At length return'd, some god inspires thy breast
To know thy kind, and here I stand confess'd.
This heaven-discover'd truth to thee consign'd,
Reserve the treasure of thy inmost mind."

ALEXANDER POPE (*Odyssey* 19.370-389)

*Penelope sets a trial involving the stringing of a mighty bow
and shooting an arrow through the openings in twelve axes.
Only Odysseus can string and shoot the bow, and with it in
his hands he leaps to the threshold and declares himself.*

54

Then did Ulysses cast his rags aside,
And, leaping to the threshold, took his stand
On its broad space, with bow and quiver filled
With arrows. At his feet the hero poured
The winged shafts, and to the suitors called:—
   "That difficult strife is ended. Now I take
Another mark, which no man yet has hit.
Now shall I see if I attain my aim,
And, by the aid of Phœbus, win renown."
   He spake; and, turning, at Antinoüs aimed
The bitter shaft,—Antinoüs, who just then
Had grasped a beautiful two-eared cup of gold,
About to drink the wine. He little thought
Of wounds and death; for who, when banqueting
Among his fellows, could suspect that one
Alone against so many men would dare,
However bold, to plan his death, and bring
On him the doom of fate? Ulysses struck

The suitor with the arrow at the throat.
The point came through the tender neck behind,
Sideways he sank to earth; his hand let fall
The cup; the dark blood in a thick warm stream
Gushed from the nostrils of the smitten man.
He spurned the table with his feet, and spilled
The viands; bread and roasted meats were flung
To lie polluted on the floor. Then rose
The suitors in a tumult, when they saw
The fallen man; from all their seats they rose
Throughout the hall, and to the massive walls
Looked eagerly; there hung no buckler there,
No sturdy lance for them to wield. They called
Thus to Ulysses with indignant words:—

  "Stranger! in evil hour hast thou presumed
To aim at men; and thou shalt henceforth bear
Part in no other contest. Even now
Is thy destruction close to thee. Thy hand
Hath slain the noblest youth in Ithaca.
The vultures shall devour thy flesh for this."

  So each one said; they deemed he had not slain
The suitor wittingly; nor did they see,
Blind that they were, the doom which in that hour
Was closing round them all. Then with a frown
The wise Ulysses looked on them, and said:—

  "Dogs! ye had thought I never would come back
From Ilium's coast, and therefore ye devoured
My substance here, and offered violence
To my maid-servants, and pursued my wife
As lovers, while I lived. Ye dreaded not
The gods who dwell in the great heaven, nor feared
Vengeance hereafter from the hands of men;
And now destruction overhangs you all."

  He spake, and all were pale with fear, and each
Looked round for some escape from death. Alone
Eurymachus found voice, and answered thus:—

  "If thou indeed be he, the Ithacan
Ulysses, now returned to thine old home,

Well hast thou spoken of the many wrongs
Done to thee by the Achaians in thy house
And in thy fields. But there the man lies slain
Who was the cause of all. Antinoüs first
Began this course of wrong. Nor were his thoughts
So much of marriage as another aim,—
Which Saturn's son denied him,—to bear rule
Himself o'er those who till the pleasant fields
Of Ithaca, first having slain thy son
In ambush. But he now has met his fate.
Spare, then, thy people. We will afterward
Make due amends in public for the waste
Here in thy palace of the food and wine.
For each of us shall bring thee twenty beeves,
And brass and gold, until thy heart shall be
Content. Till then we cannot blame thy wrath."
    Sternly the wise Ulysses frowned, and said:
"Eurymachus, if thou shouldst offer me
All that thou hast, thy father's wealth entire,
And add yet other gifts, not even then
Would I refrain from bloodshed, ere my hand
Avenged my wrongs upon the suitor-crew.
Choose then to fight or flee, whoever hopes
Escape from death and fate; yet none of you
Will now, I think, avoid that bitter doom."
    He spake. At once their knees and head grew faint,
And thus Eurymachus bespake the rest:—
    "This man, O friends, to his untamable arm
Will give no rest, but with that bow in hand,
And quiver, will send forth from where he stands
His shafts, till he has slain us all. Prepare
For combat then, and draw your swords, and hold
The tables up against his deadly shafts,
And rush together at him as one man,
And drive him from the threshold through the door.
Then, hurrying through the city, let us sound
The alarm, and soon he will have shot his last."
    He spake, and, drawing his keen two-edged sword

Of brass, sprang toward him with a dreadful cry,
Just as the great Ulysses, sending forth
An arrow, smote the suitor on the breast,
Beside the nipple. The swift weapon stood
Fixed in his liver; to the ground he flung
The sword, and, reeling giddily around
The table, fell; he brought with him to earth
The viands and the double cup, and smote
The pavement with his forehead heavily,
And in great agony. With both his feet
He struck and shook his throne, and darkness came
Over his eyes. Then rushed Amphinomus
Against the glorious chief, and drew his sword
To thrust him from the door. Telemachus
O'ertook him, and between his shoulders drove
A brazen lance. Right through his breast it went,
And he fell headlong, with his forehead dashed
Against the floor. Telemachus drew back,
And left his long spear in Amphinomus,
Lest, while he drew it forth, some one among
The Achaians might attack him with the sword,
And thrust him through or hew him down. In haste
He reached his father's side, and quickly said:—
     "Now, father, will I bring to thee a shield,
Two javelins, and a helmet wrought of brass,
Well fitted to the temples. I will case
Myself in armor, and will also give
Arms to the swineherd, and to him who tends
The beeves; for men in armor combat best."
     And wise Ulysses answered: "Bring them then,
And quickly, while I yet have arrows here
For my defence, lest, when I am alone,
They drive me from my station at the door."
     He spake. Obedient to his father's word,
Telemachus was soon within the room
In which the glorious arms were laid. He took
Four bucklers thence, eight spears, and helmets four
Of brass, each darkened with its horsehair crest,

And bore them forth, and quickly stood again
Beside his father. But he first encased
His limbs in brass; his followers also put
Their shining armor on, and took their place
Beside the wise Ulysses, eminent
In shrewd devices. He, while arrows yet
Were ready to his hand, with every aim
Brought down a suitor; side by side they fell.

W. C. BRYANT (*Odyssey* 22.1-118)

*Penelope hesitates to credit Euryclea's tidings that Odysseus
is returned. She proves his identity by private tokens, and
husband and wife are joyfully reunited.*

55   Then Eurycleia, the dear nurse, rejoined:
"What words are these, my child, that pass thy lips?
Sayst thou, then, that thy husband, who now stands
Upon thy hearthstone, never will return?
O slow of faith! but thou wert ever thus.
Come, then, I give a certain proof. I saw
Myself, when he was at the bath, the scar
Left on him by the white tusk of a boar,
And would have told thee, but he laid his hands
Upon my mouth, and would not suffer me
To bear the tidings, such his forecast was.
Now follow me; I give my life in pledge.
If I deceive thee, slay me ruthlessly."
    Then spake discreet Penelope again:
"Dear nurse, though thou in many things art wise,
Think not to scan the counsels of the gods,
Who live forever. Yet will we descend,
And meet my son, and look upon the slain,
And see the avenger by whose hand they fell."
    She spake, and from the royal bower went down,
Uncertain whether she should stand aloof
And question there her lord, or haste to him
And clasp his hands in hers and kiss his brow.
But having passed the threshold of hewn stone,

Entering she took her seat right opposite
Ulysses, in the full glow of the fire,
Against the other wall. Ulysses sat
Beside a lofty column with his eyes
Cast down, and waiting for his high-born wife
To speak when she had seen him. Long she sat
In silence, for amazement overpowered
Her senses. Sometimes, looking in his eyes,
She saw her husband there, and then again
Clad in those sordid weeds, she knew him not.
Then spake Telemachus, and chid her thus:—
    "Mother, unfeeling mother! hard of heart
Art thou; how else couldst thou remain aloof?
How keep from taking, at my father's side,
Thy place, to talk with him, and question him?
No other wife could bring herself to bear
Such distance from a husband, just returned
After long hardships, in the twentieth year
Of absence, to his native land and her.
Mother! thy heart is harder than a stone."
    And thus the sage Penelope replied:
"Dear child, my faculties are over-powered
With wonder, and I cannot question him,
Nor even speak to him, nor fix my looks
Upon his face. But if it be indeed
Ulysses, and he have returned, we soon
Shall know each other; there are tokens known
To both of us, to none but him and me."
    She ended, and the much-enduring chief
Ulysses, smiling at her words, bespake
Telemachus at once, in wingèd words:—
    "Suffer thy mother, O Telemachus,
To prove me; she will know me better soon.
My looks are sordid, and my limbs are wrapped
In tattered raiment, therefore she does think
Meanly of me, and cannot willingly
Believe that I am he. But let us now
Consider what most wisely may be done.

He who hath slain, among a tribe of men,
A single one with few to avenge his death,
Flees from his kindred and his native land;
But we have slain the champions of the realm,
The flower of all the youth of Ithaca.
Therefore, I pray thee, think what shall be done."
    And then discreet Telemachus replied:
"Look thou to that, dear father; for they say
That thou of all mankind wert wont to give
The wisest counsels. None of mortal birth
In this was deemed thy peer. We follow thee
With cheerful hearts; nor will our courage fail,
I think, in aught that lies within our power."
    Ulysses, the sagacious, answered thus:
"Then will I tell thee what I deem most wise.
First take the bath, and then array yourselves
In tunics, bid the palace-maidens choose
Fresh garments; let the godlike bard, who bears
The clear-toned harp, be leader, and strike up
A melody to prompt the festive dance,
That all may say who hear it from without,—
Whether the passers by or dwellers near,—
'It is a wedding.' Else throughout the land
The rumor of the slaughter we have wrought
Among the suitors may have spread before
We reach our wooded farm, and there consult
Beneath the guidance of Olympian Jove."
    He spake; they hearkened and obeyed. They took
The bath, and then they put their garments on.
The maids arrayed themselves; the godlike bard
Took the curved harp, and woke in all the love
Of melody, and of the graceful dance.
The spacious pile resounded to the steps
Of men and stately women in their mirth,
And one who stood without was heard to say:—
    "Some one, no doubt, has made the long-wooed queen
His bride at last; a worthless woman she,
Who could not, for the husband of her youth,

Keep his fair palace till he came again."
    Such words were said, but they who uttered them
Knew little what had passed. Eurynome,
The matron of the palace, meantime took
Magnanimous Ulysses to the bath
In his own dwelling, smoothed his limbs with oil,
And threw a gorgeous mantle over him
And tunic. Pallas on the hero's head
Shed grace and majesty; she made him seem
Taller and statelier, made his locks flow down
In curls like blossoms of the hyacinth,
As when a workman skilled in many arts,
And taught by Pallas and Minerva, twines
A golden border round the silver mass,
A glorious work; so did the goddess shed
Grace o'er his face and form. So from the bath
He stepped, like one of the immortals, took
The seat from which he rose, right opposite
Penelope, and thus addressed the queen:—
    "Lady, the dwellers of the Olympian heights
Have given thee an impenetrable heart
Beyond all other women. Sure I am,
No other wife could bring herself to bear
Such distance from a husband just returned
After long hardships, in the twentieth year
Of absence, to his native land and her.
Come, nurse, prepare a bed, where by myself
I may lie down; an iron heart is hers."
    To this the sage Penelope replied:
"Nay, sir, 'tis not through pride or disregard,
Or through excess of wonder, that I act
Thus toward thee. Well do I remember thee
As thou wert in the day when thy good ship
Bore thee from Ithaca. Bestir thyself,
Dame Eurycleia, and make up with care
A bed without the chamber, which he framed
With his own hands; bear out the massive bed,
And lay upon it seemly coverings,

Fleeces and mantles for his nightly rest."
     She spake to try her husband; but, displeased,
Ulysses answered thus his virtuous queen:—
     "O woman, thou hast said unwelcome words.
Who hath displaced my bed? That task were hard
For long-experienced hands, unless some god
Hath come to shift its place. No living man,
Even in his prime of years, could easily
Have moved it, for in that elaborate work
There was a mystery; it was I myself
Who shaped it, no one else. Within my court
There grew an olive-tree with full-leaved boughs,
A tall and flourishing tree; its massive stem
Was like a column. Round it I built up
A chamber with cemented stones until
The walls were finished; then I framed a roof
Above it, and put on the well-glued doors
Close fitting. Next I lopped the full-leaved boughs,
And, cutting off the trunk above the root,
Smoothed well the stump with tools, and made of it
A post to bear the couch. I bored the wood
With wimbles, placed it on the frame, and carved
The work till it was done, inlaying it
With silver, gold, and ivory. I stretched
Upon it thongs of oxhide brightly dyed
In purple. Now, O wife, I cannot know
Whether my bed remains as then it was,
Or whether some one from the root has hewn
The olive trunk, and moved it from its place."
     He spake, and her knees faltered and her heart
Was melted as she heard her lord recount
The tokens all so truly; and she wept,
And rose, and ran to him, and flung her arms
About his neck, and kissed his brow, and said:—
     "Ulysses, look not on me angrily,
Thou who in other things art wise above
All other men. The gods have made our lot
A hard one, jealous lest we should have passed

Our youth together happily, and thus
Have reached old age. I pray, be not incensed,
Nor take it ill that I embraced thee not
As soon as I beheld thee, for my heart
Has ever trembled lest some one who comes
Into this isle should cozen me with words;
And they who practice fraud are numberless.
The Argive Helen, child of Jupiter,
Would ne'er have listened to a stranger's suit
And loved him, had she known that in the years
To come the warlike Greeks would bring her back
To her own land. It was a deity
Who prompted her to that foul wrong. Her thought
Was never of the great calamity
Which followed, and which brought such woe on us.
But now, since thou, by tokens clear and true,
Hast spoken of our bed, which human eye
Has never seen save mine and thine, and those
Of one handmaiden only, Actoris,—
Her whom my father gave me when I came
To this thy palace, and who kept the door
Of our close chamber,—thou hast won my mind
To full belief, though hard it was to win."
    She spake, and he was moved to tears; he wept
As in his arms he held his dearly loved
And faithful wife. As welcome as the land
To those who swim the deep, of whose stout bark
Neptune has made a wreck amidst the waves,
Tossed by the billow and the blast, and few
Are those who from the hoary ocean reach
The shore, their limbs all crested with the brine,
These gladly climb the sea-beach, and are safe,—
So welcome was her husband to her eyes.
    W. C. BRYANT (*Odyssey* 23.69-239)

HESIOD

Next in time to Homer, but of a totally different social climate, is the Boeotian poet Hesiod. Where Homer is concerned with heroes who glorify and transfigure life, Hesiod faces life with prudential maxims and a gospel of work. Works and Days begins with an invocation to Zeus and a criticism of unfair gains.

56 Pierian Muses whose songs glorify, hither!
Speak of Zeus your father, chant his praises.
Through him are mortals famed or unfamed;
sung or unsung are men by the high will of Zeus.
Easily does Zeus make strong, and easily the strong lays low;
easily he minishes the proud, and the obscure enlarges;
easily he straightens the crooked, and the haughty blasts—
even Zeus, who thunders on high and inhabits the loftiest
    dwellings.
Hearken, mark and hear, and with righteousness direct your
    judgments:
Sooth, Perses, are the things I would tell.
    Not single was the breed of strife upon earth—
two there were. One when he understood, a man would
    praise,
the other blame; wholly diverse their spirit.
Evil war one nurtures and carnage—wicked she!
Her none loves, but by will of the immortals
of necessity men pay Strife her homage.
The other black Night bare first; her lofty Zeus
in ether dwelling fixed at earth's roots.
Better is she for men; even the feckless she rouses to labor,
stirs appetite for work when one man watches another,
a richer, zealous to plow and plant and set his house in order.

Neighbor vies with neighbor in pursuit of wealth. Such strife
is good for mortals. Potter competes with potter, carpenter
with carpenter; beggar envies beggar, and poet poet.

These things store in your heart, Perses. Your spirit
let not mischief-loving Strife deter from work, spying
and eavesdropping market-square wrangles. Scant time
for wrangles and gossip who possesses not livelihood
safe-stored for a year, Earth's produce, Demeter's foison.
This supplied, dispute and contest a neighbor's holdings.
Not again can you so deal. With judgments straight
adjudge we our quarrel; Zeus' judgments are these, and best.
Our heritage we already divided; yet you the greater part
did seize and carry off, swelling the bribe-guzzling princes,
all-willing to judge such a cause. Fools!
They know not how far the half exceeds the whole,
how wholesome mallows and asphodel for victuals.
Livelihood the gods keep hid from mankind; easily else
would a day's work keep you a year, aye, without working.
Soon would you put your rudder by, over the smoke;
futile the labor of oxen and of mules that toil.

Moses Hadas (*Works and Days* 1-46)

*Man must live by the sweat of his brow because of a Fall, in
which a light-headed woman was involved.*

Zeus in the wrath of his heart hath hidden the means of **57**
    subsistence—
Wrathful because he once was deceived by the wily Prome-
    theus.
Therefore it was he devised most grievous troubles for mortals.
Fire he hid: yet that, for men, did the gallant Prometheus
Steal in a hollow reed, from the dwelling of Zeus the Adviser,
Nor was he seen by the ruler of gods, who delights in the
    thunder.
Then, in his rage at the deed, cloud-gathering Zeus did
    address him:
Iapetionides, in cunning greater than any,

"Thou in the theft of fire and deceit of me art exulting,
Source of regret for thyself and for men who shall be here-
after.
I, in the place of fire, will give them a bane, so that all men
May in spirit exult and find in their misery comfort!"
Speaking thus, loud laughed he, the father of gods and of
mortals.
Then he commanded Hephaistos, the cunning artificer,
straightway
Mixing water and earth, with speech and force to endow it,
Making it like in face to the gods whose life is eternal.
Virginal, winning and fair was the shape: and he ordered
Athene
Skilful devices to teach her, the beautiful works of the weaver.
Then did he bid Aphrodite the golden endow her with beauty,
Eager desire and passion that wasteth the bodies of mortals.
Hermes, guider of men, the destroyer of Argus, he ordered,
Lastly, a shameless mind to bestow and a treacherous nature.
So did he speak. They obeyed Lord Zeus, who is offspring of
Kronos.
Straightway, out of the earth, the renowned artificer fashioned
One like a shame-faced maid, at the will of the ruler of
Heaven.
Girdle and ornaments added the bright-eyed goddess Athene
Over her body the Graces divine and noble Persuasion
Hung their golden chains; and the Hours with beautiful
tresses
Wove her garlands of flowers that bloom in the season of
Springtime.
All her adornments Pallas Athene fitted upon her.
Into her bosom, Hermes the guide, the destroyer of Argus,
Falsehood, treacherous thoughts and a thievish nature im-
parted:
Such was the bidding of Zeus who heavily thunders; and
lastly,
Hermes, herald of gods, endowed her with speech, and the
woman
Named Pandora, because all the gods who dwell in Olympos

Gave her presents, to make her a fatal bane unto mortals.
When now Zeus had finished this snare so deadly and certain,
Famous Argus slayer, the herald of gods, he commanded,
Leading her thence, as a gift to bestow her upon Epimetheus.
He, then, failed to remember Prometheus had bidden him
  never
Gifts to accept from Olympian Zeus, but still to return them
Straightway, lest some evil befall thereby unto mortals.
So he received her—and then, when the evil befell, he re-
  membered.
Till that time, upon earth were dwelling the races of mortals,
Free and secure from trouble and free from wearisome labour;
Safe from painful diseases that bring mankind to destruction
Since full swiftly in misery age unto mortals approacheth.
Now with her hands, Pandora the great lid raised from the
  vessel,
Letting them loose: and grievous the evil for men she pro-
  vided.
Hope yet lingered, alone, in the dwelling securely imprisoned,
Since she under the edge of the lid had tarried and flew not
Forth: too soon Pandora had fastened the lid of the vessel.
Such was the will of Zeus, cloud-gatherer, lord of the aegis.
Numberless evils beside to the haunts of men had departed,
Full is the earth of ills, and full no less are the waters.
Freely diseases among mankind, by day and in darkness
Hither and thither may pass and bring much woe upon
  mortals:
Voiceless, since of speech high-counselling Zeus has bereft
  them.
    W. C. Lawton (*Works and Days* 47-105)

*Rapine is natural for animals, but not, as we hear in the
sequel, for man.*

    Once a hawk said this to a nightingale—   50
    The robber had the singer in his claws,
    High up among the clouds, and Philomel,
    Trembling, and nipped in those sharp crooked talons,

Bewailed; whereat the hawk savagely screamed:
"Why pipe, my friend? I am too strong to heed;
I take you where I will, for all your singing;
To eat you if I like, or let you go;
And he's a fool that fights against his fate.
He loses, and gets shame, beside his tears."
    EDWIN ARNOLD (*Works and Days* 203-211)

*Justice reports the deeds of men to Zeus, who sends du
requital:*

59   But they who never from the right have strayed,
Who as the citizen the stranger aid,
They and their cities flourish; genial Peace
Dwells in their borders, and their youth increase:
Nor Jove, whose radiant eyes behold afar,
Hangs forth in heaven the signs of grievous war.
Nor scathe nor famine on the righteous prey;
Feasts, strewn by earth, employ their easy day:
The oak is on their hills; the topmost tree
Bears the rich acorn, and the trunk the bee:
Burdened with fleece their panting flocks: the face
Of woman's offspring speaks the father's race:
Still prosper they, nor spread in ships the sail;
For life's abundance gifts the fruitful vale.
But o'er the wicked race, to whom belong
The thought of evil and the deed of wrong,
Saturnian Jove, of wide-beholding eyes,
Bids the dark signs of retribution rise:
States rue the wrongs a sinful man has done,
And all atone the wickedness of one.
The god sends down his angry plagues from high,
Famine and pestilence; in heaps they die.
He smites with barrenness the marriage bed,
And generations moulder with the dead:
Again in vengeance of his wrath he falls
On their great hosts and breaks their tottering walls;

Arrests their navies on the ocean plain,
And whelms their strength with mountains of the main.
        C. A. ELTON (*Works and Days* 225-247)

The second part of Works and Days *is a Farmer's Calendar.
Here is a description of winter:*

Beware the January month: beware   **60**
Those hurtful days, that keenly piercing air
Which flays the steers; when wide o'er fell and flood
Ice in its curdled masses nips the blood.
From Thracia, nurse of steeds, comes rushing forth,
O'er the broad sea, the whirlwind of the north,
And moves it with his breath; earth roars through all
Its woodlands; oaks of towering foliage fall,
And thick branch'd pines, as in his fitful swell
He sweeps the hollows of the mountain dell:
He stoops to earth; the crash is heard around,
The boundless forest rolls the roar of sound.
Now shrink the beasts, and shuddering as they run,
The gust, low crouch'd, with cowering bodies, shun.
Thick is the hairy coat, the shaggy skin,
But that all-chilling breath shall pierce within:
Not his rough hide can then the ox avail;
The long-hair'd goat defenceless feels the gale:
Yet vain the north wind's rushing strength to wound
The flock, with thickening fleeces fenced around.
The old man bends him double in the blast,
Whose harmless breath the tender virgin pass'd:
Home-keeping she with her own mother dwells,
Yet innocent of Venus' golden spells,
And bathing her soft limbs, and with smooth balm
Anointing, in the shelter and the calm
Of that her secret chamber, nightly so
Seeks her safe couch, while wintry tempests blow.
Now gnaws the boneless polypus his feet,
Starved midst bleak rocks, his desolate retreat:

For now no more the sun's refracted ray
Through seas transparent lights him to his prey;
O'er the swarth Ethiop rolls his bright career,
And slowly gilds the Grecian hemisphere.
And now the horn'd and unhorn'd kind,
Whose lair is in the wood, sore famish'd grind
Their sounding jaws, and frozen and quaking fly
Where oaks the mountain dells imbranch on high;
They seek to couch in thickets of the glen,
Or lurk deep shelter'd in the rocky den.
Like aged men, who, propp'd on crutches, tread
Tottering with broken strength and stooping head,
So move the beasts of earth, and creeping low,
Shun the white flakes, and dread the drifting snow.
  C. A. ELTON (*Works and Days* 504-535)

Hesiod's other major work is his Theogony, *which is a kind
of systematization and regularization of the functions of the
various gods and of their relationship to one another. The
principal factor in the systematization and reform of Greek
religion has to do with the victory of the Olympians, who
represent the new order, over the unreasoning Titans. The
following passage describes Tartarus, where the Titans were
relegated after their defeat.*

81
    Amid the foremost, towering in the van,
The war-unsated Gyges, Briareus,
And Cottus, bitterest conflict waged: for they
Successive thrice a hundred rocks in air
Hurled from their sinewy grasp: with missile storm
The Titan host o'ershadowing, them they drove,
Vain-glorious as they were, with hands of strength
O'ercoming them, beneath th' expanse of earth
And bound with galling chains, so far beneath
This earth, as earth is distant from the sky:
So deep the space to darksome Tartarus.
A brazen anvil rushing from the sky
Through thrice three days would toss in airy whirl,

Nor touch this earth, till the tenth sun arose:
Or down earth's chasm precipitate revolve,
Nor till the tenth sun rose attain the verge
Of Tartarus. A fence of massive brass
Is forged around: around the pass is rolled
A night of triple darkness; and above
Impend the roots of earth and barren sea.
There the Titanic gods in murkiest gloom
Lie hidden: such the cloud-assembler's will:
There in a place of darkness, where vast earth
Has end: from thence no egress open lies:
Neptune's huge hand has closed with brazen gates
The mouth: a wall environs every side.
There Gyges, Cottus, high-souled Briareus,
Dwell vigilant: the faithful sentinels
Of Ægis-bearer Jove. Successive there
The dusky Earth, and darksome Tartarus,
The sterile Ocean, and the starry Heaven,
Arise and end, their source and boundary.
A dread and ghastly wilderness, abhorred
E'en by the gods; a vast vacuity:
Might none the space of one slow-circling year
Touch the firm soil, that portal entered once,
But him the whirls of vexing hurricanes
Toss to and fro. E'en by immortals loathed
This prodigy of horror. There too stand
The mansions drear of gloomy Night, o'erspread
With blackening vapours: and before the doors
Atlas upholding heaven his forehead rears,
And indefatigable hands. There Night
And Day, near passing, mutual greeting still
Exchange, alternate as they glide athwart
The brazen threshold vast. This enters, that
Forth issues; nor the two can one abode
At once constrain. This passes forth and roams
The round of earth; that in the mansion waits,
Till the due season of her travel come.
Lo! from the one the far-discerning light

Beams upon earthly dwellers; but a cloud
Of pitchy blackness veils the other round:
Pernicious Night: aye-leading in her hand
Sleep, Death's half-brother: sons of gloomy Night
There hold they habitation, Death and Sleep;
Dread deities: nor them the shining Sun
E'er with his beam contemplates, when he climbs
The cope of heaven, or when from heaven descends.
Of these the one glides gentle o'er the space
Of earth and broad expanse of ocean waves,
Placid to man. The other has a heart
Of iron; yea, the heart within his breast
Is brass, unpitying: whom of men he grasps
Stern he retains: e'en to immortal gods
A foe. The hollow-sounding palaces
Of Pluto strong, the subterranean god,
And stern Proserpina, there full in front
Ascend: a grisly dog, implacable,
Holds watch before the gates: a stratagem
Is his, malicious: them who enter there,
With tail and bended ears he fawning soothes:
But suffers not that they with backward step
Repass: whoe'er would issue from the gates
Of Pluto strong and stern Proserpina,
For them with marking eye he lurks; on them
Springs from his couch, and pitiless devours.

    There, odious to immortals, dreadful Styx
Inhabits: refluent Ocean's eldest-born:
She from the gods apart forever dwells
In far-re-echoing mansions, with arched roofs
Of loftiest rock o'erhung: and all around
The silver columns lean upon the skies.

    Swift-footed Iris, nymph of Thaumas born,
Takes with no frequent embassy her way
O'er the broad main's expanse, when haply strife
Be risen, and midst the gods dissension sown:
And if there be among th' Olympian race
Who falsehood utters, Jove sends Iris down

To bring the great oath in a golden ewer:
The far-famed water, from steep, sky-capped rock
Distilling in cold stream. Beneath wide Earth
Abundant from the sacred river-head,
Through shades of blackest night, the Stygian horn
Of ocean flows: a tenth of all the streams
To the dread oath allotted. In nine streams
Circling the round of earth and the broad seas,
With silver whirlpools twined in many a maze,
It falls into the deep: one stream alone
Flows from the rock; a mighty bane to gods.
Who of immortals, that inhabit still
Olympus topped with snow, libation pours
And is forsworn, he one whole year entire
Lives reft of breath: nor yet approaches once
The nectared and ambrosial sweet repast:
But still reclines on the spread festive couch
Mute, breathless; and a mortal lethargy
O'erwhelms him: but, his malady absolved
With the great round of the revolving year,
More ills on ills afflictive seize: nine years
From ever-living deities remote
His lot is cast: in council nor in feast
Once joins he, till nine years entire are full:
The tenth again he mingles with the blest
Societies, who fill th' Olympian courts.
So great an oath the deities of heaven
Decreed the water of eternal Styx,
The ancient stream, that sweeps with wandering waves
A rugged region, where of dusky Earth,
And darksome Tartarus, and Ocean waste,
And starry Heaven, the source and boundary
Successive rise and end: a dreary wild
And ghastly: e'en by deities abhorred.

There gates resplendent rise; the threshold brass;
Immovable; on deep foundations fixed;
Self-framed. Before them the Titanic gods
Abide, without the assembly of the Blest,

Beyond the gulf of darkness. There beneath
The ocean-roots, th' auxiliaries renowned
Of Jove who rolls the hollow-pealing thunder,
Cottus and Gyges in near mansions dwell:
But He that shakes the shores with dashing surge,
Hailing him son, gave Briareus as bride
Cymopolia, prize of brave desert.

    C. A. ELTON (*Theogony* 713-819)

HOMERIC HYMNS

*The so-called Homeric Hymns, dating from the seventh and
sixth centuries B.C., include some of the finest poetry and
most revealing religious documents of the Greek legacy. More
than any other ancient Greek writing, the* Hymn to Demeter
*dating to the seventh century B.C., breathes the beauty of
holiness. The* Hymn *is a sacred writ of the Eleusinian Mys-
teries, in which the regeneration of vegetation becomes a
paradigm for the regeneration of man.*

62

Ceres! to thee belongs the votive lay,
Whose locks in radiance round thy temples play,
And Proserpine, whom, distant from thy sight,
Fierce Pluto bore to realms of endless night.
For thus decreed the god whose piercing eyes
Trace every act, whose thunder shakes the skies,
That she, whose hands the golden sickle bear,
And choicest product of the circling year,
Rich fruits, and fragrance-breathing flowers, should know
The tender conflicts of maternal woe.
    In Nysia's vale, with nymphs a lovely train,
Sprung from the hoary father of the main,
Fair Proserpine consumed the fleeting hours
In pleasing sports, and plucked the gaudy flowers.
    Around them wide the flamy crocus glows,

Through leaves of verdure blooms the opening rose;
The hyacinth declines his fragrant head,
And purple violets deck th' enamelled mead.
The fair narcissus far above the rest,
By magic formed, in beauty rose confessed.
So Jove, t' ensnare the virgin's thoughtless mind,
And please the ruler of the shades, designed.
   He caused it from the opening earth to rise,
Sweet to the scent, alluring to the eyes.
Never did mortal or celestial power
Behold such vivid tints adorn a flower.
From the deep root an hundred branches sprung,
And to the winds ambrosial odours flung;
Which, lightly wafted on the wings of air,
The gladdened earth and heaven's wide circuit share
The joy-dispensing fragrance spreads around,
And ocean's briny swell with smiles is crowned.
   Pleased at the sight, nor deeming danger nigh,
The fair beheld it with desiring eye:
Her eager hand she stretched to seize the flower,
(Beauteous illusion of th' ethereal power!)
When, dreadful to behold, the rocking ground
Disparted—widely yawned a gulf profound!
Forth-rushing from the black abyss, arose
The gloomy monarch of the realm of woes,
Pluto, from Saturn sprung. The trembling maid
He seized, and to his golden car conveyed.
Borne by immortal steeds the chariot flies:
And thus she pours her supplicating cries:
   "Assist, protect me, thou who reign'st above,
Supreme and best of gods, paternal Jove!"
But ah! in vain the hapless virgin rears
Her wild complaint: nor god nor mortal hears!
Not to the white-armed nymphs with beauty crowned,
Her loved companions, reached the mournful sound.
   Pale Hecate, who in the cell of night
Muses on youthful pleasure's rapid flight;
And bright Hyperion's son, who decks the skies

With splendour, only heard the virgin's cries
Invoke the father of th' ethereal powers.
But he, at distance from their airy bowers,
Sits in his hallowed fane; his votaries hears,
Accepts their offerings, and rewards their prayers.
While hell's dread ruler in his car conveyed
'o realms of darkness the reluctant maid.

Long as she viewed the star-bespangled skies,
And ocean's many-teeming waters rise;
While earth's gay verdure fled not from her view,
Nor Phoebus yet his cheerful light withdrew;
So long the ray of hope illumed her breast,
Nor sunk her soul, undaunted though distressed.
Her mother still she thought would meet her sight,
And friendly powers who dwelt in realms of light.
E'en ocean's depths resounded to her cry,
And lofty mountains towering to the sky!

At length, the shrieks of woe her mother hears;
Her heavenly breast the shaft of anguish tears.
The blooming wreath she from her brow unbinds,
Rends her bright locks, and gives them to the winds:
Then (mournful emblem of her inward woes!)
A sable veil athwart her shoulders throws.
As some fond bird her ravished young deplores,
And every secret shade in vain explores;
To seek the fair she flies o'er sea and land,
The burning torches waving in her hand.
Nor gods nor men the author of her woes
Unfold: no birds of omened flight disclose.

Nine tedious days in vain the queen adored
The various regions of the earth explored;
Nor did she taste, while she her course pursued,
The balmy nectar or ambrosial food;
Nor ever in the cool translucent wave,
Toil's sweet relief, her form of beauty lave.

On the tenth morn, as, chasing night's dull gloom,
Aurora's beams the purpled east illume,
Pale Hecate before her view appeared;

Her hand the faintly-gleaming taper reared,
And thus began: "O thou! to whom we owe
Those joys the season's circling flight bestow;
What god, what mortal dared the impious deed,
That makes a heavenly breast with sorrow bleed?
I heard thy daughter's voice implore relief;
Unknown to me the author of her grief."

   She ceased; nor did the goddess make reply,
But sudden waved the flaming torch on high,
And sought the ruler of the day; whose sight
From the pure regions of unclouded light
All actions views. Before his car they came;
The burning car and horses breathing flame
Stopped sudden. Ceres thus: "O Phoebus! hear!
My fame, my ancient dignity revere!
If e'er my blessings gave thy soul delight,
Those blessings now by friendship's act requite.
A daughter late was mine of beauteous form—
(Sweet, tender plant, uprooted by a storm!)
Distant I heard her loud-lamenting cries;
But fate severe denied her to my eyes.
O thou! who, crowned with ether's purest light,
Through earth and ocean dart'st thy boundless sight,
Tell me what god, what mortal, has conveyed
Reluctant from these arms my darling maid?"

   "Daughter of Rhea!" he replied, "I hear
With grief thy wrongs, and dignity revere.
Blame not th' ethereal race: from heaven's dread king,
Who dwells 'mid black'ning clouds, thy sorrows spring.
Pluto, by his decree, the virgin bore
Where, darkly frowning on th' infernal shore,
His lofty palace stands. No more repine;
No cause for anguish nor for shame is thine.
He, brother to the god who rules on high,
Now hails her empress of the lower sky:
For Saturn's awful race superior reign
O'er heaven, o'er hell, and earth-encircling main."

   He said, and then (his course no more delayed)

Spoke to his fiery steeds: his steeds obeyed.
Whirled rapid onward through th' illumined skies,
The flame-robed chariot kindles as it flies:
Swift, as when rushing through the blaze of day,
Darts the fierce eagle on his distant prey.
　　But deeper anguish rends the mother's soul,
And thoughts of vengeance in her bosom roll;
She shuns th' imperious power who rules on high,
And quits th' immortal synod of the sky.
Then, furious from Olympus' airy height
To earth precipitates her rapid flight.
There, mingling with the race of man, she shares
Their various toils; consumed with grief appears
Her beauteous form; unknown from shore to shore
She roves; till Celeus' hospitable door
Receives her steps. He in Eleusis reigned,
Where still her rites and honors are maintained.
　　Beside a path, while o'er her drooping head
His grateful shade the verdant olive spread,
As by her feet Parthenius' waters flow,
She sits, a pallid spectacle of woe.
Her faded cheeks no more with beauty bloomed,
But now the form of wrinkled age assumed.
She seemed like those whom each attractive grace
Forsakes, when time with wrinkles marks the face;
From whom the Cyprian power indignant flies,
Her gifts refuses, and her charms denies;
Who, in some regal dome, by fate severe,
Are doomed to nurse and serve another's heir.
　　Four gentle nymphs, light-moving o'er the plain,
Approach; four brazen urns their arms sustain:
Great Celeus was their sire: he bade them bring
The limpid water from Parthenius' spring.
Lovely they seemed as heaven's immortal powers:
Youth's purple light and beauty's opening flowers
Glowed on their cheeks: Callidice the fair,
And meek Clausidice with pensive air;
Then Demo, and Callithoe's riper grace

Appeared, the eldest of the lovely race.
They hail the power unknown, (for mortal eyes
How hard to penetrate a god's disguise!)
"Who and whence art thou, dame! whose brow appears
Marked by the traces of revolving years?
Why dost thou shun yon peopled town? In grief
Why lonely sit?—there thou wilt find relief:
There, matrons like thyself, who long the load
Of life have borne, and traced its rugged road,
Employed in labors such as best engage
The pleased attention of declining age,
With tender maids, thy sorrows shall condole,
And acts of friendship cheer thy drooping soul!"

"Hail! nymphs unknown!" the goddess thus rejoined,
"Accept the tribute of a grateful mind.
Would you the story of my sorrows know,
Attend to no fictitious tale of woe.

"Reluctant from the Cretan coast I came;
Dear native land! and Doris is my name.
To ruffians' force who plough the wat'ry way,
I fell a helpless, unresisting prey.
The bark bounds swiftly o'er the liquid main,
And soon the coast of Thoricus we gain.
The vessel safely moored, a female band
Prepare the banquet on the neighb'ring strand;
Whilst wide around us eve's gray vapors rise,
And her dim shades roll slowly through the skies.
But, deeply-musing on my woes, I pine,
Nor share the feast nor taste the cheerful wine.
When through the sky night's deeper gloom was spread,
Unnoticed, trembling o'er the beach I fled.
The spoiler's lust of gold I rendered vain;
Unransomed, thus escaped the galling chain
Of servitude, long time from shore to shore
I wandered; various toils and perils bore.
To me e'en now unknown, ere you unfold,
The land I tread, the people I behold.

"To you, ye virgins! may th' ethereal powers

Who o'er Olympus dwell in airy bowers,
Shed choicest favors! may your consorts prove
Of lovely form, deserving of your love!
And be your children with such beauty blest,
As hope can image in a parent's breast!
Then, gentle maids, in pity to my woes,
How best I can obtain relief, disclose;
In yonder town with pleasure I'll engage
In tasks best suited to my feeble age.
Well-skilled in household toils, to please my lord
The couch I'll spread, and crown the festive board;
Or should a child be trusted to my care,
These arms shall nurse him and these knees shall bear."

    She ceased. The loveliest of a lovely line
Callidice, replied: "No more repine!
But know, whate'er th' immortal gods ordain,
It is our part to suffer, not complain:
Enough for us that justice rules their mind,
Whose wisdom, like their power, is unconfined.
The chiefs who here supreme dominion hold
Be it my task, O stranger! to unfold:
Through whom Eleusis hostile rage defies;
Beneath whose care yon guardian ramparts rise;
From whom protecting law derives its force,
And awful justice holds her steady course:
Triptolemus, of deep-revolving mind,
Diocles noble, Polyxenus kind;
With every milder grace Eumolpus crowned,
And stately Dolichus in arms renowned.
Superior to the rest o'er these domains
Our honoured sire, the mighty Celeus, reigns.
Each chief a lovely consort boasts, who guides
Domestic labours, and at home presides:
Not one of them who would thy suit reject,
But soothe thy sorrows and thy age respect:
For sure, thou seem'st of more than mortal race,
Though time with wrinkles marks thy pallid face.
But if thou here wilt rest, without delay

We'll to our mother's ears thy tale convey.
If she approves, accept a welcome there:
An only child, an unexpected heir,
Born to his parents in declining age,
Our darling pleasure will thy cares engage.
Shouldst thou preserve him (kindly thus employed)
Till ripening manhood make thy labours void,
Such gifts hereafter he'll on thee bestow,
As those will envy most who best shall know."
    The virgin ceased; nor aught the goddess said,
But bowed submissive her assenting head.
The liquid crystal fills their polished urns:
Each nymph exulting to the town returns.
    Arrived at Celeus' dome, they quick disclose
The stranger's humble suit and tale of woes
To Metaneira: pleased at the request,
Maternal fondness glowing in her breast,
She bids them to the matron thus declare,
That ample treasures should reward her care.
    Like the kine's lowing race, that sportive bound
Along the plain with flowery verdure crowned;
Or the sleek fawn, when he at first perceives
Spring's genial warmth, and crops the budding leaves;
Thus joyful through the beaten road they passed,
With robes collected to promote their haste.
Their tresses, like the crocus' flamy hue,
In waving radiance round their shoulders flew.
    Now to the place where sate the heavenly dame
Beside the murmuring stream, the virgins came.
Their mother's suit they urge, nor she denies;
While thoughts of sorrow in her bosom rise,
Wrapt in the sable veil her course she bends;
The robe dark-flowing to her feet descends.
    Soon they approach to Celeus' stately gate;
Within the lofty hall the mother sate
Beside the threshold; frequent to her breast
The child, the darling of her heart, she pressed.
Each nymph to greet her much-loved parent flies,

While Ceres distant stands in humble guise.
    Lo! suddenly, before their wondering sight,
Her form increasing, to the temple's height
Ascends; her head with circling rays is crowned,
And wide th' ethereal splendour spreads around!
    Awe, veneration, seized the mother's breast,
And pallid fear was on her cheeks impressed;
Upstarting from her couch, she'd fain resign
The seat resplendent to her guest divine;
With looks unwilling she the suit denies,
And fixes on the ground her radiant eyes.
But kind Iambe with a modest mien
A seat provided for the seasons' queen;
A lambkin's snowy fleece she o'er it spread:
Still, deeply musing, naught the goddess said,
But round her head the dusky mantle drew,
To hide her deep-felt anguish from their view.
    "Be it thy care to nurse this lovely boy,
Child of my age, an unexpected joy
By favouring gods bestowed! should, through thy cares,
My Demophon arrive at manhood's years,
Others shall at thy happier state repine,
Such high rewards, such treasure shall be thine."
    "O woman! favoured by the powers of heaven,
To whom the gods this beauteous child have given,"
Ceres replied, "I take with joy thy heir;
No nurse unskilled receives him to her care;
Nor magic spell, nor roots of mighty power,
From earth's dark bosom torn at midnight hour,
Shall hurt thy offspring; to defeat each charm,
And herb malignant of its power disarm,
Full well I know." She said, and to her breast
The infant clasped, and tenderly caressed.
    Thus Ceres nursed the child. Exulting joy
Reigned in his parents' hearts. Meanwhile the boy
Grew like an offspring of ethereal race;
Health crowned his frame and beauty decked his face.
No mortal food he ate; the queen adored

Around him oft ambrosial odours poured;
Oft as the child was on her bosom laid,
She heavenly influence to his soul conveyed.
At night, to purge from earthly dross his frame,
She kindled on the earth th' annealing flame;
And, like a brand unmarked by human view,
Amid the fire wide-blazing frequent threw
Th' unconscious child: his parents wond'ring trace
Something divine, a more than mortal grace
Shine in his form; and she designed the boy,
To chance superior and to time's annoy,
Crowned with unceasing joys in heaven should reign:
Those thoughts a mother's rashness rendered vain!
　　One fatal night, neglectful of repose,
Her couch forsaking, Metaneira rose;
And from her secret stand beheld the flame
Receive the infant. Terror shakes her frame!
She shrieks in agony; she smites her thighs;
And thus she pours her loud-lamenting cries:
　　"O Demophon, my child! this stranger guest,
What causeless rage, what frenzy has possessed?
Consuming flames around thy body roll,
And anguish rends thy mother's tortured soul!"
　　Wrath seized the goddess; her immortal hands
Sudden she plunged amid the fiery brands;
And full before th' afflicted mother's view
On the cold floor the blameless infant threw,
And furious thus began: "O mortals vain!
Whose folly counteracts what gods ordain!
Who, lost in error's maze, will never know
Approaching blessings from impending woe!
Long for the rashness that thy soul possessed,
Shall keen reflection agonize thy breast.
For, by that oath which binds the powers supreme
I swear! by sable Styx, infernal stream!
Else had thy son in youth's perpetual prime
Shared heavenly joys, and mocked the rage of time.
But now 'tis past! from fate he cannot fly!

Man's common lot is his—he breathes to die!
But since a goddess on her knee caressed
Thy child, since oft he slumbered on her breast,
Fame shall attend his steps, and bright renown
With wreaths unfading shall his temples crown.
In future times, torn by discordant rage,
Eleusis' sons commutual war shall wage.

"Know then that Ceres, from whose bounty flow
Those blessings the revolving years bestow,
Who, both from gods and man's frail race demands
Her honours due, before thy presence stands.
Away, and let Eleusis' sons unite,
Where steep Callichorus' projecting height
Frowns o'er the plain, a stately fane to rear:
Her awful rites its goddess shall declare.
There with pure hearts upon the hallowed shrine
Your victims slay, and soothe a power divine!"

This said; the front of age so late assumed
Dissolved; her face with charms celestial bloomed.
The sacred vesture that around her flew
Through the wide air ambrosial odours threw;
Her lovely form with sudden radiance glowed;
Her golden locks in wreaths of splendour flowed.
Through the dark palace streamed a flood of light,
As cloud-engendered fires illume the night
With dazzling blaze. Then swiftly from their view,
Urged by indignant rage, the goddess flew.

In Metaneira's breast amazement reigned:
Silent she stood; nor long her knees sustained
Their tottering weight; she sunk in grief profound;
The child neglected, shrieking on the ground
Beside her lay: his agonizing cries
The sisters hear, and from their couches rise:
They snatch him from the floor; the fire suppressed
One lights anew; one fondly to her breast
The infant folds; by filial duty swayed,
Another hastes to Metaneira's aid.

And now they gathered round th' afflicted child,
And bathed his beauteous form with dust defiled:
With broken sobs he ceased not to complain;
A different nurse he sought, but sought in vain.
     RICHARD HOLE (*Hymn to Demeter* 1-291)

*Demeter's withdrawal leaves the earth scorched and barren,
and the plaints of men constrain the gods to pacify Demeter.
Persephone is restored to her, but it is ordained that she shall
spend half of each year with her mother and half with the
ruler of the nether world. The shrine of Eleusis and its ritual
is established; the revivification of vegetation which its cult
symbolizes is made to apply also to the life of man.*

Thrice happy he among the favoured few   **63**
To whom 'tis given those glorious rites to view!
A fate far different the rejected share;
Unblest, unworthy her protecting care,
They'll perish: and with chains of darkness bound,
Be plunged forever in the gulf profound!
Her laws established, to the realms of light
With Proserpine she wings her towering flight:
The sacred powers assume their seat on high,
Beside the god whose thunders shake the sky.
Happy, thrice happy he of human race,
Who proves deserving their benignant grace!
Plutus, who from his unexhausted stores
To favoured mortals boundless treasure pours,
Th' auspicious deities to him shall send;
And prosperous fortune shall his steps attend.
     And now, O Ceres! at thy hallowed shrine
Submissive bow the Eleusinian line:
Antron's dark rocks re-echo with thy praise,
And sea-surrounded Paros thee obeys.
Goddess! through whom the seasons' circling flight
Successive blessings pours, and new delight;
And thou, O lovely Proserpine! reward

With honoured age and tranquil joys the bard
Who sings your acts; and soon his voice he'll raise,
And other strains shall celebrate your praise.
    RICHARD HOLE (*Hymn to Demeter* 480-495)

Chillier latitudes and two millennia of a more puritanical re
ligion make it difficult for us to realize that the Hymn t
Hermes *is in fact a devout celebration of a deity whose func*
tions are indispensable in human society. Light-heartednes
is not necessarily frivolous, and Shelley's gay version is no
to be read as a burlesque.

64

Sing, Muse, the son of Maia and of Jove,
    The Herald-child, king of Arcadia
And all its pastoral hills, whom, in sweet love
    Having been interwoven, modest May
Bore Heaven's dread Supreme. An antique grove
    Shadowed the cavern where the lovers lay
In the deep night, unseen by Gods or Men,
And white-armed Juno slumbered sweetly then.

Now, when the joy of Jove had its fulfilling,
    And Heaven's tenth moon chronicled her relief,
She gave to light a babe all babes excelling,
    A schemer subtle beyond all belief,
A shepherd of thin dreams, a cow-stealing,
    A night-watching, and door-waylaying thief,
Who 'mongst the Gods was soon about to thieve,
And other glorious actions to achieve.

The babe was born at the first peep of day;
    He began playing on the lyre at noon,
And the same evening did he steal away
    Apollo's herds. The fourth day of the moon,
On which him bore the venerable May,
    From her immortal limbs he leaped full soon,
Nor long could in the sacred cradle keep,
But out to seek Apollo's herds would creep.

Out of the lofty cavern wandering
    He found a tortoise, and cried out—'A treasure!'
(For Mercury first made the tortoise sing)
    The beast before the portal at his leisure
The flowery herbage was depasturing,
    Moving his feet in a deliberate measure
Over the turf. Jove's profitable son
Eying him laughed, and laughing thus begun:—

'A useful godsend are you to me now,
    King of the dance, companion of the feast,
Lovely in all your nature! Welcome, you
    Excellent plaything! Where, sweet mountain beast,
Got you that speckled shell? Thus much I know,
    You must come home with me and be my guest;
You will give joy to me, and I will do
All that is in my power to honor you.

'Better to be at home than out of door,
    So come with me; and though it has been said
That you alive defend from magic power,
    I know you will sing sweetly when you're dead.'
Thus having spoken, the quaint infant bore,
    Lifting it from the grass on which it fed
And grasping it in his delighted hold,
His treasured prize into the cavern old.
        P. B. SHELLEY (*Hymn to Hermes* 1-38)

*Having fashioned the lyre and having sung to it the loves of
his mother and Zeus, the infant proceeds to steal the cows of
Apollo.*

Seized with a sudden fancy for fresh meat,   65
He in his sacred crib deposited
    The hollow lyre, and from the cavern sweet
Rushed with great leaps up to the mountain's head,
    Revolving in his mind some subtle feat

Of thievish craft, such as a swindler might
Devise in the lone season of dun night.

Lo! the great Sun under the ocean's bed has
    Driven steeds and chariot. The child meanwhile strode
O'er the Pierian mountains clothed in shadows,
    Where the immortal oxen of the God
Are pastured in the flowering unmown meadows
    And safely stalled in a remote abode.
The archer Argicide, elate and proud,
Drove fifty from the herd, lowing aloud.

He drove them wandering o'er the sandy way,
    But, being ever mindful of his craft,
Backward and forward drove he them astray,
    So that the tracks which seemed before, were aft;
His sandals then he threw to the ocean spray,
    And for each foot he wrought a kind of raft
Of tamarisk and tamarisk-like sprigs,
And bound them in a lump with withy twigs.
        P. B. SHELLEY (*Hymn to Hermes* 63-83)

He slaughters and feasts on the cattle, and returns to h
cradle before dawn.

66   He arrived back at the sacred peak of Kyllene at dawn; o
the long way he encountered no one, neither of the blesse
gods nor of mortal men; nor did the dogs bark. Hermes th
lucky son of Zeus entered the house by slipping sideway
through the keyhole, in the shape of a breath of air in a
tumn, like a mist. He made straight for the cave and we
to the inner sanctuary, stepping softly with his feet: he mad
no sound on the hard floor. Noble Hermes hastened to o
cupy his cradle: he wrapped the baby blankets round h
shoulders and lay like an infant child wriggling the cove
round his legs with his fingers, and clutching the lovely to
toise shell in his left hand.

    Nevertheless he did not escape his mother's watchful ey

he was a goddess no less than he was a god. She spoke to him and said: "Where have you been, you devious schemer? What have you been up to, coming here in the nighttime and showing your shameless face? I see now that either you're going to go right out of the front door in Apollo's hands, with adamantine chains around your sides, or else you will make a career of prowling through the hills. Go back where you came from; when your father made you, he made a deal of trouble for mortal men and for the immortal gods."

Hermes answered his mother with a speech which revealed his shrewdness: "Mother mine, why do you throw all this at me as if I were an infant child who does not know any bad words, who is timid, and afraid of his mother's scoldings? I intend to take up whatever career is best, working all the time for myself and for you. We belong to the immortal gods: we will not put up with staying here, denied the gifts and prayers that are our due, as you advise. It is better to spend our days in the pleasant company of the immortals, in wealth, prosperity, and abundance, than to sit at home in a dreary cave. In rank I intend to get the same divine honor as Apollo. If my father does not give it to me, then I will attempt—and this is within my power—to be the prince of thieves. And if the son of noble Leto tracks me down, I think he will find something he had not expected, something too big for him: I will go to Pytho and break into his great house; there I will find plenty of beautiful tripods and bowls and gold to carry away. Just you wait and see."

N. O. Brown (*Hymn to Hermes* 142-181)

Apollo has searched in vain for his lost cattle, and now comes to Maia's cave.

And Phœbus stooped under the craggy roof   67
    Arched over the dark cavern. Maia's child
Perceived that he came angry, far aloof,
    About the cows of which he had been beguiled;
And over him the fine and fragrant woof
    Of his ambrosial swaddling clothes he piled,

As among firebrands lies a burning spark
Covered, beneath the ashes cold and dark.

There, like an infant who had sucked his fill
    And now was newly washed, and put to bed,
Awake, but courting sleep with weary will,
    And gathered in a lump, hands, feet, and head,
He lay, and his belovèd tortoise still
    He grasped, and held under his shoulder-blade.
Phœbus the lovely mountain-goddess knew,
Not less her subtle, swindling baby, who

Lay swathed in his sly wiles. Round every crook
    Of the ample cavern for his kine Apollo
Looked sharp; and when he saw them not, he took
    The glittering key, and opened three great hollow
Recesses in the rock, where many a nook
    Was filled with the sweet food immortals swallow;
And mighty heaps of silver and of gold
Were piled within—a wonder to behold!

And white and silver robes, all overwrought
    With cunning workmanship of tracery sweet;
Except among the Gods there can be nought
    In the wide world to be compared with it.
Latona's offspring, after having sought
    His herds in every corner, thus did greet
Great Hermes:—'Little cradled rogue, declare
Of my illustrious heifers, where they are!

'Speak quickly! or a quarrel between us
    Must rise, and the event will be that I
Shall hurl you into dismal Tartarus,
    In fiery gloom to dwell eternally;
Nor shall your father nor your mother loose
    The bars of that black dungeon; utterly
You shall be cast out from the light of day,
To rule the ghosts of men, unblessed as they.'

To whom thus Hermes slyly answered:—'Son
  Of great Latona, what a speech is this!
Why come you here to ask me what is done
  With the wild oxen which it seems you miss?
I have not seen them, nor from any one
  Have heard a word of the whole business;
If you should promise an immense reward,
I could not tell more than you now have heard.

'An ox-stealer should be both tall and strong,
  And I am but a little new-born thing,
Who, yet at least, can think of nothing wrong.
  My business is to suck, and sleep, and fling
The cradle-clothes about me all day long,—
  Or half asleep, hear my sweet mother sing,
And to be washed in water clean and warm,
And hushed and kissed and kept secure from harm.

'Oh, let not e'er this quarrel be averred!
  The astounded Gods would laugh at you, if e'er
You should allege a story so absurd
  As that a new-born infant forth could fare
Out of his home after a savage herd.
  I was born yesterday—my small feet are
Too tender for the roads so hard and rough.
And if you think that this is not enough,

'I swear a great oath, by my father's head,
  That I stole not your cows, and that I know
Of no one else, who might, or could, or did.
  Whatever things cows are I do not know,
For I have only heard the name.' This said,
  He winked as fast as could be, and his brow
Was wrinkled, and a whistle loud gave he,
Like one who hears some strange absurdity.
          P. B. SHELLEY (*Hymn to Hermes* 228-280)

Apollo seizes the culprit and carries him to the court o
Zeus, where he arraigns him. This is Hermes' reply.

68
    'Great Father, you know clearly beforehand
       That all which I shall say to you is sooth;
    I am a most veracious person, and
       Totally unacquainted with untruth.
    At sunrise Phœbus came, but with no band
       Of Gods to bear him witness, in great wrath,
    To my abode, seeking his heifers there,
    And saying that I must show him where they are,

    'Or he would hurl me down the dark abyss.
       I know that every Apollonian limb
    Is clothed with speed and might and manliness,
       As a green bank with flowers—but, unlike him,
    I was born yesterday, and you may guess
       He well knew this when he indulged the whim
    Of bullying a poor little new-born thing
    That slept, and never thought of cow-driving.

    'Am I like a strong fellow who steals kine?
       Believe me, dearest Father—such you are—
    This driving of the herds is none of mine;
       Across my threshold did I wander ne'er,
    So may I thrive! I reverence the divine
       Sun and the Gods, and I love you, and care
    Even for this hard accuser—who must know
    I am as innocent as they or you.
       P. B. SHELLEY (*Hymn to Hermes* 368-382)

Eventually Hermes pacifies Apollo with his music; Apollo
enchanted, and makes a bond of amity and mutual respec
with his roguish little brother.

69
    "You butcher of cattle, cunning schemer, hard worker, goo
entertainer, what you have invented there is worth the fif
cattle. From this moment, I think we can settle our dispu

eacefully. But tell me now, ingenious son of Maia, was this
niracle yours from the time of your birth, or did some mortal
r immortal present you with a wonderful gift and teach you
his inspired music? This miracle of song is new to my ears;
have never heard it from any man nor yet from any of the
ods who live on Mount Olympus—only from you, you cun-
ing son of Zeus and Maia. What art, what muse, what skill
s this that governs ungovernable sorrows? Truly here are
hree in one to be had for the asking—gaiety, love, and
weet sleep. I, too, belong to the fellowship of the Olympian
Muses, whose life is spent in dances, in the glorious paths of
nusic, in the beauty of song with the lovely accompaniment
f flutes; but never has my heart been so touched by any
alent displayed by young men at their banquet entertain-
nents. I am amazed, son of Maia, at this lovely music you
nake upon the lyre. Since you show that you possess precious
kills, in spite of your small size, sit down, my friend, and
isten to the words of your elders. Surely an honored rank
mong the immortal gods shall be yours and your mother's.
This I solemnly declare: upon this dogwood spear I swear that
will make you the noble and wealthy messenger of the gods;
will give you fine gifts and to the very end I will never de-
eive you."

N. O. Brown (*Hymn to Hermes* 436-462)

*Aphrodite presides over a function essential to life, and it is
appropriate that the* Hymn to Aphrodite *should celebrate a
divine seduction. Worshipful devotion rather than titillation
is the mood of the singer.*

Sing, Muse! the force and all-informing fire   **70**
Of Cyprian Venus, goddess of desire;
Her charms th' immortal minds of gods can move,
And tame the stubborn race of men to love:
The wilder herds and ravenous beasts of prey
Her influence feel, and own her kindly sway:
Through pathless air and boundless ocean's space
She rules the feathered kind and finny race:

Whole Nature on her sole support depends,
And far as life exists her care extends.
  Of all the num'rous host of gods above,
But three are found inflexible to love:
Blue-eyed Minerva free preserves her heart,
A virgin unbeguiled by Cupid's art;
In shining arms the martial maid delights,
O'er war presides, and well-disputed fights;
With thirst of fame she first the hero fired,
And first the skill of useful arts inspired;
Taught artists first the carving tool to wield,
Chariots with brass to arm, and form the fenceful shield;
She first taught modest maids in early bloom
To shun the lazy life, and spin or ply the loom.
  Diana next the Paphian queen defies,
Her smiling arts and proffered friendship flies;
She loves with well-mouthed hounds and cheerful horn,
Or silver-sounding voice to wake the Morn,
To draw the bow or dart the pointed spear,
To wound the mountain boar, or rouse the woodland deer;
Sometimes of gloomy groves she likes the shades,
And there of virgin-nymphs the chorus leads;
And sometimes seeks the town, and leaves the plains,
And loves society where Virtue reigns.
  The third celestial power averse to love
Is Virgin Vesta, dear to mighty Jove,
Whom Neptune sought to wed and Phoebus wooed,
And both with fruitless labour long pursued;
For she, severely chaste rejected both,
And bound her purpose with a solemn oath,
A virgin life inviolate to lead;
She swore, and Jove assenting bowed his head.
But since her rigid choice the joys denied
Of nuptial rites and blessings of a bride,
The bounteous Jove with gifts that want supplied.
High on a throne she sits amidst the skies,
And first is fed with fumes of sacrifice;
For holy rites to Vesta first are paid,

d on her altar first-fruit off'rings laid;
Jove ordained in honour of the maid.
These are the powers above and only these,
hom love and Cytherea's arts displease:
f other beings none in earth or skies
er force resists or influence denies.
ith ease her charms the Thunderer can bind,
d captivate with love th' almighty mind:
ven he, whose dread commands the gods obey,
bmits to her and owns superior sway;
slaved to mortal beauties by her power,
e oft descends his creatures to adore;
hile to conceal the theft from Juno's eyes,
me well-dissembled shape the god belies;
no, his wife and sister, both in place
d beauty first among th' ethereal race,
hom all transcending in superior worth
ise Saturn got, and Cybele brought forth,
d Jove, by never-erring counsel swayed,
he partner of his bed and empire made.
  But Jove at length, with just resentment fired,
he laughing queen herself with love inspired;
vift through her veins the sweet contagion ran,
d kindled in her breast desire of mortal man,
hat she, like other deities might prove
he pains and pleasures of inferior love,
d not insultingly the gods deride,
hose sons were human by the mother's side:
hus Jove ordained she now for man should burn,
d bring forth mortal offspring in her turn.
  Among the springs which flow from Ida's head,
is lowing herds the young Anchises fed,
hose godlike form and face the smiling queen
eheld, and loved to madness soon as seen.
o Cyprus straight the wounded goddess flies,
here Paphian temples in her honour rise,
d altars smoke with daily sacrifice.
oon as arrived she to her shrine repaired,

Where ent'ring quick, the shining gates she barred.
The ready Graces wait, her bath prepare,
And oint with fragrant oils her flowing hair;
Her flowing hair around her shoulder spreads,
And all adown ambrosial odour sheds:
Last in transparent robes her limbs they fold,
Enriched with ornaments of purest gold;
And thus attired her chariot she ascends,
And Cyprus left, her flight to Troy she bends.

On Ida she alights, then seeks the seat,
Which loved Anchises chose for his retreat;
And ever as she walked through lawn or wood,
Promiscuous herds of beasts admiring stood.
Some humbly follow, while some fawning meet,
And lick the ground, and crouch beneath her feet:
Dogs, lions, wolves, and bears, their eyes unite,
And the swift panther stops to gaze with fixed delight:
For every glance she gives soft fire imparts,
Enkindling sweet desire in savage hearts.
Inflamed with love all single out their mates,
And to their shady dens each pair retreats.

Meantime the tent she spies so much desired,
Where her Anchises was alone retired,
Withdrawn from all his friends and fellow-swains,
Who fled their flocks beneath, and sought the plains;
In pleasing solitude the youth she found,
Intent upon his lyre's harmonious sound.
Before his eyes Jove's beauteous daughter stood,
In form and dress a huntress of the wood;
For had he seen the goddess undisguised,
The youth with awe and fear had been surprised.
Fixed he beheld her, and with joy admired
To see a nymph so bright and so attired;
For from her flowing robe a lustre spread,
As if with radiant flame she were arrayed:
Her hair, in part disclosed, in part concealed,
In ringlets fell, or was with jewels held;
With various gold and gems her neck was graced,

And orient pearls heaved on her panting breast:
Bright as the moon she shone, with silent light,
And charmed his sense with wonder and delight.

Thus while Anchises gazed, through every vein
A thrilling joy he felt and pleasing pain.
At length he spake: "All hail, celestial fair!
Who humbly dost to visit earth repair:
Whoe'er thou art, descended from above,
Latona, Cynthia, or the Queen of Love,
All hail! all honour shall to thee be paid;
Or art thou Themis? or the Blue-eyed maid?
Or art thou fairest of the Graces three,
Who with the gods share immortality?
Or else some nymph, the guardian of these woods,
These caves, these fruitful hills, or crystal floods?
Whoe'er thou art, in some conspicuous field
to thy honour will an altar build,
Where holy off'rings I'll each hour prepare;
Oh! prove but thou propitious to my prayer!
Grant me among the Trojan race to prove
A patriot worthy of my country's love;
Blessed in myself, I beg I next may be
Blessed in my children and posterity;
Happy in health, long let me see the sun,
And, loved by all, late may my days be done."

He said.—Jove's beauteous daughter thus replied:
Delight of human-kind, thy sex's pride!
Honoured Anchises! You behold in me
No goddess blessed with immortality,
But mortal I, of mortal mother came,
Otreus my father, (you have heard the name,)
Who rules the fair extent of Phrygia's lands
And all her towns and fortresses commands.
When yet an infant I to Troy was brought;
There was I nursed, and there your language taught:
Then wonder not if, thus instructed young,
I like my own can speak the Trojan tongue.
In me one of Diana's nymphs behold:

Why thus arrived I shall the cause unfold.
  "As late our sports we practised on the plain,
I and my fellow nymphs of Cynthia's train,
Dancing in chorus, and with garlands crowned,
And by admiring crowds encompassed round,
Lo! hov'ring o'er my head I saw the god
Who Argus slew, and bears the golden rod;
Sudden he seized, then bore me from their sight,
Cutting through liquid air his rapid flight.
O'er many states and peopled towns we passed,
O'er hills and valleys, and o'er deserts waste;
O'er barren moors, and o'er unwholesome fens,
And woods where beasts inhabit dreadful dens:
Through all which pathless way our speed was such,
We stopt not once the face of earth to touch.
Meantime he told me, while through the air we fled,
That Jove ordained I should Anchises wed,
And with illustrious offspring bless his bed.
This said, and pointing to me your abode,
To heaven again upsoared the swift-winged god.
Thus of necessity to you I come,
Unknown and lost, far from my native home.
But I conjure you, by the throne of Jove,
By all that's dear to you, by all you love,
By your good parents, (for no bad could e'er
Produce a son so graceful, good, and fair,)
That you no wiles employ to win my heart,
But let me hence an untouched maid depart;
Inviolate and guiltless of your bed,
Let me be to your house and mother led:
Me to your father and your brothers show,
And our alliance first let them allow:
Let me be known, and my condition owned,
And no unequal match I may be found.
Equality to them my birth may claim,
Worthy a daughter's or a sister's name,
Though for your wife of too inferior fame.
Next let ambassadors to Phrygia haste,

To tell my father of my fortunes past,
And ease my mother in that anxious state
Of doubts and fears which cares for me create.
They in return shall presents bring from thence
Of rich attire, and sums of gold immense:
You in peculiar shall with gifts be graced,
In price and beauty far above the rest.
This done, perform the rites of nuptial love,
Grateful to men below and gods above."

She said, and from her eyes shot subtle fires,
Which to his heart insinuate desires:
Resistless love invading thus his breast,
The panting youth the smiling queen addressed.

"Since mortal you, of mortal mother came,
And Otreus you report your father's name,
And since th' immortal Hermes from above,
To execute the dread commands of Jove,
Your wondrous beauties hither has conveyed,
A nuptial life with me henceforth to lead;
Know, now, that neither gods nor men have power
One minute to defer the happy hour;
This instant will I seize upon thy charms,
Mix with thy soul, and melt within thine arms:
Though Phoebus, armed with his unerring dart,
Stood ready to transfix my panting heart;
Though death, though hell, in consequence attend,
Thou shalt with me the genial bed ascend."

He said, and sudden snatched her beauteous hand;
The goddess smiled, nor did th' attempt withstand,
But fixed her eyes upon the hero's bed,
Where soft and silken coverlets were spread,
And over all a counterpane was placed,
Thick sown with furs of many a savage beast,
Of bears, and lions, heretofore his spoil,
And still remained the trophies of his toil.

Now to ascend the bed they both prepare,
And he with eager haste disrobes the fair.
Her sparkling necklace first he laid aside,

Her bracelets next, and braided hair untied:
And now his busy hand her zone unbraced,
Which girt her radiant robe around her waist;
Her radiant robe at last aside was thrown,
Whose rosy hue with dazzling lustre shone.

The Queen of Love the youth thus disarrayed,
And on a chair of gold her vestments laid.
Anchises now (so Jove and Fate ordained)
The sweet extreme of ecstasy attained;
And mortal he was like th' immortals blessed,
Not conscious of the goddess he possessed.

But when the swains their flocks and herds had fed,
And from the flowery field returning led
Their sheep to fold, and oxen to the shed,
In soft and pleasing chains of sleep profound
The wary goddess her Anchises bound.
Then gently rising from his side and bed,
In all her bright attire her limbs arrayed.

And now her fair-crowned head aloft she rears,
Nor more a mortal, but herself, appears;
Her face refulgent, and majestic mien,
Confessed the goddess, Love's and Beauty's queen.

Then thus aloud she calls: "Anchises! wake;
Thy fond repose and lethargy forsake;
Look on the nymph who late from Phrygia came,
Behold me well—say if I seem the same."

At her first call the chains of sleep were broke,
And starting from his bed Anchises woke;
But when he Venus viewed without disguise,
Her shining neck beheld and radiant eyes,
Awed and abashed he turned his head aside,
Attempting with his robe his face to hide:
Confused with wonder and with fear oppressed,
In winged words he thus the queen addressed:

"When first, O Goddess, I thy form beheld,
Whose charms so far humanity excelled,
To thy celestial power my vows I paid,
And with humility implored thy aid;

But thou, for secret cause to me unknown,
Didst thy divine immortal state disown.
But now I beg thee, by the filial love
Due to thy father, aegis-bearing Jove,
Compassion on my human state to show,
Nor let me lead a life infirm below;
Defend me from the woes which mortals wait,
Nor let me share of men the common fate;
Since never man with length of days was blessed
Who in delights of love a deity possessed."
  To him Jove's beauteous daughter thus replied:
"Be bold, Anchises: in my love confide;
Nor me nor other god thou need'st to fear,
For thou to all the heavenly race art dear.
Know from our loves thou shalt a son obtain,
Who over all the realm of Troy shall reign;
From whom a race of monarchs shall descend,
And whose posterity shall know no end;
To him thou shalt the name Aeneas give,
As one for whose conception I must grieve,
Oft as I think he to exist began
From my conjunction with a mortal man."

  WILLIAM CONGREVE (*Hymn to Aphrodite* 1-201)

*As a sort of exculpation Aphrodite cites the examples of
Ganymede and Tithonus, both Trojans like Anchises, who
were loved by Zeus and Aurora respectively. She then prom-
ises that the child she will bear will be nurtured in infancy
by the nymphs and then delivered to Anchises.*

    "More to instruct thee, when five years shall end,   **71**
  I will again to visit thee descend,
  Bringing thy beauteous son to charm thy sight,
  Whose godlike form shall fill thee with delight;
  Him will I leave thenceforward to thy care,
  And will that with him thou to Troy repair;
  There if inquiry shall be made, to know
  To whom thou dost so bright an offspring owe,

Be sure thou nothing of the truth detect,
But ready answer make as I direct:
Say of a sylvan nymph the fair youth came,
And Calycopis call his mother's name;
For shouldst thou boast the truth, and madly own
That thou in bliss hadst Cytherea known,
Jove would his anger pour upon thy head,
And with avenging thunder strike thee dead.
Now all is told thee, and just caution given;
Be secret thou, and dread the wrath of heaven."
    She said, and sudden soared above his sight,
Cutting through liquid air her heavenward flight.
    All hail, bright Cyprian Queen! thee first I praise,
Then to some other power transfer my lays.

        WILLIAM CONGREVE (*Hymn to Aphrodite* 276-293

*Many of the Homeric Hymns are quite short—for example
the* Hymn to Earth Mother of All.

72   O universal Mother, who dost keep
From everlasting thy foundations deep,
Eldest of things, Great Earth, I sing of thee!
All shapes that have their dwelling in the sea,
All things that fly, or on the ground divine
Live, move, and there are nourished—these are thine;
These from thy wealth thou dost sustain; from thee
Fair babes are born, and fruits on every tree
Hang ripe and large, revered Divinity!

    The life of mortal men beneath thy sway
Is held; thy power both gives and takes away.
Happy are they whom thy mild favors nourish;
All things unstinted round them grow and flourish.
For them endures the life-sustaining field
Its load of harvest, and their cattle yield
Large increase, and their house with wealth is filled.
Such honored dwell in cities fair and free,
The homes of lovely women, prosperously;

Their sons exult in youth's new budding gladness,
And their fresh daughters, free from care or sadness,
With bloom-inwoven dance and happy song,
On the soft flowers the meadow-grass among,
Leap round them sporting; such delights by thee
Are given, rich Power, revered Divinity.

Mother of gods, thou wife of starry Heaven,
Farewell! be thou propitious, and be given
A happy life for this brief melody,
Nor thou nor other songs shall unremembered be.

    P. B. SHELLEY (*Hymn to Earth Mother of All*)

BATRACHOMYOMACHIA

*Deeply as they revered their heroic poetry, it would have been
strange if the volatile Greeks had not parodied it. There is no
compelling reason to date the Battle of the Frogs and the
Mice later than the sixth century B.C. Though the ancients do
not mention it, we know that it enjoyed a great vogue among
the Byzantines. There is no social criticism in the poem; its
fun is in the incongruity of ascribing heroic motives and ac-
tions to insignificant animals. The names are of course all
meaningful; Physignathus, for example, is "Inflated Cheeks,"
and Psycarpax is "Granary Plunderer."*

To fill my rising song with sacred fire,
Ye tuneful Nine, ye sweet celestial quire!
From Helicon's embowering height repair,
Attend my labours, and reward my prayer;
The dreadful toils of raging Mars I write,
The springs of contest, and the fields of fight;
How threatening mice advanc'd with warlike grace,
And wag'd dire combats with the croaking race.
Not louder tumults shook Olympus' towers,

73

When earth-born giants dar'd immortal powers.
These equal acts an equal glory claim,
And thus the Muse records the tale of Fame.
    Once on a time, fatigu'd and out of breath,
And just escap'd the stretching claws of Death,
A gentle mouse, whom cats pursued in vain,
Fled swift of foot across the neighbouring plain,
Hung o'er a brink, his eager thirst to cool,
And dipp'd his whiskers in the standing pool;
When near a courteous frog advanc'd his head,
And from the waters, hoarse-resounding, said,
    "What art thou, stranger? what the line you boast?
What chance has cast thee panting on our coast?
With strictest truth let all thy words agree,
Nor let me find a faithless mouse in thee.
If worthy friendship, proffer'd friendship take,
And entering view the pleasurable lake;
Range o'er my palace, in my bounty share,
And glad return from hospitable fare:
This silver realm extends beneath my sway,
And me, their monarch, all its frogs obey.
Great Physignathus I, from Peleus' race,
Begot in fair Hydromede's embrace,
Where, by the nuptial bank that paints his side,
The swift Eridanus delights to glide.
Thee too, thy form, thy strength, and port, proclaim
A scepter'd king, a son of martial fame;
Then trace thy line, and aid my guessing eyes."
Thus ceas'd the frog, and thus the mouse replies.
    "Known to the gods, the men, the birds that fly
Through wild expanses of the midway sky,
My name resounds; and if unknown to thee,
The soul of great Psycarpax lives in me,
Of brave Troxartas' line, whose sleeky down
In love compress'd Lychomile the brown.
My mother she, and princess of the plains
Where'er her father Pternotractas reigns.
Born where a cabin lifts its airy shed,

With figs, with nuts, and vary'd dainties fed.
But, since our natures nought in common know,
From that foundation can a friendship grow?
These curling waters o'er thy palace roll:
But man's high food supports my princely soul:
In vain the circled loaves attempt to lie
Conceal'd in flaskets from my curious eye.
In vain the tripe that boasts the whitest hue,
In vain the gilded bacon shuns my view,
In vain the cheeses, offspring of the pail,
Or honey'd cakes, which gods themselves regale;
And as in arts I shine, in arms I fight,
Mix'd with the bravest, and unknown to flight;
Though large to mine the human form appear,
Not man himself can smite my soul with fear;
Sly to the bed with silent steps I go,
Attempt his finger, or attack his toe,
And six indented wounds with dextrous skill,
Sleeping he feels, and only seems to feel.
Yet have we foes which direful dangers cause,
Grim owls with talons arm'd, and cats with claws,
And that false trap, the den of silent Fate,
Where Death his ambush plants around the bait:
All dreaded these, and dreadful o'er the rest
The potent warriors of the tabby vest,
If to the dark we fly, the dark they trace,
And rend our heroes of the nibbling race.
But me, nor stalks nor waterish herbs delight,
Nor can the crimson radish charm my sight,
The lake-resounding frogs' selected fare,
Which not a mouse of any taste can bear."
    As thus the downy prince his mind exprest,
His answer thus the croaking king addrest:
    "Thy words luxuriant on thy dainties rove,
And, stranger, we can boast of bounteous Jove:
We sport in water, or we dance on land,
And born amphibious, food from both command.
But trust thyself where wonders ask thy view,

And safely tempt those seas, I'll bear thee through:
Ascend my shoulders, firmly keep thy seat,
And reach my marshy court, and feast in state."
He said, and bent his back; with nimble bound
Leaps the light mouse, and clasps his arms around,
Then wondering floats, and sees with glad survey
The winding banks resembling ports at sea.
But when aloft the curling water rides,
And wet with azure wave his downy sides,
His thoughts grow conscious of approaching woe,
His idle tears with vain repentance flow,
His locks he rends, his trembling feet he rears,
Thick beats his heart with unaccustomed fears;
He sighs, and, chill'd with danger, longs for shore:
His tail extended forms a fruitless oar,
Half drench'd in liquid death his prayers he spake,
And thus bemoan'd him from the dreadful lake:
    "So pass'd Europa through the rapid sea,
Trembling and fainting all the venturous way;
With oary feet the bull triumphant rode,
And safe in Crete depos'd his lovely load.
Ah, safe at last, may thus the frog support
My trembling limbs to reach his ample court!"
As thus he sorrows, death ambiguous grows,
Lo! from the deep a water-hydra rose;
He rolls his sanguin'd eyes, his bosom heaves,
And darts with active rage along the waves.
Confus'd the monarch sees his hissing foe,
And dives, to shun the sable fates below.
Forgetful frog! the friend thy shoulders bore,
Unskill'd in swimming, floats remote from shore.
He grasps with fruitless hands to find relief,
Supinely falls, and grinds his teeth with grief;
Plunging he sinks, and struggling mounts again,
And sinks, and strives, but strives with Fate in vain.
The weighty moisture clogs his hairy vest,
And thus the prince his dying rage exprest:
    "Nor thou, that fling'st me floundering from thy back,

As from hard rocks rebounds the shattering wrack,
Nor thou shalt 'scape thy due, perfidious king!
Pursued by vengeance on the swiftest wing!
At land thy strength could never equal mine,
At sea to conquer, and by craft, was thine.
But Heaven has gods, and gods have searching eyes:
Ye mice, ye mice, my great avengers rise!"
  This said, he sighing gasp'd, and gasping dy'd.
His death the young Lychopynax espy'd,
As on the flowery brink he pass'd the day,
Bask'd in the beams, and loiter'd life away.
Loud shrieks the mouse, his shrieks the shore repeat,
The nibbling nation learn their hero's fate:
Grief, dismal grief ensues; deep murmurs sound,
And shriller fury fills the deafen'd ground.
From lodge to lodge, the sacred heralds run
To fix their council with the rising Sun;
Where great Troxartas crown'd in glory reigns,
And winds his lengthening court beneath the plains.
Psycarpax' father, father now no more!
For poor Psycarpax lies remote from shore;
Supine he lies! the silent waters stand,
And no kind billow wafts the dead to land.
  When rosy-finger'd morn had ting'd the clouds,
Around their monarch-mouse the nation crowds,
Slow rose the sovereign, heav'd his anxious breast,
And thus the council, fill'd with rage, addrest:
  "For lost Psycarpax much my soul endures,
'Tis mine the private grief, the public yours.
Three warlike sons adorn'd my nuptial bed,
Three sons, alas! before their father dead!
Our oldest perish'd by the ravening cat,
As near my court the prince unheedful sat.
Our next, an engine fraught with danger drew,
The portal gap'd, the bait was hung in view,
Dire arts assist the trap, the Fates decoy,
And men unpitying kill'd my gallant boy!
The last, his country's hope, his parent's pride,

Plung'd in the lake by Physignathus dy'd;
Rouse all to war, my friend! avenge the deed;
And bleed that monarch, and his nation bleed."

His words in every breast inspir'd alarms,
And careful Mars supply'd their host with arms.
In verdant hulls despoil'd of all their beans,
The buskin'd warriors stalk'd along the plains:
Quills aptly bound their bracing corselet made,
Fac'd with the plunder of a cat they flay'd:
The lamp's round boss affords them ample shield;
Large shells of nuts their covering helmet yield,
And o'er the region, with reflected rays,
Tall groves of needles for their lances blaze:
Dreadful in arms the marching mice appear;
The wondering frogs perceive the tumult near,
Forsake the waters, thickening form a ring,
And ask, and hearken, whence the noises spring.
When near the crowd, disclos'd to public view,
The valiant chief Embasichytros drew:
The sacred herald's sceptre grac'd his hand,
And thus his word express'd his king's command:

"Ye frogs! the mice, with vengeance fir'd, advance,
And deck'd in armour shake the shining lance:
Their hapless prince by Physignathus slain,
Extends incumbent on the watery plain.
Then arm your host, the doubtful battle try;
Lead forth those frogs that have the soul to die."

The chief retires, the crowd the challenge hear,
And proudly swelling yet perplex'd appear:
Much they resent, yet much their monarch blame,
Who, rising, spoke to clear his tainted fame:

"O friends! I never forc'd the mouse to death,
Nor saw the gasping of his latest breath.
He, vain of youth, our art of swimming try'd,
And, venturous, in the lake the wanton dy'd.
To vengeance now by false appearance led,
They point their anger at my guiltless head;
But wage the rising war by deep device,

And turn its fury on the crafty mice.
Your king directs the way; my thoughts, elate
With hopes of conquest, form designs of fate.
Where high the banks their verdant surface heave,
And the steep sides confine the sleeping wave,
There, near the margin, clad in armour bright,
Sustain the first impetuous shocks of fight:
Then, where the dancing feather joins the crest,
Let each brave frog his obvious mouse arrest;
Each strongly grasping, headlong plunge a foe,
Till countless circles whirl the lake below;
Down sink the mice in yielding waters drown'd;
Loud flash the waters; and the shores resound:
The frogs triumphant tread the conquer'd plain,
And raise their glorious trophies of the slain."

He spake no more, his prudent scheme imparts
Redoubling ardour to the boldest hearts.
Green was the suit his arming heroes chose,
Around their legs the greaves of mallows close;
Green were the beets about their shoulders laid,
And green the colewort, which the target made.
Form'd of the vary'd shells the waters yield,
Their glossy helmets glisten'd o'er the field:
And tapering sea-reeds for the polish'd spear,
With upright order pierc'd the ambient air.
Thus dress'd for war, they take th' appointed height,
Poise the long arms, and urge the promis'd fight.

But now, where Jove's irradiate spires arise,
With stars surrounded in ethereal skies,
(A solemn council call'd) the brazen gates
Unbar; the gods assume their golden seats:
The sire superior leans, and points to show
What wondrous combats mortals wage below:
How strong, how large, the numerous heroes stride,
What length of lance they shake with warlike pride!
What eager fire their rapid march reveals!
So the fierce Centaurs ravag'd o'er the dales;
And so confirm'd, the daring Titans rose,

Heap'd hills on hills, and bid the gods be foes.
   This seen, the Power his sacred visage rears,
He casts a pitying smile on worldly cares,
And asks what heavenly guardians take the list,
Or who the mice, or who the frogs assist?
   Then thus to Pallas: "If my daughter's mind
Have join'd the mice, why stays she still behind?
Drawn forth by savoury steams they wind their way,
And sure attendance round thine altar pay,
Where, while the victims gratify their taste,
They sport to please the goddess of the feast."
   Thus spake the ruler of the spacious skies.
But thus, resolv'd, the blue-ey'd maid replies:
"In vain, my father! all their dangers plead;
To such thy Pallas never grants her aid.
My flowery wreaths they petulantly spoil,
And rob my crystal lamps of feeding oil.
(Ills following ills!) but what afflicts me more,
My veil that idle race profanely tore.
The web was curious, wrought with art divine;
Relentless wretches! all the work was mine!
Along the loom the purple warp I spread,
Cast the light shoot, and crost the silver thread;
In this their teeth a thousand breaches tear,
The thousand breaches skilful hands repair,
For which, vile earthly duns thy daughter grieve
(The gods, that use no coin, have none to give,
And learning's goddess never less can owe;
Neglected learning gains no wealth below).
Nor let the frogs to win my succour sue,
Those clamorous fools have lost my favour too.
For late, when all the conflict ceas'd at night,
When my stretch'd sinews work'd with eager fight,
When spent with glorious toil, I left the field,
And sunk for slumber on my swelling shield;
Lo, from the deep, repelling sweet repose
With noisy croakings half the nation rose:

Devoid of rest, with aching brows I lay,
Till cocks proclaim'd the crimson dawn of day.
Let all, like me, from either host forbear,
Nor tempt the flying furies of the spear;
Let heavenly blood (or what for blood may flow)
Adorn the conquest of a meaner foe.
Some daring mouse may meet with wondrous odds,
Though gods oppose, and brave the wounded gods.
O'er gilded clouds reclin'd, the danger view,
And be the wars of mortals scenes for you."
   So mov'd the blue-ey'd queen; her words persuade,
Great Jove assented, and the rest obey'd.
   Now front to front the marching armies shine,
Halt ere they meet, and form the lengthening line:
The chiefs conspicuous seen and heard afar,
Give the loud signal to the rushing war;
Their dreadful trumpets deep-mouth'd hornets sound,
The sounding charge remurmurs o'er the ground;
E'en Jove proclaims a field of horrour nigh,
And rolls his thunder through the troubled sky.

      THOMAS PARNELL (*Batrachomyomachia* 1-201)

*The remaining third of the poem describes the single combats
of the heroes. The gods intervene, and finally send a formi-
dable auxiliary force of crabs to save the hard-pressed frogs.*

XENOPHANES

*Hexameter verse was used in the sixth century B.C. by a series
of thinkers who made the transition to rational philosophy.
The first of the group is Xenophanes of Colophon; the first
piece offered below is in praise of decent conviviality, and
the second criticizes the adulation bestowed upon athletic
victors.*

74   Now the floor is clean, and our hands,
           And the cups. A boy crowns us with plaited garlands;
           Another offers sweet-scented oil;
           And the mixing-bowl stands by, full of good cheer.
           The wine is ready, and says it will never betray us
           With its mild bouquet, breathing from the jars.
           On the altar, frankincense sheds holy fragrance.
           Cold is the water, and fresh, and pure.
           Brown loaves lie at hand; the table of honor
           Is laden with cheeses and with rich honey.
           The midst of the altar is adorned with flowers;
           Song and merriment reign through the house.
           First, men who are glad should sing God's praises,
           With auspicious words and pure thoughts.
           After we have poured libations, asking
           For strength to act rightly—this should be chosen first—
           There's no harm in drinking as much as you can carry
           And still get home, unassisted—unless you're old.
           We commend the man who shows he has drunk wisely,
           Who has mind, and voice, to speak of noble things;
           Not to pursue battles of Titans, giants
           And centaurs—fantasies of long ago—
           Or quarrels and brawling; there's no help in these.
           To be always mindful of the gods is good.
                EMILY ANN WOLFF (*Xenophanes* 1)

75   Why, if one should win a victory in the foot-race
           Or the five events, in the land hallowed to Zeus
           Where Pisa flows, in Olympia; or be first
           In wrestling, or the brutal boxing-match,
           Or that dread contest called pankration,
           He would be glorious in the townsmen's eyes,
           And have a seat of honor at the games,
           And meals provided at the public table
           By the city, and a gift that he would cherish.
           If he won with horses, he'd still have these rewards,
           Though he'd not be worthy, as I am. For our art
           Is better than the strength of men and horses.

This is a senseless custom; nor is it just
To give brawn preference over goodly wisdom.
If a skilled boxer be among the people,
Or a winner in pentathlon or wrestling-match,
Or even in running, which is most admired
Wherever men compete in deeds of strength—
For all that, a state would not be better-governed.
Small joy would a city have from such as these,
From victories in the games by Pisa's stream;
Such things do not enrich a city's treasure.
EMILY ANN WOLFF (*Xenophanes* 2)

PARMENIDES

*The central figure in the Eleatic school of philosophy was a
mystic and something of a poet. The first fragment of Par-
menides here presented is an account of a revelation; the
others treat of his theory of being.*

The horses bore me as far as my desire,   **76**
conveyed me amply, as they led me on
to stand within the far-famed Way of the Daimon
who leads the knowing man through all the cities.
Here was I borne; for here did the thoughtful horses
bear me, drawing the chariot. Meanwhile maidens
guided the way.
    The axle blazing round within the naves
sent forth a piping cry, urged on by the wheels
which whirled to either side as towards the light
the maidens of the Sun in haste conveyed me,
who left the halls of Night, and dropped their veils.
There are the gates of the paths of Night and Day,
fitted about with threshold of stone and the lintel;
themselves on high are filled by mighty doors,
and Dike avenging holds the answering keys.

Her did the maids entreat with soothing words,
with skill persuade her to loose the fastened bolt
from off the gates; these swinging back in turn
on brazen posts fitted with nails and studs
disclosed a gaping gulf between the doors,
and straight through them the maidens held the car,
and held the horses straight along the highway.
    The goddess with her hand took my right hand,
received me kindly, spoke to me these words:
"Welcome! youth who comest to our halls,
joined with deathless drivers, borne by steeds,
for no ill Fate, but Themis and Dike
have sent thee forth to come upon this road:
far is it from the beaten way of men.
And all things must thou needst inquire now,
both of rounded Truth the heart unquaking
and Views of men in which is no true trust;
but these things wilt thou surely learn as well,
in what way there was need that *the things which seem*
should be acceptable to men since through the Whole
all things they penetrate."
        CHARLES H. KAHN (*Parmenides* 1)

77   Thou shalt know the nature of the Sky,
and all the signs within the Aither there,
and the works unseen of the Sun's pure shining torch,
and whence they arose; and the revolving deeds
of the round-faced Moon, and thou shalt know its growth;
and the encompassing Heaven, whence it grew,
and how Ananke took and bound it fast
to hold the limits of the stars.
        CHARLES H. KAHN (*Parmenides* 10)

78   The narrower bands were filled with unmixed Fire;
those after these with Night, and in among them
rushes their lot of flame. And in their midst
the Daimon is, who guides and steers all things,
begins all painful birth and intercourse,

sending the female on to meet the male,
and the male to the female.

    CHARLES H. KAHN (*Parmenides* 12)

For this shall never prevail, that the things which are not **79**
are; but from this way of search hold back thy thought
nor let thyself be forced upon this way
by oft-tried habit here along to aim
a heedless eye, resounding ear and tongue,
but judge by Reason this disputed proof
spoken by me. The only tale which yet
remains to tell of the Way is that *it is*;
and many signs there are upon this path
that it *is* Unborn and is without Destruction,
for Whole is it of limb and still unquaking
and without fatal End, nor *was* it ever
nor *will* it be, since now it *is* Together
All and One, Containing; for what Birth
wilt thou seek for it? How and whence
could it increase? I shall not let thee say
nor think it came from *what is not*,
for it is unuttered and unthought, *that it is not*;
and what need could have stirred it up to grow
rather now than then, if it began
from Nothing? Therefore must it altogether
Be, or not at all; and never yet
will trustful strength release it that aught else
besides itself should rise from out *What is*,
since Dike has not loosed it from her shackles
free to Birth and Death, but holds her grip.
The Judgment on these things resides in this:
it is or is not. With Necessity
in our decision was it judged already
to leave the one unknown and without name
(for it is no truthful path), but that the other
is and is of Truth. How then may *what is*
go down in Death or how might it be born?
For if it came-to-be, it *is* not, nor

if ever it is-to-be. So thus is Birth
utterly quenched and Death is not to be heard of.
Nor may it be divided, for the Whole
is of like kind, nor is there aught more here
than in another place nor any less
which might prevent it holding fast together.
But all is full of *what is*, and thus it stands
continuous all; for *what is* draws nigh to *what is*.
      CHARLES H. KAHN (*Parmenides* 7-8)

EMPEDOCLES

*Empedocles of Agrigentum in Sicily was probably the best
poet of the three. He is the remote ancestor of Lucretius
in conceiving and expressing philosophic doctrine in poetic
form. The first selection here given describes the cosmic proc-
ess; the second alludes to expiation and metempsychosis.*

80

I will report a twofold truth. Now grows
The One from Many into being, now
Even from the One disparting come the Many.
Twofold the girth, twofold the death of things:
For, now, the meeting of the Many brings
To birth and death; and, now, whatever grew
From out their sundering, flies apart and dies.
And this long interchange shall never end.
Whiles into One do all through Love unite;
Whiles too the same are rent through hate of Strife.
And in so far as is the One still wont
To grow from Many, and the Many, again,
Spring from primeval scattering of the One,
So far have they a birth and mortal date;
And in so far as the long interchange
Ends not, so far forever established gods
Around the circle of the world they move.

But come! but hear my words! For knowledge gained
Makes strong thy soul. For as before I spake,
Naming the utter goal of these my words,
I will report a twofold truth. Now grows
The One from Many into being, now
Even from the One disparting come the Many,—
Fire, Water, Earth and awful heights of Air;
And shut from them apart, the deadly Strife
In equipoise, and Love within their midst
In all her being in length and breadth the same.
Behold her now with mind, and sit not there
With eyes astonished, for 'tis she inborn
Abides established in the limbs of men.
Through her they cherish thoughts of love, through her
Perfect the works of concord, calling her
By name Delight or Aphrodite clear.
She speeds revolving in the elements,
But this no mortal man hath ever learned—
Hear thou the undelusive course of proof:
Behold those elements own equal strength
And equal origin; each rules its task;
And unto each its primal mode; and each
Prevailing conquers with revolving time.
And more than these there is no birth nor end;
For were they wasted ever and evermore,
They were no longer, and the great All were then
How to be plenished and from what far coast?
And how, besides, might they to ruin come,
Since nothing lives that empty is of them?—
No, these are all, and, as they course along
Through one another, now this, now that is born—
And so forever down Eternity.

  W. E. Leonard

There is a word of Fate, an old decree
And everlasting of the gods, made fast
With amplest oaths, that whosoe'er of those
Far spirits, with their lot of age-long life,

  81

Do foul their limbs with slaughter in offense,
Or swear forsworn, as failing of their pledge,
Shall wander thrice ten thousand weary years
Far from the Blessed, and be born through time
In various shapes of mortal kind, which change
Ever and ever troublous paths of life:
For now Air hunts them onward to the Sea;
Now the wild Sea disgorges them on Land;
Now Earth will spue toward beams of radiant Sun;
Whence he will toss them back to whirling Air—
Each gets from other what they all abhor.
And in that brood I too am numbered now,
A fugitive and vagabond from heaven,
As one obedient unto raving Strife.
                    W. E. LEONARD

CALLINUS

The first variation from heroic hexameter poetry is elegiac, in which each hexameter line is followed by another curtailed by a syllable at middle and end. Elegiac poetry was recited to the accompaniment of a flute. The curtailed lines made it less stately and formulaic than heroic poetry, and it is in fact more personal in tone. Perhaps elegy was originally, as in modern usage, funereal; ultimately it was erotic; but in all our ancient specimens elegy is used for admonition or exhortation to military or civic virtue.

Our earliest specimen of elegy is Callinus' spirited exhortation, apparently to his fellow Ephesians, to fight bravely against the Cimmerians who were invading Asia Minor in the seventh century B.C.

82   How long will ye slumber? when will ye take heart
        And fear the reproach of your neighbors at hand?

Fie! comrades, to think ye have peace for your part
Whilst the sword and the arrow are wasting our land!
Shame! grasp the shield close! cover well the bold breast!
Aloft raise the spear as ye march on the foe!
With no thought of retreat, with no terror confessed,
Hurl your last dart in dying, or strike your last blow.
Oh, 'tis noble and glorious to fight for our all,—
For our country, our children, the wife of our love!
Death comes not the sooner; no soldier shall fall,
Ere his thread is spun out by the sisters above.
Once to die is man's doom; rush, rush to the fight!
He cannot escape though his blood were Jove's own.
For a while let him cheat the shrill arrow by flight;
Fate will catch him at last in his chamber alone.
Unlamented he dies;—unregretted. Not so,
When, the tower of his country, in death falls the brave;
Thrice hallowed his name amongst all, high or low,
As with blessings alive, so with tears in the grave.

    H. N. COLERIDGE

TYRTAEUS

According to later Athenian gossip Tyrtaeus, Callinus' Spartan contemporary, was a lame schoolmaster from Athens; actually he was from Lesbos. His poems constituted a kind of sacred book from which young Spartans were to learn courage.

From never-vanquished Hercules ye boast
    That ye are sprung: be bold then, for away
Zeus turns not from us; never let the host
    Of foes by numbers fill you with dismay.

But each, direct against the foremost foe
    His shield extend; prepared this hated breath

83

To render, and no fonder love to show
  For the sun's beams than for the shades of death.

The deeds of tears-causing Ares how bright!
  How dire the shock of battle ye have known!
And ye by turns have proved pursuit and flight,
  Until, brave youths, of both too weary grown.

Of those who dare at once, with constant mind,
  To charge, and closing 'gainst the foe make head,
Few fall, while they protect the ranks behind;
  But in the timid all their soul is dead.

What ills attend the men whose deeds are base?
  Words justly to relate one scarce can find;
For it is ever counted a disgrace,
  Him who from battle flees to wound behind.

Shameful a corse is tumbled on the sand,
  Through the back wounded by a spear's point keen:
With feet apart, then, let each firmly stand,
  And with lip hard compressed his teeth between.

And let each guard, with broad protecting shield,
  His thighs and legs, his shoulders and his breast;
Let him his powerful spear with right hand wield,
  And shake above his head his dreadful crest.

Let each who bears a buckler learn to fight,
  Doing brave deeds, nor from the conflict go;
But, rushing close, let him essay to smite,
  Or with long lance or sword, the meeting foe:

Foot placed 'gainst foot, buckler with buckler closed,
  While breast, crest, helmet, breast, crest, helmet touch;
Let him fight well against the men opposed,
  And his sword's hilt or spear-shaft try to clutch.

But yon light troops disperst along the field,
    Yet near the well-armed ranks, assail the foe;
And from behind the shelter of a shield,
    Each ponderous stones or polisht javelins throw.
    ANONYMOUS (*Tyrtaeus* 8)

84

A man I would not name, I would not prize
    For racer's swiftness or for wrestler's force;
Nor though he had the Cyclops' strength and size,
    Or left the Thracian north-wind in his course;

Nor though Tithonos he in form surpast;
    Midas and Cynaras in golden store;
Pelops Tantalides in empire vast;
    Nor though Adrastos' honied tongue he bore;

Nor though the fame of all save valour keen,
    Were his—for good he is not in the fight
Who cannot look on slaughter's bloody scene,
    Nor feel in closing with the foe delight.

But valour is 'mongst men the chief renown,
    And most becoming for a youth to bear.
A public good that man is to his town,
    And all his people, who will firmly dare,

Amid the foremost of the warlike band,
    With feet apart, base flight forgetting all;
Exposing life, with constant mind to stand,
    And to his comrades courage give to fall.

Good is such a man in war; he turns to flight
    The fiercest phalanx of the rushing foe,
And by his single, unassisted might,
    The tide of battle bids no further go.

When falling in the van he life must yield,
    An honour to his sire, his town, his state—

His breast oft mangled through his circling shield,
    And gasht in front through all his armour's plate—

Him young and old together mourn: and then
    His city swells his funeral's sad array;
His tomb, his offspring, are renowned 'mongst men—
    His children's children, to the latest day.

His glory or his name shall never die,
    Though 'neath the ground, he deathless shall remain,
Whom fighting steadfastly, with courage high,
    For country and for children Mars has slain.

But if he 'scape the fate of death's long sleep,
    And bear victorious conquest's bright renown,
Then young and old shall him in honour keep,
    Till full of joys he to the shade sink down.

Advanced in years, he holds an honoured place
    Amongst his townsmen, who in reverence meet,
Or justice towards him fail not; but in grace,
    Both young and old him cede the chiefest seat.

Then to such warlike worth as this to attain,
    And such a high reward of honour bright,
Let each one strive, with eager soul, to gain,
    With dauntless valour bearing him in fight.
        ANONYMOUS (*Tyrtaeus* 9)

MIMNERMUS

*Mimnermus of Colophon, who lived later in the seventh cen-
tury, introduces into elegiac the voluptuous tone character-
istic of Asia Minor. The first selection here given celebrates
love, the second laments fleeting life.*

What is joy of life apart from Venus the golden?   **85**
  I should prefer to die when ye move me no more,
Sweet clandestine delights, and friendship and gifts slyly
    proffered!
  Even the flowers of youth, dear unto woman and man,
Vanish and fade so soon, for hateful old age comes upon us,
  Striking the good and the bad equally cruelly down.
Then, indeed, do worrisome cares and sorrows assail us,
  Nor do we take delight seeing the bright shining sun,
But we are hateful to children, and objects of scorn unto
    women!
  Such is the bane of old age fastened by God upon man.
    N. H. DOLE (*Mimnermus* 1)

We, like the leaves of many-blossomed Spring,   **86**
When the sun's rays their sudden radiance fling
In growing strength, on earth, a little while,
Delighted, to see youth's blooming flowerets smile.
Not with that wisdom of the Gods endued,
To judge aright of evil and of good.
Two Fates, dark-scowling, at our side attend;
Of youth, of life, each points the destined end,
Old age and death: the fruit of youth remains
Brief, as the sunshine scattered o'er the plains:
And when these fleeting hours have sped away,
To die were better than to breathe the day.
A load of grief the burdened spirit wears;
Domestic troubles rise; penurious cares;
One with an earnest love of children sighs;
The grave is opened and he childless dies:
Another drags in pain his lingering days,
While slow disease upon his vitals preys.
Nor lives there one, whom Jupiter on high
Exempts from years of mixt calamity.
    C. A. ELTON (*Mimnermus* 2)

SOLON

Solon, a prime designer of Athenian democracy and accounted one of the Seven Sages, is also the first literary figure of Athens. His elegiac verses all inculcate moral, political, or martial virtue.

87 O ye splendid children of Memory and Zeus the Olympian,
    Pierian Muses, hear! Heed me now as I pray!
Happiness in the eyes of the gods ever blessed, O grant me,
    And to enjoy good repute in the eyes of mankind!
Let me be sweet to my friends, to my enemies let me be
    bitter;
    Win from the ones respect, fill the others with fear!
Soothly I fain would have riches, but never would gain them
    unjustly.
    All together the last Justice came on the earth.
Wealth, if the gods confer it, remains an unbroken posses-
    sion,
    Standing faithfully by from foundation to roof.
But the power that men honour, born of violence, lawless,
    Action unjust obeys, prisoner is by restraint.
Ate, the goddess of Mischief, quickly takes part in the matter.
    Tiny it is at first—soon it spreads like a fire,
Smouldering when it begins, but finally ending in anguish.
    Thus for mortal men insolent deeds cannot thrive.
Zeus as he sits on high foresees the ending of all things.
    Sudden as when the wind scatters the clouds in the Spring.
Stirring the depths of the waste sea with its infinite billows,
    Wreaking destruction fierce over the wheat-fruitful lands.
Then when it sweeps thro the skies, the lofty seats of im-
    mortals
    Clear it leaves them again, freed from the veil of the fogs.

Then the might of the sun shines down on the wide fertile
    regions
  Beautiful, filled with the works built by the labours of man.
Such is the retribution of Zeus, that comes all-impartial,
  Not like a mortal man's, quickly stirred into wrath.
Not forever will he escape and hide from the judgment
  Who has a sinful heart; nay! at the last he is doomed.
One may pay it today and another may pay it tomorrow.
  Yet if they seem to escape, if the doom of the gods
Following, do not attain them while still in the land of the
    living,
  Under the fatal ban, guiltless, their children are curst.

  N. H. DOLE

*A great contribution to democracy was Solon's "disburden-
ment" ordinance, by which mortgages (marked by inscribed
stones) which deprived freemen of their civic rights were
canceled. The following makes reference to this legislation.*

Which of the aims that spurred me to unite **88**
the people—which did I leave abandoned, unattained?
Star-witness be, to help me in my cause,
before the court of time, black Earth,
majestic mother of the Olympian gods:
the mortgage stones which everywhere impaled her
did I remove, from bondage set her free.
To Athens, homeland founded by the gods,
I gave back many men who, lawfully or no,
were sold as slaves abroad: some the constraint
of debts had exiled, and roaming the wide earth
they stilled their Attic tongue; others at home
a master held in fear, degraded slaves:
I liberated them. And through my power,
with force and justice in true harmony,
I did the work and lived up to my promise.
And laws I wrote for villain and for noble,
and set the rule of justice straight for all

alike. A man of greed and evil counsels,
if he had cracked the whip which then I held,
could not have curbed the people. Had I willed
to do what then pleased my opponents, or again
what their opponents planned in turn for them,
this city would have lost full many men.
This was the reason why against all sides
I built a bulwark—a wolf at bay 'midst a pack of hounds.

   MARTIN OSTWALD

THEOGNIS

To confront the rising democracy of Solon we have the trucu-lent aristocracy of Theognis of Megara (late sixth century), for whom blood and breed are paramount and who deplores the obliteration of class distinctions by new wealth. Theognis alone of the lyric poets has come down in an independent manuscript tradition, but the 1400 lines we have seem merely an accretion, for they contain recognizable quotations from other poets and from Theognis himself. The first passage cited is the earliest claim of a poet to have conferred immortality upon his addressee, in this case Cyrnus; the remainder is typi-cal of gnomic poetry.

89   Lo, I have given thee plumes wherewith to skim
               The unfathomed deep, and lightly hover around
               Earth's huge circumference. Thou shalt be found
         At banquets on the breath of pæan and hymn:
         To shrill-voiced pipes with lips of seraphim,
               Lovely young men thy rapturous fame shall sound;
               Yea, when thou liest lapped in noiseless ground,
         Thy name shall live, nor shall oblivion dim
         Thy dawn of splendour. For these lands, these isles,
               These multitudinous waves of refluent seas,
               Shall be thy pleasure ground where-through to roam,

Borne by no steed, but wafted by the smiles
  Of Muses violet-crowned, whose melodies,
    While earth endures, shall make all earth thy home.
      JOHN ADDINGTON SYMONDS (*Theognis* 237-252)

To rear a child is easy, but to teach   **90**
Morals and manners is beyond our reach;
To make the foolish wise, the wicked good,
That science never yet was understood.
  The sons of Esculapius, if their art
Could remedy a perverse and wicked heart,
Might earn enormous wages! But, in fact,
The mind is not compounded and compact
Of precept and example; human art
In human nature has no share or part.
Hatred of vice, the fear of shame and sin,
Are things of native growth, not grafted in:
Else wise and worthy parents might correct
In children's hearts each error and defect:
Whereas we see them disappointed still,
No scheme nor artifice of human skill
Can rectify the passions or the will.

Our commonwealth preserves its former frame,
Our common people are no more the same:
They that in skins and hides were rudely dress'd
Nor dreamt of law, nor sought to be redress'd
By rules of right, but in the days of old
Flock'd to the town, like cattle to the fold,
Are now the brave and wise; and we, the rest,
(Their betters nominally, once the best)
Degenerate, debasèd, timid, mean!
Who can endure to witness such a scene?
Their easy courtesies, the ready smile,
Prompt to deride, to flatter, and beguile!
Their utter disregard of right or wrong,
Of truth or honour!—Out of such a throng
(For any difficulties, any need,

For any bold design or manly deed)
Never imagine you can choose a just
Or steady friend, or faithful in his trust.
    But change your habits! let them go their way!
Be condescending, affable, and gay!

I walk by rule and measure, and incline
To neither side, but take an even line;
Fix'd in a single purpose and design.
With learning's happy gifts to celebrate,
To civilize and dignify the state:
Not leaguing with the discontented crew,
Nor with the proud and arbitrary few.

The generous and the brave, in common fame,
From time to time encounter praise or blame;
The vulgar pass unheeded; none escape
Scandal or insult in some form or shape.
Most fortunate are those, alive or dead,
Of whom the least is thought, the least is said.
Court not a tyrant's favour, nor combine
To further his iniquitous design;
But, if your faith is pledg'd, though late and loth,
If covenants have pass'd between you both,
Never assassinate him! keep your oath!
But should he still misuse his lawless power
To trample on the people, and devour,
Depose or overturn him; anyhow!
Your oath permits it, and the gods allow.

The sovereign single person—what cares he
For love or hate, for friend or enemy?—
His single purpose is utility.

If popular distrust and hate prevail,
If saucy mutineers insult and rail,
Fret not your eager spirit,—take a line
Just, sober, and discreet, the same as mine.

Let no persuasive art tempt you to place
Your confidence in crafty minds and base;—
How can it answer? Will their help avail
When danger presses, and your foes assail?
The blessing which the gods in bounty send,
Will they consent to share it with a friend?

No!—To bestrew the waves with scatter'd grain,
To cultivate the surface of the main,
Is not a task more absolutely vain
Than cultivating such allies as these,—
Fickle and unproductive as the seas.

Such are all baser minds, never at rest,
With new demands importunately press'd,
A new pretension or a new request;
Till, foil'd with a refusal of the last,
They disavow their obligations past.

But brave and gallant hearts are cheaply gain'd,
Faithful adherents, easily retain'd;
Men that will never disavow the debt
Of gratitude, or cancel or forget.

Waste not your efforts, struggle not, my friend,
Idle and old abuses to defend:
Take heed! the very measures that you press
May bring repentance with their own success.

Rash angry words, and spoken out of season,
When passion has usurp'd the throne of reason,
Have ruin'd many.—Passion is unjust,
And, for an idle transitory gust
Of gratified revenge, dooms us to pay
With long repentance at a later day.

The gods send Insolence to lead astray
The man whom Fortune and the Fates betray;
Predestin'd to precipitate decay.
Wealth nurses Insolence, and wealth, we find,
When coupled with a poor and paltry mind,

Is evermore with insolence combin'd.
   Never in anger with the meaner sort
Be mov'd to a contemptuous retort,
Deriding their distresses; nor despise
In hasty speech their wants and miseries.
   Jove holds the balance, and the gods dispense
For all mankind riches and indigence.

Join with the world; adopt with every man
His party views, his temper, and his plan;
Strive to avoid offence, study to please,
Like the sagacious inmate of the seas,
That an accommodating colour brings,
Conforming to the rock to which he clings;
With every change of place changing his hue;
The model for a statesman such as you.

Let not a base calumnious pretence,
Exaggerating a minute offence,
Move you to wrong a friend; if, every time,
Faults in a friend were treated as a crime,
Here upon earth no friendship could have place.
But we, the creatures of a faulty race
Amongst ourselves, offend and are forgiven:
Vengeance is the prerogative of heaven.

Schemes unadvisable and out of reason
Are best adjourn'd—wait for a proper season!
Time and a fair conjuncture govern all.
Hasty ambition hurries to a fall;
A fall predestin'd and ordain'd by heaven:
By a judicial madness madly driven,
Mistaking and confounding good and evil,
Men lose their senses, as they leave their level.

A trusty partisan, faithful and bold,
Is worth his weight in silver or in gold,
For times of trouble.—But the race is rare;

Steady determin'd men, ready to share
Good or ill fortune!—such, if such there are,
Could you survey the world, and search it round,
And bring together all that could be found,
The largest company you could enroll,
A single vessel could embark the whole!—
So few there are! the noble manly minds
Faithful and firm, the men that honour binds;
Impregnable to danger and to pain
And low seduction in the shape of gain,

From many a friend you must withhold your plans;
No man is safe with many partisans,
No secret!—With a party, sure but small,
Of bold adherents, trusty men withal,
You may succeed: else ruin must ensue,
Inevitable, for your friends and you.

An exile has no friends! no partisan
Is firm or faithful to the banish'd man;
A disappointment and a punishment,
Harder to bear, and worse than banishment.

Happy the man, with worldly wealth and ease,
Who, dying in good time, departs in peace.
Nor yet reduc'd to wander as a stranger
In exile and distress and daily danger;
To fawn upon his foes, to risk the trial
Of a friend's faith, and suffer a denial!

No mean or coward heart will I commend
In an old comrade or a party friend:
Nor with ungenerous, hasty zeal decry
A noble-minded gallant enemy.
Not to be born—never to see the sun—
No worldly blessing is a greater one!
And the next best is speedily to die,
And lapt beneath a load of earth to lie!

You, great Apollo, with its walls and towers
Fenc'd and adorn'd of old this town of ours!
Such favour in thy sight Alcathous won,
Of Pelops old the fair and manly son.
Now, therefore, in thy clemency divine,
Protect these very walls, our own and thine!
Guide and assist us, turn aside the boast
Of the destroying haughty Persian host!

So shall thy people each returning spring
Slay fatted hecatombs, and gladly bring
Fair gifts, with chaunted hymns and lively song,
Dances and feasts, and happy shouts among:
Before thy altar, glorifying thee,
In peace and health and wealth, cheerful and free.

Yet much I fear the faction and the strife,
Throughout our Grecian cities, raging rife,
And their wild councils. But do thou defend
This town of ours, our founder and our friend!

Wide have I wander'd, far beyond the sea,
Even to the distant shores of Sicily,
To broad Eubœa's plentiful domain,
With the rich vineyards in its planted plain;
And to the sunny wave and winding edge
Of fair Eurotas, with its reedy sedge;
Where Sparta stands in simple majesty,
Among her manly rulers, there was I!
Greeted and welcom'd (there and everywhere)
With courteous entertainment, kind and fair;
Yet still my weary spirit would repine,
Longing again to view this land of mine.

Henceforward no design nor interest
Shall ever move me, but the first and best,
With learning's happy gift to celebrate,
To adorn and dignify my native state.
The song, the dance, music and verse agreeing,
Will occupy my life, and fill my being:
Pursuits of elegance and learnèd skill

(With good repute and kindness and good will,
Among the wiser sort) will pass my time
Without an enemy, without a crime;
Harmless and just with every rank of men,
Both the free native and the denizen.
    J. H. Frere (*Theognis*, cento)

ARCHILOCHUS

Archilochus of Paros wrote elegiacs but also introduced iambics—and gave that form the connotation "scurrilous" which it retained throughout antiquity. The iambic marks a further relaxation of the formalism of the hexameter, and Archilochus, himself the son of an aristocratic father and slave mother, uses the meter to express scorn, hatred, sarcasm, resignation, and vindictiveness. In the aristocratic code the loss of a shield is a major crime; Archilochus can boast of losing his:

Some Thracian strutteth with my shield;   **91**
    For, being somewhat flurried,
I left it in a wayside bush,
    When from the field I hurried;
A right good targe, but I got off,
    The deuce may take the shield;
I'll get another just as good
    When next I go afield.
    Paul Shorey (*Archilochus* 6)

For general he wants no dandy but a tough little man:

I do not like a swagger captain   **92**
    Who stands with legs apart,
Or wears his hair in flowing ringlets,
    Or shaves with careful art.

But give me one of slender stature,
  With well-turned legs and smart,
Who walks along unfaltering, strong,
  While courage fills his heart.
          N. H. DOLE (*Archilochus* 58)

Nor is he envious of wealth:

93   The wealth of gold-abounding Croisos
                   Is no concern to me;
                 Ambition offers no temptation;
                   From envy I am free.
                 The god's affairs I do not question;
                   No monarch would I be.
                 I am content, where'er I'm sent,
                   With mediocrity.
                         N. H. DOLE (*Archilochus* 25)

*But Archilochus can also show mature reflection, as in the
following selections:*

94   Tossed on a sea of troubles, Soul, my Soul,
                   Thyself do thou control;
                 And to the weapons of advancing foes
                   A stubborn breast oppose:
                 Undaunted mid the hostile might
                 Of squadrons burning for the fight.

                 Thine be no boasting when the victor's crown
                   Wins thee deserved renown;
                 Thine no dejected sorrow, when defeat
                   Would urge a base retreat:
                 Rejoice in joyous things—nor overmuch
                   Let grief thy bosom touch
                 Midst evil, and still bear in mind
                 How changeful are the ways of humankind.
                         WILLIAM HAY (*Archilochus* 66)

Bows will not avail thee, **95**
Darts and slings will fail thee,
    When Mars tumultuous rages
    On wide-embattled land:
Then with falchions clashing,
Eyes with fury flashing,
    Man with man engages
    In combat hand to hand.
But most Eubœa's chiefs are known,
    Marshalled hosts of spearmen leading
    To conflict, whence is no receding,
To make this—war's best art—their own.
    J. H. MERIVALE (*Archilochus* 1)

Leave the gods to order all things; **96**
    Often from the gulf of woe
They exalt the poor man, grovelling
    In the gloomy shades below;
Often turn again and prostrate
    Lay in dust the loftiest head,
Dooming him through life to wander,
    Reft of sense and wanting bread.
    J. H. MERIVALE (*Archilochus* 56)

These lines are on an eclipse of the sun:

Naught, now, can pass belief; in Nature's ways **97**
No strange anomaly our wonder raise.
The Olympian Father hangs a noon-day night
O'er the sun's disk and veils its glittering light.
Fear falls on man. Hence miracles, before
Incredible, are counted strange no more.
Stand not amazed if beasts exchange the wood
With dolphins and exist amid the flood;
These the firm land exchange for sounding waves,
And those find pleasure in the mountain caves.
    C. A. ELTON (*Archilochus* 74)

Excessive water calls for abundant wine:

98   Come then, my friend, and seize the flask,
    And while the deck around us rolls,
Dash we the cover from the cask
    And crown with wine our flowing bowls.
While the deep hold is tempest-tost,
    We'll strain bright nectar from the lees;
For though our freedom here be lost
    We drink no water on the seas.
    J. H. MERIVALE (*Archilochus* 4)

And here are some reflections on friends lost at sea:

99   Blaming the bitterness of this sorrow, Perikles, no man
    in all our city can take pleasure in festivities:
such were the men the surf of the rolling sea washed under,
    all of us go with hearts aching against our ribs
for misery. Yet against such grief that is past recovery
    the gods, dear friend, have given us strong endurance to be
our medicine. Such sorrows are variable. They beat now
    against ourselves, and we take the hurt of the bleeding sore.
Tomorrow it will be others who grieve, not we. From now on
    act like a man, and put away these feminine tears.
    RICHMOND LATTIMORE (*Archilochus* 9)

SEMONIDES

In the hands of Semonides of Amorgos iambic makes a complete break with the aristocratic tradition and turns to ordinary interests of middle-class society. Here is Semonides' essay on women.

100   In the beginning God made various kinds of women
with various minds. He made one from the hairy sow,

that one whose house is smeared with mud, and all within
lies in dishevelment and rolls along the ground,
while the pig-woman in unlaundered clothing sits
unwashed herself among the dunghills, and grows fat.

God made another woman from the mischievous
vixen, whose mind gets into everything. No act
of wickedness unknown to her; no act of good
either, because the things she says are often bad
but sometimes good. Her temper changes all the time.

One from a bitch, and good-for-nothing like her mother.
She must be in on everything, and hear it all.
Out she goes ranging, poking her nose everywhere
and barking, whether she sees anyone about
or not. Her husband cannot make her stop by threats,
neither when in a rage he knocks her teeth out with
a stone, nor when he reasons with her in soft words,
not even when there's company come, and she's with them.
Day in, day out, she keeps that senseless yapping up.

The gods of Olympus made another one of mud
and gave her lame to man. A woman such as this
knows nothing good and nothing bad. Nothing at all.
The only thing she understands is how to eat,
and even if God makes the weather bad, she won't,
though shivering, pull her chair up closer to the fire.

One from the sea. She has two different sorts of mood.
One day she is all smiles and happiness. A man
who comes to visit sees her in the house and says:
"There is no better wife than this one anywhere
in all mankind, nor prettier." Then, another day
there'll be no living with her, you can't get within
sight, or come near her, or she flies into a rage
and holds you at a distance like a bitch with pups
cantankerous and cross with all the world. It makes
no difference whether they are friends or enemies.

The sea is like that also. Often it lies calm
and innocent and still, the mariner's delight
in summer weather. Then again it will go wild
and turbulent with the thunder of big crashing waves.
This woman's disposition is just like the sea's
since the sea's temper also changes all the time.

One was a donkey, dusty-gray and obstinate.
It's hard to make her work. You have to curse and tug
to make her do it, but in the end she gets it done
quite well. Then she goes to her corner-crib and eats.
She eats all day, she eats all night, and by the fire
she eats. But when there's a chance to make love, she'll take
the first one of her husband's friends who comes along.

One from a weasel—miserable stinking thing.
There's nothing pretty about her. She has no kind
of charm, no kind of sweetness, and no sex appeal.
She's always crazy to make love and go to bed,
but makes her husband—if she has one—sick, when he
comes near her. And she steals from neighbors. She's all bad.
She robs the altar and eats up the sacrifice.

One was begotten from the maned, fastidious mare.
She manages to avoid all housework and the chores
of slaves. She wouldn't touch the mill, or lift a sieve,
or sweep the dung from the house and throw it out of doors,
or squat by the fire. Afraid the soot will make her dirty.
She makes her husband boon-companion to Hard Times.
She washes the dirt off her body every day
twice at least, three times some days, and anoints herself
with perfume, and forever wears her long hair combed
and shadowed deep with flowers. A woman such as this
makes, to be sure, a lovely wife for someone else
to look at, but her husband finds her an expense
unless he is some tyrant or a sceptered king
who can indulge his taste for luxuries like her.

One was a monkey; and this is the very worst,
most exquisite disaster Zeus has wished on men.
Hers is the ugliest face of all. When such a woman
walks through the village, everybody turns to laugh.
Her neck's so short that she can scarcely turn her head.
Slab-sided, skinny-legged. Oh, unhappy man
who has to take such a disaster in his arms!
Yet she has understanding of all tricks and turns,
just like a monkey. If they laugh, she doesn't mind.
Don't expect any good work done by her. She thinks
of only one thing, plans for one thing, all day long:
how she can do somebody else the biggest harm.

One from a bee. The man is lucky who gets her.
She is the only one no blame can settle on.
A man's life grows and blossoms underneath her touch.
She loves her husband, he loves her, and they grow old
together, while their glorious children rise to fame.
Among the throngs of other women this one shines
as an example. Heavenly grace surrounds her. She
alone takes no delight in sitting with the rest
when the conversation's about sex. It's wives like this
who are God's gift of happiness to mortal men.
These are the thoughtful wives, in every way the best.

But all those other breeds come to us too from God
and by his will. And they stay with us. They won't go.
For women are the biggest single bad thing Zeus
has made for us. Even when a wife appears to help,
her husband finds out in the end that after all
she didn't. No one day goes by from end to end
enjoyable, when you have spent it with your wife.
She will not stir herself to push the hateful god
Hard Times—that most unwelcome caller—out of doors.
At home, when a man thinks that by God's grace or by
men's good will, there'll be peace for him and all go well,
she finds some fault with him and starts a fight. For where

there is a woman in the house, no one can ask
a friend to come and stay with him, and still feel safe.
Even the wife who appears to be the best-behaved
turns out to be the one who lets herself go wrong.
Her husband gawps and doesn't notice; neighbors do,
and smile to see how still another man gets fooled.
Each man will pick the faults in someone else's wife
but boast of his own each time he speaks of her. And yet
the same thing happens to us all. But we don't see.
For women are the biggest single bad thing Zeus
has made for us; a ball-and-chain; we can't get loose
until in the end a quarrel over a woman starts
a war, and we all volunteer, and go to hell.

    RICHMOND LATTIMORE

SAPPHO

*Where elegy and iamb are written in series of identical lines,
to be intoned to instrumental accompaniment, true lyric,
whether solo or choral, is written in strophes, to be sung.*

*For us solo lyric begins with Sappho of Lesbos (early sixth
century), whom antiquity with one voice acclaimed the great-
est in her art.*

101   Throned in splendor, deathless, o Aphrodite
    child of Zeus, charm-fashioner, I entreat you
    not with griefs and bitternesses to break my
        spirit, o goddess;

    standing by me rather, if once before now
    far away you heard, when I called upon you,
    left your father's dwelling place and descended
        yoking the golden

chariot to exquisite doves, who drew you
down in speed aslant the black world, the bright air
trembling at the heart to the pulse of countless
        fluttering wingbeats.

Swiftly then they came, and you, blessed lady,
smiling on me out of immortal beauty
asked me what affliction was on me, why I
        called thus upon you,

what beyond all else I would have befall my
tortured heart: "Whom then would you have Persuasion
force to serve desire in your heart? Who is it,
        Sappho, that hurt you?

Though she now escape you, she soon will follow;
though she take not gifts from you, she will give them:
though she love not, yet she will surely love you
        even unwilling."

In such guise come even again and set me
free from doubt and sorrow; accomplish all those
things my heart desires to be done; appear and
        stand at my shoulder.
        RICHMOND LATTIMORE (*Sappho* 1)

Peer of the gods he seemeth to me, the blissful   **102**
Man who sits and gazes at thee before him,
Close beside thee sits, and in silence hears thee
        Silverly speaking,

Laughing love's low laughter. Oh this, this only
Stirs the troubled heart in my breast to tremble!
For should I but see thee a little moment,
        Straight is my voice hushed;

Yea, my tongue is broken, and through and through me
'Neath the flesh impalpable fire runs tingling;

Nothing see mine eyes, and a noise of roaring
  Waves in my ear sounds;

Sweat runs down in rivers, a tremor seizes
All my limbs, and paler than grass in autumn,
Caught by pains of menacing death, I falter,
  Lost in the love-trance.
        JOHN ADDINGTON SYMONDS (*Sappho* 2)

103 Some there are who say that the fairest thing seen
on the black earth is an array of horsemen,
some, men marching, some would say ships, but I say
  she whom one loves best

is the loveliest. Light were the work to make this
plain to all. Since she who surpassed in beauty
all mortality beside, Helen, chose that
  man as the noblest

who destroyed the glory of Troy entirely.
Not the thought of child, nor beloved parents,
was remembered, after the Queen of Cyprus
  won her at first sight.

Since young brides have hearts that can be persuaded
easily, light things, palpitant to passion
as am I, remembering Anaktoria
  who has gone from me

and whose lovely walk and the shining pallor
of her face I would rather see before my
eyes than Lydia's chariots in all their glory
  armored for battle.
        RICHMOND LATTIMORE (*Sappho* 13)

104 Like the sweet apple which reddens upon the topmost bough,
A-top on the topmost twig,—which the pluckers forgot some-
  how,—

Forgot it not, nay, but got it not, for none could get it till
    now.

Like the wild hyacinth flower, which on the hills is found,
Which the passing feet of the shepherds for ever tear and
    wound,
Until the purple blossom is trodden into the ground.
    D. G. ROSSETTI (*Sappho* 93 and 94)

       The moon hath left the sky;   **105**
       Lost is the Pleiads' light;
       It is midnight
       And time slips by;
       But on my couch alone I lie.
         JOHN ADDINGTON SYMONDS (*Sappho* 52)

       Oh, my sweet mother, 'tis in vain,   **106**
       I cannot weave as once I wove,
       So 'wildered is my heart and brain
       With thinking of that youth I love.
         THOMAS MOORE (*Sappho* 90)

Thou liest dead, and there will be no memory left behind   **107**
Of thee or thine in all the earth, for never didst thou bind
The roses of Pierian streams upon thy brow; thy doom
Is now to flit with unknown ghosts in cold and nameless
    gloom.
    EDWIN ARNOLD (*Sappho* 68)

This dust was Timas'; ere her bridal hour   **108**
She lies in Proserpina's gloomy bower;
Her virgin playmates from each lovely head
Cut with sharp steel their locks, the strewments for the dead.
    C. A. ELTON (*Sappho* 119)

O Hesperus! Thou bringest all things home;   **109**
All that the garish day hath scattered wide;

The sheep, the goat, back to the welcome fold;
Thou bring'st the child, too, to his mother's side.
     W. H. APPLETON (*Sappho* 95)

ALCAEUS

*Sappho's older contemporary Alcaeus was also from Lesbos,
and tradition affirmed that there was a connection between
the two. Alcaeus was much imitated by Horace, who spoke
of his propensities to fighting, drinking, and loving, which,
with his political interests, are illustrated in the following
pieces. The ship in the first piece is presumably the ship of
state, in the second an actual ship.*

110
I cannot understand how the winds are set
against each other. Now from this side and now
     from that the waves roll. We between them
          run with the wind in our black ship driven

hard pressed and laboring under the giant storm.
All round the mast-step washes the sea we shipped.
     You can see through the sail already
          where there are opening rents within it.

The forestays slacken. . . .

     Now jettison all cargo; ride out
          best as we can in the pounding surfbeat.

They say that, beaten hard by the running seas,
the ship herself no longer will fight against
     the wildness of the waves, would rather
          strike on the reefs underneath, and founder.
     RICHMOND LATTIMORE (*Alcaeus* 18, 19, 154)

Be with me now, leaving the Isle of Pelops,   **111**
mighty sons of Zeus and of Leda, now in
kindliness of heart appear to me, Kastor
    and Polydeukes:

you who wander over the wide earth, over
all the sea's domain on your flying horses
easily delivering mortal men from
    death and its terror:

swept in far descent to the strong-built vessel's
masthead you ride shining upon the cables,
through the weariness of the dark night bringing
    light to the black ship.

RICHMOND LATTIMORE (*Alcaeus* 14)

The fighting man's joy in good weapons is gloriously expressed
in lines on the poet's armory.

Glitters with brass my mansion wide,   **112**
The roof is decked on every side
    In martial pride;
With helmets ranged in order bright,
And plumes of horse-hair nodding white,
    A gallant sight—
Fit ornament for warrior's brow—
And 'round the walls in goodly row
    Refulgent glow
Stout greaves of brass like burnished gold,
And corselets there in many a fold
    Of linen rolled;
And shields that in the battle fray
The routed losers of the day
    Have cast away.
Euboean falchions too are seen,
With rich embroidered belts between
    Of dazzling sheen;

And gaudy surcoats piled around,
And spoils of chiefs in war renowned
      May there be found.
These, and all else that here you see
Are fruits of glorious victory
      Achieved by me.
            J. H. MERIVALE (*Alcaeus* 15)

And here wine is suggested as a prophylactic for winter.

113   Zeus rains upon us, and from the sky comes down
      enormous winter. Rivers have turned to ice. . . .

      Dash down the winter. Throw a log on the fire
      and mix the flattering wine (do not water it
            too much) and bind on round our foreheads
            soft ceremonial wreaths of spun fleece.

      We must not let our spirits give way to grief.
      By being sorry we get no further on,
            my Bukchis. Best of all defences
            is to mix plenty of wine, and drink it.
            RICHMOND LATTIMORE (*Alcaeus* 34)

ANACREON

Anacreon's poetry typifies the grace and urbanity of Ionia.
Though his subjects are wine, women, and song, he is never-
theless a sincere and serious poet who deals maturely with an
important if circumscribed sphere of human experience. A
number of his poems complain that the onset of old age
makes him less attractive to women.

114   The women tell me every day
      That all my bloom has past away.

"Behold," the pretty wantons cry,
"Behold this mirror with a sigh;
The locks upon thy brow are few,
And, like the rest, they're withering too!"
Whether decline has thinn'd my hair,
I'm sure I neither know nor care;
But this I know, and this I feel,
As onward to the tomb I steal,
That still as death approaches nearer,
The joys of life are sweeter, dearer;
And had I but an hour to live,
That little hour to bliss I'd give.

  THOMAS MOORE

Why with Scorn-reverting Eye,   **115**
Pretty Thracian Filley, why
Me as skill-less and unwise,
Fly you, Cruel! and despise?
  Scorner, could I once attain
O'er thy Neck to throw the rein,
Swift with raptur'd Speed would I
Urge thee round the Goal of Joy.
  O'er the daisy-painted Mead,
Lightly bounding now you feed;
'Time some happy Lord ascend,
Skill'd thy stubborn Pride to bend.

  JOSEPH ADDISON

*Anacreon's mood and manner attracted many imitators. The
so-called Anacreontics, which aroused the enthusiasm of eight-
eenth and nineteenth century readers, cannot be the master's
own but are an accumulation of centuries. Here are some of
the most charming.*

Of th' Atrides I would sing,   **116**
Or the wand'ring Theban king;
But when I my lute did prove,

Nothing it would sound but love;
I new strung it, and to play
Hercules' labours did essay;
But my pains I fruitless found;
Nothing it but love would sound:
Heroes then farewell, my lute
To all strains but love is mute.
          THOMAS STANLEY (*Anacreontics* 1)

117

Horns to bulls wise Nature lends;
Horses she with hoofs defends;
Hares with nimble feet relieves;
Dreadful teeth to lions gives;
Fishes learns through streams to slide;
Birds through yielding air to glide;
Men with courage she supplies;
But to women these denies;
What then gives she? Beauty: this
Both their arms and armour is;
She, that can this weapon use,
Fire and sword with ease subdues.
          THOMAS STANLEY (*Anacreontics* 2)

118

I not care for Gyges' sway,
Or the Lydian sceptre weigh;
Nor am covetous of gold,
Nor with envy kings behold;
All my care is to prepare
Fragrant unguents for my hair;
All my care is where to get
Roses for a coronet;
All my care is for to-day;
What's to-morrow who can say?
Come then, let us drink and dice,
And to Bacchus sacrifice,
Ere death come and take us off,
Crying, Hold! th' hast drunk enough.
          THOMAS STANLEY (*Anacreontics* 15)

If thou dost the number know   **119**
Of the leaves on every bough,
If thou can'st the reckoning keep
Of the sands within the deep;
Thee of all men will I take,
And my love's accomptant make.
Of Athenians first a score
Set me down; then fifteen more;
Add a regiment to these
Of Corinthian mistresses:
For the most renown'd for fair
In Achaea, sojourn there;
Next our Lesbian Beauties tell;
Those that in Ionia dwell;
Those of Rhodes and Caria count;
To two thousand they amount.
Wonder'st thou I love so many?
'Las of Syria we not any,
Egypt yet, nor Crete have told,
Where his orgies Love doth hold.
What to those then wilt thou say
Which in eastern Bactria,
Or the western Gades remain?
But give o'er, thou toil'st in vain;
For the sum which thou dost seek
Puzzles all arithmetic.

    THOMAS STANLEY (*Anacreontics* 32)

Painter, by unmatch'd desert   **120**
Master of the Rhodian art,
Come, my absent mistress take,
As I shall describe her; make
First her hair, as black as bright,
And if colours so much right
Can but do her, let it too
Smell of aromatic dew;
Underneath this shade, must thou
Draw her alabaster brow;

Her dark eye-brows so dispose
That they neither part nor close,
But by a divorce so slight
Be disjoin'd, may cheat the sight:
From her kindly killing eye
Make a flash of lightning fly,
Sparkling like Minerva's yet
Like Cythera's mildly sweet:
Roses in milk swimming seek
For the pattern of her cheek:
In her lip such moving blisses,
As from all may challenge kisses;
Round about her neck (outvying
Parian stone) the Graces flying;
And o'er all her limbs at last
A loose purple mantle cast;
But so ordered that the eye
Some part naked may descry,
An essay by which the rest
That lies hidden may be guess'd.
  So, to life th' hast come so near,
    All of her, but voice, is here.
      THOMAS STANLEY (*Anacreontics* 28)

121

Away, away, ye men of rules,
What have I to do with schools?
They'd make me learn, they'd make me think,
But would they make me love and drink?
Teach me this, and let me swim
My soul upon the goblet's brim;
Teach me this, and let me twine
Some fond, responsive heart to mine,
For age begins to blanch my brow,
I've time for nought but pleasure now.

  Fly, and cool my goblet's glow
At yonder fountain's gelid flow;
I'll quaff, my boy, and calmly sink

This soul to slumber as I drink.
Soon, too soon, my jocund slave,
You'll deck your master's grassy grave;
And there's an end—for ah, you know
They drink but little wine below!
    THOMAS MOORE (*Anacreontics* 52)

Yes—loving is a painful thrill,
And not to love more painful still;
But oh, it is the worst of pain,
To love and not be lov'd again!
Affection now has fled from earth,
Nor fire of genius, noble birth,
Nor heavenly virtue, can beguile
From beauty's cheek one favouring smile.
Gold is the woman's only theme,
Gold is the woman's only dream.
Oh! never be that wretch forgiven—
Forgive him not, indignant Heaven!
Whose grovelling eyes could first adore,
Whose heart could pant for sordid ore.
Since that devoted thirst began,
Man has forgot to feel for man;
The pulse of social life is dead,
And all its fonder feelings fled!
War too has sullied Nature's charms,
For gold provokes the world to arms:
And oh! the worst of all its arts,
It rends asunder loving hearts.
    THOMAS MOORE (*Anacreontics* 29)

122

Cupid, as he lay among
Roses, by a bee was stung.
Whereupon, in anger flying
To his mother, said thus, crying,
"Help, oh help, your boy's a-dying!"
"And why, my pretty lad?" said she.
Then, blubbering, replied he,

123

"A winged snake has bitten me,
Which country people call a bee."
At which she smiled; then with her hairs
And kisses drying up his tears,
"Alas," said she, "my wag! if this
Such a pernicious torment is;
Come, tell me, then, how great's the smart
Of those thou woundest with thy dart!"

    ROBERT HERRICK (*Anacreontics* 35)

'24

Happy insect! what can be
In happiness compared to thee?
Fed with nourishment divine,
The dewy morning's gentle wine!
Nature waits upon thee still,
And thy verdant cup does fill;
'Tis filled wherever thou dost tread
Nature's self's thy Ganymede.
Thou dost drink, and dance, and sing,
Happier than the happiest king!
All the fields which thou dost see,
All the plants belong to thee;
All that summer hours produce,
Fertile made with early juice.
Man for thee does sow and plough;
Farmer he, and landlord thou!
Thou dost innocently joy;
Nor does thy luxury destroy.
The shepherd gladly heareth thee,
More harmonious than he.
Thee country hinds with gladness hear,
Prophet of the ripened year!
Thee Phoebus loves and does inspire,
Phoebus is himself thy sire.
To thee of all things upon earth,
Life is no longer than thy mirth.
Happy insect! happy thou,
Dost neither age nor winter know!

But when thou'st drunk, and danced, and sung
Thy fill, the flowery leaves among,
(Voluptuous and wise withal,
Epicurean animal!)
Sated with thy summer feast,
Thou retir'st to endless rest.

   ABRAHAM COWLEY (*Anacreontics* 34)

The black earth tipples rain,   **125**
The earth is sucked by trees,
The seas the rivers drain,
The sun drinks up the seas;
And the moon drinks the sun;
Why, then, will any one
Contend with me, who think
That all the world should drink?

   EDWIN ARNOLD (*Anacreontics* 21)

As I once in wanton play,   **126**
Binding up a chaplet lay,
Mid the roses on the ground,
Cupid fast asleep, I found.
Straightway, by his wings, well-pleased,
I the little archer seized,
Who so oft had vexed my soul,
And within my flowing bowl
Plunged him deep, then swallowed up,
Him, and all that filled the cup.

   ABRAHAM COWLEY (*Anacreontics* 6)

ALCMAN

Choral lyric is a peculiarly Greek institution, in which repre-
sentatives of various groups in the community—men, women,
boys, girls—participated. It was employed in various festivals

*and provided the beginning for Greek tragedy. Choral lyric
first received official recognition in Sparta, where its master
was Terpander. Of him there are no substantial remains, but
of his successor Alcman (seventh century B.C.) we have por-
tions of a* partheneion, *or chorus for girls, recovered from a
papyrus. The opening deals with a myth of Heracles; the
portion presented below seems to reflect rivalry between the
leaders of the half-choruses.*

127   Verily there is a vengeance from on high, and happy he
that weaveth merrily one day's weft without a tear. And so,
as for me, I sing now of the light that is Agido's. Bright I see
it as the very sun's which the same Agido now invoketh to
shine upon us. And yet neither praise nor blame can I give
at all to such as she without offence to our splendid leader,
who herself appeareth as pre-eminent as would a well-knit
steed of ringing hoof that overcometh in the race, if he were
set to graze among the unsubstantial cattle of our dreams that
fly.

See you not first that the courser is of Enetic blood, and
secondly that the tresses that bloom upon my cousin Hagesi-
chora are like the purest gold? and as for her silvern face, how
shall I put it you in express words? Such is Hagesichora. . . .

For is not the fair-ankled Hagesichora here present and
abideth hard by Agido to commend our Thosteria? Then O
receive their prayers, ye Gods; for to the Gods belongeth the
accomplishment. And for the end of my song I will tell you
a passing strange thing. My own singing hath been nought;
I that am a girl have yet shrieked like a very owl from the
housetop—albeit 'tis the same girl's desire to please Aotis so
far as in her lies, seeing the Goddess is the healer of our
woe—; 'tis Hagesichora's doing, hers alone, that the maidens
have attained the longed-for peace.

For 'tis true the others have run well beside her even as
horses beside the trace-horse; but here as on shipboard the
steersman must needs have a good loud voice, and Hagesi-
chora—she may not outsing the Sirens, for they are Gods,
but I would set her higher than any child of human breed.

Aye, she sings like a very swan beside the yellow streams of
Xanthus.

   J. M. EDMONDS

*Of the lesser fragments of Alcman the lines on the calm of
nature at night are most attractive:*

The mountain brows, the rocks, the peaks are sleeping,   **128**
Uplands and gorges hush!
The thousand moorland things are stillness keeping;
The beasts under each bush
Crouch, and the hived bees
Rest in their honied ease;
In the purple sea fish lie as they were dead,
And each bird folds his wing over his head.
   EDWIN ARNOLD

ARION

*Arion (late seventh century) of whom Herodotus tells the
famous adventure with the pirates is said to have given the
dithyramb regular form. We have none of his choral work.
The hymn to Poseidon ascribed to him is surely of later date,
but may be given here nevertheless.*

Mighty master of the ocean!   **129**
Neptune of the golden trident!
Oh, Earth-shaker! Oh, Storm-maker!
Gilled things, snorting, slimy, strident,
Glide about thee in a ring,
Winnowing fins with rapid motion;
Fish with beaks and fish with backs
Bristly, and the dog-fish packs;
Silvery dolphin dear to song,
With salt-sea maids that throng

Scale-tailed nereids, one with other,
Whereof Amphitrite was mother.
EDWIN ARNOLD

IBYCUS

*Neither do we have choral work of Ibycus (sixth century),
who, in modern times, is known chiefly for the legend of the
cranes. But there is a charming bit on spring and love.*

130

What time soft zephyrs fan the trees
In the blest gardens of th' Hesperides,
Where those bright golden apples glow,
Fed by the fruitful streams that round them flow,
And new-born clusters teem with wine
Beneath the shadowy foliage of the vine;
To me the joyous season brings
But added torture on his sunny wings.
Then Love, the tyrant of my breast,
Impetuous ravisher of joys and rest,
Bursts, furious, from his mother's arms,
And fills my trembling soul with new alarms;
Like Boreas from his Thracian plains,
Cloth'd in fierce lightnings, in my bosom reigns,
And rages still, the madd'ning power—
His parching flames my wither'd heart devour:
Wild Phrensy comes my senses o'er,
Sweet Peace is fled, and Reason rules no more.
J. H. MERIVALE

SIMONIDES

Nor, except for the fragment "How hard it is to be a good man builded four-square," pieced together from quotation in Plato's Protagoras, do we have any of Simonides' choral lyric; but there is enough else to prove his worth. The following two epigrams on Thermopylae are quoted by Herodotus.

Go tell the Spartans, thou that passest by,
That here obedient to their laws we lie.
    WILLIAM L. BOWLES (*Simonides* 92)

131

This is the grave of famed Megistias, whom
    Beside Spercheius' stream the Persian slew:
A seer he, who dared to share the doom
    Of Sparta's leaders, though that doom he knew.
    G. B. GRUNDY (*Simonides* 83)

132

Here is another on the dead of Thermopylae:

Of those who at Thermopylae were slain,
    Glorious the doom, and beautiful the lot;
Their tomb an altar: men from tears refrain
    To honor them, and praise, but mourn them not.
Such sepulchre, nor drear decay
Nor all-destroying time shall waste; this right have they.
Within their grave the home-bred glory
    Of Greece was laid: this witness gives
Leonidas the Spartan, in whose story
    A wreath of famous virtue ever lives.
    JOHN STERLING (*Simonides* 3)

133

There are a number of similar official epigrams for heroic dead. Here is a general one on the long sleep of death:

134   Long, long and dreary is the night
                 That waits us in the silent grave;
             Few, and of rapid flight,
                 The years from Death we save.
             Short—ah, how short—that fleeting space;
             And when man's little race
             Is run, and Death's grim portals o'er him close,
             How lasting his repose!
                 J. H. MERIVALE (*Simonides* 39)

Tenderest of all is the poem on Danae. Immured in her tower, she was visited by Zeus in a shower of gold and gave birth to Perseus, whereupon her father Acrisius put her and her infant in a chest and cast it out to sea. Here is her lament and prayer:

135   When, in the carven chest,
             The winds that blew and waves in wild unrest
             Smote her with fear, she, not with cheeks unwet,
                 Her arms of love round Perseus set,
                 And said: "O child, what grief is mine!
             But thou dost slumber, and thy baby breast
                 Is sunk in rest,
             Here in the cheerless brass-bound bark,
             Tossed amid starless night and pitchy dark.
                 Nor dost thou heed the scudding brine
             Of waves that wash above thy curls so deep,
                 Nor the shrill winds that sweep,—
             Lapped in thy purple robe's embrace,
                 Fair little face!
             But if this dread were dreadful too to thee,
             Then wouldst thou lend thy listening ear to me;
             Therefore I cry,—Sleep, babe, and sea, be still,
             And slumber our unmeasured ill!
                 Oh, may some change of fate, sire Zeus, from thee

Descend, our woes to end!
But if this prayer, too overbold, offend
Thy justice, yet be merciful to me!"
JOHN ADDINGTON SYMONDS (*Simonides* 37)

Simonides' elegiac tone is illustrated by his retort to a claim of immortality for a monument, written by Cleobulus. This is Cleobulus' epitaph:

136

I am the maiden in bronze set over the tomb of Midas.
As long as water runs from well springs, and tall trees burgeon,
and the sun goes up the sky to shine, and the moon is brilliant,
as long as rivers shall flow and the wash of the sea's breakers,
so long remaining in my place on this tomb where the tears fall
I shall tell those who pass that Midas here lies buried.
(*Diogenes Laertius* 1.89)

This is Simonides' comment:

Who that trusts his mind could believe the man of Lindos, Cleobulus,
who against the forever flow of rivers, the spring flowers,
against sun's flame and moon gold
and the tossing of the sea, sets up the strength of a gravestone:
All things are less than the gods. That stone
even a man's hand could smash. This is the word of a fool.
RICHMOND LATTIMORE (*Simonides* 57)

PINDAR

The greatest master of choral lyric was undoubtedly Pindar (518-438), who combines a rich formalism with a dazzling and opulent imagination. Pindar's epinician odes were com-

missioned by the princes of his day to celebrate their victories
at the pan-Hellenic festivals. The First Olympian was written
in 476 B.C. for Hiero of Syracuse's victory in a horse race.

137 Best of all things is water; but gold, like a gleaming fire
by night, outshines all pride of wealth beside.
But, my heart, would you chant the glory of games,
look never beyond the sun
by day for any star shining brighter through the deserted air,
nor any contest than Olympia greater to sing.
It is thence that the song winds strands
in the hearts of the skilled to celebrate
the son of Kronos. They come their ways
to the magnificent board of Hieron,

who handles the scepter of dooms in Sicily, rich in flocks,
reaping the crested heads of every excellence.
There his fame is magnified
in the splendor of music, where
we delight at the friendly table. Then take the Dorian lyre
          from its peg,
if any glory of Pisa or Pherenikos
slide with delight beneath your heart,
when by Alpheus waters he sped
his bulk, with the lash laid never on,
and mixed in the arms of victory his lord,

king of Syracuse, delighting in horses; and his fame shines
among strong men where Lydian Pelops went to dwell,
Pelops that he who clips the earth in his great strength,
Poseidon, loved when Klotho lifted him out
of the clean cauldron, his shoulder gleaming ivory.
Great marvels in truth are these, but tales
told and overlaid with elaboration of lies
amaze men's wits against the true word.

Grace, who brings to fulfilment all things for men's delight,
granting honor again, many a time makes

things incredible seem true.
Days to come are the wisest witnesses.
It is better for a man to speak well of the gods; he is less to
    blame.
Son of Tantalos, against older men I will say
that when your father summoned the gods
to that stateliest feast at beloved Sipylos,
and gave them to eat and received in turn,
then he of the shining trident caught you up,

his heart to desire broken, and with his horses and car of gold
carried you up to the house of Zeus and his wide honor,
where Ganymede at a later time
came for the same desire in Zeus.
But when you were gone, and men from your mother looked,
    nor brought you back,
some man, a neighbor, spoke quietly for spite,
how they took you and with a knife
minced your limbs into bubbling water
and over the table divided and ate
flesh of your body, even to the last morsel.

I cannot understand how a god could gorge thus; I recoil.
Many a time disaster has come to the speakers of evil.
If they who watch on Olympos have honored
any man, that man was Tantalos; but he was not
able to swallow his great fortune, and for his high stomach
drew a surpassing doom when our father
hung the weight of the stone above him.
He waits ever the stroke at his head and is divided from joy.

That life is too much for his strength; he is buckled fast in
    torment,
agony fourth among three others, because he stole
and gave to his own fellowship
that ambrosia and nectar
wherewith the gods made him immortal. If any man thinks
    to swindle

God, he is wrong. Therefore, they sent his son
back to the fleeting destiny of man's race.
And when at the time of life's blossoming
the first beard came to darken his cheek,
he thought on winning a bride ready at hand,

Hippodameia, the glorious daughter of a king in Pisa.
He walked alone in the darkness by the gray sea,
invoking the lord of the heavy trident,
and he appeared clear at his feet.
He spoke: "Look you, Poseidon, if you have had any joy of
        my love
and the Kyprian's sweet gifts, block the brazen spear
of Oinomaos, and give me the fleeter chariot
by Elis' river, and clothe me about in strength.
Thirteen suitors he has killed now, and ever
puts aside the marriage of his daughter.

The great danger never descends upon a man without
        strength;
but if we are destined to die, why should one sit
to no purpose in darkness and find a nameless old age
without any part of glory his own? So my way
lies this hazard; yours to accomplish the end."
He spoke, with words not wide of the mark.
The god, increasing his fame, gave him
a golden chariot and horses never weary with wings.

Breaking the strength of Oinomaos, he took the maiden and
        brought her to bed.
She bore him six sons, lords of the people, blazing in valor.
Now he lies at the Alpheus
crossing, mixed with the mighty dead.
His tomb is thronged about at the altar where many strangers
        pass; but the glory
of Pelops looks afar from Olympia
in the courses where speed is matched with speed
and a man's force harsh at the height.

And the winner the rest of his lifetime
keeps happiness beside him sweeter than honey

as far as the games go; but the good that stays by day and
     abides with him
is best that can come to a man. Be it my work to crown
in the rider's rhythm and strain
of Aiolis that king. I believe
there is no man greater both ways, for wisdom in beautiful
     things and power's weight
we shall ever glorify by skill in the folds of song.
Some god stands ever about you, musing
in his mind over what you do,
Hieron. May he not leave you soon.
So shall I hope to find once more

even a sweeter word's way to sing and help the chariot
     fleeting,
coming again to the lifting hill of Kronos. For me
the Muse in her might is forging yet the strongest arrow.
One man is excellent one way, one in another; the highest
fulfils itself in kings. Oh, look no further.
Let it be yours to walk this time on the height.
Let it be mine to stand beside you
in victory, for my skill at the forefront of the Hellenes.

   RICHMOND LATTIMORE (*Olympian* 1)

*The First Isthmian celebrates the victory in the chariot race
won, probably in 480 B.C., by Herodotus of Thebes, Pindar's
own home town. Herodotus had driven his own chariot
(which was unusual), and so the allusions to famous chariot-
ers of the heroic age are apposite.*

Thebes of the golden shield, my mother, I will put
your errand beyond other necessity that is upon me.
Let not Delos of the rocks that is my delight
begrudge me; for what delights the good
more than parents in their graciousness? Give way,

138

island of Apollo; by God's grace I shall achieve a twofold
    task, the delight of both,

making a song of dancing to Phoibos of the uncut hair
in wave-washed Keos among the men of the sea,
likewise for the Isthmos, that shoulder that dykes the surf.
It has granted garlands from games won
six times to the host of the sons of Kadmos, splendor
of fair success for their own land, on whose soil Alkmana bore
    a child

fearless, for the savage hounds of Geryon shivered before him.
But I will give Herodotos his meed for the four-horse chariot
    race;
and for reins guided by no hands other than his own
I will implicate him in song for Kastor or Iolaos.
These two in Lakedaimon and Thebes were the mightiest
    charioteers among heroes.

In all trials of strength they won most prizes,
and their houses were made magnificent with tripods,
cauldrons, dishes of gold. The feel
of garlands given in token of victory
was theirs. That excellence is a clear shining
they had alike in the naked race and the course of warriors
    among clattering shields,
for the way of the javelin's flight thrown from their hands
and the cast of the stone discus.
There was no pentathlon then, but for each event
the end lay in itself.
And often and again, binding their brows with the clustered
branched garlands, by Dirke's waters they appeared; and be-
    side Eurotas,

the son of Iphikles, dweller among the breed of the Sown
    Men;
and among Achaians Kastor the Tyndarid of the high house
    at Therapne.

Farewell both: I must bring the sweep of my song about
to Poseidon and the holy Isthmos and the strands of On-
      chestos,
to speak aloud in this man's honor the glorious destiny of
      Asopodoros, his father,

and Orchomenos with its ancestral acres
that in sympathy accepted him, he
being stricken and in the unhappiness of shipwreck,
out of the sea immeasurable; now
the fortune in this house has come back, to stand
once more high in its happiness of old; the man who has had
      labor of mind wins forethought also.

But if every temper of him is disposed toward virtue
both ways, by outlay and endurance of toil,
toward such finding the goal we should bring lordly
praise, freely and with heart not begrudging;
for it is a light gift for a man well skilled
to find the right word for various labors achieved and build
      up splendor in all men's sight.

And, in truth, each man delights in the price befitting work
      done—
shepherd, plowman, fowler, or one who lives by the sea.
The strain of warding off incessant hunger is on all men,
but he who in contests or in war achieves the delicate glory
is magnified to be given the supreme prize, splendor of speech
      from citizen and stranger.

It befits us now to hymn the son of Kronos
the earth-shaker, our neighbor and benefactor,
in requital, the lord of the running of horses,
and to speak, Amphitryon,
of your sons, and the hollow of Minyas,
and the glorious grove of Demeter, Eleusis, and Euboia,
      where the ways curve;

your precinct in Phylake, Protesilaos, I bring likewise,
yours, and of the Achaian men.
But to speak of all that Hermes, god of games,
has bestowed on Herodotos
for horses racing, the song's measure is straitened
to prevent me. Indeed, many a time the thing left silent
    makes for happiness.

May he be lifted on the shining wings of the Muses,
the melodious, and fill his hands with choice leafage won
from Pytho also and Olympian games by Alpheus, and bring
    honor
upon seven-gated Thebes. But if a man keep wealth a secret
    thing in his house
and laugh at each encounter, he knows not that he appoints
    to Hades a life without glory.
    RICHMOND LATTIMORE (*Isthmian 1*)

BACCHYLIDES

*Pindar's principal rival was Simonides' nephew Bacchylides
(fifth century), whose work is of the same character as Pindar's, but far tamer. Ode 16, here presented, deals with the
myth of Theseus and the voyage to Crete. It was possibly
intended as a paean to Apollo.*

139   The dark-prowed ship through surges cleft her way
            To Crete, and battle-bider Theseus bare
        With all those doomed to be the man-bull's prey,
            Twice seven Ionian children passing-fair.
        The north-wind smote on her far-gleaming sail
            By grace of Pallas, aegis-brandisher.
        Then goads of love-crowned Kypris, stings of bale,
            Began in Minos' tyrant heart to stir,

That he refrained him not from outrage proud,
    But on the cheek of one white girl he laid
A wanton hand. Eriboia shrieked aloud
    Unto Pandion's scion bronze-arrayed.
And Theseus saw the deed: full height he sprung;
    Sudden beneath his brows flashed his dark eye,
As indignation's bitter anguish stung
    His soul, and unto Minos did he cry:
'Ha! *thou* a son of Zeus most mightiest—
    Or base-born churl that knoweth not to rein
In righteousness the brute within his breast?
    From outrage arrogant those hands refrain!

What weird soever the resistless Fate
    God-sent, and scales of Justice, shall ordain
That cup, what time it cometh, soon or late,
    Will we receive, and to the dregs will drain.
But now—forbear thy caitiff purpose thou!
    If Phoinix' noble child of gracious name
Bare thee indeed to Zeus 'neath Ida's brow
    To be the chief of men in power and fame,
Me too the child of Pittheus wealth-renowned
    In union with Poseidon the Sea-king
Bare to a God. The Nereids violet-crowned
    Over her head a golden veil did fling.
Therefore, thou captain of Crete's war-array,
    I warn thee, this thy wantonness refrain
That breeds but grief; for verily I would pray
    Never to see dawn's lovesome light again,
If thou by force hadst wrought thy foul intent
    On any of this fair young company.
Nay, we will try the steel's arbitrament
    Ere then! The issue shall with Heaven lie.'

Thus far he spake, that hero battle-peerless;
    And all the shipmen with amazement heard
The warrior's stern defiance utter-fearless.

But Helios' kinsman's wrath was fury-stirred.
A web whose warp and woof held life's perdition
  He wove, and cried: 'Supreme in might, hear me,
Zeus, father! If the white-armed maid Phoenician
  In very truth did bear me unto thee,
Now unto me do thou send down from heaven
  A token none shall fail to understand,
Thy swift bolt of the fiery-streaming levin!
  But thou—if to the Shaker of the land
Aithra the maid Troezenian truly bore thee,
  For proof thereof, this golden signet-ring
Whose splendour flashes on mine hand before thee,
  Up from the dark deep sea-floor do thou bring.
Ay, cast thy body down to thy sire's dwelling!
  So shalt thou know if He doth hear my prayer,
Kronion, lord of thunder terror-kneeling,
  Whose sway is over all things everywhere.'

That daring prayer by Zeus the all-puissant one
  Was heard, and he vouchsafed to Minos then
Transcendent honour, to his own dear son
  Granting a grace all-manifest to men.
The lightning flashed. He saw that welcome sign:
  To glorious heaven the king war-steadfast raised
His hands—'Thou seest, Theseus, yon divine
  Boon wherewith Zeus,' he cried, 'his son hath graced.
Thou then into the thunder-tolling sea
  Leap! so shall Kronos' Son who gave thee birth,
Poseidon, the Sea-king, bestow on thee
  Renown transcendent through green-vestured earth.'
He spake: shrank Theseus' heart from that essay
  No whit; upon the strong-knit stern he stood
And leapt. The sea's white-blossomed mead straightway
  Welcomed him in, and closed o'er him the flood.
Then gladness thrilled the soul of Zeus's son.
  He gave command to hold adown the wind
The goodly-fashioned ship fast flying on—
  But Fate prepared far other ways to find.

Hard-thrusting blew the North astern; the pine
   Sped fast. But Athens' children quaked with fear,
Deeming he leapt to death beneath the brine,
   And from their flower-bright eyes shed many a tear.
But dolphins, haunters of the watery ways,
   Upstayed the mighty Theseus: onward fast
They bore the hero to the dwelling-place
   Of his Sire, Lord of Steeds. And so he passed
Into the palace-halls where Gods abode;
   And there with trembling awe he looked upon
Blest Nereus' glorious daughters. Far and wide
   Flame-like a splendour from their bright limbs shone;
And twined about the glory of their hair
   Did fillets golden-braided gleam and glance;
And joyance filled their hearts, as here, as there
   Softly their feet were floating in the dance.
And there he saw his sire's belovèd bride
   Throned in that goodly palace of the sea:
Imperial Amphitrite lovely-eyed
   Clad him in purple-rippling bravery.

She laid withal a wreath of rich adorning
   On his crisped hair, of fadeless roses wrought
Dark-splendid, which upon her bridal morning
   She of the love-wiles, Aphrodite, brought.
No miracle of the high Gods' devising
   To men whose hearts are right is past belief.
By that ship's taper stern from sea-gulfs rising
   There was he! With what thoughts he smote the chief
Of Cnossian men aghast, when midst the plashing
   Wave-crests he rose unwetted! Oh, he seemed
A marvel! On his limbs the sunlight-flashing
   Gifts of the Gods with heavenly radiance gleamed.
And up from hyaline halls there came a crying,
   The chanting of the Sea-maids splendour-throned
In new-born rapture. The great deep replying
   Echoed their joy with voices thunder-toned.
Then from the deck hard by they sang the paean,

Those youths and maids in accents sweetly blent.
O Delian, may thy soul by choir-hymns Keian
  Glow gladdened! Grant fair fortune heaven-sent!
    ARTHUR S. WAY (*Bacchylides* 16)

Here are some fine lines of Bacchylides on the charms of peace:

140 To mortal men Peace giveth these good things:
Wealth, and the flowers of honey-throated song;
  The flame that springs
On craven altars from fat sheep and kine,
Slain to the gods in heaven; and, all day long,
Games for glad youths, and flutes, and wreaths, and circling
  wine.
Then in the steely shield swart spiders weave
  Their web and dusky woof:
Rust to the pointed spear and sword doth cleave;
  The brazen trump sounds no alarms;
Nor is sleep harried from our eyes aloof,
But with sweet rest my bosom warms:
The streets are thronged with lovely men and young,
And hymns in praise of boys like flames to heaven are flung.
    JOHN ADDINGTON SYMONDS (*Bacchylides* 13)

DELPHIAN ORACLE

Of numerous recorded utterances of the oracle at Delphi those reported by Herodotus are surely genuine. The following replies to the Athenians before the Persian invasion of 480 B.C. he ascribes to the priestess Aristonice:

141 Wretches, why sit ye here? Fly, fly to the ends of creation,
Quitting your homes, and the crags which your city crowns
  with her circlet.

Neither the head, nor the body is firm in its place, nor at
    bottom
Firm the feet, nor the hands, nor resteth the middle un-
    injur'd.
All—all ruined and lost. Since fire, and impetuous Ares,
Speeding along in a Syrian chariot, hastes to destroy her.
Not alone shalt thou suffer; full many the towns he will level,
Many the shrines of the gods he will give to a fiery destruc-
    tion.
Even now they stand with dark sweat horribly dripping,
Trembling and quaking for fear, and lo! from the high roofs
    trickleth
Black blood, sign prophetic of hard distresses impending.
Get ye away from the temple, and brood on the ills that
    await ye!

    GEORGE RAWLINSON (*Herodotus* 7.140)

*When the dejected Athenians made a second appeal they
heard the following:*

Pallas has not been able to soften the lord of Olympus,
Though she has often prayed him, and urged him with ex-
    cellent counsel.
Yet once more I address thee in words than adamant firmer.
When the foe shall have taken whatever the limit of Cecrops
Holds within it, and all which divine Cithaeron shelters,
Then far-seeing Zeus grants this to the prayers of Athena;
Safe shall the wooden wall continue for thee and thy children.
Wait not the tramp of the horse, nor the footman mightily
    moving
Over the land, but turn your back to the foe, and retire ye.
Yet shall a day arrive when ye shall meet him in battle.
Holy Salamis, thou shalt destroy the offspring of women,
When men scatter the seed, or when they gather the harvest.

    GEORGE RAWLINSON (*Herodotus* 7.141)

The "wooden wall," it may be remembered, Themistocles
interpreted as the Athenian navy.

HYBRIAS

A skolion *was a song sung at aristocratic banquets; a number of skolia seem to be embedded in Theognis. Nothing is known of the Hybrias to whom the following is attributed:*

143
My wealth's a burly spear and brand,
And a right good shield of hides untanned,
   Which on my arm I buckle:
With these I plough, I reap, I sow,
With these I make sweet vintage flow,
   And all around me truckle.
But your wights that take no pride to wield
A massy spear and well-made shield,
   Nor joy to draw the sword:
O, I bring those heartless, hapless drones,
Down in a trice on their marrow-bones,
   To call me king and lord.
          THOMAS CAMPBELL

CALLISTRATUS

Nor is anything known of Callistratus; his skolion celebrates the famous tyrannicides Harmodius and Aristogeiton, who delivered Athens from the rule of Hipparchus in 514 B.C.

144
In a wreath of myrtle I'll wear my glaive,
Like Harmodius and Aristogeiton brave,
   Who, striking the tyrant down,
   Made Athens a freeman's town.

Harmodius, our darling, thou art not dead!
Thou liv'st in the isles of the blest, 'tis said,
  With Achilles first in speed,
  And Tydides Diomede.

In a wreath of myrtle I'll wear my glaive,
Like Harmodius and Aristogeiton brave,
  When the twain on Athena's day
  Did the tyrant Hipparchus slay.

For aye shall your fame in the land be told,
Harmodius and Aristogeiton bold,
  Who, striking the tyrant down,
  Made Athens a freeman's town.
      JOHN CONINGTON

SWALLOW SONG

There were many popular work songs, begging songs, ceremonial songs. The Swallow Song *was sung by children as they went from house to house.*

She is here, she is here, the swallow!
Fair seasons bringing, fair years to follow!
      Her belly is white,
      Her back black as night!
      From your rich house
      Roll forth to us
      Tarts, wine, and cheese:
      Or if not these,
      Oatmeal and barley-cake
      The swallow deigns to take.
What shall we have? or must we hence away?
Thanks, if you give: if not, we'll make you pay!
      The house-door hence we'll carry;

145

Nor shall the lintel tarry;
From hearth and home your wife we'll rob;
She is so small,
To take her off will be an easy job!
Whate'er you give, give largess free!
Up! open, open, to the swallow's call!
No grave old men, but merry children we!
        JOHN ADDINGTON SYMONDS

AESCHYLUS

It was out of choral lyric that tragedy developed, and in construction the choral odes of Aeschylus (525-456 B.C.) are very like those of Pindar, though their spirit is very different. In Suppliants, *for example, Aeschylus' earliest play, the chorus at once sets forth a view of Zeus like that of an Old Testament prophet:*

146 Secure it falls upon its feet, not upon its back,
whatever thing is decreed to fulfilment by Zeus' nod;
through thicket and shadow stretch the paths of his under-
        standing
and no speculation can spy them out.
From the high towers of their hopes he hurls men to utter
        ruin,
yet no armed violence need he array;
all that is divine is effortless.
From the holy throne where he is firmly seated,
somehow he carries his thought into deed.
        MOSES HADAS (*Suppliants* 90-104)

And later in the same play:

147 To whom of the gods could I more fitly appeal?
Thou, Lord, art our father, thine own hand has planted us,

thou art the ancient artificer of our race,
thou Zeus whose breath prospereth all things.
He sits not upon his throne 'neath another's suzerainty,
no humbler dominion does he hold 'neath a mightier power,
he honors no sovereignty of higher seat;
with him the deed is as the word,
swiftly to execute what his counselling mind brings forth.

    MOSES HADAS (*Suppliants* 590-599)

In Persians *the messenger tells how the Greek Squadron began the battle of Salamis.*

      The morn, all beauteous to behold,   **148**
Drawn by white steeds bounds o'er the enlightened earth;
At once from ev'ry Greek with glad acclaim
Burst forth the song of war, whose lofty notes
The echo of the island rocks return'd,
Spreading dismay through Persia's hosts, thus fallen
From their high hopes; no flight this solemn strain
Portended, but deliberate valour bent
On daring battle; while the trumpet's sound
Kindled the flames of war. But when their oars,
The paean ended, with impetuous force
Dash'd the resounding surges, instant all
Rush'd on in view: in orderly array
The squadron on the right first led, behind
Rode their whole fleet; and now distinct we heard
From ev'ry part this voice of exhortation:—
"Advance, ye sons of Greece, from thraldom save
Your country, save your wives, your children save,
The temples of your gods, the sacred tomb
Where rest your honour'd ancestors; this day
The common cause of all demands your valour."

    ROBERT POTTER (*Persians* 377-405)

In Seven against Thebes *the chorus upon its entry is terrified
of the approaching enemy, and in imagination sees destruc-
tion approaching ever closer.*

[I]

149

O wailing and sorrow, O wailing and woe!
Their tents they have left, many-banded they ride,
And onward they tramp with the prance of pride,
    The horsemen of the foe.
The dark-volumed dust-cloud that rides on the gale,
Though voiceless, declares a true messenger's tale;
With clattering hoofs, on and on still they ride;
It swells on my ear, loud it rusheth and roareth,
As a fierce wintry torrent precipitous poureth,
Rapidly lashing the mountain side.

Hear me ye gods, and ye goddesses hear me!
The black harm prevent that swells near and more near
    me!
As a wave on the shore when the blast beats the coast,
So breaks o'er the walls, from the white-shielded host,
The eager war-cry, the sharp cry of fear,
And near still it rolls, and more near.

*In the following A and B denote semichoruses, and AB tutti
passages.*

[II]

A To which of the gods and the goddesses now
    Shall I pay my vow?
B Shall I cling to the altar, and kneeling embrace
    The guardian gods of the Theban race?
AB Ye blissful Olympians, throned sublime,
    In the hour of need, in the urgent time,
        May the deep drawn sigh
        And the heart's strong cry
    Ascend not in vain to your seats sublime!
A Heard ye the shield's rattle, heard ye the spear?

In this dark day of dole,
  With chaplet and stole
Let us march to the temples, and worship in fear!

B I heard the shield's rattle, and spear clashed on spear
  Came stunning on my ear.

AB O Ares, that shines in the helmet of gold,
  Thine own chosen city wilt thou behold
      To slavery sold?
  O Ares, Ares, wilt thou betray
    Thy Theban home today?

[III]

Patron gods that keep the city,
Look, look down upon our woe,
Save this band of suppliant virgins
From the harsh enslaving foe!
For a rush of high-plumed warriors
Round the city of the free,
By the blast of Ares driven,
Roars like billows of the sea.
Father Jove the consummator,
Save us from the Argive spear;
For their bristling ranks enclose us,
And our hearts do quake with fear,
And their steeds with ringing bridles
Knell destruction o'er the land;
And seven chiefs, with lance in hand,
Fixed by lot to share the slaughter,
At the seventh gate proudly stand.
Save us, Pallas, war-delighting
Daughter of immortal Jove!
Save us, lord of billowy ocean!
God of pawing steeds, Poseidon,
Join thine aid to his above,
And with thy fish-piercing trident
Still our hearts, our fears remove.
Save us, Ares! father Ares,
Father now thy children's need!

Save us Cypris, mother of Thebans,
For we are thy blood indeed!
Save us, save us, Wolf-Apollo,
Be a wolf against the foe!
Whet thine arrows, born of Leto,
Leto's daughter bend thy bow!

[IV]

A   I hear the dread roll of the chariots of war!
AB   O holy Hera!
B   And the axles harsh-creaking with dissonant jar!
AB   O Artemis dear!
A   And the vext air is madded with quick-brandished spears.
B   To Thebes, our loved city, what hope now appears?
A   And when shall the gods bring an end to our fears?
B   Hark! hark! stony hail the near rampart is lashing!
AB   O blest Apollo!
A   And iron-bound shield against shield is clashing!
AB   The issue of war with the gods abideth,
The doubtful struggle great Jove decideth.
O Onca, blest Onca, whose worshippers ever
Invoke thee, the queen of the Oncan gate,
The seven-gated city deliver, deliver,
Thou guardian queen of the gate.

[V]

Gods and goddesses almighty!
Earthly and celestial powers!
Of all good things consummators,
Guardians of the Theban towers!
Save the spear-encompassed city
From a foreign-speaking foe!
Hear the virgin band, that prays thee
With the out-stretched arms of woe!
Gods and demigods! the city
Aid that on your aid depends,
Watch around us, and defend us;
He is strong whom God defends.

Bear the incense in remembrance
Of our public sacrifice;
From a people rich in offerings
Let no prayer unanswered rise!

J. S. BLACKIE (*Seven against Thebes* 77-181)

While Hephaestus and Strength were riveting Prometheus to the desolate cliff he remained silent. This is his first utterance after he has been left alone. The concluding lines herald the approach of the chorus of sea-nymphs.

O holy Æther, and swift-winged Winds,   **150**
And River-wells, and laughter innumerous
Of yon sea-waves! Earth, mother of us all,
And all-viewing cyclic Sun, I cry on you,—
Behold me a god, what I endure from gods!
   Behold, with throe on throe
   How, wasted by this woe,
I wrestle down the myriad years of time!
   Behold, how fast around me,
The new King of the happy ones sublime
Has flung the chain he forged, has shamed and bound
   me!
Woe, woe! to-day's woe and the coming morrow's
I cover with one groan. And where is found me
   A limit to these sorrows?
And yet what word do I say? I have foreknown
Clearly all things that should be; nothing done
Comes sudden to my soul; and I must bear
What is ordained with patience, being aware
Necessity doth front the universe
With an invincible gesture. Yet this curse
Which strikes me now, I find it hard to brave
In silence or in speech. Because I gave
Honour to mortals, I have yoked my soul
To this compelling fate. Because I stole
The secret fount of fire, whose bubbles went
Over the ferule's brim, and manward sent

Art's mighty means and perfect rudiment,
That sin I expiate in this agony,
Hung here in fetters, 'neath the blanching sky.
          Ah, ah me! what a sound,
What a fragrance sweeps up from a pinion unseen
Of a god, or a mortal, or nature between,
Sweeping up to this rock where the earth has her bound,
To have sight of my pangs or some guerdon obtain.
Lo, a god in the anguish, a god in the chain!
          The god, Zeus hateth sore
          And his gods hate again,
As many as tread on his glorified floor,
Because I loved mortals too much evermore.
Alas me! what a murmur and motion I hear,
          As of birds flying near!
          And the air undersings
          The light stroke of their wings—
And all life that approaches I wait for in fear.
     ELIZABETH B. BROWNING (*Prometheus* 88-127)

In Agamemnon *Clytemnestra tells how relays of beacons
from Troy brought the news of her husband's victory:*

151   From Ida fleet Hephaestus shot the spark;
          And flaming straightway leapt the courier fire
          From height to height; to Hermaean rock
          Of Lemnos, first from Ida; from the isle
          The Athoan steep of mighty Jove received
          The beaming beacon; thence the forward strength
          Of the far-travelling lamps strode gallantly
          Athwart the broad sea's back. The flaming pine
          Rayed out a golden glory like the sun,
          And winged the message to Macistus' watch-tower.
          There the wise watchman, guiltless of delay,
          Lent to the sleepless courier further speed;
          And the Messapian station hailed the torch
          Far-beaming o'er the floods of the Euripus.
          There the grey heath lit the responsive fire,

Speeding the portioned message; waxing strong,
And nothing dulled across Asopus' plain
The flame swift darted like the twinkling moon,
And on Cithaeron's rocky heights awaked
A new receiver of the wandering light.
The far-sent ray, by the faithful watch not spurned,
With bright addition journeying, bounded o'er
Gorgopus' lake and Aegiplanctus' mount,
Weaving the chain unbroken. Hence it spread
Not scant in strength, a mighty beard of flame,
Flaring across the headlands that look down
On the Saronic gulf. Speeding its march,
It reached the neighbour-station of our city,
Arachne's rocky steep; and thence the halls
Of the Atridae recognized the signal,
Light not unfathered by Idaean fire.
Such the bright train of my torch-bearing heralds,
Each from the other fired with happy news,
And last and first was victor in the race.
Such the fair tidings that my lord hath sent,
A sign that Troy hath fallen.

> J. S. BLACKIE (*Agamemnon* 281-316)

*Poignancy not usually associated with Aeschylus characterizes
these lines from* Agamemnon *describing Menelaus' loneliness
when Helen has deserted him:*

So much he mourns the queen beyond the seas
A phantom queen will walk about his hall.
No statue, though so fair, can do him ease,
Can aught but sadness to his heart recall,
For in the lovely, cold, and silent head
    The spirit of love is dead.
Sometime the shadowy mockeries of night
    Will come before his weary sight
        Bringing a false delight.
In vain his outstretched arms would keep
The fleeting shape his dreaming eyes discern.

152

The vision fades away, nor will return,
Companion of the winged path of sleep.
        J. C. WORDSWORTH (*Agamemnon* 416-426)

Aeschylus' Eumenides shows how the old law of blood for
blood has been replaced by a new rule of reason, operating
through a regularly constituted court. The Eumenides are in
the end reconciled to a new and beneficent function, but are
at first extremely loath to surrender their ancient prerogatives:

153 O ye youngster gods!
ye my statutes old
have ridden down and snatched them from my aged grasp.
And I, all-scorned, forlorn, in this my grievous spite
but murmur? nay do—what?
Let's make us—destructful—to th' folk here!
on this country, ugh!
casting grief-avenging drops! venom! venom from our heart!
a rain noisome to
this land; whence shall come
a tetter eating buds and babes, Io for Right!
darting upon this ground,
and scatter health-destroying pest-spots on the soil.
I have endured hardships immense,
'th ill-starred girls of Night, we of unseemly sorrows.
        J. F. DAVIES (*Eumenides* 759-774)

Athena attempts to soothe them, but they continue:

154 Me, me suffer this!
bah!
me with the thoughts of eld!
o'er earth vainly roam!
bah!
a scorned hateful thing!
I breathe furious rage,
and each form of spite.
Oy, oy, da, bah!

what is this smart that creeps under my ribs? O mark
my wrath, mother, O
Night! for the rude-of-hand tricks of the gods have reft
me of my ancient rights, setting me down for naught.

   J. F. DAVIES (*Eumenides* 787-799)

*The epitaph which Aeschylus wrote for himself is remarkable
in that it refers to his soldiery but says nothing of his poetry:*

Athenian Aeschylus, Euphorion's son,   **155**
  In fertile Gela lies, beneath this stone.
His might the sacred grove of Marathon
  Has witnessed, and the deep-tressed Mede has known.

   HUGH MACNAGHTEN

SOPHOCLES

*In Sophocles (496-406) the choral odes tend to be more or-
thodox, the speeches of the heroes more intense. The latter
quality is illustrated in Ajax' solitary farewell before plung-
ing his sword into his body, in Ajax.*

Thou that makest high heaven thy chariot course,   **156**
O Sun, when gazing on my fatherland,
Draw back thy golden rein, and tell my woes
To the old man, my father, and to her
Who nursed me at her bosom,—my poor mother!
There will be wailing through the echoing walls
When—but away with thoughts like these! the hour
Brings on the ripening deed. Death, death! look on me—
Did I say Death? —it was a waste of words;
We shall be friends hereafter.
                      'Tis the Day,
Present and breathing round me, and the car
Of the sweet sun, that never shall again

Receive my greeting! —Henceforth time is sunless,
And day a thing that is not! Beautiful Light,
My Salamis—my country, and the floor
Of my dear household-hearth; and thou, bright Athens,
Thou—for thy sons and I were boys together—
Fountains and rivers, and ye Trojan plains,
I loved you as my fosterers—fare ye well!
Take, in these words, the last earth hears from Ajax.
All else unspoken; in a spectre-land
I'll whisper to the dead.

    E. BULWER-LYTTON (*Ajax* 845-865)

When, in Sophocles' play named for her, Antigone demon-
strates her readiness to suffer immolation for her conviction,
the chorus is moved to sing the wonders of man:

157

Many the forms of life,
Wondrous and strange to see,
But nought than man appears
More wondrous and more strange.
He, with the wintry gales,
O'er the white foaming sea,
'Mid wild waves surging round,
Wendeth his way across:
Earth, of all Gods, from ancient days the first,
Unworn and undecayed.
He, with his ploughs that travel o'er and o'er,
Furrowing with horse and mule,
Wears ever year by year.

The thoughtless tribe of birds,
The beasts that roam the fields,
The brood in sea-depths born,
He takes them all in nets
Knotted in snaring mesh,
Man, wonderful in skill.
And by his subtle arts
He holds in sway the beasts

That roam the fields, or tread the mountain's height;
  And brings the binding yoke
Upon the neck of horse with shaggy mane,
    Or bull on mountain crest,
    Untamable in strength.

And speech, and thought as swift as wind,
And tempered mood for higher life of states,
    These he has learnt, and how to flee
    Or the clear cold of frost unkind,
    Or darts of storm and shower,
Man all-providing. Unprovided, he
Meeteth no chance the coming days may bring;
    Only from Hades, still
    He fails to find escape,
Though skill of art may teach him how to flee
From depths of fell disease incurable.

So, gifted with a wondrous might,
Above all fancy's dreams, with skill to plan,
    Now unto evil, now to good,
    He turns. While holding fast the laws,
    His country's sacred rights,
That rest upon the oath of Gods on high,
High in the State: an outlaw from the State,
    When loving, in his pride,
    The thing that is not good;
Ne'er may he share my hearth, nor yet my thoughts,
Who worketh deeds of evil like to this.

  E. H. PLUMPTRE (*Antigone* 332-374)

*And when, in the same play, Haemon displays his readiness
to give all for love, the chorus sings the first ode to love in
Greek:*

O Love, in every battle victor owned;   **158**
    Love, rushing on thy prey,
  Now on a maiden's soft and blooming cheek,

In secret ambush hid;
Now o'er the broad sea wandering at will,
    And now in shepherd's folds;
Of all the Undying Ones none 'scape from thee,
    Nor yet of mortal men
Whose lives are measured as a fleeting day;
And who has thee is frenzied in his soul.

Thou makest vile the purpose of the just,
    To his own fatal harm;
Thou hast stirred up this fierce and deadly strife,
    Of men of nearest kin;
The charm of eyes of bride beloved and fair
    Is crowned with victory,
And dwells on high among the powers that rule,
    Equal with holiest laws;
For Aphrodite, she whom none subdues,
Sports in her might and majesty divine.
    E. H. PLUMPTRE (*Antigone* 781-805)

The account of the imaginary chariot race in Electra *is a
stirring bit of sports-reporting:*

159   They took their stand where the appointed judges
Had cast their lots and ranged their rival cars.
Rang out the brazen trump! Away they bound,
Cheer the hot steeds and shake the slackened reins;
As with a body the large space is filled
With the huge clangor of the rattling cars.
High whirl aloft the dust-clouds; blent together,
Each presses each and the lash rings; and loud
Snort the wild steeds, and from their fiery breath,
Along their manes and down the circling wheels
Scatter the flaking foam. Orestes still—
Aye, as he swept around the perilous pillar
Last in the course, wheeled in the rushing axle;
The left rein curbed,—that on the dexter hand

Flung loose. —So on erect the chariots rolled!
Sudden the Aenian's fierce and headlong steeds
Broke from the bit—and, as the seventh time now
The course was circled, on the Libyan car
Dashed their wild fronts: then order changed to ruin:
Car crashed on car; the wide Crissaean plain
Was sea-like strewed with wrecks; the Athenian saw,
Slackened his speed, and wheeling round the marge,
Unscathed and skillful, in the midmost space,
Left the wild tumult of that tossing storm.
Behind, Orestes, hitherto the last,
Had yet kept back his coursers for the close;
Now one sole rival left—on, on he flew,
And the sharp sound of the impelling scourge
Rang in the keen ears of the flying steeds.
He nears, he reaches—they are side by side—
Now one—the other—by a length the victor.
The courses all are past—the wheels erect—
All safe—when, as the hurrying coursers round
The fatal pillar dashed, the wretched boy
Slackened the left rein: on the column's edge
Crashed the frail axle: headlong from the car
Caught and all meshed within the reins, he fell;
And masterless the mad steeds raged along!
Loud from that mighty multitude arose
A shriek—a shout! But yesterday such deeds,
Today such doom! Now whirled upon the earth,
Now his limbs dashed aloft, they dragged him—those
Wild horses—till all gory from the wheels
Released; —and no man, not his nearest friends,
Could in that mangled corpse have traced Orestes.
They laid the body on the funeral pyre;
And while we speak, the Phocian strangers bear,
In a small, brazen, melancholy urn,
That handful of cold ashes to which all
The grandeur of the Beautiful hath shrunk.

    E. BULWER-LYTTON (*Electra* 709-763)

The first choral ode of Oedipus the King, *filled with anguish and foreboding and supplication, sets the psychologic mood for what follows.*

160 Lord of the Pythian treasure,
                 What meaneth the word thou hast spoken?
                    The strange and wondrous word
                       Which Thebes hath heard,
Oh! it hath shaken our hearts to a faltering measure.
           A token, O Paian, a token!
                 What is thy boon to us?
                 Shall it come soon to us,
        Shall it be long ere the circle bend
           Full round to the fatal end?
                 Answer us, daughter of Hope!
                    Voice born immortal of golden Hope!

First therefore thou be entreated,
                 Divine unapproachable maiden,
        And Artemis with thee, our aid to be,
In the mid mart of our city majestical seated,
                 And Phoibos the archer death-laden!
                    By your affinity
                    Helpfullest trinity,
           Help us! And as in the time gone by
              Ye have bowed to our plaintive cry,
                 Bowed to our misery sore:
                 So come to us now as ye came before!

Ah me! it is a world, a world of woe,
Plague upon the height and plague below!
        And they mow us with murderous glaive,
        And never a shield to save!
Never a fruit of the earth
                 Comes to the birth,
                 And in vain, in vain
Is the cry and the labour of mothers, and all for a fruitless
                 pain!

Away, away,
Ghost upon ghost they are wafted away:
 One with another they die,
 Swifter than flame do they fly
  From life, from light, from day!

Ah me! it is a world, a world of dead,
Feverous and foul with corpses spread:
 And they lie as they lie, unbefriended.
Where are the mothers and where are the wives?
 They are fled, fled for their lives
  To the altars to pray
There to lie, to sigh
 And to pray, and to pray unattended,
  With choir and cry
Lamentation and litany blended.
And only, O Maiden, by thee may our marred state be
   mended!

The field of plague, whose swordless hand
Burns like battle thro the land
 With wild tempestuous wailing all about him—
O cross his track and turn him back!
 O meet him, thou, and rout him!
  Let him sink again
   Deep in the deepest main!
 Let him mingle in horrible motion
  With the wildest ocean!
(For still what scapes the cruel night
Cruel day destroys it quite!)
  But oh! with thunder-stroke
  Let our enemy and thine be broke—
   O Zeus!—
Father!—let him know thy wrath, thy wrath divine!

  O God of light, from lightsome bow
Cast abroad thy fiery snow,
Like morsels cast thy arrowy, fiery snow!

And thou, O mountain maiden pure
His sister, stand our champion sure,
   Stand and strow
    Arrows as fire below!
Thou too—thou art Theban— O Bacchos
Thou— art thou not Theban?— O Bacchos
  In rosy bloom, elate and strong,
  Lead thy madding train along,
    Until thy fiery chase
Hunt the demon from the place,
    Afar, afar!
O follow, follow him far, afar!
  A. W. VERRALL (*Oedipus the King* 151-215)

When, in Philoctetes, *the crippled and marooned hero finds that he has been cheated of his divine bow and his hopes of home-coming by the seemingly ingenuous Neoptolemus, he gives vent to passion and despair:*

161 Thou fire, thou utter monster, thou hateful masterpiece of subtle villainy,—how hast thou dealt with me,—how hast thou deceived me! And thou art not ashamed to look upon me, thou wretch, the suppliant who turned to thee for pity? In taking my bow, thou hast despoiled me of my life. Restore it, I beseech thee,—restore it, I implore thee, my son! By the gods of thy fathers, do not rob me of my life! Ah me! No—he speaks to me no more; he looks away,—he will not give it up!

O ye creeks and headlands, O ye wild creatures of the hills with whom I dwell, O ye steep cliffs! to—for to whom else can I speak?—to you, my wonted listeners, I bewail my treatment by the son of Achilles: he swore to convey me home,—to Troy he carries me: he clinched his word with the pledge of his right hand,—yet hath he taken my bow,—the sacred bow, once borne by Heracles son of Zeus,—and keeps it, and would fain show it to the Argives as his own.

He drags me away, as if he had captured a strong man,—and sees not that he is slaying a corpse, the shadow of a vapour, a mere phantom. In my strength he would not have taken me,—no, nor as I am, save by guile. But now I have been tricked, unhappy that I am. What shall I do? Nay, give it back,—return, even now, to thy true self! What sayest thou? Silent? Woe is me, I am lost!

Ah, thou cave with two-fold entrance, familiar to mine eyes, once more must I return to thee,—but disarmed, and without the means to live. Yes, in yon chamber my lonely life shall fade away; no winged bird, no beast that roams the hills shall I slay with yonder bow; rather I myself, wretched one, shall make a feast for those who fed me, and become a prey to those on whom I preyed; alas, I shall render my life-blood for the blood which I have shed,—the victim of a man who seemed innocent of evil!

R. C. JEBB (*Philoctetes* 927-960)

When Oedipus, old now as well as blind, asks the chorus what place he has reached, they reply:

> To a land rich in goodly horses
> hast thou come at length:
> no fairer resting-place
> doth the wide earth know
> than white Colonus.
> Here dwelleth ever the clear-voiced nightingale
> and uttereth her song
> in the green-brak'd thickness
> of the glades;
> wine-dark is the ivy
> of her haunts
> and untrodden is the god's green bower,
> rich in gleaming fruits,
> unscourg'd by sun,
> unswept by any storm.
>
> And here flourisheth
> amid the dew of heaven
> the fair-clustering narcissus-flower

162

through all its days,
a goodly crown divine;
here, too, doth bloom the crocus,
golden-ray'd.

Nor do the ever-wakeful fountains,
whence flow the waters of Cephisus,
cease from their task;
but ever and unceasingly
doth the stream
o'er earth's rich bosom
pursue unsullied paths,
swift to bring increase.
Neither have the Muses
in their choric dance
shunned this fair resting-place,
nor yet the goddess of the golden rein.
    H. N. COUCH (*Oedipus at Colonus* 668-694)

*Besides seven complete plays a number of fragments of
Sophocles have been preserved; selections from* Aletes, Lovers
of Achilles, Colchian Women, *and* Tereus *follow:*

163   Hard it is that impious men, of base forebears
sprung, should yet prosper and flourish,
while those that are good and of good men
descended, should labor ill-starred.
Nay, mortals should not by heaven
so be treated; to the pious among men
should some manifest advantage from the gods
descend, and to their opposites the wicked
condign punishment for their wickedness.
So should none proven base prosper and flourish.
    MOSES HADAS

164   Bitter-sweet is the ailment called love.
Not unfairly might I give it this similitude:

when shining frost has fallen, and boys
with both hands grasp its crystal firmness,
delightful at first is the pleasure they take;
but then it melts, and they cannot let go,
nor avail to retain the treasure in their hands.
Just so the same yearning drives your lover,
drives him to act, not to act, over and again.

    MOSES HADAS

Girls, look you, Kupris is not Kupris only: **165**
In her one name names manifold are blended;
For she is Death, imperishable power,
Frenetic fury, irresistible longing,
Wailing and groaning. Her one force includes
All energy, all languor, and all violence.
Into the vitals of whatever thing
Hath breath of life, she sinks. Who feeds her not?
She creeps into the fishes of the sea
And the four-footed creatures of dry land,
Shakes 'mid the birds her own aerial plumes,
Sways beasts and mortal men and gods above.
Which of the gods hath she not thrown in wrestling?
If right allows, and to speak truth is right,
She rules the heart of Zeus. Without or spear
Or sword, I therefore bid you know, Dame Kupris
Fells at a blow of gods and men the counsels.

    JOHN ADDINGTON SYMONDS

Now am I nought—abandoned: oftentimes   **166**
I've noticed how to this we women fall,
How we are nought. In girlhood and at home
Our life's the sweetest life men ever know,
For careless joy is a glad nurse to all:
But when we come to youth, gleeful and gay,
Forth are we thrust, and bought and sold and bartered,
Far from our household gods, from parents far;
Some to strange husbands, to barbarians some,
To homes uncouth, to homes foul with shame.

Yea, let but one night yoke us, all these things
Must needs forthwith be praised and held for fair.
    JOHN ADDINGTON SYMONDS

EURIPIDES

*In Euripides (480-406 B.C.), though the characters still bear
the heroic names of legend, they tend to be recognizable as
contemporary types; and the choral odes tend to be detach-
able interludes. In the selection from* Alcestis *given below,
for example, the speaker Heracles had been drinking. Adme-
tus' courtesy had forbidden him to tell his guest that he was
in mourning for Alcestis. Now Heracles reproaches the butler
for his sad expression:*

167   Why look'st so solemn and so thought-absorbed?
        To guests a servant should not sour-faced be,
        But do the honors with a mind urbane.
        While thou, contráriwise, beholding here
        Arrive thy master's comrade, hast for him
        A churlish visage, all one beetle-brow—
        Having regard to grief that's out-of-door!
        Come hither, and so get to grow more wise!
        Things mortal—know'st the nature that they have?
        No, I imagine! whence could knowledge spring?
        Give ear to me, then! For all flesh to die,
        Is nature's due; nor is there any one
        Of mortals with assurance he shall last
        The coming morrow: for, what's born of chance
        Invisibly proceeds the way it will,
        Not to be learned, no fortune-teller's prize.
        This, therefore, having heard and known through me,
        Gladden thyself! Drink! Count the day-by-day
        Existence thine, and all the other—chance!
        Ay, and pay homage also to by far

The sweetest of divinities for man,
Kupris! Benignant Goddess will she prove!
But as for aught else, leave and let things be!
And trust my counsel, if I seem to speak
To purpose—as I do, apparently.
Wilt not thou, then,—discarding overmuch
Mournfulness, do away with this shut door,
Come drink along with me, be-garlanded
This fashion? Do so, and—I well know what—
From this stern mood, this shrunk-up state of mind,
The pit-pat fall o' the flagon-juice down throat
Soon will dislodge thee from bad harborage!
Men being mortal should think mortal-like:
Since to your solemn, brow-contracting sort,
All of them,—so I lay down law at least,—
Life is not truly life but misery.
        ROBERT BROWNING (*Alcestis* 779-802)

*When he discovers the facts Heracles determines to reward
Admetus by recovering Alcestis from the dead:*

O much-enduring heart and hand of mine!   **168**
Now show what sort of son she bore to Zeus,
That daughter of Elektruon, Tiruns' child,
Alkmené! for that son must needs save now
The just-dead lady: ay, establish here
I' the house again Alkestis, bring about
Comfort and succor to Admetos so!
I will go lie in wait for Death, black-stoled
King of the corpses! I shall find him, sure,
Drinking, beside the tomb, o' the sacrifice:
And if I lie in ambuscade, and leap
Out of my lair, and seize—encircle him
Till one hand join the other round about—
There lives not who shall pull him out from me,
Rib-mauled, before he let the woman go!
But even say I miss the booty,—say,
Death comes not to the boltered blood,—why then,

Down go I, to the unsunned dwelling-place
Of Koré and the king there,—make demand,
Confident I shall bring Alkestis back,
So as to put her in the hands of him
My host, that housed me, never drove me off:
Though stricken with sore sorrow, hid the stroke,
Being a noble heart and honoring me!
Who of Thessalians, more than this man, loves
The stranger? Who, that now inhabits Greece?
Wherefore he shall not say the man was vile
Whom he befriended,—native noble heart!
ROBERT BROWNING (*Alcestis* 837-860)

Medea (in Medea) reproaches Jason for his ingratitude:

169 Rotten, heart-rotten, that is the word for you.
Words, words, magnificent words. In reality a craven.
You come to me, you come, my worst enemy!
It's not bravery, you know, not valor, to face your victims.
No! It's humanity's ugliest sore, Shamelessness.
But thank you for coming. To tell your wickedness
will disburden my heart, and you 'twill hurt to hear.
This is the sum of my tale: I saved you, saved your life!
MOSES HADAS and J. H. MCLEAN (*Medea* 465-476)

After Aegeus has promised Medea eventual asylum in Athens,
the chorus sings the praise of that city:

170 Of old are Erechtheus' folk favored of heaven.
Children of the blessed are they,
sprung of hallowed land trodden of no foeman's foot.
Their food is glorious wisdom. Their skies
are always clear, and lightly do they walk
a land where on a time fair Harmony
nine chaste daughters bore, the Muses of Pieria.
Aphrodite, 'tis told, once quickened that land
with sprinklings from fair Cephissus, and breathed over it
breezes soft and fragrant.

With roses sweet-smelling is her hair ever wreathed;
ever she sends the Loves to assist at Wisdom's court.
Without their help is no good thing wrought.

MOSES HADAS and J. H. McLEAN (*Medea* 824-845)

After the chorus of Hippolytus *has heard Phaedra's confession, it hymns the power of love.*

Love distills desire upon the eyes,
love brings bewitching grace into the heart
of those he would destroy.
I pray that love may never come to me
with murderous intent,
in rhythms measureless and wild.
Not fire nor stars have stronger bolts
than those of Aphrodite sent
by the hand of Eros, Zeus' child.

In vain by Alpheus' stream,
in vain in the halls of Phoebus' Pythian shrine
the land of Greece increases sacrifice.
But Love the King of Men they honour not,
although he keeps the keys
of the temple of desire,
although he goes destroying through the world
author of dread calamities
and ruin when he enters human hearts.

The Oechalian maiden who had never known
the bed of love, known neither man nor marriage
the Goddess Cypris gave to Heracles.
She took her from the home of Eurytus,
maiden unhappy in her marriage song,
wild as a Naiad or a Bacchanal,
with blood and fire, a murderous hymenaeal!

O holy walls of Thebes and Dirce's fountain
bear witness you, to Love's grim journeying:

171

once you saw Love bring Semele to bed,
lull her to sleep, clasped in the arms of Death,
pregnant with Dionysus by the thunder king.
Love is like a flitting bee in the world's garden
and for its flowers, destruction is in his breath.

    DAVID GRENE (*Hippolytus* 525-564)

*Later in the same play, the chorus wishes to leave all human
troubles behind and fly away.*

172 Would that I were under the cliffs, in the secret hiding-places
          of the rocks,
that Zeus might change me to a winged bird
and set me among the feathered flocks.
I would rise and fly to where the sea
washes the Adriatic coast,
and to the waters of Eridanus.
Into that deep-blue tide,
where their father, the Sun, goes down,
the unhappy maidens weep
tears from their amber-gleaming eyes
in pity for Phaethon.

I would win my way to the coast,
apple-bearing Hesperian coast,
of which the minstrels sing.
Where the Lord of the Ocean
denies the voyager further sailing,
and fixes the solemn limit of Heaven
which Giant Atlas upholds.
There the streams flow with ambrosia
by Zeus' bed of love,
and holy earth, the giver of life,
yields to the Gods rich blessedness.

O Cretan ship with the white sails,
from a happy home you brought her,
my mistress over the tossing foam, over the salty sea,

to bless her with a marriage unblest.
Black was the omen that sped her here,
black was the omen for both her lands,
for glorious Athens and her Cretan home,
as they bound to Munychia's pier
the cables' ends with their twisted strands
and stepped ashore on the continent.

The presage of the omen was true;
Aphrodite has broken her spirit
with the terrible sickness of impious love.
The waves of destruction are over her head,
from the roof of her room with its marriage bed,
she is tying the twisted noose.
And now it is around her fair white neck!
The shame of her cruel fate has conquered.
She has chosen good name rather than life:
she is easing her heart of its bitter load of love.

    DAVID GRENE (*Hippolytus* 732-775)

Andromache *is a war play, filled with contempt of Sparta and
its ways. Here Andromache upbraids Menelaus:*

O ye inhabitants of Sparta, the whole human race loathes **173**
you. Your counsels are full of treachery. Masters of the lie
you are, ever planning wickedness. Your minds are crooked,
hypocritical, always devious. Justice is thwarted by your suc-
cesses in Greece. What crimes are not found among you?
Where does murder thrive more? Or sordid greed? Are you
not always found saying one thing and thinking another? My
curse on you! For me this death sentence is not so hard as you
expect. I died long ago, on that day when the hapless city of
the Phrygians was destroyed and my noble husband, whose
spear often drove you to your ship, making a craven sailor
out of a craven soldier. Now it is to a woman that the war-
rior shows his grim face. You will slay me. Then slay. With
no flatteries on my tongue I will take leave of you and your
daughter. You are great in Sparta. Well, I was great in Troy.

If I am now in misery, don't you gloat; you too may some
day fare likewise.

     MOSES HADAS and J. H. McLEAN (*Andromache* 445-464)

In Hecuba *the ghost of Achilles has demanded the sacrifice of*
Polyxena; this is the herald's description of the horror.

174   The whole vast concourse of the Achaean host
Stood round the tomb to see your daughter die.
Achilleus' son taking her by the hand,
Placed her upon the mound, and I stayed near;
And youths, the flower of Greece, a chosen few,
With hands to check thy heifer, should she bound,
Attended. From a cup of carven gold,
Raised full of wine, Achilleus' son poured forth
Libation to his sire, and bade me sound
Silence throughout the whole Achaean host.
I, standing there, cried in the midst these words:
    "Silence, Achaians! let the host be still!
Hush, hold your voices!" Breathless stayed the crowd;
But he: "O son of Peleus, father mine,
Take these libations pleasant to thy soul,
Draughts that allure the dead: come, drink the black
Pure maiden's blood wherewith the host and I
Sue thee: be kindly to us, loose our prows,
And let our barks go free: give safe return
Homeward from Troy to all, and happy voyage."
Such words he spake, and the crowd prayed assent.
Then from the scabbard, by its golden hilt,
He drew the sword, and to the chosen youths
Signaled that they should bring the maid; but she,
Knowing her hour was come, spake thus and said:
    "O men of Argos, who have sacked my town,
Lo, of free will I die! let no man touch
My body: boldly will I stretch my throat.
Nay, but I pray you set me free, then slay;
That free I thus may perish: 'mong the dead,
Being a queen, I blush to be called slave."

The people shouted, and King Agamemnon
Bade the youths loose the maid and set her free:
She, when she heard the order of the chiefs,
Seizing her mantle, from the shoulder down
To the soft centre of her snowy waist
Tore it, and showed her breasts and bosom fair
As in a statue. Bending then with knee
On earth, she spake a speech most piteous:
   "See you this breast, O youth? if breast you will,
Strike it; take heart: or if beneath my neck,
Lo! here my throat is ready for your sword!"
He willing not, yet willing, pity-stirred
In sorrow for the maiden, with his blade
Severed the channels of her breath: blood flowed;
And she, though dying, still had thought to fall
In seemly wise, hiding what eyes should see not.
But when she breathed her life out from the blow,
Then was the Argive host in divers ways
Of service parted; for some, bringing leaves,
Strewed them upon the corpse; some piled a pyre,
Dragging pine trunks and boughs; and he who bore none,
Heard from the bearers many a bitter word:
   "Standest thou, villain? Has thou then no robe,
No funeral honors for the maid to bring?
Wilt thou not go and get for her who died
Most nobly, bravest-souled, some gift?" Thus they
Spake of thy child in death, O thou most blest
Of women in thy daughter, most undone!
     JOHN ADDINGTON SYMONDS (*Hecuba* 521-582)

In Hercules *the chorus of Thebans sing the labors of Heracles:*

Even a dirge, can Phoibos suit

175

In song to music jubilant
For all its sorrow: making shoot
His golden plectron o'er the lute,
Melodious ministrant.
And I, too, am of mind to raise,

Despite the imminence of doom,
A song of joy, outpour my praise
To him—what is it rumor says?—
Whether—now buried in the ghostly gloom
Below ground—he was child of Zeus indeed,
Or mere Amphitruon's mortal seed—
To him I weave the wreath of song, his labor's meed.
For, is my hero perished in the feat?
The virtues of brave toils, in death complete,
These save the dead in song,—their glory-garland meet!

First, then, he made the wood
Of Zeus a solitude,
Slaying its lion-tenant; and he spread
The tawniness behind—his yellow head
Enmuffled by the brute's, backed by that grin of dread.
The mountain-roving savage Kentaur-race
He strewed with deadly bow about their place,
Slaying with winged shafts: Peneios knew,
Beauteously-eddying, and the long tracts too
Of pasture trampled fruitless, and as well
Those desolated haunts Mount Pelion under,
And, grassy up to Homolé, each dell
Whence, having filled their hands with pine-tree plunder,
Horse-like was wont to prance from, and subdue
The land of Thessaly, that bestial crew.
The golden-headed spot-backed stag he slew,
That robber of the rustics: glorified
Therewith the goddess who in hunter's pride
Slaughters the game along Oinoé's side.
And, yoked abreast, he brought the chariot-breed
To pace submissive to the bit, each steed
That in the bloody cribs of Diomede
Champed and, unbridled, hurried down that gore
For grain, exultant the dread feast before—
Of man's flesh: hideous feeders they of yore!
All as he crossed the Hebros' silver-flow
Accomplished he such labor, toiling so

For Mukenaian tyrant; ay, and more—
He crossed the Melian shore
And, by the sources of Amauros, shot
To death that strangers'-pest
Kuknos, who dwelt in Amphanaia: not
Of fame for good to guest!

And next, to the melodious maids he came,
Inside the Hesperian court-yard: hand must aim
At plucking gold fruit from the appled leaves,
Now he had killed the dragon, backed like flame,
Who guards the unapproachable he weaves
Himself all round, one spire about the same.
And into those sea-troughs of ocean dived
The hero, and for mortals calm contrived,
Whatever oars should follow in his wake.
And under heaven's mid-seat his hands thrust he,
At home with Atlas: and, for valor's sake,
Held the gods up their star-faced mansionry.
Also, the rider-host of Amazons
About Maiotis many-streamed, he went
To conquer through the billowy Euxine once,
Having collected what an armament
Of friends from Hellas, all on conquest bent
Of that gold-garnished cloak, dread girdle-chase!
So Hellas gained the girl's barbarian grace
And at Mukenai saves the trophy still—
Go wonder there, who will!

And the ten thousand headed hound
Of many a murder, the Lernaian snake
He burned out, head by head, and cast around
His darts a poison thence,—darts soon to slake
Their rage in that three-bodied herdsman's gore
Of Erutheia. Many a running more
He made for triumph and felicity,
And, last of toils, to Haides, never dry
Of tears, he sailed: and there he, luckless, ends

His life completely, nor returns again.
The house and home are desolate of friends,
And where the children's life-path leads them, plain
I see,—no step retraceable, no god
Availing, and no law to help the lost!
The oar of Charon marks their period,
Waits to end all. Thy hands, these roofs accost!—
To thee, though absent, look their uttermost!

But if in youth and strength I flourished still,
Still shook the spear in fight, did power match will
In these Kadmeian co-mates of my age,
They would,—and I,—when warfare was to wage,
Stand by these children; but I am bereft
Of youth now, lone of that good genius left!

But hist, desist! for here come these,—
Draped as the dead go, under and over,—

Children long since—now hard to discover—
Of the once so potent Herakles!
And the loved wife dragging, in one tether
About her feet, the boys together;
And the hero's aged sire comes last!
Unhappy that I am! Of tears which rise,—
How am I all unable to hold fast,
Longer, the aged fountains of these eyes!

    ROBERT BROWNING (*Hercules* 348-450)

In Ion *Creusa thinks that Apollo ravished and then forsook her. This is her reproach to the god:*

176 You that make music from the seven voices of the lyre,
    drawing from the lifeless horns of oxen strains of lovely
        music—
  yours is the reproach, son of Leto,
  that I will publish to the bright light of day.
  You came to me with the sunlight in your golden hair

when I was gathering the yellow flowers in the folds of my
    robe,
the flowers that shone like golden suns.
You caught the white wrists of my hands
and drew me screaming "Mother, Mother" to the bed in that
    cave.
Divine seducer, you drew me there,
and shamelessly you worked the pleasure of Cypris.
And I bore you a son—O misery!
And in fear of my mother I cast him upon your bed,
upon the cruel couch where cruelly you ravished me,
me the hapless girl.
Woe is me, woe!
And now my boy is gone,
fowls of the air have torn and devoured him,
my boy—and yours, cruel god.
But you only play your lyre and sing songs of triumph!
    Ho, son of Leto, you I call,
You who sit on your throne of gold
and give holy answers from earth's center:
I will shout a word into your ear.
Vile seducer!
To my husband who has done you no kindness,
you have given a son and heir;
but my child, yes and yours (where is your heart?)
is gone, the prey of the birds,
reft from his mother's swaddling clothes.
Delos hates you, the young laurels hate you,
beside the soft leaved palm,
where Leto bore you in a holy birth
by the seed of Zeus.

    Moses Hadas and J. H. McLean (*Ion* 881-922)

*Her true plight gives a macabre quality to mad Cassandra's
wedding song in* Trojan Women:

> Lift your foot high in the dance.   **177**
> Joy, oh joy! for my father's happiest fortunes.

Sacred is the dance. Lead us now, Apollo.
I sacrifice to you in the grove of bay trees.
Hymen, O Hymenaeus, Hymen.
Dance, mother, and laugh;
Wind your feet with mine in the dance beloved.
Call on the marriage god
In happiest song, on the bride.
Come, women of Phrygia in your beautiful robes
Sing of my marriage and the bridegroom
Fated to my bed.

    G. M. A. GRUBE (*Trojan Women* 325-440)

In Iphigenia among the Taurians *the chorus of Greek women held captive in a barbarian land sings wistfully of Greece and the homeward voyage.*

178   Halcyon, that from the wave-swept reef
Sendest thy notes of sorrow and lonely yearning,
    Well understood of hearts discerning
That hear therein thy endless song of grief
    Over thy long-lost mate,
A wingless halcyon here laments her fate
    In notes too like to thine,
Longing for Greece and kindly Artemis
Whose dwelling on the shore of Cythnus is,
    Where palm-trees wave their fine
And delicate fans, and high the laurel springs
    And the god-given olive grey,
So dear to Leto, when she bore her daughter
    There where the round lake's whirling water
Hears how the swan, the Muses' follower, sings
    His clear, melodious lay.

    O bitter memory of my tears
That day my city fell before the invader,
    When the dark galley of the raider
Bore me afar amid the thronging spears
    And sweep of many an oar.

Here was I sold, on this wild, alien shore,
    And here my lot ordained,
To wait on royal Agamemnon's child,
Who serves thy altars, Huntress of the wild,
    With human slaughter stained,
Envying the life that no delight has known;
    For easier grows familiar grief.
It is the change that fills our hearts with sadness;
    To live awhile in joy and gladness
And then to taste of sorrow, that alone
    Is sorrow past relief.

    But thee, lady, the Argive ship
    Soon will bear thee to thy home,
And the whistling reed of the mountain Pan
Will put good speed in the rhythmic dip
    Of the fifty oars in the foam.
And Phœbus, revealer of truth to man,
With heavenly voice and magic touch of hand
    Upon the seven-toned shell
Will bring thee safely to the shining land
    Wherein the Athenians dwell.
Me thou wilt leave here, condemned to stay
    While thy swift oars toss up the spray.
The wind blows fair and the sheets even now
Are stretching the sail to the galley's prow
    That carries thee away.

    Might I follow that path divine
    Where the Sun-god rides in light
And wing my way home o'er the sundering main
And on the chambers that once were mine
    Descend from my weary flight.
    Would I might come to the dance again
When to the music of the marriage song
    I left my mother's side
And joined my young companions 'mid the throng
    In rhythmic steps allied,

And rivalled my fellows in the race
Of comely movement, youthful grace,
In rich array of embroidery rare
And in the delicate wealth of hair
    That shadowed o'er my face.
        J. C. WORDSWORTH
        (*Iphigenia among the Taurians* 1089-1150)

Helen *turns on the story that it was only a wraith that was
taken to Troy, while Helen herself was safe in Egypt. Here
the chorus prays for her happy voyage home.*

179   Fair be thy speed, Sidonian ship!
Thine oars, familiar to the oarsman's grip,
    Fall fast, and make the surges bound,
    And lead along the dolphin train,
        While all around
    The winds forego to vex the main,
        And the mariners hear
    The sea-king's daughter calling clear,
"Now, sails to the breeze, fling out, fling out,
Now pull, strong arms, to the cheering shout;
Speed royal Helen, away and away,
To Argos home, to the royal bay."

What sacred hour, when festal tide
Shall bring fair Helen to Eurotas' side?
    Say, shall the Spartan maidens dance
    Before Leucippis then? Or meet
        That day perchance
    At Pallas' gate? Or shall they greet
        Thee, lost so long,
    With lost Hyacinthus' nightly song,
How Phoebus slew him with a quoit far-flown,
And yearly the maidens with mourning atone?
There is one of them, Helen, one fair of the fair,
Who will not be wife till her mother be there!

O for wings to fly
Where the flocks of fowl together
Quit the Afric sky,
Late their refuge from the wintry weather!
All the way with solemn sound
Rings the leader's clarion cry
O'er dewless deserts and glad harvest-ground.
We would bid them as they go,
Neck by neck against the cloud
Racing nightly neath the stars,
When Eurotas rolls below,
Light and leave a message loud,
How princely Menelaus, proud
With conquest, cometh from the Dardan wars.

Come, eternal Pair,
Come, Twin Brethren, from your heaven ascended;
Down the steep of air
Drive, by many a starry glance attended!
Mid the waters white and blue,
Mid the rolling waves be there,
And brotherly bring safe your sister through.
Airs from heaven, serene and pure,
Breathe upon her; bless and speed;
Breathe away her cruel shame!
Never her did Paris lure,
Never won her (as they rede)
Of Aphrodite for his meed,
Nor thither led, where never yet she came!
A. W. VERRALL (*Helen* 1451-1511)

Orestes *opens with the hero lying sick and his sister Electra
tending him. The chorus comes to inquire about his health.*

ELECTRA: O dearest maidens, tread with feet of wool;   **180**
Come softly, make no rustling, raise no cry:
For though your kindness be right dear to me,
Yet to wake him will work me double mischief.

CHORUS: Softly, softly! let your tread
    Fall upon the ground like snow!
    Every sound be dumb and dead:
    Breathe and speak in murmurs low!

ELECTRA: Further from the couch, I pray you; further yet,
    and yet away!

CHORUS: Even so, dear maid, you see that I obey.

ELECTRA: Ah, my friend, speak softly, slowly,
    Like the sighing of a rush.

CHORUS: See I speak and answer lowly
    With a stealthy smothered hush.

ELECTRA: That is right: come hither now; come boldly for-
    ward to my side;
    Come, and say what need hath brought you: for at
    length with watching tried,
    Lo, he sleeps, and on the pillow spreads his limbs and
    tresses wide.

CHORUS: How is he? dear lady, say:
    Let us hear your tale and know
    Whether you have joy today,
    Whether sorrow brings you low.

ELECTRA: He is breathing still, but slightly groaning in his
    sleep alway.

CHORUS: Oh, poor man! but tell us plainer what you say.

ELECTRA: Hush! or you will scare the pleasant
    Sleep that to his eyelid brings
    Brief oblivion of the present.

CHORUS: Ah, thrice wretched race that springs
    Burdened with the god-sent curses of abhorred deeds.

ELECTRA: Ah, me!
    Guilty was the voice of Phoebus, when enthroned for
    prophecy,

He decreed my mother's murder—mother murdered
    guiltily!

CHORUS: Look you, lady, on his bed,
How he gently stirs and sighs!

ELECTRA: Woe is me! His sleep hath fled,
Frightened by your noisy cries!

CHORUS: Nay, I thought he sleeping lay.

ELECTRA: Hence, I bid you, hence away
From the bedside, from the house!
    Cease your noise;
    Subdue your voice;
Stay not here to trouble us!

CHORUS: He is sleeping, and you rightly caution us.

ELECTRA: Holy mother, mother Night!
Thou who sheddest sleep on every weary wight!
Arise from Erebus, arise
With plumy pinions light:
Hover o'er the house of Atreus; and upon our aching eyes
Wearied with woe,
With grief brought low,
Solace bring 'mid miseries.

(*To Chorus*)   Silence! Hush! what noise was this?
Can you ne'er your tongue restrain,
And allow soft slumber's kiss
To refresh his fevered brain?

CHORUS: Tell me, lady, what the close
Of his grief is like to be?

ELECTRA: Death. Naught else will end his woes.
Lo, he fasts continually.

CHORUS: Alas! Alas! his fate is sure.

ELECTRA: By the promise to make pure
Hands a mother's lifeblood stained,

Phoebus brought
Woe, and wrought
All the grief that we have gained.

CHORUS: Just it was to slay the slayer; yet the deed with
crime was fraught.

ELECTRA: Thou art dead: oh, thou art dead,
Mother, who didst bear me! mother, who didst shed
A father's blood, and slay
The children of thy bed!
We are dying, we are dying, like the dead, and weak as
they:
For thou art gone,
And I am wan,
Weeping, sighing night and day!
Look upon me, friends, behold
How my withered life must run,
Childless, homeless, sad and cold,
Comfortless beneath the sun.

CHORUS: Come hither, maid Electra, to the couch:
Lest haply he should breathe his life away
Unheeded: I like not this deep dead languor.

ORESTES (awaking):   O soothing Sleep! dear friend! best
nurse of sickness!
How sweetly came you in my hour of need.
Blest Lethe of all woes, how wise you are,
How worthy of the prayers of wretched men!
Whence came I to this place? How journeyed I?
I cannot think: my former mind is vanished.
        JOHN ADDINGTON SYMONDS (Orestes 136-216)

In Bacchae the chorus hymns holiness and admonishes rever-
ent piety:

181
On tongues uncurbed by reverent awe,
On foolish hearts that heed not law
An evil end shall come;

But quiet life and prudent mind
Remain unshaken by the wind,
   A wall about the home.
What though their dwellings be so far from ours,
Yet human deeds are watched by heavenly powers,
And 'tis no wisdom to be over-wise,
    To think high thoughts and strange
    Beyond a mortal spirit's range.
   Short is our life, and swiftly flies
     And large ambition brings
But restless discontent with present things.
    Such idle fantasies, I deem,
    Are worthy of a madman's dream,
     From wits perverted rise.
   J. C. WORDSWORTH (*Bacchae* 386-401)

*Iphigenia at Aulis, about to be sacrificed, appeals to her
father's pity:*

Had I, my father, Orpheus' gift of speech,   **182**
So that the very rocks would come to life
Hearing my song, and could my words but charm
All whom I wished, to that I had recourse.
But now my only talent is my tears,
And these are yours; they are my only strength.
Your knees I touch with this my suppliant body
Which unto you my mother bore. Spare me!
I am so young; the light of life is sweet.
Compel me not to see the world below.
I was the first who ever called you father,
Me first you named your child, and on your knees
I first have kissed you and been kissed in turn.
   G. M. A. GRUBE (*Iphigenia in Aulis* 1211-1222)

*Euripides' Cyclops is the only satyr play that has survived.
The satyrs who form the chorus are bound in servitude to the
Cyclops; here is their entry song:*

183

Where has he of race divine
  Wandered in the winding rocks?
Here the air is calm and fine
  For the father of the flocks;
Here the grass is soft and sweet,
And the river-eddies meet
In the trough beside the cave,
Bright as in their fountain wave.
Neither here, nor on the dew
  Of the lawny uplands feeding?
Oh, you come!—a stone at you
  Will I throw to mend your breeding;
Get along, you hornèd thing,
Wild, seditious, rambling!

An Iacchic melody
  To the golden Aphrodite
Will I lift, as erst did I
  Seeking her and her delight
With the Mænads whose white feet
To the music glance and fleet.
Bacchus, O belovèd, where,
Shaking wide thy yellow hair,
Wanderest thou alone, afar?
  To the one-eyed Cyclops, we,
Who by right thy servants are,
  Minister in misery,
In these wretched goat-skins clad,
  Far from thy delights and thee.
          P. B. SHELLEY (*Cyclops* 41-52, 63-81)

*The lines following are ostensibly addressed to the Cyclops
but in fact refer to Odysseus, who is to deliver the satyrs from
him:*

184

One with eyes the fairest
  Cometh from his dwelling;
Some one loves thee, rarest,

Bright beyond my telling.
In thy grace thou shinest
Like some nymph divinest,
In her caverns dewy;
All delights pursue thee,
Soon pied flowers, sweet-breathing,
Shall thy head be wreathing.

P. B. SHELLEY (*Cyclops* 511-518)

Euripides is very quotable, and hence his fragments are numerous. Here is a prayer to Peace from the lost Cresophontes:

Peace, deep and rich,   **185**
of gods immortal the fairest,
I yearn for you: so long you tarry!
I fear old age and its bleakness
will overtake me ere again I see
your grace and your beauty
and lovely dances and songs
and garlanded merry-makers.
Come, lady Peace, come to our city;
ward hateful contention from our dwellings,
and bitter strife whose pleasure is the sharp sword.

MOSES HADAS

*And here, like Xenophanes before him, Euripides ridicules
the exaggerated honors heaped on athletes:*

Of the myriad afflictions that beset Hellas   **186**
none is worse than the breed of athletes.
Never, first of all, do they understand the good life,
nor could they. How can a man enslaved to his jaws,
subject to his belly, increase his patrimony?
Nor to abide poverty, to row in fortune's stream
are they able; they have not learned the fair art
of confronting the insoluble. Shining in youth
they stride about like statues in the square.

But comes astringent age, they shrink in rags.
Blameworthy is the custom of the Hellenes
who for such men make great concourses
to honor idle sports—for feasting's sake.
What nimble wrestler, fleet runner, sinewy
discus thrower, agile boxer, has benefited his city
by his firsts? Fight our enemy discus in hand?
In mellay of shields box the foe from the fatherland?
Confronted with steel, such silliness none remembers.
'Tis the wise and the good we should crown with bay,
who best guide the state, the prudent and the just,
whoso by discourse averts evil actions, banishes
strife and contention. Prowess of such sort
is to all the city a boon, to all Hellenes.

                    MOSES HADAS

THUCYDIDES

The following epitaph on Euripides is usually ascribed to Thucydides (471-401 B.C.) but may be by Timotheus:

187   To Hellas' bard all Hellas gives a tomb:
                    On Macedon's far shore his relics sleep:
                Athens, the pride of Greece, was erst his home,
                    Whom now all praise and all in common weep.
                F. A. PALEY

TIMOTHEUS

A friend of Euripides, and his teacher in music, was Timotheus of Miletus (late fifth century B.C.), whose language was as extravagant as his composition. In the following ex-

ARISTOPHANES 259

tract from his Persians (*a nome for solo performance with musical accompaniment*), *a drowning Persian addresses the sea; the "hempen bonds" allude to the bridge over the Hellespont:*

Bold as thou art, ere now thou hast had thy boisterous throat **188** bound fast in hempen bonds; and now my king—aye mine— will plow thee with hill-born pines, and will encompass thy navigable plains with his far-roaming rays. O thou frenzied thing, hated from of old, who treacherously embraces me, while the breeze sweeps over thy surge! —So spake he, panting with strangled breath, as he spat forth the grim sea-dew, belching from his mouth the brine of the deep.

    R. C. JEBB

ARISTOPHANES

Aristophanes (450-385) *is remarkable not only for Rabelaisian humor, but also for serious political and social criticism and for exquisite lyrics. In* Archarnians *the charcoal burner Dicaeopolis ridicules the causes of the Peloponnesian War, which was then in its sixth year:*

    First, I detest the Spartans most extremely; **189**
And wish, that Neptune, the Taenarian deity,
Would bury them in their houses with his earthquakes.
For I've had losses—losses, let me tell ye,
Like other people; vines cut down and injured.
But, among friends (for only friends are here),
Why should we blame the Spartans for all this?
For people of ours, some people of our own,
Some people from amongst us here, I mean;
But not the people (pray remember that);
I never said the people,—but a pack

Of paltry people, mere pretended citizens,
Base counterfeits, went laying informations,
And making a confiscation of the jerkins
Imported here from Megara; pigs moreover,
Pumpkins, and pecks of salt, and ropes of onions,
Were voted to be merchandise from Megara,
Denounced, and seized, and sold upon the spot.
　　Well, these might pass, as petty local matters.
But now, behold, some doughty drunken youths
Kidnap, and carry away from Megara,
The courtesan Simaetha. Those of Megara,
In hot retaliation, seize a brace
Of equal strumpets, hurried forth perforce
From Dame Aspasia's house of recreation.
So this was the beginning of the war,
All over Greece, owing to these three strumpets.
For Pericles, like an Olympian Jove,
With all his thunder and his thunderbolts,
Began to storm and lighten dreadfully,
Alarming all the neighbourhood of Greece;
And made decrees, drawn up like drinking songs,
In which it was enacted and concluded,
That the Megarians should remain excluded
From every place where commerce was transacted,
With all their ware—like 'old care'—in the ballad:
And this decree, by land and sea, was valid.
　　Then the Megarians, being all half starved,
Desired the Spartans, to desire of us,
Just to repeal those laws; the laws I mention'd,
Occasion'd by the stealing of those strumpets.
And so they begg'd and pray'd us several times;
And we refused; and so they went to war.
You'll say, 'They should not.' Why, what should they have
　　done?
Just make it your own case; suppose the Spartans
Had mann'd a boat, and landed on your islands,
And stolen a pug puppy from Seriphos;

Would you then have remain'd at home inglorious?
Not so, by no means; at the first report,
You would have launch'd at once three hundred galleys,
And fill'd the city with the noise of troops;
And crews of ships, crowding and clamouring
About the muster-masters and pay-masters;
With measuring corn out at the magazine,
And all the porch choked with the multitude;
With figures of Minerva, newly furbish'd,
Painted and gilt, parading in the streets;
With wineskins, kegs, and firkins, leeks and onions;
With garlic cramm'd in pouches, nets, and pokes;
With garlands, singing girls, and bloody noses.
Our arsenal would have sounded and resounded
With bangs and thwacks of driving bolts and nails;
With shaping oars, and holes to put the oar in;
With hacking, hammering, clattering and boring;
Words of command, whistles and pipes and fifes.

   J. H. FRERE (*Acharnians* 509-554)

Clouds *ridicules the new education and makes a special butt
of Socrates. This is the entrance song of the chorus of clouds
when they are summoned by Socrates:*

    Cloud-maidens that float on forever,   **190**
      Dew-sprinkled, fleet bodies, and fair,
    Let us rise from our Sire's loud river,
      Great Ocean, and soar thro the air
    To the peaks of the pine-covered mountains
      Where the pines hang as tresses of hair!
    Let us seek the watch-towers undaunted,
      Where the well-watered corn-fields abound,
    And thro murmurs of rivers nymph-haunted
      The song of the sea-waves resound;
    And the sun in the sky never wearies
      Of spreading his radiance around!
          Let us cut off the haze

Of the mists from our band
Till with far-seeing gaze
We may look on the land!

Cloud maidens that bring the rain-shower,
   To the Pallas-loved land let us wing,
To the land of stout heroes and Power,
   Where Kekrops was hero and king,
Where honour and silence is given
   To the mysteries that none may declare,
Where are gifts of the high gods in heaven
   And a people that knows no fear;
Where stand lofty-rooft temples,
   And statues well-carven and fair;
Where are feasts to the happy immortals
   When the sacred procession draws near,
Where garlands make bright the bright portals
   At all seasons and months of the year;
               And when Spring days are here,
Then we tread to the wine-god a measure
In Bacchanal dance and in pleasure,
   Mid the contests of sweet-singing choirs,
      And the crash of loud lyres!
OSCAR WILDE (*Clouds* 275-290, 299-313)

Strepsiades, who is a kind of Sancho Panza, will endure any discomfort to be admitted to Socrates' Think-shop:

191   So now let them do with me just what they will;
      I give them my carcase for good or for ill,
      To experience beatings, and hunger, and thirst,
      And dandruff, and cold, or be flayed if they durst,
      On condition they teach me the method to find
      An escape from my debts, and I'm thought by mankind
      Bold, nimble-tongued, impudent, anxious to rise,
      A blackguard, a gluer-together of lies,
      An inventor of words, a lover of suits,
      A law-book, a rattle, a cunning old boots,

An auger, a strap, a dissembling old bags,
A puddle of grease, an indulger in brags,
A goad-riddled slave, an impertinent dog,
A twister, a teaser, a gluttonous hog.
If passers-by speak of me thus, I am ripe
  For whatever they think to be proper;
And, if such is their wish, let them tear out my tripe
  And give it the Scholars for supper.

    B. D. WALSH (*Clouds* 439-456)

*What may be described as the earliest idyllic poetry of the
Greeks is Aristophanes' description of rural beatitude in*
Peace:

Ah, there's nothing half so sweet as when the seed is in **192**
    the ground,
God a gracious rain is sending, and a neighbour saunters
    round.
'O Comarchides!' he hails me: 'how shall we enjoy the hours?
Drinking seems to suit my fancy, what with these benignant
    showers.
Therefore let three quarts, my mistress, of your kidney-beans
    be fried,
Mix them nicely up with barley, and your choicest figs pro-
    vide;
Syra run and shout to Manes, call him in without delay,
'Tis no time to stand and dawdle pruning out the vines to-
    day,
Nor to break the clods about them, now the ground is soak-
    ing through.
Bring me out from home the fieldfare, bring me out the
    siskins two,
Then there ought to be some beestings, four good plates of
    hare beside
(Hah! unless the cat purloined them yesterday at eventide;
Something scuffled in the pantry, something made a noise and
    fuss);
If you find them, one's for father, bring the other three to us.

Ask Aeschinades to send us myrtle branches green and strong;
Bid Charinades attend us, shouting as you pass along.
                    Then we'll sit and drink together,
                    God the while refreshing, blessing
                        All the labour of our hands.'
        B. B. ROGERS (*Peace* 1140-1158)

Richest of all the comedies in fantasy is Birds, *in which an ideal community is established in the air. Here is the hoopoe's serenade to the nightingale, and then his summons to the other birds:*

193   Awake! awake!
                    Sleep no more my gentle mate!
                    With your tiny tawny bill,
                    Wake the tuneful echo shrill,
                        On vale or hill;
                    Or in her airy rocky seat,
                    Let her listen and repeat
                    The tender ditty that you tell,
                        The sad lament,
                        The dire event,
                    To luckless Itys that befell.
                        Thence the strain
                        Shall rise again,
                        And soar amain,
                    Up to the lofty palace gate,
                    Where mighty Apollo sits in state
                    In Jove's abode, with his ivory lyre,
                    Hymning aloud to the heavenly choir.
                    While all the gods shall join with thee
                        In a celestial symphony. . . .
                            Hoop! hoop!
                            Come in a troop,
                            Come at a call,
                            One and all,
                            Birds of a feather,
                            All together.

    Birds of an humble gentle bill
      Smooth and shrill,
Dieted on seeds and grain,
Rioting on the furrow'd plain,
    Pecking, hopping,
    Picking, popping,
Among the barley newly sown.
    Birds of bolder louder tone,
    Lodging in the shrubs and bushes,
Mavises and Thrushes.
On the summer berries browsing,
On the garden fruits carousing,
All the grubs and vermin smouzing.
    You that in an humbler station,
With an active occupation,
Haunt the lowly watery mead,
Warring against the native breed,
    The gnats and flies, your enemies;
In the level marshy plain
Of Marathon pursu'd and slain.

    You that in a squadron driving
From the seas are seen arriving,
    With the Cormorants and Mews
Haste to land and hear the news!
    All the feather'd airy nation,
Birds of every size and station,
Are convened in convocation.
    For an envoy queer and shrewd
    Means to address the multitude,
And submit to their decision
A surprising proposition,
For the welfare of the state
    Come in a flurry,
    With a hurry-scurry,
Hurry to the meeting and attend to the debate.
    J. H. FRERE (*Birds* 209-259)

In a part of the parabasis the chorus explains the advantage
of wings.

194 Nothing can be more delightful than the having wings to
            wear!
          A spectator sitting here, accommodated with a pair,
          Might for instance (if he found a tragic chorus dull and
            heavy)
          Take his flight and dine at home, and if he did not choose to
            leave ye,
          Might return in better humour when the weary drawl was
            ended.
          Introduce then wings in use—believe me, matters will be
            mended:
           Patroclides would not need to sit there and befoul his seat
          Flying off, he might return, eased in a moment, clean and
            neat.
          If a gallant should the husband on the Council-bench behold
          Of a gay and charming lady, one whom he had loved of old,
          Off at once he'd fly to greet her, have a little converse sweet
          Then be back or e'er ye missed him, calm and smiling in his
            seat.
          Trust me, wings are all in all! Diitrephes has mounted quicker
          Than the rest of our aspirants, soaring on his wings of wicker:
          Basket-work and crates and hampers first enabled him to fly,
          First a captain, then promoted to command the cavalry;
          With his fortunes daily rising, office and preferment new,
          An illustrious, enterprising, airy, gallant Cockatoo.
              J. H. FRERE (*Birds* 786-800)

          And this is the chorus' appeal for the prize.

195 To the judges of the prize, we wish to mention in a word
          The return we mean to make, if our performance is preferr'd.
            First, then, in your empty coffers you shall see the sterling
              Owl,
          From the mines of Laurium, familiar as a common fowl;
          Roosting among the bags and pouches, each at ease upon his
            nest;

Undisturb'd, rearing and hatching little broods of interest:
If you wish to cheat in office, but are inexpert and raw,
You should have a Kite for agent, capable to gripe and claw;
Cranes and Cormorants shall help you to a stomach and a
    throat
When you feast abroad; but if you give a vile, unfriendly vote,
Hasten and provide yourselves, each, with a little silver plate,
Like the statues of the gods, for the protection of his pate;
Else, when forth abroad you ramble on a summer holiday,
We shall take a dirty vengeance, and befoul your best array.

    J. H. FRERE (*Birds* 1101-1115)

In Thesmophoriazusae *the chorus of women justifies their sex against the calumnies of Euripides.*

> They're always abusing the women,
>   As a terrible plague to men:
> They say we're the root of all evil,
>   And repeat it again and again;
> Of war and quarrels and bloodshed,
>   All mischief, be what it may:
> And pray, then, why do you marry us,
>   If we're all the plagues you say?
> And why do you take such care of us,
>   And keep us so safe at home,
> And are never easy a moment,
>   If ever we chance to roam?
> When you ought to be thanking heaven
>   That your Plague is out of the way—
> You all keep fussing and fretting—
>   "Where *is* my Plague today?"
> If a Plague peeps out of the window,
>   Up go the eyes of the men;
> If she hides then they all keep staring
>   Until she looks out again.
>   W. L. COLLINS
>   (*Thesmophoriazusae* 785-799)

196

Aristophanes represents Aeschylus as parodying Euripides'
manner in this song in Frogs. *The humor consists not only in*
sound effects but in endowing commonplace persons and
events with high pathos and ornate language. "Ida's chil-
dren, men of Crete," for example, refers simply to the Athe-
nian police.

197   O gloom of night
                              With sable light
What send'st thou me, what dismal dream
      Forth from the Invisible,
        Servant of the Lord of Hell,
          Soul-less, in whom a soul doth dwell,
      Child of the murky night,
      A gruesome, fearful sight,
      In death's dark robes bedight,
With eyes that gleam with slaughter, slaughter,
                              And talons fell?
      Handmaids, kindle the taper's gleam!
Fetch in your pitchers the dew from the rivers, and heat me
      some water,
      To wash the god-sent dream away.
                              O thou Lord of the sea!
                              'Tis even so. O ye
Who dwell with me here
                              These portents see:
Glyce hath stol'n my Chanticleer,
                              And gone is she!
      Nymphs on the mountain born!
      Kitchenmaid! hands on her lay!
There I sat at my work, ah! wretch forlorn,
      Spin-in-in-inning with my hands
      The spindle full of flaxen strands,
Weaving a skein that early tomorrow
      To market I'ld bear,
      And barter it there.
But he, on pinion tips so light
      Has fled, has fled, to heaven's height,

   And left me sorrow, sorrow;
And tear-drops, tear-drops, from my eyes
   I shed, I shed, in piteous wise.
      But, Ida's children! men of Crete!
      Seize your bows, and come to my aid!
         Nimbly ply your legs, and meet
      In a circle round my home.
      And let the fair net-wielding maid
         Artemis, with her puppies come
            Through the house everywhere.
Thou too, Zeus' daughter, raise on high
   The two-fold torchlights' glare,
   In keenest hands, O Hecate!
   And into Glyce's house for me
   Cast beams of light, that entering, I
         May catch the robber there!
   A. D. COPE (*Frogs* 1331-1363)

*In Plutus the unhappiness due to inequable distribution of
wealth is to be remedied by curing Plutus of his blindness.
But Poverty insists on its own serviceableness:*

O dotards both, most easily seduced from wisdom's train,   **198**
Fellows in silliness of speech and enterprise insane,
I say you will not profit, if you get your hearts' desire;
For, should his vision, as of old, the god of wealth acquire,
And himself redistribute, giving all an equal part,
None then will study science, and none then will practise
      art;
But art and science vanished from amongst you, who will go
To work the forge, to build the ship, to turn the wheel, to
      sew,
To mould the brick out of the clay, to put the boot together,
To do the washing of the clothes, to tan the hide to leather,
To plough the plain, and Deo's fruit in harvest time collect,
If man can live in idleness and all these works neglect? . . .
No more for you sound sleep in bed, for beds will not be
      made;

Nor upon rugs; for who will weave whose purse has gold in-
    side?
You'll have no liquid perfume to offer to your bride,
Nor, to adorn her, costly robes of bright and varied hue;
But, if you can't have all these things, what is wealth worth
    to you?
Now I can find you all you want, can give you all you crave;
For I sit by the craftsman like a mistress by her slave,
And so, because he's needy and is not with riches fed,
I make him labour with his hands to earn his daily bread.

    W. R. KENNEDY (*Plutus* 508-517, 528-535)

EUPOLIS

*Aristophanes' principal rivals in Old Comedy were Cratinus
and Eupolis, whose themes and treatment were apparently
very like Aristophanes'. Political interest is shown in the fa-
mous lines on Pericles.*

199   A statesman who in speaking all surpassed
    And far out-distanced like a runner fast.
    Once past them, none could catch him; "yards ahead
    His word-flow keeps," in all debates 'twas said.
    Not merely eloquence, but more, a charm
    Sat on his lips, wild passions to disarm.
    The only man who could the influence bring
    To make men *feel*—and leave behind the sting.

    F. A. PALEY

METAGENES

*The Cockaigne theme, a glutton's Eldorado, was common
and sometimes progressed into a genuine utopia. Here is a*

fragment of Metagenes, another contemporary of Aristoph-anes.

200

> This river Crathis rolls us down
> Huge buns of self-made dough, baked brown;
> One other stream, the Sybaris hight,
> Bears on its current, pleasing sight!
> Relays of loaves and hunks of meat,
> Plaice plunging, ready cooked to eat,
> While lesser streamlets all about
> Run with baked squids and crabs and trout;
> With sausages or mince-meats rare,
> Here crisp-fried smelts, prime herrings there.
> Into your mouth dressed collops tumble;
> Or at your feet in glorious jumble;
> Sponge cakes on every side abound,
> Like neighbours closely grouped around.
>
> F. A. PALEY

EPICHARMUS

Epicharmus of Sicily (fifth century) wrote not comedies but mimes, from which Plato is said to have learned the art of dialogue. The following fragment describes the character of the "parasite," who was to become a fixture in New Comedy:

201

> Invite me to dinner, I'm sure to accept;
> With no invitation I may show up yet.
> I'm gracious at table, and 'tis my boast
> To amuse the guests and to praise the host;
> I take his side in any discussion,
> Abuse his opponent with a good deal of passion.
> I eat and drink till I can't hold more,
> Then leave, and struggle to find my door;
> For without a servant to light the way

Stumbling alone in the dark I stray,
And when I encounter the city guards,
If they only lash me I thank my stars;
Home I come with my brains so wet,
That I sleep uncovered with no regret
As long as the wine fumes hold me yet.
      CHARLES H. KAHN

PRAXILLA

*Among famous poetesses of the fifth century were Corinna,
teacher and rival of Pindar, and Praxilla, of whom a single
couplet may be cited:*

202 A girlish face is what appears through the lattice-slot;
      The woman's body 'neath the face—alas that showeth not.
        MOSES HADAS

PARRHASIUS

*The famous painter, who lived about 400 B.C., asserts his
pride:*

203   Though men believe it not this thing I know—
              Art's utmost bourne has been achieved by me;
          Beyond the bound I set no man can go;
              Yet is no mortal work from cavil free.
        WALTER LEAF (*Athenaeus* 12.543c)

PLATO

A number of epigrams are ascribed to the philosopher Plato
(429-337 B.C.). The following are on Aster ("Morning
star"), on the Athenian dead at Ecbatana, on Lais' mirror, on
Dion of Syracuse, and on Aristophanes:

Thou wert the morning star among the living,   **204**
   Ere thy fair light had fled;
Now, having died, thou art as Hesperus, giving
   New splendour to the dead.
     P. B. SHELLEY (Diogenes Laertius 3.29)

Goodbye to the Aegean   **205**
that swelling strikes the coast,
Eretria and our neighbors
in Athens. Dead and lost
on Persian plains expanding
in endless length we lie,
and so we seize the moment
to tell the sea Goodbye.
     RALPH GLADSTONE (Pal. Anth. 7.256)

Lais of the haughty smile,   **206**
The despair of Greece erewhile,
Whose doors fond gallants wont to crowd,
Hath her glass to Venus vowed:
"Since what I am I will not see,
And cannot what I used to be."
     F. E. GARRETT (Pal. Anth. 6.1)

For Priam's queen and daughters at their birth   **207**
   The fates weaved tears into their web of life;
But for thee, Dion, in thy hour of mirth,

When triumph crowned thy honourable strife,
Thy gathering hopes were poured upon the sand:
Thee, still thy countrymen revere, and lay
In the broad precincts of thy native land,
Thee,—love for whom once took my wits away.
CHARLES MERIVALE (*Diogenes Laertius* 3.29)

208

The Graces, seeking for a shrine,
Whose glories ne'er should cease,
Found, as they strayed, the soul divine
Of Aristophanes.
CHARLES MERIVALE

ARISTOTLE

Aristotle (384-322) no less than Plato wrote verse. The following hymn to virtue was dedicated to King Hermeias of Atarneus, his connection by marriage.

209

Virtue, to men thou bringest care and toil;
Yet thou art life's best, fairest spoil!
O virgin Goddess, for thy beauty's sake
To die is delicate in this our Greece,
Or to endure of pain the stern strong ache!
Such fruit for our soul's ease
Of joys undying, dearer far than gold
Or home or soft-eyed sleep, dost thou unfold.
It was for thee the seed of Zeus,
Stout Heracles, and Leda's twins did choose
Strength-draining deeds, to spread abroad thy name:
Smit with the love of thee
Aias and Achilleus went smilingly
Down to Death's portal, crowned with deathless fame.
Now since thou art so fair,
Leaving the lightsome air

Atarneus' Hero hath died gloriously.
Wherefore immortal praise shall be his guerdon:
His goodness and his deeds are made the burden
   Of songs divine
  Sung by Memory's daughters nine,
Hymning of hospitable Zeus the might
And friendship firm as Fate in Fate's despite.
    JOHN ADDINGTON SYMONDS

EPITAPH FOR CHAERONEIA

Public epitaphs for heroic dead continued to be written. Here is the epitaph, almost Simonidean, written for those fallen at Chaeroneia (336 B.C.), which happens to be quoted by Demosthenes.

These are the patriot brave, who side by side   **210**
Stood to their arms, and dash'd the foeman's pride:
Firm in their valour, prodigal of life,
Hades they chose the arbiter of strife;
That Greeks might ne'er to haughty victors bow,
Nor thraldom's yoke, nor dire oppression know;
They fought, they bled, and on their country's breast
(Such was the doom of heaven) these warriors rest.
Gods never lack success, nor strive in vain,
But man must suffer what the fates ordain.
    C. R. KENNEDY (*On the Crown* 289)

PROCESSIONAL FOR DEMETRIUS POLIORCETES

After Greek democracy was extinguished at Chaeroneia, the Successors (of Alexander) ruled and became objects of abject flattery. Here Demetrius Poliorcetes (end of fourth century B.C.) is hailed as a god:

211

See how the mightiest gods, and best-beloved
    Towards our town are winging!
For lo, Demeter and Demetrius
    This glad day is bringing!
She to perform her daughter's solemn rites;
    Mystic pomps attend her:
He, joyous as a god should be, and blithe,
    Comes with laughing splendor.
Show forth your triumph! Friends all, troop around!
    Let him shine above you!
Be you the stars to circle him with love;
    He's the sun to love you.
Hail, offspring of Poseidon, powerful god,
    Child of Aphrodite!
The other gods keep far away from earth;
    Have no ears, though mighty;
They are not, or they will not hear us wail:
    Thee our eye beholdeth;
Not wood, not stone, but living, breathing, real,
    Thee our prayer enfoldeth.
First give us peace! Give, dearest, for thou canst:
    Thou art Lord and Master!
The Sphinx, who not on Thebes, but on all Greece
    Swoops to gloat and pasture;
The Ætolian, he who sits upon his rock,

Like that old disaster;
He feeds upon our flesh and blood, and we
    Can no longer labor;
For it was ever thus the Ætolian thief
    Preyed upon his neighbor;
Him punish thou, or if not thou, then send
    Œdipus to harm him,
Who'll cast his Sphinx down from his cliff of pride,
    Or to stone will charm him.

    JOHN ADDINGTON SYMONDS

ERINNA

*Epigrams, sepulchral and votive, continued to be written at
all periods. Here is an epigram for her friend Baucis written
by Erinna about 350 B.C.:*

Pillars of death! carved sirens! tearful urn!   **212**
    In whose sad keeping my poor dust is laid,
To those who near my tomb their footsteps turn,
    Stranger or Greek, bid hail! and say, a maid
Rests in her bloom below; her sire the name
    Of Baucis gave; her birth and lineage high;
And say her bosom friend Erinna came,
    And on this marble graved her elegy.

    C. A. ELTON (*Pal. Anth.* 7.710)

ANTIPHANES

*Where the tragic poet dealt with "Thebes or Pelops' line, or
the tale of Troy divine," the comic poet had to invent plot
and character. Here Antiphanes, a poet of Middle Comedy,
complains of his harder lot.*

213   The tragic poet's a happy man;
            No other writer can crib as he can.
            His lines are all known; he hasn't to find them.
            The audience waits; he only reminds them.
            If he says "Oedipus," they know the rest;
            His father Laius and his Mother Iocaste,
            Two daughters, more than one son,
            What he will suffer and what he has done.
            A cue like "Alcmaeon" is as good as another:
            Even the kids know he killed his mother
            In a crazy fit, and then soon enough
            Adrastus pops on and off in a huff.
            When the play gets stuck and needs a last scene,
            He lifts his finger, and out rolls the machine
            Bearing the god, and all is well.
            But we comic poets don't have it so swell;
            The whole plot must be new, new names, new scenes,
            A novel conclusion, and original themes.
            If our characters fumble so much as a line,
            They're hissed off the stage in double-quick time;
            But Teucros and Peleus can muff as they please.
                    CHARLES H. KAHN

Antiphanes also illustrates the comic preoccupation with food and especially fish.

214   No creature's so unlucky as a fish!
            When caught, to die at once it well might wish,
            And in the stomach snugly buried lie;
            But now on salesman's slab left high and dry
            More stale it gets, until some greedy ass
            Who has no eyes to see shall chance to pass.
            To him the festering corpses to remove
            The right is given (for something more than *love*).
            He brings them home, but straightway from him throws
            His parcel when its odour meets his nose.
                    F. A. PALEY

ANAXANDRIDES

The comic preoccupation with questions of marriage may be illustrated by a fragment from another author of Middle Comedy, Anaxandrides.

> A man who doubts if he should marry,   **215**
> Or thinks he has good cause to tarry,
> Is foolish if he takes a wife,
> The source of half the plagues in life!
> A poor man to a rich wife sold
> Exchanges liberty for gold.
> If she has nothing, then, 'tis true
> There is a different ill to rue;
> For now he has, for all his need,
> Two mouths instead of one to feed.
> Perhaps she's ugly; married life
> Thenceforth is never-ending strife!
> Perhaps she's pretty; then *your* boast
> Is made by all your friends their toast.
> Does ugly, handsome, poor, or rich,
> Bring most ill luck? —I know not which.
> > F. A. PALEY

ALEXIS

The most prolific author of Middle Comedy was Menander's uncle Alexis. Here is a jibe at philosophers.

> "Flesh that hath life eat not," Pythagoras said.   **216**
> I don't: those big fish from the shop were dead.
> I eat fat lamb—but not alive, of course;

Baked liver too is sometimes a resource.
If voice or life in collops can be shown,
Then I'm a cannibal, I'm bound to own.

All things they search for those who have the mind
To persevere by toil and pains may find.
Yon distant orbs that in the heavens shine,
Their risings, settings, ruled by hand divine,
The planets' paths, the sun's eclipse, we know:
How much more common movements here below!
  F. A. PALEY

MENANDER

The most fully preserved New Comedy is Menander's Arbitrants. The charcoal man Davus had found an exposed infant and presented it, but without the trinkets attached to it, to the shepherd Syriscus. Syriscus now pleads on the baby's behalf before the arbiter Smicrines, who, unbeknownst to all, is the baby's grandfather.

217 All alone this fellow found
The baby. Yes, and all of this he's telling now
He tells correctly, father, and it happened so.
I do not contradict. I did entreat and beg
And I received it from him. Yes, he tells the truth.
A certain shepherd, fellow labourer of his,
With whom he had been talking, then brought word to me
That with the baby he had found some ornaments.
To claim these things, see, father, he is here himself!
Give me the baby, wife.

  (Takes the child from his wife's arms.)
                    Now, Davus, here from you

He's asking back the necklace and birth-tokens too,
For he declares that these were placed upon himself
For his adorning, not for eking out your keep.
I too join in, and ask for them, as guardian—
On giving him you made me that. (*To Smicrines*) And now,
      good sir,
Methinks 'tis yours to settle whether it be right
These golden trinkets and whatever else there be,
As given by his mother, whosoe'er she was,
Be put by for the baby till he come of age,
Or this footpad who stripped him is to have these things,
That others own, provided that he found them first!
"Why didn't I," you'll say, "when first I took the child,
Demand them then of you?" It was not then as yet
Within my power to speak thus in the child's behalf,
And even now I'm here demanding no one thing
That's mine, mine only. "Windfall! Share-all!" None of that!
No "finding" when 'tis question of a person wronged.
That is not "finding," nay, but outright filching that!
And look at this too, father. Maybe this boy here
Was born above our station. Reared 'mongst working-folk
He will despise our doings, his own level seek
And venture on some action suiting noble birth:
Will go a-lion hunting; carry arms; or run
A race at games. You've seen the actors act, I know,
And all of this you understand. Those heroes once,
Pelias, Neleus, by an aged man were found,
A goatherd in his goatskin dressed as I am now,
And, when he noticed they were better born than he,
He tells the matter, how he found, how took them up,
He gave them back their wallet, with birth-tokens filled.
And thus they found out clearly all their history,
And they, the one-time goatherds, afterwards were kings.
But had a Davus found those things and sold them off,
That he might profit by twelve drachmas for himself,
Through all the coming ages they had been unknown
Who were such great ones and of such a pedigree.
And so it is not fitting, father, that I here

Should rear his body and that Davus seize meanwhile
His life's hope for the future, make it disappear.
A youth about to wed his sister once was stopped
By just such tokens. One a mother found and saved,
And one a brother. Since, O father, all men's lives
Are liable to dangers, we must watch, look out,
With forethought far ahead for what is possible.
"Well, if you are not suited, give him back," says he.
This is his stronghold in the matter, as he thinks.
But that's not just. If you must give up what is his,
Then in addition do you claim to have the child
That more securely you may play the rogue again
If some of his belongings Fortune has preserved?
I've said my say. (*To Smicrines*) Give verdict as you hold is
    just.
      F. G. ALLINSON (*Arbitrants* 77-135)

*When Charisius who, unbeknownst to both, had been his
wife's seducer, discovers the truth, he reproaches himself for
having rejected her for an offense in which he was equally
guilty.*

218 The sinless saint I was, mine eyes on honour fixed!
Could scan the noble and disgraceful, which is which,
Myself so innocent and spotless in my life!—
Right well and very fittingly the power divine
Has used me—here but human I'm shown up to be.
"You thrice-unlucky, puffed-up boastful chatterer,
Your wife's involuntary ill-luck you'll not bear.
But I will show that you have stumbled just as much.
To you she'll then be kind, but you dishonour her,
And you shall be shown up to have become at once
A luckless and a loutish and unfeeling man.
Most like indeed to your thoughts then was what but now
She said unto her father: 'Partner of his life
I come and, being such, I must not shirk ill-luck
When it befalls.' But you were high and mighty, you!"
      F. G. ALLINSON (*Arbitrants* 693-707)

Aside from the considerable fragments of a handful of Menander's plays recovered from papyri, there are numerous substantial and attractive quotations. Here are two of the best known:

Whom the gods love die young; that man is blest   **219**
Who having viewed at ease this solemn show
Of sun, stars, ocean, fire, doth quickly go
Back to his home with calm uninjured breast.
Be life or short, or long, 'tis manifest
Thou ne'er wilt see things goodlier, Parmeno,
Than these; then take thy sojourn here as though
Thou wert some playgoer or wedding-guest.
The sooner sped, the safelier to thy rest,
Well-furnished, foe to none, with strength at need,
Shalt thou return; while he who tarries late,
Faints on the road out-worn, with age oppressed,
Harassed by foes whom life's dull tumults breed;
Thus ill dies he for whom death long doth wait.
    JOHN ADDINGTON SYMONDS

Being a man, ask not release from pain,   **220**
But strength to bear pain, from the gods above;
If thou wouldst fain escape all woe for aye,
Thou must become god, or, if not, a corpse.
    JOHN ADDINGTON SYMONDS

The middle-class affinities of New Comedy are illustrated by the following from Menander:

Don't talk of birth and family; all those   **221**
Who have no natural worth on that repose.
Blue blood, grand pedigree, illustrious sires
He boasts of, who to nothing more aspires.
What use long ancestry your *pride* to call?
One must have had them to be born at all!
And those who have no pedigree to show,
Or who their grandsires were but scantly know,

From change of homes or lack of friends at need,
And so have lost all record of their breed,
Are not more "low-born" than your men of blood;
An Ethiop's well-born, if he makes for good!
>   F. A. PALEY

PHILEMON

*Menander's principal rival appears to have been Philemon.
Here are two fragments:*

222   Happy the animals! *they* do not bother
Their heads about this question and another;
None makes inquiries, none need take the trouble
To prove that black is white, or single double.
No self-inflicted woes, no cares have they;
All their own nature, their own laws obey.
We mortals live a life not worth the living,
To laws and politics attention giving,
For sons providing, pedigrees unwinding,
Yet some excuse for worry always finding.
>   F. A. PALEY

223   A happy creature is your snail indeed!
Just where he pleases he can live and feed.
And if a neighbour gives him any bother,
With house on back he moves off to another.
>   F. A. PALEY

DIPHILUS

*The third in the triad with Menander is Diphilus, who may
be represented by the following.*

When I am asked by some rich man to dine,   **224**
I mark not if the walls and roof are fine,
Nor if the vases such as Corinth prizes—
But *solely* how the smoke from cooking rises.
If dense it runs up in a column straight,
With fluttering heart the dinner-hour I wait.
If, thin and scant, the smoke-puffs sideway steal,
Then I forebode a thin and scanty meal.
      F. A. PALEY

LYCOPHRON

*The only extant example of Alexandrian tragedy is the
Alexandra of Lycophron, a single prophecy in 1430 iambic
trimeters spoken by Cassandra (Alexandra) to her gaoler for
transmission to Priam on the day that Paris left Troy for the
rape of Helen. The first selection is the introduction.*

Mark then my words, for I will speak, O King,   **225**
Though long the task, and tedious be the toil;
For not with sweet and soothing blandishment
Flowed from the Maiden's lips the gentle stream
Of oracles benign, but sounds of woe
Burst dreadful, as she chewed the laurel leaf,
And ever and anon, like the black Sphinx,

Poured the full tide of enigmatic song.
All shalt thou hear, which Memory can retain,
And through th' obscure of prophecies explore
Thine uncouth way; for now the barriers yield,
And o'er th' enchanted ground mine eager soul
Starts like a steed, and wings her rapid flight.

The Morn had left thy brother's bed, the couch
Of aged Tithon, near to Cerne's isle,
And o'er the misty mountain-tops had flown
Jocund, upborne on Pegasëan wing;
The busy crew their moorings had unloosed,
And heaved their heavy anchors from the sand:
And now th' Idëan Daughters of the grove
Spread their white wings athwart the Hellespont,
Walking with insect feet upon the waves
Beyond Calydna's isle; their swelling sails,
White as the plumage of the crane, were filled
With breezes issuing from the stormy North:
When, phrenzied as a moon-struck Bacchanal,
CASSANDRA wandered upon Ate's hills,
Hills crowned with thousand herds, and poured aloud
Presaging sounds, and prophecies of woe.
        LORD ROYSTON (*Alexandra* 1-30)

This picture follows the landing of the Greeks:

226   Now Mars showers down a fiery sleet, and winds
His trumpet-shell, distilling blood, and now,
Knit with the Furies and the Fates in dance,
Leads on the dreadful revelry; the fields
With iron harvests of embattled spears
Gleam; from the towers I hear a voice of woe
Rise to the stedfast Empyréan; crowds
Of zoneless matrons rend their flowing robes,
And sobs and shrieks cry loud unto the night
One woe is past!—Another woe succeeds!
        LORD ROYSTON (*Alexandra* 249-257)

This is the penalty for Ajax' sacrilege:

Greece

For this one crime, aye for this one, shall weep   **227**
Myriads of sons; no funeral urn, but rocks
Shall hearse their bones; no friends upon their dust
Shall pour the dark libations of the dead;
A name, a breath, an empty sound remains,
A fruitless marble warm with bitter tears
Of sires, and orphan babes, and widowed wives!
        LORD ROYSTON (*Alexandra* 365-372)

And here is an obscure prophecy of the founding of Rome:

"Visions of glory, crowd not on my soul;"   **228**
Immortal sons of an immortal sire,
Bound on your brows (so valour should be crowned)
The laurelled meed of conquest shall entwine;
O'er earth and seas extends your dread domain,
Powerful of realms; o'er empires and o'er waves
In solemn majesty your sceptred hand
Rules far and wide, and shakes the conquering spear.
Not yet, my country, no, nor yet thy fame
Shall fade in darkness; such a martial pair,
Twin Lions, shall my Kinsman leave, who springs
From Chœras and the Castnian Queen, well skilled
To pour the honied words, or guide the war.
        LORD ROYSTON (*Alexandra* 1226-1235)

*The conquests of Alexander are enigmatically foreshadowed
in the following:*

Then woes, and wars, and wasting tides of blood,   **229**
Shall sweep conflicting armies from the world;
For some in plains shall bow their heads to death,
And some on ridges of the mountain rock,
And some on seas shall sink beneath the wave,

All murdered: nor till then shall grisly War
Sheath his fell sword, and break his iron car,
Till sprung from Dardan seed from Æacus,
Thesprotian, Chaladræan, forth shall rush
The Lion form, and ranging for revenge
Spring from his lair, and lap his kindred blood:
Round him in fawning blandishment shall cower
And cringe, and crook the hinges of their knees,
The chiefs of ancient Argolis, and yield
Sceptres, and realms, and diadems, and thrones.
            LORD ROYSTON (*Alexandra* 1435-1445)

*What the prophecy of the concluding lines refers to remains
a puzzle:*

230   But when athwart the empty-vaulted heaven
Six times of years have rolled, War shall repose
His lance, obedient to my Kinsman's voice;
Who rich in spoils of monarchs shall return
With friendly looks, and carollings of love,
While Peace sits brooding upon seas and land.
            LORD ROYSTON (*Alexandra* 1446-1450)

CLEANTHES

*The religious fervor of which Stoicism was capable is illus-
trated in the hymn of Cleanthes (331-232 B.C.), the most
spiritual which has survived from pagan antiquity.*

231   O God most glorious, called by many a name,
Nature's great King, through endless years the same;
Omnipotence, who by thy just decree
Controllest all, hail, Zeus, for unto thee
Behoves thy creatures in all lands to call.
We are thy children, we alone, of all

On earth's broad ways that wander to and fro,
Bearing thine image wheresoe'er we go.
Wherefore with songs of praise thy power I will forth show.
Lo! yonder heaven, that round the earth is wheeled,
Follows thy guidance, still to thee doth yield
Glad homage; thine unconquerable hand
Such flaming minister, the levin-brand
Wieldeth, a sword two-edged, whose deathless might
Pulsates through all that Nature brings to light;
Vehicle of the universal Word, that flows
Through all, and in the light celestial glows
Of stars both great and small. O King of Kings
Through ceaseless ages, God, whose purpose brings
To birth whate'er on land or in the sea
Is wrought, or in high heaven's immensity;
Save what the sinner works infatuate.
Nay, but thou knowest to make crooked straight:
Chaos to thee is order: in thine eyes
The unloved is lovely, who didst harmonize
Things evil with things good, that there should be
One Word through all things everlastingly.
One Word—whose voice alas! the wicked spurn;
Insatiate for the good their spirits yearn:
Yet seeing see not, neither hearing hear
God's universal law, which those revere,
By reason guided, happiness who win.
The rest, unreasoning, divers shapes of sin
Self-prompted follow: for an idle name
Vainly they wrestle in the lists of fame:
Others inordinately riches woo,
Or dissolute, the joys of flesh pursue.
Now here, now there they wander, fruitless still,
For ever seeking good and finding ill.
Zeus the all-bountiful, whom darkness shrouds,
Whose lightning lightens in the thunder clouds;
Thy children save from error's deadly sway:
Turn thou the darkness from their souls away:
Vouchsafe that unto knowledge they attain;

For thou by knowledge art made strong to reign
O'er all, and all things rulest righteously.
So by thee honoured, we will honour thee,
Praising thy works continually with songs,
As mortals should; nor higher meed belongs
E'en to the gods than justly to adore
The universal law for evermore.

      JAMES ADAM

ARATUS

*Didactic poetry was a specialty of the Alexandrians, and we
have long poems by Nicander on such unlikely themes as
poisons and their antidotes. The best of the class is the
Phainomena of Aratus (315-240 B.C.), which is a kind of
versified handbook of astronomy. The spirited opening shows
the poet's Stoicism and suggests dependence on Cleanthes.*

232   Let us begin with Zeus, the power we mortals never leave
Unsaluted. Zeus fills all the city streets,
All the nations' crowded marts; fills the watery deeps
And havens; every labour needs the aid of Zeus.
His children are we. He benignant
Raises high signals, summoning man to toil,
And warning him of life's demands: tells when the sod is
      fittest
For oxen and harrows; tells the auspicious hours
For planting the sapling and casting every seed.
'Twas he who set the beacons in the sky,
And grouped the stars, and formed the annual round
Of constellations, to mark unerringly
The days when labour is crowned first with increase.
Him therefore men propitiate first and last.
Hail, father, mighty marvel! hail! mighty benefactor!
Thyself and those who begot thee! And ye too, Muses,

Gracious influences, hail! and while I essay to tell of skies
What mortal may tell, guide right my wandering lay.

E. POSTE (*Phainomena* 1-18)

The show-piece of the poem is the description of Virgo *in the
Zodiac:*

Below the Waggoner's feet   **23**
Lo the Virgin, in her hand a glittering ear of corn.
Whether born of Astræus, whom they call
The old sire of heaven, or from whomsoever sprung,
Her favour be upon us. The story runs,
That earth was once her home,
And that she mixed in human throngs, nor ever shunned
Society of man or woman of olden times;
But sate among them, immortal though she were,
And bore the name of Justice: and summoning the elders
In solemn senate or wide market-place,
She sang in thrilling strains the notes of equal law.
As yet they knew not baleful strife
Nor parted interests' bitter feud nor battle;
But lived a life all unalloyed, far from the dangerous sea,
And no ships brought their food from foreign lands;
But oxen and the plough and throned Justice
Yielded ten thousandfold to all their needs, with distribution
    due.
These things were when earth nurtured the golden race.
The silver race she visited more rarely with somewhat altered
    mood,
No longer finding the spirits of former days:
Yet she consorted with the silver race.
At eve she would come from the echoing mountains
Uncompanioned, nor had she gentle words for any:
But when she hill-ward drew the thronging crowds,
Her voice was stern, upbraiding their crimes.
No more, said she, at their invocations would she meet them
    face to face.
'How base a progeny sprang from golden sires!

And viler shall they be whom ye beget,
And wars shall break forth, and unholy blood
Stain the earth, and sin bring penal woe.'
After such speech she would hie mountain-ward, and leave
    the human tribes
Straining eager gaze on her retiring form.
But when that generation died, and there was born
A brazen generation, more pernicious than their sires,
Who forged the felon sword
For hostile foray, and tasted the blood of the ox that drew
    the plough,
Justice, loathing that race of men,
Winged her flight to heaven; and fixed her station in that
    region
Where still by night is seen
The Virgin goddess, near to bright Bootes.

    E. POSTE (*Phainomena* 96-136)

CALLIMACHUS

Callimachus is the perfect embodiment of Alexandrianism.
His is the elaborate art of the miniature. His metrical pre-
cision makes Homer slipshod; his erudition, Milton a school-
boy. But, except in his epigrams, polish and learning leave
little room for anything else. Where the Homeric Hymns
are written by and for believers, those of Callimachus are
written by an artist for a special "literary" audience. The
version of the first hymn, given below, is somewhat curtailed,
especially at beginning and end, but its spirit is remarkably
faithful.

Hymn to Zeus

                   Great Rhea,
234 Pregnant, to high Parrhasia's cliffs retired,
And wild Lycaeus, black with shading pines:

Holy retreat! Sithence no female hither,
Conscious of social love and nature's rites,
Must dare approach, from the inferior reptile
To woman, form divine. There the blest parent
Ungirt her spacious bosom, and discharged
The ponderous birth: she sought a neighbouring spring
To wash the recent babe: in vain: Arcadia,
(However streamy) now adust and dry,
Denied the goddess water; where deep Melas,
And rocky Cratis flow, the chariot smoked,
Obscure with rising dust: the thirsty traveller
In vain required the current, then imprisoned
In subterraneous caverns: forests grew
Upon the barren hollows, high o'ershading
The haunts of savage beasts, where now Iaon
And Erimanth incline their friendly urns.

  Thou too, O Earth, great Rhea said, bring forth;
And short shall be thy pangs. She said; and high
She reared her arm, and with her sceptre struck
The yawning cliff; from its disparted height
Adown the mount the gushing torrent ran,
And cheered the valleys: there the heavenly mother
Bathed, mighty king, thy tender limbs: she wrapt them
In purple bands: she gave the precious pledge
To prudent Neda, charging her to guard thee,
Careful and secret: Neda, of the nymphs
That tended the great birth, next Philyre
And Styx, the eldest. Smiling, she received thee,
And conscious of the grace, absolved her trust:
Not unrewarded; since the river bore
The favourite virgin's name: fair Neda rolls
By Lerpion's ancient walls, a faithful stream.
Fast by her flowery banks the sons of Arcas,
Favourites of Heaven, with happy care protect
Their fleecy charge; and joyous drink her wave.

  Thee, God, to Cnossus Neda brought: the nymphs
And Corybantes thee, their sacred charge,
Received: Adraste rocked thy golden cradle:

The goat, now bright amidst her fellow stars,
Kind Amalthea, reacht her teat distent
With milk, thy early food: the sedulous bee
Distilled her honey on thy purple lips.
    Around, the fierce Curetes (order solemn
To thy foreknowing mother!) trod tumultuous
Their mystic dance, and clanged their sounding arms;
Industrious with the warlike din to quell
Thy infant cries and mock the ear of Saturn:
Swift growth, and wondrous grace, O heavenly Jove,
Waited thy blooming years: inventive wit,
And perfect judgment, crowned thy youthful act.
That Saturn's sons received the threefold empire
Of Heaven, of ocean, and deep hell beneath,
As the dark urn and chance of lot determined,
Old poets mention, fabling. Things of moment
Well-nigh equivalent and neighbouring value
By lot are parted: but high Heaven, thy share,
In equal balance laid 'gainst sea or hell,
Flings up the adverse scale, and shuns proportion.
Wherefore not chance, but power, above thy brethren
Exalted thee, their king. When thy great will
Commands thy chariot forth, impetuous strength,
And fiery swiftness wing the rapid wheels,
Incessant; high the eagle flies before thee,
And oh! as I and mine consult thy augur,
Grant the glad omen: let thy favourite rise
Propitious, ever soaring from the right.
    Thou to the lesser gods hast well assigned
Their proper shares of power: thy own, great Jove,
Boundless and universal. Those who labour
The sweaty forge, who edge the crooked scythe,
Bend stubborn steel, and harden gleaming armour,
Acknowledge Vulcan's aid. The early hunter
Blesses Diana's hand, who leads him safe
O'er hanging cliffs, who spreads his net successful,
And guides the arrow thro' the panther's heart.
The soldier, from successful camps returning

With laurel wreathed, and rich with hostile spoil,
Severs the bull to Mars. The skilful bard,
Striking the Thracian harp, invokes Apollo,
To make his hero and himself immortal.
Those, mighty Jove, meantime, thy glorious care,
Who model nations, publish laws, announce
Or life or death, and found or change the empire.
Man owns the power of kings; and kings of Jove.
MATTHEW PRIOR

Hymn to Apollo

What force, what sudden impulse, thus can make   **235**
The laurel-branch, and all the temple shake!
Depart, ye souls profane; hence, hence! O fly
Far from this holy place! Apollo's nigh;
He knocks with gentle foot; the Delian palm
Submissive bends, and breathes a sweeter balm:
Soft swans, high hovering, catch th' auspicious sign,
Wave their white wings, and pour their notes divine.
Ye bolts, fly back; ye brazen doors, expand,
Leap from your hinges, Phœbus is at hand.
Begin, young men, begin the sacred song,
Wake all your lyres, and to the dances throng,
Remembering still, the Power is seen by none
Except the just and innocent alone;
Prepare your minds, and wash the spots away,
That hinder men to view th' all-piercing ray,
Lest ye provoke his favouring beams to bend
On happier climes, and happier skies ascend:
And lo! the Power, just opening on the sight,
Diffuses bliss, and shines with heavenly light.
Nor should the youthful choir with silent feet,
Or harps unstrung, approaching Phœbus meet,
If soon they wish to mount the nuptial bed,
To deck with sweet perfumes the hoary head,
On old foundations lofty walls to build,
Or raise new cities in some distant field.

Ye listening crowds, in awful silence hear
Apollo's praises, and the song revere;
Even raging seas subside, when poets sing
The bow, the harp of the Lycorean king:
Nor Thetis, wretched mother, dares deplore
Her lov'd, her lost Achilles, now no more!
But thrill'd with awe, she checks her grief and pain,
When Io Pæan sounds along the main.
The weeping rock, once Niobe, suspends
Its tears a while, and mute attention lends;
No more she seems a monument of woe,
Nor female sighs through Phrygian marble flow.
Sound Io! Io! such the dreadful end
Of impious mortals, that with gods contend;
Who dares high heaven's immortal powers engage,
Against our king a rebel war would wage,
And who rebels against our sovereign's sway
Would brave the bright far-shooting god of day.
But rich rewards await the grateful choir
That still to Phœbus tune the living lyre;
From him all honour springs, and high above
He sits in power, at the right hand of Jove.
Beyond the day, beyond the night prolong
The sacred theme, to charm the god of song.
Let all resound his praise; behold how bright
Apollo shines in robes of golden light;
Gold are his quiver, harp, and Lyctian bow,
And his fair feet with golden sandals glow.
All-bright in gold appears the Power divine,
And boundless wealth adorns his Delphic shrine.
Immortal youth and heavenly beauty crown
His cheeks, unshaded by the softest down,
But his fair tresses drop ambrosial dews,
Distil soft oils, and healing balm diffuse:
And on what favour'd city these shall fall,
Life, health, and safety guard the sacred wall.

To great Apollo various arts belong,
The skill of archers and the powers of song;

By him the sure events of lots are given,
By him the prophet speaks the will of heaven,
And wise physicians, taught by him, delay
The stroke of fate, and turn disease away.
　　But we to Nomius, heavenly shepherd cry,
Since he, for young Admetus, left the sky;
When burning with desire, he deign'd to feed
A mortal's coursers on Amphrysus' mead.
His herds increas'd, and overspread the ground,
Kids leapt, and sportive lambkins frisk'd around,
Where'er Apollo bent his favouring eyes,
The flocks with milk abounded, grew in size,
And pregnant ewes, that brought one lamb before,
Now dropt a double offspring on the shore.
Ere towns are built, or new foundations laid,
We still invoke the great Apollo's aid,
And oracles explore; for with delight
He views new cities rising on the sight;
And Phœbus' self the deep foundations lays.
The god, but four years old, in former days,
First rais'd a structure on th' Ortygian ground
Close by the lake that ever circles round;
When young Diana, skill'd in hunting, laid
Unnumber'd goats, on Cynthus' mountain, dead:
The careful goddess brought their heads away,
And gave them to the glorious god of day;
He broke the horns, and rais'd with artful toil
A wondrous altar from the sylvan spoil,
Plac'd rows on rows, in order still dispos'd,
Which he with circling walls of horn enclos'd;
And from this model, just in every part,
Apollo taught mankind the builder's art.
　　Besides Apollo show'd my native place
To Battus, and the fam'd Theræan race,
A crow propitious sent, that flew before,
And led the wanderers to the Libyan shore.
Apollo, marking from unclouded skies,
Beheld Cyrene's lofty towers arise,

And faithful swore, that Egypt's king should gain
The new-built city and the fertile plain.

To tuneful Phœbus, sacred god of song,
In various nations, various names belong;
Some Boëdromius, Clarius some implore,
But nam'd Carneus on my native shore.
Thee, great Carneus! Sparta first possess'd,
Next Thera's isle was with thy presence bless'd;
You cross'd the swelling main from Thera's bowers,
And then resided in Cyrene's towers.
The sixth from Œdipus convey'd the god
From Lacedæmon o'er the watery road
To Thera's isle; but brought from Thera's strand
By blameless Battus to Asbystis' land.
He rais'd a temple to record thy praise,
Appointed annual feasts, on solemn days,
In fair Cyrene; sacred hymns resound,
And slaughter'd bulls lie bleeding on the ground.

Io! Carnean Phœbus! all must pay
Their vows to thee, and on thine altars lay
Green herbs and painted flowers, when genial spring
Diffuses sweetness from Favonius' wing;
But when stern winter his dark power displays
With yellow crocus feed the rising blaze:
So flames unceasing deck thy hallow'd shrine,
And breathe sweet odours to thy power divine.

With transport Phœbus views the war-like dance,
When fierce Bellona's sons in arms advance,
And, with brown Libyan virgins, tread the ground,
When annual the Carnean feast comes round;
Nor yet Alcides' sons had Cyrene seen,
Her crystal fountain and extended green;
But through Azilis' woods the wanderers stray'd,
And hid their heads within the dusky shade,
When Phœbus standing on the hornèd hill
Beheld the forest and the murmuring rill,
And show'd the warriors to his lovely bride,

Cyrene fair attending at his side,
Who kill'd the lion on Myrtusa's rocks,
That tore the god Eurypylus's flocks.
Apollo saw not from the realms above
A city more deserving of his love;
No rising town, no mighty state obtain'd
Such gifts from Phœbus as Cyrene gain'd,
In dear remembrance of the ravish'd dame,
That crown'd his love, and gave the city's name.
Nor were her sons ungrateful, but bestow'd
Superior honours on their guardian god.

Now Io! Io Pæan! rings around
As first from Delphi rose the sacred sound,
When Phœbus swift descending deign'd to show
His heavenly skill to draw the golden bow.
For when no mortal weapons could repel
Enormous Python horrible and fell,
From his bright bow incessant arrows flew,
And, as he rose, the hissing serpent slew.
Whilst Io! Io Pæan! numbers cry,
Haste, launch thy darts; for surely from the sky
Thou cam'st the great preserver of mankind,
As thy fair mother at thy birth design'd.

An equal foe, pale Envy, late drew near,
And thus suggested in Apollo's ear:
I hate the bard who pours not forth his song
In swelling numbers, loud, sublime, and strong;
No lofty lay should in low murmurs glide,
But wild as waves, and sounding as the tide.
Fierce with his foot indignant Phœbus spurn'd
Th' invidious monster, and in wrath return'd:
Wide rolls Euphrates' wave, but soil'd with mud,
And dust and slime pollute the swelling flood:
For Ceres still the fair Melissæ bring
The purest water from the smallest spring,
That softly murmuring creeps along the plain,
And falls with gentle cadence to the main.

Propitious Phœbus thus thy power extend,
And soon shall Envy to the shades descend.
    H. W. TYTLER

And here are some of Callimachus' epigrams. The first is much expanded, but a classic in its own right:

236 They told me, Heraclitus, they told me you were dead,
They brought me bitter news to hear and bitter tears to shed.
I wept as I remember'd how often you and I
Had tired the sun with talking and sent him down the sky.

And now that thou art lying, my dear old Carian guest,
A handful of grey ashes, long, long ago at rest,
Still are thy pleasant voices, thy nightingales, awake:
For Death, he taketh all away, but these he cannot take.
    (2) WILLIAM CORY

237 Here lie I, Timon; who, alive, all living men did hate:
Pass by, and curse thy fill; but pass and stay not here thy gait.
    (3) W. SHAKESPEARE

238 Here Dicon's son, Acanthian Saon lies
In sacred sleep: say not a good man *dies*.
    (11) LORD NEAVES

239 Now would to God swift ships had ne'er been made!
Then, Sopolis, we had not mourned thy shade—
    Dear son of Diocleides seaward sent!
Now somewhere in deep seas thy corse is tost
Hither and thither—and for whom we lost
    We find thy name an empty monument.
    (19) W. M. HARDINGE

240 Rests Charidas beneath this tomb? "Here I
Son of Arimnas of Cyrene lie."
Charidas! what's below? "Eternal night."
What your returns to earth? "A falsehood quite."
And Pluto? "But a fable: all as one,
Body and soul are ended and undone.
Soft words you'd have of me, I speak the true,

An ox in Hades fares as well as you."
   (15) R. G. MacGregor

This morning we beheld with streaming eyes   **241**
The flames from Melanippus' body rise;
At eve fair Basile resign'd her breath,
Disdaining to survive a brother's death;
With frantic hands she gave the deadly blow
That sent her soul to gloomy shades below.
Two mighty ills the wretched sire must mourn,
And weep around a son and daughter's urn;
Old Aristippus sunk in grief appears,
And old Cyrene melts in briny tears.
   (22) H. W. Tytler

ADDAEUS

*There were numerous other epigrammatists, in Greece as in
Alexandria. Addaeus of Macedonia (about 320 B.C.) has the
following:*

    The ox, rewarded for his pains,   **242**
       Is spared the butcher's cruel stroke.
    Now, lowing on the grassy plains,
       He hymns his freedom from the yoke.
      Earl of Cromer (*Pal. Anth.* 6.228)

ANYTE

*One of the favorite forms of Anyte of Tegea (about 300
B.C.) was the epigram on a building or statue. Here are her
lines on statues of Venus and of Hermes:*

    Seaward the gentle Cyprian loves to gaze,   **243**
      And call the sailor back to Love and Home.

Trembling, the loud-resounding billows praise
   The goddess fair, who rose from out the foam.
      EARL OF CROMER (*Pal. Anth.* 9.144)

244   Here in the orchard's breezy nook
   I Hermes stand,
And from the crossroads overlook
   The plashing strand.
Here to the wayfarer forspent
   Repose I bring;
Cold gushing from the earth is sent
   A limpid spring.
      WALTER LEAF (*Pal. Anth.* 9.314)

SIMMIAS

Simmias of Rhodes (about 300 B.C.) has a fine epitaph for Sophocles:

245   Wind, gentle evergreen, to form a shade
Around the tomb where Sophocles is laid;
Sweet ivy, wind thy boughs, and intertwine
With blushing roses and the clustering vine:
Thus will thy lasting leaves, with beauties hung,
Prove grateful emblems of the lays he sung;
Whose soul, exalted like a god of wit,
Among the Muses and the Graces writ.
      ANONYMOUS (*Pal. Anth.* 7.22)

ASCLEPIADES

*Asclepiades of Samos (about 290 B.C.) is a first-class poet,
to whom Theocritus expressed his indebtedness. His epigrams
are among the best in their kind, at once tender and sharply
cut.*

Snow and hail and flash and gloom—   **246**
darken the earth in storm!
Until your thunders bring my doom
I never shall conform,
but in the face of yet worse odds
hail Love with wine and song,
for he is strong among the gods
who now drags me along:—
my master now who once was yours,
when, Zeus, at his persuasion,
you sought your love through brazen doors—
a glittering invasion.
    WILLIAM WALLACE AND MARY WALLACE
    (*Pal. Anth.* 7.22)

Hermione   **247**
was roguishly
engaged in play
with me one day,
when round her waist I found a band
bright worked in gold with this command:
*Love me and leave
And never grieve
If others too
Do as you do.*
    WILLIAM WALLACE AND MARY WALLACE
    (*Pal. Anth.* 5.58)

248   Demetrios, go to the market and
           get me some fish from Amyntas—
           don't worry, you won't have to count them
           yourself, for I know he won't stint us:
           three shiners and ten little carp and
           two dozen small shrimps. And don't potter
           about! So be off—wait! Six wreaths . . . and
           ask Tryphera too, I forgot her!
                    WILLIAM WALLACE AND MARY WALLACE
                    (*Pal. Anth.* 5.185)

249   This small, delightful book Erinna wrote;
           its little size betrays her nineteen years.
           Yet few indeed have struck so true a note:
           Had death not come, whose name had equalled hers?
                    WILLIAM WALLACE AND MARY WALLACE
                    (*Pal. Anth.* 7.11)

250   I, Valour, wretched maid, sit here forlorn
           By Ajax' tomb, my locks for sorrow shorn:
           Grieved at my heart, among the Greeks to see
           Crafty and base deceit preferred to me.
                    LORD NEAVES (*Pal. Anth.* 7.145)

251   In less than two and twenty years
           my cares have worn me out.
           The young loves laugh to see my tears;
           and if I die?—Without a doubt
           they'll roll, unheeding, as before,
           their ivory dice upon the floor.
                    WILLIAM WALLACE AND MARY WALLACE
                    (*Pal. Anth.* 12.46)

POSIDIPPUS

Asclepiades was one of a circle of poets of which other members were his friends Posidippus and Hedylus. Here is Posidippus on love and on wine:

Trust not to tears, Philaenis, nay,
  Nor think that you deceive me.
You love me best of all you say?
  I know it well, believe me.

Whilst I am here your vows are true;
  No love could be sincerer,
Until another come to you
  Then he will be the dearer.
  J. A. POTT (*Pal. Anth.* 5.186)

252

With Bacchus' shower soak us all,
  O Attic demijohn.
Let thy rain impartial fall
  Our merry club upon.

Zeno, the dying swan, is dead;
  Cleanthes cannot sing;
Love reigneth till we go to bed,
  Our sweet and bitter king.
  W. R. PATON (*Pal. Anth.* 5.134)

253

The following pensive lines are attributed to Posidippus, but alternatively to Plato Comicus:

What course of life should wretched mortals take?
In courts hard questions large contention make:

254

Care dwells in houses, labour in the field,
Tumultuous seas affrighting dangers yield.
In foreign lands thou never canst be blessed;
If rich, thou art in fear; if poor, distressed.
In wedlock frequent discontentments swell;
Unmarried persons as in deserts dwell.
How many troubles are with children born;
Yet he that wants them counts himself forlorn.
Young men are wanton, and of wisdom void;
Gray hairs are cold, unfit to be employed.
Who would not one of these two offers choose,
Not to be born, or breath with speed to lose?
    JOHN BEAUMONT (*Pal. Anth.* 9.359)

METRODORUS

*The proper response to Posidippus' gloom are these lines by
the Epicurean Metrodorus:*

255

In every way of life true pleasure flows:
Immortal fame from public action grows:
Within the doors is found appeasing rest;
In fields the gifts of nature are expressed.
The sea brings gain, the rich abroad provide
To blaze their names, the poor their wants to hide:
All households best are governed by a wife;
His cares are light who leads a single life:
Sweet children are delights which marriage bless;
He that hath none disturbs his thoughts the less.
Strong youth can triumph in victorious deeds;
Old age the soul with pious motions feeds.
All states are good, and they are falsely led
Who wish to be unborn or quickly dead.
    JOHN BEAUMONT (*Pal. Anth.* 9.360)

HEDYLUS

The third of the group is least fully represented. Here is one of Hedylus on drink:

> Crown high the cup and pass it round,   **256**
>   For subtle thought and rare
> Or miracle of honeyed sound
>   Perchance is lurking there.
>
> Full draughts of Chian let me taste
>   If ye would stir my wit,
> For life is but an arid waste
>   Except we moisten it.
>   J. A. POTT

LEONIDAS OF TARENTUM

Leonidas of Tarentum (about 280) is represented by about a hundred poems in the Palatine Anthology. The following are on Erinna, an old fisherman, an old shepherd, and the brevity of life.

> Erinna, songstress of the honeyed lay,   **257**
> Was wooed by Death, and could not say him nay.
> Still the wise maiden, with her parting breath,
> True to the Muses, sang "Ah! envious Death!"
>   EARL OF CROMER (*Pal. Anth.* 7.13)

> Here lies old Theris: death has set him free   **258**
> From tossing like a gull upon the sea.

His weels and seines, his coble with one oar,
The fish, the rocks will never see him more.
And yet no autumn gale, no tempest's rage
Brought to its end the full tale of his age.
Within the wattled cabin where he lay
Life's lamp burned low and slowly died away.
Nor wife nor children dear were with him then,
This tomb was built by fellow fishermen.
    F. A. Wright (*Pal. Anth.* 7.295)

259   Shepherds, ye that haunt these rocks
With your goats and fleecy flocks,
Grant a boon of simple worth,
For the sake of Mother Earth
And the Queen of Shades below;
Let my sheep and kidlings go
Bleating, while the gentle swain
Pipes to them a soothing strain,
On a rustic hillock set;
Let my village neighbours met,
Soon as spring renews the bloom,
Crop the meads to deck my tomb.
May the ewe's prest udder shed
Sweet libation o'er my bed.
E'en the dead have grace to give
Boons in turn to them who live.
    Walter Leaf (*Pal. Anth.* 7.657)

260 Measureless time or ever thy years, O man, were reckon'd;
    Measureless time shall run over thee low in the ground.
And thy life between is—? The flick of a flying second,
    A flash, a point—or less, if a lesser thing can be found.
    Edwyn Bevan (*Pal. Anth.* 7.472)

NOSSIS

Nossis (early third century) was reputed to be a very passion-
ate poetess; what we have is sweet but tame, for example,

> Pretty Nossis vows that she   **261**
> Spurns the honey of the bee,
> But that Cupid can distil
> Sweets the cup of joy to fill.
> Who Venus hates can never know
> What roses in her garden grow.
>   EARL OF CROMER *(Pal. Anth. 5.170)*

MOERO

Moero, of about the same period, was an epic poetess and the
mother of a tragic poet. The following seems to be a dedica-
tion for an artificial cluster of grapes:

> Abrim with Dionysos' wine   **262**
> Thou liest, daughter of the vine,
> In Aphrodite's golden fane.
> Thy mother never may again
> A twining tendril 'round thee throw,
> Nor bid a nectarous leaf shading thy head to grow.
>   W. C. LAWTON *(Pal. Anth. 6.119)*

APOLLONIUS OF RHODES

The erudite Argonautica, whose subject is Jason's quest of the Golden Fleece, was written to disprove Callimachus' thesis that long epics could no longer be written. In keeping with the spirit of the age, Jason's prowess is mainly in the lists of love. The first considerable adventure, for example, is the stop at Lemnos, which was inhabited only by women. Here they dally, and have to be recalled to their task by Heracles.

263
So did he chide with the band; was none dared meet his eye,

Neither look in his face, nor was any man found that essayed reply.

But straight from his presence, to make their departing ready, they went

In haste; and the women came running, so soon as they knew their intent.

And as when round the beautiful lilies the wild bees hum at their toil,

From their hive in the rock forth pouring; the dew-sprent meadow the while

Around them rejoiceth, and hovering, stooping, now and again

They sip of the sweet flower-fountains—in such wise round the men

Forth streamed the women with yearning faces, making their moan;

And with hands caressing and soft sad words did they greet each one,

Beseeching the Blessed to grant them a home-coming void of bane.

Yea, so doth Hypsipyle pray, as her clinging fingers strain

The hand of Jason, and stream her tears with the parting-
pain:
  "Go thou, and thee may the Gods with thy comrades
scathless bring
Back to the home-land, bearing the Fleece of Gold to the
king,
Even as thou wilt, and thine heart desireth: and this mine
isle,
And my father's sceptre withal, shall wait for thee the while,
If haply, thine home-coming won, thou wouldst choose to
come hither again.
Thou couldst gather from other cities a host unnumbered of
men
Lightly—ah, but the longing shall never awaken in thee;
Yea, and mine own heart bodeth that this shall never be!
Yet O remember Hypsipyle whilst thou art far away,
And when home thou hast won; and leave me a word that thy
love shall obey
With joy, if the Gods shall vouchsafe me to bear a son to my
lord."
    A. S. WAY (*Argonautica* 1.875-898)

*The first great trial is the passage through the Symplegades,
or Clashing Rocks, which is effected with the help of Athene.*

Long did the heroes with King Phineus bide,   **264**
While every day at morn or eventide
The men of Thrace brought them rich gifts and rare
To court the favor of the King, that there
Full sweet it seemed to rest. But at the last
They shipped the oars, and raised the well-braced mast,
After that they had built of stones and sods
Beside the sea twelve altars to the gods,
And sacrificed thereon. Then they embarked,
And ready for the voyage again they harked
To Phineus' words, and wise Euphemus bore
In hand the shrinking dove. So from the shore
They cast the hawsers loose, and, gathering way,

Drove the swift Argo through the dashing spray,
And Pallas watched the voyagers outward bound.
Now, when they neared the narrow, crooked sound,
And saw on either bow the rocky clift
Skyward upreared without a break or rift,
And underneath the ship the eddies leap
And slap against the bow, a dread 'gan creep
Over their hearts; and ever more the crash
Of those dire rocks smote on their ears, with clash
Of booming breakers on the sea-washed brow
Of cape and headland. Then upon the prow
Stalwart arose Euphemus, and did stand
Before them all, the gray dove in his hand,
And at the call of Tiphys from the poop
Each heartily upon his oar did stoop,
Trusting the helmsman's might to steer them straight
Out through the perils of that fearful gate
Where ship had never swum. But when the last
Of all the headlands rounded had been passed,
And now they saw the dread rocks gape apart,
Within each hero melted then his heart.
Euphemus then cast forth the dove to fly;
All ceased to row and looked, as down the high
And narrow cleft of rocks the swift bird flew.
Quickly the dread rocks closed, but she was through
Ere with a grinding crash they met. Then splashed
The spray in clouds aloft, and the seas dashed
To the vast heaven thundering with the shock,
While in the hollow caverns of the rock
Deep boomed the washing waves, and o'er the clift
Was blown the white foam!
                Straight the eddying drift
Whirled the good ship around. The rocks had shorn
The dove's tail feathers, but herself was borne
Unscathed from out them, and the heartened rowers
Shouted; but Tiphys bade them ply their oars
With all their strength, for now the rocks again
Were opening, so they rowed with might and main.

Yet trembling held them, till the returning swell
Rushed back and bore them 'twixt the cliffs. Then fell
Dire terror on them, for above them all
Certain destruction threatened from each wall.
And now before them stretched the open sea
Beyond the rocks' mouth, when all suddenly
A mighty wave rose up before the bow
Curving and steep as some abrupt cliff's brow,
And when they saw it hang above them there
One moment ere it overwhelmed, despair
Bowed their averted heads. But Tiphys' skill,
Easing the good ship as she labored still
Beneath the oars avoided yet this death,
And all the great wave slid away beneath
The keel, but surging, bore the ship, uplift
In air, astern, far from the rocky clift.
Then rose Euphemus yet again, and paced
From bow to stern along the Argo's waist
Amidst the rowers, urging each by name
To spend his whole soul in his stroke for shame;
And so again with shouts each drove the oar.
But howsoe'er the ship gave way before
Their strokes, yet twice so fast abaft was borne
The Argo, tho' the oars like bows of horn
Bent with the heroes' strength. Then once again
Came a great curving billow from the main,
And now the tall ship rose and rode the sea,
And as it shook her off, plunged mightily
Down, down into the hollow of the wave;
But midst the rocks the eddying swirls that lave
The beetling walls, held back the Argo, and
The echoing crags crept near on either hand,
Until they touched the timbers of the ship.
Then great Athene with the mighty grip
Of her left hand sundered the rocks in twain,
And with her right hand pushed the ship amain
That forth she flew swift as a feathered shaft.
Yet Argo lost the high curved poop abaft

The rudders, which was barely caught and crushed
As the great rocks hurtling together rushed.
Then Pallas, when she saw the peril passed,
Returned to high Olympus. But steadfast,
Forever moveless, sundered but a space,
Now keeps each rooted rock its fated place;
For the just gods had doomed them to this fate
When once a living man should pass that gate.
And now the heroes breathed once more, and shook
The icy terror from them, and dared look
Half timidly upon the sky and sea
Spread out before them ever endlessly;
And they were silent, midst new life and dear,
For their wide eyes had seen dark Hades near.

L. P. CHAMBERLAYNE (*Argonautica* 2.528-611)

The heart of the Argonautica *is the third book, which tells
the loves of Jason and Medea. By the contrivance of Hera
and Athene Eros shoots an arrow at Medea, and this is its
effect:*

265
A sudden transport seiz'd the melting maid:
The god, exulting now, no longer staid.
The glowing shaft the virgin's heart inspires,
And in her bosom kindles amorous fires.
On Jason beamed the splendour of her eyes;
Her swoln breast heav'd with unremitting sighs:
The frantic maid had all remembrance lost,
And the soft pain her sickening soul engross'd.
As some good housewife, who, to labour born,
Fresh to her loom must rise with early morn;
Studious to gain what human wants require,
In embers heap'd preserves the seeds of fire;
Renew'd by these the brand rekindling burns,
And all the glowing heap to ashes turns:
Thus, kindling slow, love's secret flames invade,
And torture, as they rise, the troubled maid;

Her changeful cheeks the heartfelt anguish show,
Now pale they turn, now like the ruby glow.
> FRANCIS FAWKES (*Argonautica* 3.285-298)

Medea's first sight of Jason is overwhelming, and leaves her
in an agony of pity and fear for him. In her bed at night she
dreams, and is in a torment of indecision:

Now as she lay upon her couch awhile   9.66
>   Deep slumber calmed Medea's fevered breast,
>   Yet visions such as trouble and beguile
>   Afflicted spirits came to break her rest,
>   And she imagined in her dream, their guest
>   Had come unto the city of the king
>   And undertaken such a perilous test
>   Not for the fleece, but rather coveting
Her for his wedded wife and homeward her to bring.

Now she herself was struggling, as it seemed,
>   With those fire-breathing oxen, unafraid,
>   And easily prevailed: and now she dreamed
>   Her father heeded not the promise made,
>   For upon Jason, not on her, was laid
>   That task; whereon a sharp contention rose
>   Between him and the stranger, and they prayed
>   That she herself their quarrel would compose.
She passed her father by and that adventurer chose.

Thereat her parents, sore discomforted,
>   Cried out in indignation, and their cries
>   Roused her from sleep; she started up in dread,
>   All quivering, and with wide and anxious eyes
>   Peered round her room, if she might recognize
>   From whence that sound had risen; and hardly yet
>   Recovering, broke forth into deep-drawn sighs:
>   "Alas, what heavy dreams my soul beset.
Those heroes' coming, sure, great mischief will beget.

" 'Tis for yon stranger that such deep dismay
    Afflicts me; let him go and seek a bride
    In his own land Achæa far away,
    And let me in my father's house abide
    A maiden still. Yet will I lay aside
    My fear and shame and prove my sister's heart,
    Whether she will entreat me to provide
    Some means whereby he may perform his part.
She for her children fears, and that would ease my smart."

This said, she rose and crossed the chamber floor
    To find her sister, barefoot and arrayed
    In but one robe; now opened she the door,
    Now passed the threshold, but even there was stayed
    By shame, and turned into her room, afraid;
    Again went forward and returned again,
    So idly to and fro her footsteps strayed.
    Shame held her back, when she to go was fain,
And love still urged her on, whene'er she would remain.

Thrice she went forth, thrice back into her room,
    Then, wrung by anguish, on her bed lay prone.
    Even as a bride mourns the young husband's doom
    Whom sire or brethren lately made her own,
    Nor wills her grief should openly be shown
    But in pure shame her handmaids would avoid,
    And sitting in her chamber weeps alone
    For him whom fate so early has destroyed
Ere in each other's sweet society they joyed.

Burning with grief yet silently the while,
    Eying her widowed bed, she mourns apart,
    Lest women's tongues should chide her and revile;
    So wept Medea.
    J. C. WORDSWORTH (*Argonautica* 3.617-664)

*Even after she has arranged to help Jason she is again plunged
into an agony of doubt and shame:*

Now over earth was spread the veil of night   **267**
    And weary sailors wandering o'er the deep
    Looked towards the Bear and towards Orion's light
    That guide them from on high their course to keep.
    The wayfarer, the warder sighed for sleep,
    And in the folds of heavy slumber bound
    The mother for her dead forgot to weep.
    No voice of man was heard nor barking hound
But silence and the dark wrapped all the city round.

But on Medea's eyes no slumber came,
    Such care for Jason all her thoughts possessed,
    Fearing the mighty bulls, whose breath of flame
    Was like to slay him in that perilous quest,
    And fast the heart was trembling in her breast
    Like to the light that quivers on a wall
    From water in a pail not come to rest.
    Now here, now there the flickering beam will fall
And idly to and fro goes dancing through the hall.

So quivered in her breast the troubled heart,
    The tears of pity falling from her eyes.
    Through her soft body ran the burning smart
    And thrilled her nerves with tingling agonies
    And fastened deep within her neck, where lies
    The region pain most sharply visiteth
    When to the heart Love's stinging arrow flies.
    And now those charms against the fiery breath
Her purpose was to give, and now to share his death.

Then neither would she die nor give him aid
    But bear her sorrow, quiet and resigned.
    Doubting she sat, and wavered long, and said:
    "Woe's me, which evil shall I choose, who find

Such torment every way beset my mind?
   No remedy, but still it burns the more.
   Would Artemis with arrows swift and kind
   Had slain me ere I saw the man, before
Thy sons, Chalciope, sailed for the Achæan shore.

"Some god or Fury sent them hitherward
   To be my woe and ruin. Let him die
   There on the field, if such be Fate's award.
   How could I give, without discovery,
   The magic charms? discovered, how reply?
   What means can I devise to aid the chief?
   Can I meet him alone, no comrade nigh?
   Alas, but if he suffer death, my grief
Will never at such cost find comfort or relief.

"That were for me a sad and evil hour.
   Avaunt all shame and honour then, I say,
   And let the man, delivered by my power,
   Where'er he please to wander take his way.
   But when he has prevailed, that very day
   May death be mine by strangling with the noose
   Or tasting drugs that bring life to decay.
   Yet even when dead will evil tongues and loose
Mock me, and all the folk pursue me with abuse.

"Yea, all the Colchian women far and wide
   Will spread the deep dishonour of her name
   Who in her fondness for a stranger died
   And yielding to mad passion brought to shame
   Her father's house. Such then will be my fame.
   Far better were it by an instant doom
   To save myself from all disgrace and blame,
   This very night to perish in my room
Ere ever thus to blast my honour I presume."

She spake, and fetched a casket where she kept
   Full many a drug of good effect or ill,

And setting this upon her knees she wept,
The tears upon her bosom falling still,
So miserable a fate she must fulfil.
Long she her doom lamented, yet designed
To reach unto her lips the drugs that kill.
And now the casket she unloosed to find
The poison that should end her destiny unkind.

But suddenly the dread of hideous death
And speechless horror on her spirit fell,
And long she sat aghast with panting breath,
While all the pleasing cares that weave the spell
Of life, all joys that with the living dwell
Came thronging to her heart; she thought once more,
As maidens will, of comrades loved so well,
And the sweet sun grew sweeter than before
And all things in her sight a fairer semblance wore.

And now she put the casket from her knee,
So Hera changed her heart, nor longer space
Sat she in doubt but rather longed to see
The dawn, that she might bring unto the place
The promised charms and meet him face to face;
And oft did she unbolt the door, intent
To watch for morning's first and faintest trace.
And now at last the welcome light was sent
And through the awakened town a rising murmur went.

J. C. WORDSWORTH (*Argonautica* 3.744-824)

When the seer Mopsus accompanies Jason to the tryst he is
roundly scolded by a Hera-inspired crow:

"A sorry prophet this, a witless seer,
    Who hath not yet for all his skill divined
    What even to children is right plain and clear,
    That never maiden was so bold of mind
    To give a youth one loving word and kind
    When strangers were at hand nor would retire.

268

Go, foolish prophet, ignorant and blind!
Never did Cypris thy dull heart inspire,
Nor feltest thou the breath of warm desire."

.   .   .   .

So shrewdly he advised and they approved.
Meanwhile Medea played and sang among
Her company, but all her thought still moved
Towards the hero's coming, and no song
She raised her voice unto might please her long
But still broke off in restless discontent.
Nor could she keep her eyes upon the throng
Of handmaids, but her looks were ever sent
Far off along the path on other solace bent.

And many a time she trembled and came nigh
Even to swooning at the fancied sound
Of steps, or when some gust of wind passed by.
But now her eyes his wished-for coming found;
Onward he came, high striding o'er the ground,
As bright as Sirius rising o'er the deep,
Whose light shines clear above the stars around
But smites with deadly pestilence the sheep;
So beautiful came he and made her spirit leap,

But with him love and all love's sorrows came.
Wildly the heart within her bosom beat
And her fair cheeks were blushing red as flame;
Upon her eyes fell darkness and her feet
Could neither bear her forwards nor retreat
But stood as though into the earth they grew.
Now when they saw her and the stranger meet
The handmaids of Medea all withdrew
Unto a place apart and left alone those two.

And they stood face to face, voiceless and still,
Like oaks or lofty pine-trees that have taken
Firm root together on the self-same hill,

That stand all silent, by the winds forsaken,
But murmur low soon as their leaves are shaken;
So these were silent till the gentle wind
Of coming Love their voices should awaken.
But Jason knew some passion filled her mind,
Heaven-sent, and spake to her in flattering words and kind.

. . . .

So spake he, and she turned her eyes aside,
Sweetly as nectar smiling at his praise
That lifted up her heart with joy and pride;
Then turning once again to meet his face
What first to say she knew not for a space
But fain at once a hundred things would say;
Then drew the magic charm forth from the place
Within her fragrant girdle where it lay
And to his eager hand gave it without delay.

She would have drawn forth from her breast, indeed,
And given to him her very heart and soul,
Glad that her aid and succour he should need;
So sweetly Love her spirit did control,
Lighting a flame that like an aureole
With wondrous beauty circled Jason's head
And all the wealth of her bright glances stole.
Even as the dew upon the roses shed
Melts when the morning sun those flowers hath visited,

So all her heart was melted with delight.
Now on the ground, abashed, their eyes they cast,
Now raised their heads to meet each other's sight,
And many a smiling glance between them passed
Till she the silence broke and spoke at last.

    J. C. WORDSWORTH (*Argonautica* 3.932-1025)

*With the help of Medea's charms Jason is successful in his
trial, and the third book closes. At the beginning of the
fourth her father Aeetes suspects her complicity; she flees*

from home, joins the Argo, and lands with Jason at the wood
which holds the golden fleece and its guardian dragon:

269   So to the sacred wood those two drew nigh
              And sought there for the mighty oak whereon
              The fleece was hanging, like a cloud on high
              Red-glowing when the rising sun has shone.
              But now the serpent, as they hastened on,
              Saw them with eyes that sleep had never bound,
              Saw, and stretched forth his monstrous head anon
              And hissed so loud that all the wood around
        And either bank afar re-echoed to the sound.

        That hiss the Colchians heard whose dwellings stood
              Far off from Æa, where the waters flow
              Of Lycus, parted from the roaring flood
              Of great Araxes, and united go
              With Phasis stream, till both together throw
              Their tribute to the wide Caucasian main.
              And mothers heard far off and wakened so
              Stretched through the dark their hands in terror vain
        And caught their trembling babes unto their breasts again.

        But as from smouldering wood the spiry curls
              Of smoke arise continually on high
              And swiftly one above another whirls
              Its eddying vapour, mounting to the sky;
              So fold on fold the serpent ceaselessly
              Uncoiled his monstrous body, covered all
              With iron scales; whereat the maid drew nigh
              And unto Sleep with gentle voice did call,
        Sleep, highest of the gods, that dragon to enthral,

        And called on the night-wandering Hecate,
              The queen of hell, to favour their design.
              In fear came Jason to the snake; but he,
              Tranced by her song, slackened his rigid spine

And in the dust his body did decline
In coils outspreading like a wave that flows
Silent and dark across the sullen brine.
Yet oftentimes with threatening head he rose
And huge, wide open mouth to seize his daring foes.

But she, the while chanting her magic lay,
  Held in one hand a bowl of witches' brew
And often dipped therein a new-cut spray
Of juniper, wherewith she lightly threw
Upon his eyelids that enchanted dew,
Whose heavy scent scattered deep slumber round.
  Down sank his head, nor further onward drew,
And far behind his scaly folds unwound
Through the wide sacred wood lay trailing on the ground.

Then Jason from the bough that golden prize
  Caught at Medea's bidding, who yet stayed
And rained down slumber on the dragon's eyes,
Till Jason called her back, and she obeyed
And, turning, left the forest's gloomy shade.
  But as a maiden catches on her gown
The radiance of the moon at full displayed
When on her high-roofed chamber it looks down,
The joy of which fair sight doth all her spirit drown;

So Jason in his hands uplifted now
  The mighty trophy, from whose glitterance came
A ruddy glow on his fair cheeks and brow,
A glory on his countenance like a flame.

    J. C. WORDSWORTH (*Argonautica* 4.123-171)

*The Argonauts evade Colchian pursuit by killing Medea's
brother Absyrtus, and after many other adventures arrive at
Phaeacia. The Colchians are still in pursuit, and upon Queen
Arete's suggestion King Alcinous decides that if Medea is
still a maid she must be returned to her father, but if she is*

*married to Jason she must not be separated from him. When
the Argonauts learn this a wedding is quickly prepared in a
famous cave.*

270   To deck with honours due the bridal bed,
                Around it wide the Golden Fleece was spread.
                With sweetest flowers that deck or dale or hill,
                Th' assiduous nymphs their snowy bosoms fill.
                The Golden Fleece emits so bright a ray,
                They shone all radiant as the star of day,
                Inspiring love: the prize though strong desire
                Prompts them to touch, with reverence they retire.
                These are the daughters of the Aegean flood,
                Those, Meletaeum, haunt thy lofty wood,
                From groves, from streams, at Juno's call they ran,
                To grace the nuptials of this godlike man.
                The sacred grot, recorded still by fame,
                Bears to this day Medea's honour'd name.
                For here the nymphs, their veils around them spread,
                To nuptial joys the happy lovers led:
                And every chief, to guard the blissful spot,
                Clad in bright armour, stood before the grot,
                Lest hostile troops with rude tumultuous noise,
                Should force an entrance and distract their joys.
                Thus station'd, they protect the hallow'd ground,
                Their festive brows with leafy chaplets crown'd.
                As Orpheus struck his tuneful lyre, they sung,
                And Hymeneals round the grotto rung.
                FRANCIS FAWKES (*Argonautica* 4.1345-68)

*The king does keep his word, but the trials of the Argonauts
are far from ended. Apollonius continues to bring in every
legend that could be related to the heroes, but the relation-
ship between Jason and Medea is left where Euripides' drama
had taken the story up.*

THEOCRITUS

*The father of pastoral poetry and the truest poet of the
Hellenistic age is the Sicilian Theocritus, of the early third
century B.C. In Idyll 2 forsaken Simaetha has recourse to
magic to recall her neglectful lover.*

Where are the bay-leaves, Thestylis, and the charms?   **271**
Fetch all; with fiery wool the caldron crown;
Let glamour win me back my false lord's heart!
Twelve days the wretch hath not come nigh to me,
Nor made enquiry if I die or live,
Nor clamoured (oh unkindness!) at my door.
Sure his swift fancy wanders otherwhere,
The slave of Aphrodite and of Love.
I'm off to Timagetus' wrestling-school
At dawn, that I may see him and denounce
His doings; but I'll charm him now with charms.
So shine out fair, O moon! To thee I sing
My soft low song: to thee and Hecate
The dweller in the shades, at whose approach
E'en the dogs quake, as on she moves through blood
And darkness and the barrows of the slain.
All hail, dread Hecate: companion me
Unto the end, and work me witcheries
Potent as Circe or Medea wrought,
Or Perimede of the golden hair!
   Turn, magic wheel, draw homeward him I love.
First we ignite the grain. Nay, pile it on:
Where are thy wits flown, timorous Thestylis?
Shall I be flouted, I, by such as thou?
Pile, and still say, "This pile is of his bones."
   Turn, magic wheel, draw homeward him I love.
Delphis racks me: I burn him in these bays.

As, flame-enkindled, they lift up their voice,
Blaze once, and not a trace is left behind:
So waste his flesh to powder in yon fire!
 Turn, magic wheel, draw homeward him I love.
E'en as I melt, not uninspired, the wax,
May Mindian Delphis melt this hour with love:
And, swiftly as this brazen wheel whirls round,
May Aphrodite whirl him to my door.
 Turn, magic wheel, draw homeward him I love.
Next burn the husks. Hell's adamantine floor
And aught that else stands firm can Artemis move.
Thestylis, the hounds bay up and down the town:
The goddess stands i' the crossroads: sound the gongs.
 Turn, magic wheel, draw homeward him I love.
Hushed are the voices of the winds and seas;
But O not hushed the voice of my despair.
He burns my being up, who left me here
No wife, no maiden, in my misery.
 Turn, magic wheel, draw homeward him I love.
Thrice I pour out; speak thrice, sweet mistress, thus:
"What face soe'er hangs o'er him be forgot
Clean as, in Dia, Theseus (legends say)
Forgat his Ariadne's locks of love."
 Turn, magic wheel, draw homeward him I love.
The coltsfoot grows in Arcady, the weed
That drives the mountain-colts and swift mares wild.
Like them may Delphis rave: so, maniac-wise,
Race from his burnished brethren home to me.
 Turn, magic wheel, draw homeward him I love.
He lost this tassel from his robe; which I
Shred thus, and cast it on the raging flames.
Ah baleful Love! why, like the marsh-born leech,
Cling to my flesh, and drain my dark veins dry?
 Turn, magic wheel, draw homeward him I love.
From a crushed eft tomorrow he shall drink
Death! But now, Thestylis, take these herbs and smear
That threshold o'er, whereto at heart I cling
Still, still—albeit he thinks scorn of me—

And spit, and say, " 'Tis Delphis' bones I smear."

Exit THESTYLIS

Turn, magic wheel, draw homeward him I love.
Now all alone, I'll weep a love whence sprung,
When born? Who wrought my sorrow? Anaxo came,
Her basket in her hand, to Artemis' grove.
Bound for the festival, troops of forest beasts
Stood round, and in the midst a lioness.

Bethink thee, mistress Moon, whence came my love.
Theucharidas' slave, my Thracian nurse now dead
Then my near neighbor, prayed me and implored
To see the pageant: I, the poor doomed thing,
Went with her, trailing a fine silken train,
And gathering round me Clearista's robe.

Bethink thee, mistress Moon, whence came my love.
Now, the mid-highway reached by Lycon's farm,
Delphis and Eudamippus passed me by.
With beards as lustrous as the woodbine's gold
And breasts more sheeny than myself, O Moon,
Fresh from the wrestler's glorious toil they came.

Bethink thee, mistress Moon, whence came my love.
I saw, I raved, smit (weakling) to my heart.
My beauty withered, and I cared no more
For all that pomp; and how I gained my home
I know not: some strange fever wasted me.
Ten nights and days I lay upon my bed.

Bethink thee, mistress Moon, whence came my love,
And wan became my flesh, as 't had been dyed,
And all my hair streamed off, and there was left
But bones and skin. Whose threshold crossed I not,
Or missed what grandam's hut who dealt in charms?
For no light thing was this, and time sped on.

Bethink thee, mistress Moon, whence came my love.
At last I spake the truth to that my maid:
"Seek, an thou canst, some cure for my sore pain.
Alas, I am all the Mindian's! But begone,
And watch by Timagetus' wrestling-school:
There doth he haunt, there soothly take his rest.

Bethink thee, mistress Moon, whence came my love.
"Find him alone: nod softly: say, 'she waits';
And bring him." So I spake: she went her way,
And brought the lustrous-limbed one to my roof.
And I, the instant I beheld him step
Lightfooted o'er the threshold of my door,
   (*Bethink thee, mistress Moon, whence came my love*)
"Became all cold like snow, and from my brow
Brake the damp dewdrops: utterance I had none,
Not e'en such utterance as a babe may make
That babbles to its mother in its dreams;
But all my fair frame stiffened into wax.
   Bethink thee, mistress Moon, whence came my love.
He bent his pitiless eyes on me; looked down,
And sate him on my couch, and sitting, said:
"Thou hast gained on me, Simætha, (e'en as I
Gained once on young Philinus in the race),
Bidding me hither ere I came unasked.
   Bethink thee, mistress Moon, whence came my love.
"For I had come, by Eros I had come,
This night, with comrades twain or maybe more,
The fruitage of the Wine-god in my robe,
And, wound about my brow with ribands red,
The silver leaves so dear to Heracles.
   Bethink thee, mistress Moon, whence came my love.
"Had ye said 'Enter,' well; for 'mid my peers
High is my name for goodliness and speed:
I had kissed that sweet mouth once and gone my way.
But had the door been barred, and I thrust out,
With brand and axe would we have stormed ye then.
   Bethink thee, mistress Moon, whence came my love.
"Now be my thanks recorded, first to Love,
Next to thee, maiden, who didst pluck me out,
A half-burned helpless creature, from the flames,
And badst me hither. It is Love that lights
A fire more fierce than his of Lipara;
   (*Bethink thee, mistress Moon, whence came my love*)
"Scares, mischief-mad, the maiden from her bower,
The bride from her warm couch." He spake: and I,

A willing listener, sat, my hand in his,
Among the cushions, and his cheek touched mine,
Each hotter than its wont, and we discoursed
In soft low language. Need I prate to thee,
Sweet Moon, of all we said and all we did?
Till yesterday he found no fault with me,
Nor I with him. But lo, to-day there came
Philista's mother—hers who flutes to me—
With her Melampo's; just when up the sky
Gallop the mares that chariot rose-limbed Dawn:
And divers tales she brought me, with the rest
How Delphis loved, she knew not rightly whom:
But this she knew; that of the rich wine aye
He poured "to Love"; and at the last had fled,
To line, she deemed, the fair one's halls with flowers.
Such was my visitor's tale, and it was true:
For thrice, nay four times, daily he would stroll
Hither, leave here full oft his Dorian flask:
Now—'tis a fortnight since I saw his face.
Doth he then treasure something sweet elsewhere?
Am I forgot? I'll charm him now with charms.
But let him try me more, and by the Fates
He'll soon be knocking at the gates of hell.
Spells of such power are in this chest of mine,
Learned, lady, from mine host in Palestine.

Lady, farewell: turn ocean-ward thy steeds:
As I have purposed, so shall I fulfil.
Farewell, thou bright-faced Moon! Ye stars, farewell,
That wait upon the car of noiseless Night.
    C. S. CALVERLEY

Idyll 7, entitled Harvest Home, *is the earliest specimen of the
pastoral in which actual poets masquerade in shepherds' dress
and bear shepherds' names. Simichidas is Theocritus himself.*

Once on a time did Eucritus and I
(With us Amyntas) to the riverside
Steal from the city. For Lycopeus' sons

Were that day busy with the harvest-home,
Antigenes and Phrasidemus, sprung
(If aught thou holdest by the good old names)
By Clytia from great Chalcon—him who erst
Planted one stalwart knee against the rock,
And lo, beneath his foot Burine's rill
Brake forth, and at its side poplar and elm
Shewed isles of pleasant shadow, greenly roofed
By tufted leaves. Scarce midway were we now,
Nor yet descried the tomb of Brasilas:
When thanks be to the Muses, there drew near
A wayfarer from Crete, young Lycidas.
The horned herd was his care: a glance might tell
So much: for every inch a herdsman he.
Slung o'er his shoulder was a ruddy hide
Torn from a he-goat, shaggy, tangle-haired,
That reeked of rennet yet: a broad belt clasped
A patched cloak round his breast, and for a staff
A gnarled wild-olive bough his right hand bore.
Soon with a quiet smile he spoke—his eye
Twinkled, and laughter sat upon his lip:
"And whither ploddest thou thy weary way
Beneath the noontide sun, Simichidas?
For now the lizard sleeps upon the wall,
The crested lark folds now his wandering wing.
Dost speed, a bidden guest, to some reveller's board?
Or townward to the treading of the grape?
For lo! recoiling from thy hurrying feet
The pavement stones ring out right merrily."
Then I: "Friend Lycid, all men say that none
Of haymakers or herdsmen is thy match
At piping: and my soul is glad thereat.
Yet, to speak sooth, I think to rival thee.
Now look, this road holds holiday to-day:
For banded brethren solemnise a feast
To richly-dight Demeter, thanking her
For her good gifts: since with no grudging hand
Hath the boon goddess filled the wheaten floors.

So come: the way, the day, is thine as mine:
Try we our woodcraft—each may learn from each.
I am, as thou, a clarion-voice of song;
All hail me chief of minstrels. But I am not,
Heaven knows, o'er credulous: no, I scarce can yet
(I think) outvie Philetas, nor the bard
Of Samos, champion of Sicilian song.
They are as cicadas challenged by a frog."

    I spake to gain mine ends; and laughing light
He said: "Accept this club, as thou'rt indeed
A born truth-teller, shaped by heaven's own hand!
I hate your builders who would rear a house
High as Oromedon's mountain-pinnacle:
I hate your song-birds too, whose cuckoo-cry
Struggles (in vain) to match the Chian bard.
But come, we'll sing forthwith, Simichidas,
Our woodland music: and for my part I—
List, comrade, if you like the simpler air
I forged among the uplands yesterday.

    "Safe be my true-love convoyed o'er the main
To Mitylene—though the southern blast
Chase the lithe waves, while westward slant the Kids,
Or low above the verge Orion stand—
If from Love's furnace she will rescue me,
For Lycidas is parched with hot desire.
Let halcyons lay the sea-waves and the winds,
Northwind and Westwind, that in shores far-off
Flutters the seaweed—halcyons, of all birds
Whose prey is on the waters, held most dear
By the green Nereids: yea let all things smile
On her to Mitylene voyaging,
And in fair harbour may she ride at last.
I on that day, a chaplet woven of dill
Or rose or simple violet on my brow,
Will draw the wine of Pteleas from the cask
Stretched by the ingle. They shall roast me beans,

And elbow-deep in thyme and asphodel
And quaintly-curling parsley shall be piled
My bed of rushes, where in royal ease
I sit and, thinking of my darling, drain
With steadfast lips the liquor to the dregs.
I'll have a pair of pipers, shepherds both,
This from Acharnæ, from Lycope that;
And Tityrus shall be near me and shall sing
How the swain Daphnis loved the stranger-maid;
And how he ranged the fells, and how the oaks
(Such oaks as Himera's banks are green withal)
Sang dirges o'er him waning fast away
Like snow on Athos, or on Hæmus high,
Or Rhodope, or utmost Caucasus.
And he shall sing me how the big chest held
(All through the maniac malice of his lord)
A living goatherd: how the round-faced bees,
Lured from their meadow by the Cedar-smell,
Fed him with daintiest flowers, because the Muse
Had made his throat a well-spring of sweet song.
Happy Cometas, this sweet lot was thine!
Thee the chest prisoned, for thee the honey-bees
Toiled, as thou slavedst out the mellowing year:
And oh hadst thou been numbered with the quick
In my day! I had led thy pretty goats
About the hill-side, listening to thy voice:
While thou hadst laid thee down 'neath oak or pine,
Divine Cometas, warbling pleasantly."

    He spake and paused; and thereupon spake I.
"I too, friend Lycid, as I ranged the fells,
Have learned much lore and pleasant from the Nymphs,
Whose fame mayhap hath reached the throne of Zeus.
But this wherewith I'll grace thee ranks the first:
Thou listen, since the Muses like thee well.

    "On me the young Loves sneezed: for hapless I
Am fain of Myrto as the goats of Spring.

But my best friend Aratus inly pines
For one who loves him not. Aristis saw—
(A wondrous seer is he, whose lute and lay
Shrinèd Apollo's self would scarce disdain)—
How love had scorched Aratus to the bone.
O Pan, who hauntest Homole's fair champaign,
Bring the soft charmer, whosoe'er it be,
Unbid to his sweet arms—so, gracious Pan,
May ne'er thy ribs and shoulderblades be lashed
With squills by young Arcadians, whensoe'er
They are scant of supper! But should this my prayer
Mislike thee, then on nettles mayest thou sleep,
Dinted and sore all over from their claws!
Then mayst thou lodge amid Edonian hills
By Hebrus, in midwinter; there subsist,
The Bear thy neighbour: and, in summer, range
With the far Æthiops 'neath the Blemmyan rocks
Where Nile is no more seen! But O ye Loves,
Whose cheeks are like pink apples, quit your homes
By Hyetis, or Byblis' pleasant rill,
Or fair Dione's rocky pedestal,
And strike that fair one with your arrows, strike
The ill-starred damsel who disdains my friend.
And lo, what is she but an o'er-ripe pear?
The girls all cry 'Her bloom is on the wane.'
We'll watch, Aratus, at that porch no more,
Nor waste shoe-leather: let the morning cock
Crow to wake others up to numb despair!
Let Molon, and none else, that ordeal brave:
While we make ease our study, and secure
Some witch, to charm all evil from our door."

I ceased. He smiling sweetly as before,
Gave me the staff, "the Muses' parting gift,"
And leftward sloped tow'rd Pyxa. We the while,
Bent us to Phrasydeme's, Eucritus and I,
And baby-faced Amyntas: there we lay
Half-buried in a couch of fragrant reed

And fresh-cut vineleaves, who so glad as we?
A wealth of elm and poplar shook o'erhead;
Hard by, a sacred spring flowed gurgling on
From the Nymphs' grot, and in the sombre boughs
The sweet cicada chirped laboriously.
Hid in the thick thorn-bushes far away
The treefrog's note was heard; the crested lark
Sang with the goldfinch; turtles made their moan,
And o'er the fountain hung the gilded bee.
All of rich summer smacked, of autumn all:
Pears at our feet, and apples at our side
Rolled in luxuriance; branches on the ground
Sprawled, overweighed with damsons; while we brushed
From the cask's head the crust of four long years.
Say, ye who dwell upon Parnassian peaks,
Nymphs of Castalia, did old Chiron e'er
Set before Heracles a cup so brave
In Pholus' cavern—did as nectarous draughts
Cause the Anapian shepherd, in whose hand
Rocks were as pebbles, Polypheme the strong,
Featly to foot it o'er the cottage lawns:—
As, ladies, ye bid flow that day for us
All by Demeter's shrine at harvest-home?
Beside whose cornstalks may I oft again
Plant my broad fan: while she stands by and smiles,
Poppies and cornsheaves on each laden arm.

    C. S. CALVERLEY

*The theme of Cyclops and Galatea (Idyll 11) was a favorite
with the Hellenistic poets and was often used to show that
neither brawn nor brain is proof against the power of love.
The charming (and quite accurate) translation was published
anonymously at Oxford in 1588.*

273   O Galatea faire, why dost thou shun thy lover true?
     More tender than a Lambe, more white than cheese when it
       is new,

More wanton than a calfe, more sharpe than grapes unripe
    I finde.

You use to come, when pleasant sleepe my senses all doe
    binde.

But you are gone againe, when pleasant sleepe dooth leave
    mine eie,

And as a sheep you run, that on the plaine a Woolfe doth
    spie.

I then began to love thee, Galatê, when first of all
You with my mother came, to gather leaves of Crowtoe small
Upon our hil, when I as usher, squirde you all the waie.

Nor when I saw thee first, nor afterward, nor at this daie,
Since then could I refraine; but you, by Jove, nought set
    thereby.

But well I knowe, fair Nimphe, the verie cause why you thus
    flie.

Because upon my front, one onlie brow, with bristles strong
From one eare to the other eare, is stretched al along.

Nethe which, one eie, and on my lips a hugie nose there
    standes.

Yet I, this such a one, a thousand sheep feed on these lands.

And pleasant milke I drinke, which from the strouting bags
    is prest.

Nor want I cheese in summer, nor in Autumne of the best,
Nor yet in winter time. My cheese-rackes ever laden are,
And better can I pipe, than anie Cyclops maie compare.

O Apple, sweet, of thee, and of my selfe I use to sing,
And that at midnight oft. For thee, aleavne faunes up I
    bring,

All great with young, and foure beares whelps, I nourish up
    for thee.

But come thou hither first, and thou shalt have them all of
    me.

And let the blewish colorde Sea beat on the shore so nie.

The night with me in cave, thou shalt consume more pleas-
    antlie.

There are the shadie Baies, and there tall Cypres-trees doe
    sprout,

And there is Ivie blacke, and fertill Vines are al about.

Coole water there I have, distillèd of the whitest snowe,

A drinke devine, which out of wooddy Ætna mount doth
  flowe.

In these respects, who in the Sea and waves would rather be?

But if I seeme, as yet, too rough and savage unto thee,

Great store of Oken woode I have, and never quenchèd fire;

And I can well indure my soule to burne with thy desire,

With this my only eie, then which I nothing thinke more
  trimme.

Now woe is me, my mother bore me not with finns to
  swimme,

That I might dive to thee, that I thy dainty hand might
  kisse,

If lips thou wouldst not let; then would I Lillies bring I wis,

And tender Poppie toe, that bears a top like rattells red.

And these in summer time, but other are in winter bred,

So that I cannot bring them all at once. Now certainlie,

Ile learne to swimme of some or other stranger passing bie,

That I maie knowe what pleasure tis in water deepe to dwell.

Come forth, faire Galatê, and once got out, forget thee well

(As I doe sitting on this rocke) home to returne againe.

But feede my sheepe with me, and for to milke them take
  the paine,

And cheese to presse, and in the milke, the rennet sharpe to
  straine.

My mother only wrongeth me, and her I blame, for shee

Spake never yet to thee, one good or lovelie word of me,

And that, although shee daily sees how I awake doe pine.

But I will saie my head and feete doe ake, that shee maie
  whine

And sorrowe at the hart, because my hart with griefe is
  swolne.

O Cyclops, Cyclops, whither is thy wit and reason flowne?

If thou wouldst baskets make, and cut downe browzing from
  the tree,

And bring it to thy Lambes, a great deal wiser thou shouldst
  be!

Goe coie some present Nimphe, why dost thou follow flying
 wind?
Perhaps an other Galatê, and fairer thou shalt find.
For manie maidens in the evening tide with me will plaie,
And all doe sweetlie laugh, when I stand harkning what they
 saie,
And I some bodie seeme, and in the earth doe beare a swaie.
 ANONYMOUS

*Adoniazusae (Idyll 15) is named for the festival which cele-
brated the annual resurrection of Adonis. The mime rep-
resents the gossips Gorgo and Praxinoa (Eunoe is Praxinoa's
maid) meeting, making their way through the crowded
streets of Alexandria, and attending the service.*

GORGO: Praxinoa in?   **274**

PRAXINOA: Yes, Gorgo dear, at last!
    How late you are! See to a chair,
    A cushion, Eunoe!

GORGO: No, thank you.

PRAXINOA: Sit down.

GORGO: My body and soul! Do you know,
    I've scarcely got here alive, Praxinoa?
    There's such a crowd—such heaps of carriages,
    And horses, and fine soldiers, all full dressed:
    And then you live such an immense way off!

PRAXINOA: Why, 'twas his shabby doing. He would take
    This hole that he calls house, at the world's end.
    'Twas all to spite me, and to part us two.

GORGO: Don't talk so of your husband, there's a dear,
    Before the little one. See how he looks at you.

PRAXINOA (*to the child*):   There, don't look grave, child;
        cheer up, Zopy, sweet;
    It isn't your papa we're talking of.

GORGO: He thinks it is, though.

PRAXINOA: Oh, no—nice papa!
        (*to Gorgo*) Well, this strange body once (let us say *once*,
        And then he won't know who we're telling of),
        Going to buy some rouge and saltpeter,
        Comes bringing salt! the great big simpleton!

GORGO: And there's my precious ninny, Dioclede:
        He gave for five old ragged fleeces, yesterday,
        Ten drachmas! for mere dirt! trash upon trash!
        But come; put on your things; button away,
        Or we shall miss the show. It's the king's own;
        And I am told the queen has made of it
        A wonderful fine thing.

PRAXINOA: Aye, luck has luck.
        Well, tell us all about it; for we hear
        Nothing in this vile place.

GORGO: We haven't time.
        Workers can't throw away their holidays.

PRAXINOA: Some water, Eunoe; and then, my fine one,
        To take your rest again. Puss loves good lying.
        Come, move, girl, move; some water—water first.
        Look how she brings it! Now, then;—hold, hold, care-
            less;
        Not quite so fast; you're wetting all my gown.
        There; that'll do. Now, please the gods, I'm washed.
        The key of the great chest—where's that? Go fetch it.

GORGO: Praxinoa, that gown with the full skirts
        Becomes you mightily. What did it cost you?

PRAXINOA: Oh, don't remind me of it. More than one
        Or two good minas, besides time and trouble.

GORGO: All which you had forgotten.

PRAXINOA: Ah, ha! True;

That's good. You're quite right.—Come, my cloak, my
    cloak;
And parasol. There—help it on now, properly.
—Child, child, you cannot go. Horsey will bite.
The Horrid Woman is coming. Well, well, simpleton,
Cry, if you will; but I'll not have you lamed.
Come, Gorgo. Phrygia, take the child and play with him;
And call the dog indoors, and lock the gate.

Powers, what a crowd! how shall we get along?
Why, they're like ants! countless! innumerable!
Well, Ptolemy, you've done fine things, that's certain,
Since the gods took your father. No one nowadays
Does harm to travelers as they used to do,
After the Egyptian fashion, lying in wait—
Masters of nothing but detestable tricks;
And all alike—a set of cheats and brawlers.
Gorgo, sweet friend, what will become of us?
Here are the king's horse-guards! Pray, my good man,
Don't tread upon us so. See the bay horse!
Look how it rears! It's like a great mad dog.
How you stand, Eunoe! It will throw him certainly!
How lucky that I left the child at home!

GORGO: Courage, Praxinoa: they have passed us now;
    They've gone into the courtyard.

PRAXINOA: Good, I breathe again.
    I could never abide in all my life
    A horse and a cold snake.

GORGO (*to an old woman*):   From court, mother?

OLD WOMAN: Yes, child.

GORGO: Pray, is it easy to get in?

OLD WOMAN: The Greeks got into Troy. Everything's done
    By trying.

GORGO: Bless us! How she bustles off!
Why, the old woman's quite oracular.
But women must know everything; even what Juno
Wore on her wedding day. See now, Praxinoa,
How the gate's crowded.

PRAXINOA: Frightfully indeed.
Give me your hand, dear Gorgo; and do you
Hold fast of Eutychis's, Eunoe.
Don't let her go; don't stir an inch; and so
We'll all squeeze in together. Stick close now.
Oh me! oh me! my veil's torn right in two!
Do take care, my good man, and mind my cloak.

MAN: 'Twas not my fault, but I'll take care.

PRAXINOA: What heaps!
They drive like pigs!

MAN: Courage, old girl! all's safe.

PRAXINOA: Blessings upon you, sir, now and forever,
For taking care of us. A good, kind soul.
How Eunoe squeezes us! Do, child, make way
For your own self. There; now we've all got in,
As the man said when he was put in prison.

GORGO: Praxinoa, do look there! What lovely tapestry!
How fine and showy! One would think the gods did it.

PRAXINOA: Holy Athena! How those artists work!
How they do paint their pictures to the life!
The figures stand so like and move so like!
They're quite alive, not worked. Well, certainly,
Man's a wise creature. See now—only look—
See—lying on the silver couch, all budding,
With the young down about his face! Adonis!
Charming Adonis, charming even in Acheron!

MAN: Do hold your tongue there; chatter, chatter, chatter.
The turtles stun one with their yawning gabble.

GORGO: Hey-day! whence comes the man? What is't to you
　　　　If we do chatter? Speak where you've a right.
　　　　You're not the master here. As for that,
　　　　Our people are from Corinth, like Bellerophon.
　　　　Our tongue's Peloponnesiac; and we hope
　　　　It's lawful for the Dorians to speak Doric!

PRAXINOA: We've but one master, by the Honey-sweet,
　　　　And don't fear you nor all your empty breath.

GORGO: Hush, hush, Praxinoa, there's the Grecian girl,
　　　　A most amazing creature, going to sing
　　　　About Adonis; she that sings so well
　　　　The song of Sperchis: she'll sing something fine,
　　　　I warrant. See how sweetly she prepares!

The Song

　　　O Lady, who dost take delight
　　　In Golgos and the Erycian height
　　　And in the Idalian dell,
　　　Venus ever amiable;
　　　Lo, the long expected Hours,
　　　Slowest of the blessed powers,
　　　Yet who bring us something ever,
　　　Ceasing their soft dancing never,
　　　Bring thee back thy beauteous one
　　　From perennial Acheron.
　　　Thou, they say, from earth hast given
　　　Berenice place in heaven,
　　　Dropping to her woman's heart
　　　Ambrosia; and for this kind part
　　　Berenice's daughter—she
　　　That's Helen-like—Arsinoe,
　　　O thou many-named and shrined,
　　　Is to thy Adonis kind.
　　　He has all the fruits that now
　　　Hang upon the timely bough:
　　　He has green young garden-plots,

Basketed in silver pots;
Syrian scents in alabaster,
And whate'er a curious taster
Could desire, that women make
With oil or honey, of meal cake;
And all shapes of beast or bird,
In the woods by huntsman stirred;
And a bower to shade his state
Heaped with dill, an amber weight;
And about him Cupids flying,
Like young nightingales, that—trying
Their new wings—go half afraid,
Here and there within the shade.
See the gold! The ebony see!
And the eagles in ivory,
Bearing the young Trojan up
To be filler of Zeus' cup;
And the tapestry's purple heap,
Softer than the feel of sleep;
Artists contradict who can,
Samian or Milesian.
But another couch there is
For Adonis, close to his;
Venus has it, and with joy
Clasps again her blooming boy
With a kiss that feels no fret,
For his lips are downy yet.
Happy with her love be she;
But tomorrow morn will we
With our locks and garments flowing,
And our bosoms gently showing,
Come and take him in a throng,
To the seashore with this song:
Go, beloved Adonis, go
Year by year thus to and fro;
Only privileged demigod;
There was no such open road
For Atreides; nor the great

Ajax, chief infuriate;
Nor for Hector, noblest once
Of his mother's twenty sons;
Nor Patroclus, nor the boy
That returned from taken Troy;
Nor those older buried bones,
Lapiths and Deucalions;
Nor Pelopians, and their boldest;
Nor Pelasgians, Greece's oldest.
Bless us then Adonis dear,
And bring us joy another year;
Dearly hast thou come again,
And dearly shalt be welcomed then.

GORGO: Well, if that's not a clever creature, trust me!
Lord! What a quantity of things she knows!
And what a charming voice! 'Tis time to go though,
For there's my husband hasn't had his dinner,
And you'd best come across him when he wants it!
Good-by, Adonis darling. Come again.
LEIGH HUNT

HERODAS

*Among the most welcome of the acquisitions to Greek litera-
ture recovered from the sands of Egypt are the Mimes of
Herodas, which present artistic vignettes of the daily life
of Alexandria. Of the eight pieces recovered the first repre-
sents the visit of a bawd, Gyllis, to a young woman, Metriche,
whose lover or husband, Mandris, is absent on military serv-
ice, in order to procure her complaisance to a young gallant
named Gryllus. Thracian is Metriche's maid. The Mime
shows notable similarities to Theocritus 15 and 2.*

METRICHE (*to* THRACIAN): Hark, girl! There's some one   **275**
knocking at the door.

See who it is,—perhaps some visitor
From our country place.

THRACIAN (*shouting*):   Who knocked?

GYLLIS: I.

THRACIAN: Who are you?
Don't be afraid; come nearer.

GYLLIS: So I do.

THRACIAN: Who *are* you?

GYLLIS: I'm Philainion's mother dear,
Gyllis. Go tell your mistress that I'm here.

METRICHE: Let her in. Who is it?

THRACIAN: Gyllis.

METRICHE: Gyllis? Not
"Mamma"? Now, girl, be brisk! Well, and to what
Supreme good fortune, Gyllis, do I owe
This "angel's visit"? These five months or so
No soul, awake or sleeping, 's noticed you
Come near this doorway; by the Fates, it's true.

GYLLIS: My home's far off, child; then, the mud!—it lies
Thick in the streets, and reaches to one's thighs.
That weak I am, too,—like a fly! Dear, dear!
Age pulls us down, the shadow of death is near.

METRICHE: It's libelling Time to say so. Go along!
Why, you could crush one's life out,—you're so strong.

GYLLIS: Ah! mock away. You girls will have your fun;
But that won't warm you, when all's said and done.
Well, child, how long, now, in this widowed state,
Do you press a lonely couch, disconsolate?
Ten months have flown since Mandris went away
To Egypt, and no syllable from that day
To this he's sent you; he's forgotten *you*,

And drained the honeyed cup of love anew.
The goddess makes her home there; every kind
Of thing, both new and old, you're sure to find
In the land of Egypt: wealth, power, fame, repose,
Gymnasium, gold, young men, philosophers, shows,
The shrine of Brother and Sister, the Good King,
Wine, the Museum,—every pleasant thing
The heart of man can wish for; women, there,
In number more—by Hades' Maid I swear—
Than all the stars Heaven's front does proudly wear,
Fair as those goddesses who once, to claim
The prize of beauty, unto Paris came,
—Hope they don't hear their names. Well, there you sit,
Hugging your chair. What do you think of it,
Poor girl? You'd better mind: you'll waste away,
Youth swallowed in the ashes of decay.
Look somewhere else, steer for another port
A day or two, and merrily resort
To a new friend. The ship that tries to ride
At a single anchor may not stem the tide.
If your first love is in his grave, why then
No mortal man can raise him up again.
Besides, you know, fine weather has a close,
And angry storms succeed; and no one knows
What hidden fortune future days may bring,
For human life's a most uncertain thing.
There's no one near us, is there?

METRICHE: No one.

GYLLIS: Well,
Now you shall hear the news I came to tell.
Know that young Gryllos, Matakine's son
(She's daughter of Pataikios),—who has won
Five prizes at the games, once as a lad
At Pytho, twice at Corinth, where he had
The striplings all defeated, twice again
At Pisa, where he quite outboxed the men,—
Well off, the kind of man who'll never move

A twig from off the ground, unversed in love,
Safe as a signet,—at the late Returning
Of Mise saw you, and his heart was burning
With frenzied love in no time. Night and day
He haunts my house, and ceases not to pray,
Weeping, for help to me, his "mother dear";
In fact, his passion's killing him, I fear.
Now, Metriche, my child, this little sin,
This *one*, you surely may commit; give in
To the Goddess, lest old age should find you out.
And you'll gain doubly; you'll enjoy, no doubt,
A pleasant time, and also you'll receive
A bigger sum than you could well believe.
Just think now. Be advised in this by me;
Please do, child, in the name of Destiny.

METRICHE: Gyllis, your grey hairs steal your wits away.
By Mandris' ship, which yet will come some day,
And by Demeter, saving you, I'd stand
These speeches from no woman in the land;
For her sore words her bones should soon be sore,
And she should hate my threshold evermore.
Never bring such a tale upon your tongue
To me again, dear. Women gay and young
May listen to such harlotries as these;
Let Metriche, daughter of Pytheës,
Still "hug her chair." Nobody can poke fun
At Mandris. But enough! You "care for none
Of these things," as they say. (*To* THRACIAN) Girl, hark
     to me!
Wipe the black drinking-shell, and pour out three
Half-measures of neat wine, then, filling up
With water, hand our guest a brimming cup.

THRACIAN: There, Gyllis; there's your drink.

GYLLIS: Ah! bring it
     here.

I came about the festival, my dear,
And not to tempt you.

METRICHE: Yes, your wine's for that.

GYLLIS: I hope you've plenty of it in your vat,
          For your sake. By Demeter, this stuff's fine;
          Gyllis has never tippled better wine.
          Well, fare you well, child. Mind you take all care
          Of your own self. For me, be this my prayer,
          That Myrtale and Sime still may keep
          Young (yes, and gay), till Gyllis sleeps her sleep.
              HUGO SHARPLEY

*The Battaros of the second Mime is a brothel-keeper who is
bringing suit for damages against Thales; Thales had broken
into the establishment and carried off one of the inmates. In
the manner of a trial lawyer Battaros declares that his profes-
sion is as socially useful as that of his opponent.*

BATTAROS: Gentlemen of the jury, 'tis not birth   **276**
            That you are called to judge, nor moral worth.
            Though Thales own a ship of value quite
            Five talents, while I own—an appetite,
            Battaros, in law, is just as good as he,
            If at his hands I've suffered injury.

       [*Three mutilated lines are here omitted.*]

Men live, you know, not as they wish to do,
But as events outside compel them to.
Mennes supports him; I've Aristophon
As my supporter. Well, the first is known
As a prize-boxer, while my nominee
Is still a good garotter. Come and see
At nightfall, gentlemen, if you should doubt it;
Each bring your cloak,—and each go home without it.
I back *my* champion, and that's all about it.
He'll tell you, "I brought wheat, a plenteous store,
From Ake, and the famine raged no more."

Well, I brought girls from Tyre. How is this, pray,
A public service? He's not given away
The wheat to grind; both of us make you pay.
But if he thinks, because he plies the sea,
And wears a cloak that cost him two or three
Good Attic minas, while I live ashore,
Wrapped in a coarse coat, trailing on the floor
Shoes all in tatters,—if he thinks that therefore
He can take aught of mine that he may care for,
By force, without my leave, at night-time too,
Then the protection guaranteed by you
Means simply nothing, and your boasted joy,
Your independence, Thales will destroy.
He should know who he is, and of what clay
Compounded; he should copy me; I pay
Respect to all alike, both small and great.
Ah! those who are the roof-tree of the State,
Those who may vaunt their birth with better cause
Than can this fellow, *they* regard the laws:
No *citizen* has ever pummelled me,
Or smashed my door in (alien though I be)
At night-time, or has set my house on fire,
Or wrested from me girls I keep for hire:
But Phrygian Thales, who, I'ld have you know,
Was called Artimmes not so long ago,
Has done all this, and wantonly defied
Laws, councillors, and president beside.
Stay! Read the law, clerk, dealing with the offence
Of personal assault and violence.
(*To the usher*) And you, good sir, bung up the water-
     clock,
Until he's finished. Thales must not dock
Poor Battaros of his "last suit of clo'es
And what's beneath them," as the saying goes.

CLERK OF THE COURT: "If a free man shall wilfully assault
          Or follow a slave woman, for this fault
          The fine is double."

BATTAROS: 'Twas Chairondes thus
    Enacted, mind, not Battaros emulous
    To punish Thales. He goes on to say,—
    "If a man smash a door in, he shall pay
    A mina: if he use his fists in fight,
    A mina: if he set the house alight,
    Or force his way inside, ten minas,"—such
    The fines,—"for damage done, just twice as much."
    Yes, Thales, *he* inhabited a city;
    You don't know what that means, nor—more's the
        pity—
    How city life is ordered. Brikindera
    'S your home to-day, 'twas yesterday Abdera;
    To-morrow, if you only get a freight,
    You'll take your ship off to Phaselis straight.
    Well, lest I bore you with a rambling sort
    Of story, gentlemen, I'll cut it short;
    Thales has been the pitch, and I the mouse:
    I got an awful drubbing, and my house
    (I pay "a third" rent, neither less nor more)
    Has got charred lintels and a broken door.
    Now, Myrtale, my girl, come forward here;
    Let them all see you; don't be shy, my dear!
    Think that these jurymen whom you behold
    Are loving brothers or are fathers old.
    See, gentlemen! See how she's bruised all over,
    From the rough handling of her scoundrel lover.
    Old Age, you ought to get thank-offerings due,
    For he'ld have spirted blood, except for you,
    Like Brenkian Philip once in Samian land.
    Laughing, eh, Thales? I'm a blackguard, and
    I don't deny it. Battaros is my name,
    My grandsire was Sisymbras, of the same
    Profession, as was Sisymbriskos too,
    My father; all were pandars. But, for thew
    And muscle, I could throttle without fear
    A lion, if 'twere Thales. (*To* THALES) Now, look here!
    You love the girl perhaps; that's nothing strange.

Well, I love corn. Offer a fair exchange,
—She's yours. Or, if your gizzard is on fire,
Thrust in my hand the price that I require,
—She's yours; maltreat your own just as you please.
He's free to, gentlemen,—for, though in these
Proposals Thales is addressed, yet you
Must carefully decide with judgment true,
As you've no witnesses. But if his real
Desire's the torture, and he seeks ordeal
By slave-examination, then I tender
Myself. Come, rack me, Thales!—only render
My value into court. Why, a decision
By Minos' scales could have no more precision!
And think not, gentlemen, that you are giving
Your votes to Battaros or his way of living,
But unto all the aliens of this State.
Show how that Kos and Merops both are great;
Show what was Herakles' and Thessalos' fame,
Show how Asklepios here from Trikke came,
How Phoebe here gave Leto to the light.
Consider all of this, and guide aright
Your sober judgment; for, if now you smite
The Phrygian, he'll be better by-and-bye,
Unless the ancient proverb tells a lie.
      HUGO SHARPLEY

*Excerpts from Mime 4, finally, offer interesting specimens of
contemporary art criticism. Two women who are making
an offering to Asclepius remark to each other on the art dis-
played in the temple.*

277 KYNNO: . . . Look how the girl up there
           Is gazing at the apple! You would swear
           She'll die outright, if she can't get her apple.

    PHILE: Then that old man there! That's the way to grapple
           With a fox-goose, as that boy does! Yes, by Fate,
           The very pose! But that the stone is straight
           In front of us, you'd look for word or moan

From the figures. We shall soon be forced to own
That life itself can dwell in lifeless stone.
Look, Kynno! Myttes' daughter Battale's statue!
Why, there she stands! She might be posing at you!
All ye who know not Battale, survey
This likeness, and you'll know her any day!

.   .   .   .

PHILE: . . . If I prick that naked boy,
   Surely he'll bleed? The flesh that moulds his form
   Lies firm upon his limbs, so warm, so warm,
   Throbbing with life, upon the panel thrown:
   And if Myellos sees those tongs, you'll own,
   Or Pataikiskos, son of Lamprion,
   They're like to lose their eyeballs in their greed,
   Thinking it silver plate in very deed.
   Then, there! The ox, the man in charge, the girl
   Who walks beside, the beaked shock-headed churl,
   Aren't they just animals? But that I feel
   Above such woman's weakness, I could squeal,
   For fear the ox should hurt me; the one eye
   Shoots out a sidelong glance so threateningly.

KYNNO: Yes, dear, Apelles the Ephesian's skill
   Fails never, be the subject what you will.
   You couldn't say, "Some things that man would see,
   And others miss." No, whatsoe'er might be
   The work—perhaps a god—he planned to do,
   With swift, unerring strokes he'ld carry it through.
   May he who felt not reverence and awe
   Of him and of his works, when such he saw,
   Hang in a fuller's workshop by the feet!
     HUGO SHARPLEY

MOSCHUS

*The Sicilian Moschus (second century B.C.) is the second
name in pastoral after Theocritus. His* Fugitive Love *has been
imitated in all languages, in English by Ben Jonson.*

278   Aloud for her son Eros, Cypris cries:
               "Whoever meets with Eros on the way,
               My fugitive reporting, wins a prize,
               Even a kiss from Cypris for your pay.
               But stranger, if you lead him to my door,
               No naked kiss you'll get, but something more.

               "The child is one any could recognize
               Out of a crowd of twenty; nothing fair
               His skin, but like the fire; his shining eyes
               Are keen with crafty gleam beyond compare.
               His mind is wicked, but he prattles sweet.
               Unlike his thoughts the words he will repeat.

               "A voice of honey, but a mind of gall;
               Untamed that stripling, but with manners smooth;
               Deceptive in his nature all in all,
               He never yet was known to speak the truth;
               A sportive little playmate, bright and gay;
               But ever ruthless in his sport and play.

               "His locks are lustrous and his forehead bold;
               His hands and arms are small, but he can throw
               As far as Acheron; his missiles hold
               Forward and down to Hades' king they go.
               His body is all naked, but his mind
               Covers ideas that you can never find.

"Winged like a bird, he'll make a sudden dart,
One to another, man or maid alike;
And settle down and perch upon the heart.
His bow is small; his arrow sharp to strike.
His midget arrow up to Heaven will bear
His message through the region of the air.

"Upon his back a quiver gilded o'er
Holds bitter shafts that often wounded me.
All this is cruel indeed, but even more
Cruel his torch; though tiny it may be,
That lamp can start a conflagration dire
That Helios himself will set afire.

"If you should catch him, hold him fast and bind;
Nor pity him at all, though weeping sore;
Beware the subtle schemes he has in mind.
And if he laughs, drag him along once more;
But if he tries to kiss you as a friend,
Flee him as you would flee pain without end.

"His kiss is evil; for a venomous charm
Is on his lips; and if he chance to say,
'Take you these weapons that Mankind alarm;
Freely to you I give them all away!'
Touch not those gifts even with your fingertips,
For one and all alike in flame he dips."

                    H. H. CHAMBERLIN

*The next is a characteristic Alexandrian treatment of the
familiar story of Europa.*

Once to Europa sweetly came a dream   **279**
By Cypris sent, when the last third of Night
Its course commences near the Dawn's first gleam;
And more than honey-sweet is Sleep's delight
To sit upon men's eyelids, and their sight

As with a soft and soothing chain is bound,
And dreams that all come true swarm all around.

Fast in an upper room slept Phoenix' daughter,
Europa, still a maid, who thought to see
Two continents, the land across the water
And Asia, striving for her custody;
And either like a woman seemed to be;
One was a stranger from an alien strand
And one was like a native to the land,

Who claimed the girl her very own by right,
As born from her and nurtured day by day;
The other came with heavy-handed might
And seized the maid and carried her away,
Though not against her will, as who would say
It was Europa's fate to be the prize
Of Aegis-bearing Zeus, Lord of the Skies.

Out of her bed she leapt in sudden fright,
And wildly throbbed her heart; what seemed to be
A figment of a vision of the night
Was still before her like reality.
Long in dread darkness sitting silently
Both women she beholds with open eyes,
Till, lifting up her voice, the maiden cries:

"Who of the heavenly born sent down this doom
On me? What dreams have roused me from my bed,
While sweetly I was sleeping in my room?
What stranger did I see ere Sleep had fled?
Oh! how my heart by her was ravishèd,
And oh! how tenderly she looked and smiled,
Lifting me up as if I were her child!

"But O ye blest! fulfill my dreams for me
Unto my good!" So saying the girl uprose
And went to seek a maiden company

Of her own age. Well born were all of those;
With her they sported when the dance she chose,
Or when from mountain rills her skin would glow,
Or far afield for lilies she would go. . . .
   H. H. CHAMBERLIN (1-32)

Europa and her friends go to pick flowers; their frolic, described at considerable length is interrupted by the arrival of the disguised Zeus.

Not long it was her fate among the flowers,   280
Delighting of her soul, to be beguiled;
Not long amid the pleasant passing hours
To guard her maiden girdle undefiled;
For now as at a signal Cronos' child
Spied her and was by Cypris' dart laid low,
For she alone can even Zeus o'erthrow.

He, to escape mad Hera's jealousy,
And to beguile a maiden's guileless mind,
Concealed the form of his divinity
And changed him to a bull; but not the kind
That men would munching in a stable find,
Nor one who cuts the furrows with curved plows,
Nor one who goes to pasture with the cows,

Nor harness-broken draws a laboring wain;
All otherwise was he, with saffron hide;
Upon his brow a circle shone again
Like silver; with desire his eyes were wide;
Equally curved his horns at either side
Over his head, under the light of morn
Like semicircle of Selene's horn.

He to the meadow came, nor struck with fright
The girls when he before them would appear;
But every maiden longed with all her might,
With her own hand to touch the lovely steer;

To that delighted throng still drawing near,
Ambrosial perfume all his body yields
And overcomes the fragrance of the fields.

He stayed his steps before Europa fair;
He licked her neck to charm an innocent
Maiden; she fondled him with tender care
And wiped the foam from off his lips; and bent
Forward and kissed the bull; in blandishment
He softly bellows; surely you will say
Mygdonian music on the flute he'll play.

Kneeling before her feet he turned his head
And gazed upon Europa, showing there
His ample back; she glanced about and said
Unto her maidens long and thick of hair:
"Hither, dear comrades of my age! Come share
My joy. We all will ride upon the bull
And so we'll take our pleasure at the full.

"We all will make our bed upon his back;
And certainly to him we'll welcome be;
Of grace and gentleness he has no lack;
Unlike all other bulls he seems to me.
His mind is like a man's as all may see.
His wits he has about him of wide reach,
He needs alone the power of human speech."

She sat her down upon his back and smiled;
The rest got ready; but right speedily
The bull uprose; the girl he had beguiled
He bore away and went down to the sea;
She called her dear companions plaintively,
Turning about and raising either hand;
But none could ever come to her on land. . . .

H. H. CHAMBERLIN (72-112)

*Europa pleads for release, in vain. Zeus reveals his identity
and promises her a royal future.*

> He spoke, and what he spoke was all fulfilled.   **281**
> Crete came in sight; and Zeus his form again
> Put on; and loosed her girdle as he willed;
> The Hours prepared their couch upon the plain;
> Nor were their nuptial vows performed in vain.
> She was a bride who was a maid before,
> And to the son of Cronos children bore.
>   H. H. CHAMBERLIN (162-166)

*Transmitted under Moschus' name, but probably of different
authorship, is this lament for the pastoral poet Bion.*

Mingle your sighs with mine, ye dales, thou Dorian water,   **282**
Weep and lament, ye rivers and floods, for Bion the lovely!
Now let the groves begin their laments and gardens their
      weeping!
Henceforth, blossom and bud, shall ye breathe but the per-
      fume of sorrow;
Redden, ye roses and blush now, ye windflowers scarlet with
      anguish;
Hyacinth, babble thy letters and print "ai ai" on thy petals
Plainer than ever before, for dead is the beautiful singer!
Muses of Sicily, lift up your voices in wailing and weeping!

Nightingales, making your plaint in the leaf-hidden heart of
      the thicket,
Tell to the waters of Sicily, tell to the fount Arethusa
Tidings of woe, that Bion the herdsman is dead and that like-
      wise
Dead is his song and perished and gone is the music of Doris.
Muses of Sicily, lift up your voices in wailing and weeping!

Lift up your cry, ye swans that lament on the waters of Stry-
      mon,

Sing to me now in your mournfullest notes the songs of your
    sadness
Strains such as those that his voice rang withal in the day of
    your mourning!
Tell once more to the daughters of Oeagrus, tell to the Muses,
Tell all the nymphs of Bistonia, "Dead is the Dorian Or-
    pheus!"
Muses of Sicily, lift up your voices in wailing and weeping!

Loved of his kine that he was, no more he maketh his music,
Under the wilderness oaks no longer he sitteth and singeth.
Down in the house of Pluto a song of Lethe he singeth.
Mute are the mountains now. The cattle, both bullock and
    heifer,
Wander at large on the hills and mourn, their pasture refus-
    ing.
Muses of Sicily, lift up your voices in wailing and weeping!

Bion, the doom that destroyed thee drew tears from even
    Apollo,
Also the Satyrs mourned, and swarthy Priapus, the scarecrow,
Wept thee; the Pans do sigh for thy song, and deep in the
    woods the
Nymphs of the springs bewailed and turned their streams into
    teardrops.
Echo hides in the rocks and weeps, for mute is her voice now,
Never again may she mimic the sound of thy lips. On thy
    deathday
Trees cast their fruit, all blossom and bloom were faded and
    withered.
Ceased in its flow the milk of the ewes, of hives the sweet
    honey—
Died in the comb the honey for grief. What profits it hence-
    forth
Stripping the hives of their sweet, now thy song's honey hath
    perished?
Muses of Sicily, lift up your voices in wailing and weeping!

Never so sorrowed the dolphin along the salt shore of the
   ocean;
Nor from his perch on the high rocky cliff ever screamed so
   the eagle;
Never so wild on the long mountain ridges the plaint of the
   swallow
Thrilled; nor so harsh for the halcyon's pain rang the scream
   of her Ceyx;
Never so sounded the kingfisher's song from among the green
   billows;
Never in vales of the East so mourned for the son of the
   morning,
Fluttering over his body the dark feathered, sad bird of
   Memnon—
As they all joined in grief and lament for the passing of Bion.
Muses of Sicily, lift up your voices in wailing and weeping!

Nightingales all and swallows, birds which he once had de-
   lighted,
Birds he had taught how to pipe, flew aloft to their perch in
   the treetops;
Twittering each to the other they wailed, and the others
   responded:
"Grieve all ye mourners, ye birds of the forest, for we too are
   grieving."
Muses of Sicily, lift up your voices in wailing and weeping!

Who in the days now to come will play on thy pipes, my be-
   loved?
Who will so much as lay lip to thy reeds? Ah, who were so
   hardy?
Resonant yet with the breath of thy lips and the sound of thy
   pipings
Still in the reeds there lingers an echo, the ghost of thy music.
Pan even, him should I challenge to rival thy song, would be
   fearful
Thy pipes to press to his lips, lest even Pan should be second.
Muses of Sicily, lift up your voices in wailing and weeping!

Mourns Galatea the music she once delighted to list to,
Sitting not far from thy side on the windblown verge of the
    ocean.
Not like old Polypheme thou sangest: Him Galatea
Loathed in her beauty but thou wast to her more lief than the
    billows.
Now all forgot are the waves. On the sands of the sea beach
    she sitteth,
Lone though they be, and keepeth thy kine, O herdsman de-
    parted!
Died in one death with thee, O Bion, all gifts of the Muses—
Gone are the lips of boys and the lovely kisses of maidens!
Round thy corpse assemble the Loves to weep and bewail
    thee.
Even the Cyprian Goddess regrets thee more than the last
    kiss
Pressed but of late on the lips of her darling, her dying
    Adonis.
Muses of Sicily, lift up your voices in wailing and weeping!

This, O stream of the mightiest song, is a second bereave-
    ment,
This is a new sorrow, Meles. Of yore wast bereft of thy
    Homer,
Honey-sweet voice of Calliope; men even now tell the story
How thou didst mourn for thy beautiful son till the woe of
    thy waters
Filled all the sea with its sound. And now again for another
Child thou weepest, and yet once more thou pinest in sorrow.
Muses of Sicily, lift up your voices in wailing and weeping!

Both were beloved of the wells of song; one drank of the
    fountain
Sprung from the Muses' steed, and one Arethusa's waters.
One sang the fame of the daughter of Tyndarus, loveliest
    Helen,
Sang Menelaus, her spouse, and the mighty offspring of
    Thetis;

Bion would sing no wars, no tears, of Pan was his piping,
Herdsmen were all his song and singing he pastured his cattle,
Pan-pipes of reed he fashioned, and drew the rich milk of his
    heifers,
Taught of the kisses of boys and folded young Love to his
    bosom,
Yea, and better than all he troubled with love Aphrodite.
Muses of Sicily, lift up your voices in wailing and weeping!

Never a town far famed, my Bion, nor city but weepeth.
Ascra mourneth for thee far more than for Hesiod; Pindar's
Loss they lament less sorely than thine in Boeotian Hylae;
Never was Lesbos the lovely so sad for the loss of Alcaeus;
Never so much for her minstrel's death wept the city of Teos;
Paros laments thee, forgetting Archilochus; and for their
    Sappho
Thine is the music the maidens regret in fair Mytilene.
Muses of Sicily, lift up your voices in wailing and weeping!

Pastoral minstrels all to whom the Muses have given
Voices piercing and sweet bewail the mishap of thy dying.
Weepeth Sicelidas, glory of Samos, and of the Cretans
He whose eyes were wont to be lit with the light of his smil-
    ing,
Lycidas, weepeth for thee, and amongst the Triopian burghers
Far in the Coan isle the dirge is raised by Philetas;
Also Theocritus mourneth in Syracuse. Moreover I too
Raise the lament of Ausonian woe, not to song a mere
    stranger
But of the muse of the herdsmen, the lore thou didst teach
    thy disciples,
Yea, of the muse of the Dorians, heir. That lore thou hast
    left me,
Leaving to others thy treasure but me thy song for a portion.
Muses of Sicily, lift up your voices in wailing and weeping!

Ay me! Even the humblest of herbs when they die in the
    garden,

Mallow and parsley green and the close crisped sprouts of the
    anise,
Spring up again into life and shoot forth leaves for a new year;
We men nevertheless, the great and the mighty, we wise men,
Once we are dead, may harken no more but shut in the dark
    earth
Slumber a long and unending sleep whence we shall not
    awaken.
So shalt thou lie fast shut in the silent earth, for the wood
    nymphs
Will that alone the croak of the frog be heard from the
    marshes!
Theirs be the joy! I envy them not, no sweet song he singeth.
Muses of Sicily, lift up your voices in wailing and weeping!

Bion, that drug to thy mouth came poisonous, deadly and
    bitter,
How could it touch those lips and straightway be turned not
    to sweetness?
Who was the mortal was savage enough to mix thee or give
    thee,
While thou didst speak, the drug, and fled not the sound of
    thy singing?
Muses of Sicily, lift up your voices in wailing and weeping!

Yet none mocketh the gods for aye. Unsated with dirges
Many the tears I weep for thy doom, and were it but lawful
As the descent into Tartarus Orpheus made, as Odysseus,
As Alcides of yore, I too would go down unto Pluto's
House but to see thee again, and if unto Pluto thou singest,
That I might hear thy song. But stay, Persephone listens!
Sing her a sweet Sicilian song, some pastoral ditty.
She is of Sicily too and played on the shore beneath Aetna.
She too sang, and her songs were the Dorian. Not unrewarded
Then shall thy music be. As of yore she gave unto Orpheus
Brief though the boon should be, his wife in meed for his
    harping.

Will she not send thee, Bion, back to the hills? Were but I
　　too
Skilled so to pipe, for thy sake I too would have sung before
　　Pluto.
　　L. P. CHAMBERLAYNE

ALEXANDRIAN
EROTIC FRAGMENT

*This song, found written on the reverse of a contract on a
papyrus of the second century B.C., is the plaint of a rejected
girl and a threatening plea for reinstatement in her beloved's
affections.*

We twain with one will and one heart were united　　**283**
　　Beneath the connubial yoke,
And Cypris herself, that fair goddess of loving,
　　Our sealèd affection bespoke.

Pain seizes me ,when I remember the way
　　His kisses burned into my soul,—
He, the author of discord, who left me abandoned,
　　He, that played such a treacherous role!

Yet, despite his desertion, Love held me in thrall,—
　　Once established, Love will not depart;—
I remember his courting, forget his betrayal,
　　Nor deny he's still held in my heart.

Dear stars of the heaven, and pale queenly night,
　　My partner in passion and pain,
Bring me now, willing slave, to his side, whom fair Cypris
　　And conquering Love lead again.

The fire that burns in my soul is my guide,
  It will lead me through torments and woe;—
That deceiver of hearts, who once was so proud,
  Denies Cypris my love did bestow!

Ah! the wrong he has done me! Who knows what I suffer,
  In mad, frenzied flames am I burned!
Cast down lovers' garlands that bring rosy blushes
  To cheeks now so heartlessly spurned!

Yet my Lord, shun me not, do not leave me forever,
  Though shut out, I would enter once more;
Thy slave I must be, 'tis my passionate longing,
  I am mad for that face I adore!

Truly, Love is the author of terrible griefs!
  I'm tortured by jealousy's fires,—
Yet, outwardly silent, pretend to be strong,
  And must learn to conceal my desires.

This bitter Truth learn: if thou set thine affection
  And passion on one man alone,
Why then thou'rt a fool, because madness possesses
  Whoever is faithful to one!

Take warning! My heart becomes steel if once rage
  Be born from my spurned lamentations;—
Think'st thou I'm not mad when I seek my lone couch,
  While thou runnest to thine assignations?

Ah me! Anger rages, yet peace must return,
  For at last every wrong is made right;
Why else have we friends, who will arbitrate strife,
  And attempt severed hearts to unite?
  ANONYMOUS

ALCAEUS OF MESSENE

Alone of the poets of the Anthology Alcaeus (200 B.C.) uses the epigram for political purposes. After a victory of Philip V of Macedon he wrote:

> Zeus! since by Philip scal'd Macynus' wall,
> Shut of the Blest the brazen portals all.
> Earth and the Sea now Philip's sceptre own,
> The road Olympus-ward remains alone.
>   R. G. MacGregor (*Pal. Anth.* 9.518)

284

But when Philip disillusioned the Greeks and was defeated by Flamininus at Cynoscephalae Alcaeus puts a gruesomely mocking epigram into the mouths of the fallen Macedonians:

> Unmourn'd, unburied, traveller, we lie,
> Three myriad sons of fruitful Thessaly,
> In this wide field of monumental clay.
> Aetolian Mars had marked us for his prey;
> Or he, who, bursting from th' Ausonian fold
> In Titus' form, the waves of battle rolled,
> And taught Emathia's boastful lord to run
> So swift, that swiftest stags were by his speed undone.
>   J. H. Merivale (*Pal. Anth.* 7.247)

285

And here are lines on Pan of a more familiar type:

> Breathe, Mountain Pan, a joyous note
> On rustic pipes from ample throat;
> Pour from glad reeds thy tune, inspire
> To concert sweet the harmonious quire;
> The water nymphs around shall glance
> With cadence true in rhythmic dance.
>   Walter Leaf (*Pal. Anth.* 16.226)

286

DIONYSIUS

One of several poets called Dionysius lived before 200 B.C. and wrote this epitaph on Eratosthenes:

287   No wasting sickness, but long years of peace
        Laid thee to slumber, Eratosthenes.
        Thinker profoundest, brought to thy long rest
        Not with thy sires, on the Cyrene's breast,
        But here, a friend, though in a stranger land,
        Thou hast thy tomb on Proteus' fringe of sand.
            WALTER LEAF (*Pal. Anth.* 7.78)

DIOSCORIDES

From Dioscorides, who lived in Egypt before 200 B.C., we have, among other pieces, epigrams on Thespis and on a freed slave:

288   I, Thespis, in dramatic mould
            Cast the goat-song of old,
         A joy to simple village men.
         A goat indeed, or crate of figs, was then
         The victor's prize. Juniors in later days
         Shall alter tragedy in countless ways,
         For many inventions Time shall bring to light;
         —Yet shall mine own abide as mine of right.
           W. C. LAWTON (*Pal. Anth.* 7.410)

289 Lydian? Yes; to Timanthes foster father, and slave;
      But freed by him and laid in a free grave.

When, Master, in hale old age, closing a life without ill,
  You come down, command your slave's service still.
    WILLIAM STEBBING (*Pal. Anth.* 7.178)

ANTIPATER OF SIDON

*Antipater, whose date is about 130 B.C., has poems in many
moods, of which the following are representative:*

To Anacreon

Around thy tomb, O bard divine!   **290**
  Where soft thy hallowed brow reposes,
Long may the deathless ivy twine,
  And summer pour his waste of roses!

And many a fount shall there distill,
  And many a rill refresh the flowers;
But wine shall gush in every rill,
  And every fount yield milky showers.

Thus, shade of him whom nature taught
  To tune his lyre and soul to pleasure,
Who gave to love his warmest thought,
  Who gave to love his fondest measure;

Thus, after death, if spirits feel,
  Thou mayst, from odors round thee streaming,
A pulse of past enjoyment steal,
  And live again in blissful dreaming.
    THOMAS MOORE (*Pal. Anth.* 7.23)

To Sappho

291   Sappho thou coverest, Aeolian land!
                 The Muse who died,
         Who with deathless Muses hand in hand,
                 Sang, side by side!
         Sappho, at once of Cypris and of Love
                 The child and care;
         Sappho, that those immortal garlands wove
                 For the Muses' hair!
         Sappho, the joy of Hellas, and thy crown.
                 Ye Sisters dread,
         Who spin for mortals from the distaff down
                 The threefold thread,
         Why span ye not for her unending days,
                 Unsetting sun,
         For her who wrought the imperishable lays
                 Of Helicon?
             ANDREW LANG (*Pal. Anth.* 7.14)

On Corinth Fallen

292   Where is thy beauty, Dorian Corinth, where
                 The crown of towers, which of old was thine?
         The halls once crowded by the brave and fair,
                 The throng which flocked to many a gorgeous shrine?
         Thy beauty's wrecked. It ne'er can rise again,
                 'Tis wasted by the stern, relentless foe,
         And only we, the Nymphs from out the main
                 Abide, like halcyons, wailing o'er thy woe.
             EARL OF CROMER (*Pal. Anth.* 9.151)

293   This rudely sculptured porter-pot
         Denotes where sleeps a female sot;
         Who passed her life, good easy soul,
         In sweetly chirping o'er her bowl.
         Not for her friends or children dear
         She mourns, but only for her beer.
         E'en in the very grave, they say,

She thirsts for drink to wet her clay;
And, faith, she thinks it very wrong
This jug should stand unfilled so long.
ROBERT BLAND

BION

*Adonis died each Autumn, to be reborn the following Spring,
and the* Lament *for him ascribed to Bion (ca. 100 B.C.) was
doubtless composed for a festival like that dealt with in
Theocritus'* Adoniazusae.

I.

I mourn for Adonis—Adonis is dead,
    Fair Adonis is dead and the Loves are lamenting.
Sleep, Cypris, no more on thy purple-strewed bed:
    Arise, wretch stoled in black; beat thy breast unrelenting,
And shriek to the worlds, "Fair Adonis is dead."

294

II.

I mourn for Adonis—the Loves are lamenting.
    He lies on the hills in his beauty and death;
The white tusk of a boar has transpierced his white thigh.
    Cytherea grows mad at his thin gasping breath,
While the black blood drips down on the pale ivory,
    And his eyeballs lie quenched with the weight of his brows,
The rose fades from his lips, and upon them just parted
    The kiss dies the goddess consents not to lose,
Though the kiss of the Dead cannot make her glad-hearted:
    He knows not who kisses him dead in the dews.

III.

I mourn for Adonis—the Loves are lamenting.
    Deep, deep in the thigh is Adonis's wound,

But a deeper, is Cypris's bosom presenting.
　　The youth lieth dead while his dogs howl around,
And the nymphs weep aloud from the mists of the hill,
　　And the poor Aphrodité, with tresses unbound,
All dishevelled, unsandalled, shrieks mournful and shrill
　　Through the dusk of the groves. The thorns, tearing her
　　　　feet,
Gather up the red flower of her blood, which is holy,
　　Each footstep she takes; and the valleys repeat
The sharp cry she utters, and draw it out slowly.
　　She calls on her spouse, her Assyrian; on him
Her own youth, while the dark blood spreads over his body,
　　The chest taking hue from the gash in the limb,
And the bosom, once ivory, turning to ruddy.

IV.

Ah, ah, Cytherea! the Loves are lamenting.
　　She lost her fair spouse and so lost her fair smile:
When he lived she was fair, by the whole world's consenting,
　　Whose fairness is dead with him: woe worth the while!
All the mountains above and the oaklands below
　　Murmur, ah, ah Adonis! the streams overflow
Aphrodité's deep wail; river-fountains in pity
　　Weep soft in the hills; and the flowers, as they blow,
Redden outward with sorrow, while all hear her go
　　With the song of her sadness through mountain and city.

V.

Ah, ah, Cytherea! Adonis is dead,
　　Fair Adonis is dead—Echo answers, Adonis!
Who weeps not for Cypris, when bowing her head,
　　She stares at the wound where it gapes and astonies?
—When, ah, ah!—she saw how the blood ran away
　　And empurpled the thigh, and, with wild hands flung out,
Said with sobs, "Stay, Adonis! unhappy one, stay,
　　Let me feel thee once more, let me ring thee about
With the clasp of my arms, and press kiss into kiss!
　　Wait a little, Adonis, and kiss me again,

For the last time, beloved,—and but so much of this,
  That the kiss may learn life from the warmth of the strain!
—Till thy breath shall exude from thy soul to my mouth,
  To my heart, and, the love-charm I once more receiving,
May drink thy love in it and keep, of a truth,
  That one kiss in the place of Adonis the living.
Thou fliest me, mournful one, fliest me far,
  My Adonis, and seekest the Acheron portal,—
To Hell's cruel King goest down with a scar,
  While I weep and live on like a wretched immortal,
And follow no step! O Persephoné, take him,
  My husband!—thou'rt better and brighter than I,
So all beauty flows down to thee: *I* cannot make him
  Look up at my grief; there's despair in my cry,
Since I wail for Adonis who died to me—died to me—
    Then, I fear *thee!*—Art thou dead, my Adored?
Passion ends like a dream in the sleep that's denied to me,—
  Cypris is widowed, the Loves seek their lord
All the house through in vain. Charm of cestus has ceased
  With thy clasp! O too bold in the hunt past preventing,
Ay, mad, thou so fair, to have strife with a beast!"
  Thus the goddess wailed on—and the Loves are lamenting.

VI.

Ah, ah, Cytherea! Adonis is dead.
  She wept tear after tear with the blood which was shed,
And both turned into flowers for the earth's garden-close,
  Her tears, to the wind-flower; his blood, to the rose.

VII.

I mourn for Adonis—Adonis is dead.
  Weep no more in the woods, Cytherea, thy lover!
So, well: make a place for his corse in thy bed,
  With the purples thou sleepest in, under and over.
He's fair though a corse—a fair corse, like a sleeper.
  Lay him soft in the silks he had pleasure to fold
When, beside thee at night, holy dreams deep and deeper
  Enclosed his young life on the couch made of gold.

Love him still, poor Adonis; cast on him together
  The crowns and the flowers: since he died from the place,
Why, let all die with him; let the blossoms go wither;
  Rain myrtles and olive-buds down on his face.
Rain the myrrh down, let all that is best fall a-pining,
  Since the myrrh of his life from thy keeping is swept.
Pale he lay, thine Adonis, in purples reclining;
  The Loves raised their voices around him and wept.
They have shorn their bright curls off to cast on Adonis;
One treads on his bow,—on his arrows, another,—
One breaks up a well-feathered quiver, and one is
  Bent low at a sandal, untying the strings,
  And one carries the vases of gold from the springs,
While one washes the wound,—and behind them a brother
  Fans down on the body sweet air with his wings.

VIII.

Cytherea herself, now, the Loves are lamenting.
  Each torch at the door Hymenæus blew out;
And, the marriage-wreath dropping its leaves as repenting,
  No more "Hymen, Hymen," is chanted about.
But the *ai ai* instead—"ai alas" is begun
  For Adonis, and then follows "ai Hymenæus!"
The Graces are weeping for Cinyris' son,
  Sobbing low each to each, "His fair eyes cannot see us!"
Their wail strikes more shrill than the sadder Dioné's.
The Fates mourn aloud for Adonis, Adonis,
Deep chanting; he hears not a word that they say:
  He *would* hear, but Persephoné has him in keeping.
—Cease moan, Cytherea: leave pomps for to-day,
  And weep new when a new year refits thee for weeping.
    ELIZABETH B. BROWNING

MELEAGER

Meleager of Gadara (about 75 B.C.) is an important name in the history of European poetry. His preoccupation with colors and scents and with romantic love are both as charming as they are new. Here are poems on his Heliodora:

I'll twine white violets and the myrtle green;   **295**
Narcissus will I twine and lilies sheen;
I'll twine sweet crocus and the hyacinth blue;
And last I twine the rose, love's token true:
That all may form a wreath of beauty, meet
To deck my Heliodora's tresses sweet.
    GOLDWIN SMITH (*Pal. Anth.* 5.147)

Tears to thee even beneath the earth, my Heliodora,   **296**
I offer as love's last long pledge,
tears that fall with bitterness untold.
With ceaseless sorrowing at thy tomb
I vow this last token of my longing,
of my devotion and my love.
Bitter, bitter is my grief for thee,
belovèd e'en in death,
and idle is the grace I pay
to Acheron.
Where now is my belovèd flower?
Stolen to the home of Death!
Dust covereth my flower in all her loveliness.
Oh, mother Earth, who nourisheth all things,
do thou enfold gently to thy breast
my Heliodora, flower of my devotion,
wept of all mankind.
    H. N. COUCH (*Pal. Anth.* 7.476)

This is for a bride who died on her wedding day:

297 That morn which saw me made a bride,
The evening witnessed that I died.
Those holy lights, wherewith they guide
Unto the bed the bashful bride,
Served but as tapers for to burn,
And light my relics to their urn.
This epitaph which here you see,
Supplied the epithalamy.
  ROBERT HERRICK (*Pal. Anth.* 7.182)

Here is a beautiful spring song:

298 The gusts of winter are gone, the sky no longer lowers,
Spring with her smiles is here, Spring with her purple flowers.
The dark earth crowns herself with grassy chaplets green.
The blooming woods are tressed with leafage of new sheen.
The meadows all do laugh with bursting of the rose—
Drenched with the quickening dew, at dawn their buds un-
    close.
The shepherd's heart is glad, his clear pipe wakes the hill.
The little frisking kids with joy the goatherds thrill.
Over the wide sea-waves fearless the shipmen sail,
Their bellying canvass filled with Zephyr's harmless gale.
Once more with ivy flowers their locks the feasters twine
And shout, "Hail! Bacchus, hail! thou giver of the vine!"
Busy about the hive, the bees with cunning skill
The fair white waxen comb with newdript honey fill.
On all sides round the birds do sound with their jargon
    shrill—
The halcyon over the waves, the swallow about the eaves,
The swan on the river's shore, the nightingale in the leaves.
If then the earth is gay, and the trees of the wood rejoice,
And the shepherd joys in his pipe and the flocks at the shep-
    herd's voice,
And the sea is alive with ships and the shore with the dancers'
    feet,

And the air with the song of bird and drone of bee, 'tis meet
That the poet too with song the coming of Spring should
  greet.
  L. P. CHAMBERLAYNE (*Pal. Anth.* 9.363)

*In the first of the two pieces following Cupid is advertised as
a runaway, and in the second he is offered for sale:*

Lost a boy! A runaway!   **299**
  Raise the hue and cry O!
From his bed at break of day
  Naughty Love did fly O!
Fleet he is, a quiver bears,
  Wings upon his shoulder;
Saucy laugh and dainty tears;
  None can chatter bolder.
What his country none can tell,
  Nor his sire before him;
Land and sea and heaven and hell
  Swear they never bore him.
All disown him, all detest;
  Hurry! While you're staying
Sure the rascal in some breast
  Other snares is laying.
Ho, you rogue! I spy your lair!
  Now you cannot fly, sir,
Lurking with your arrow there
  In my Zeno's eye, sir!
    WALTER LEAF (*Pal. Anth.* 5.177)

Let him be sold, though still he sleep   **300**
upon his mother's breast!
let him be sold! why should I keep
so turbulent a pest?

For winged he was born, he leers,
and sharply with his nails

he scratches, and amid his tears
oft laughs the while he wails.

Withal and further, glances keen
he plies, devoid of shame,
a ceaseless babbler, wild, nor e'en
to his own dear mother tame.

An utter monster: on that ground
sold he shall be today:
if any trader outward bound
would buy a boy, this way!

But see, in tears beseecheth he:
nay, thee no more I sell:
fear not, with my Zenophile
remain thou here to dwell.

    WALTER HEADLAM (*Pal. Anth.* 5.178)

PHILODEMUS

Philodemus was an Epicurean philosopher from Gadara and had Piso for his patron at Rome. Cicero, who knew him, respected him as a philosopher but was shocked at his lascivious epigrams. The first of the following selections is an invitation to Piso; the others are the sort Cicero objected to.

301
    To Piso from his pet friend—
    This letter, Sir, to you I send,
    And beg you graciously to come
    Tomorrow to my humble home.

    At four o'clock I you invite
    To celebrate our annual rite;

A feast of friendship and of verse
Sweeter than Homer can rehearse.

'Tis true we have no vintage wine
Or fatted paunch whereon to dine.
Yet if you will but smile on me
Our meal a banquet soon will be.
        F. A. WRIGHT (*Pal. Anth.* 11.44)

What feet she has, what legs, what waist, what thighs,   **302**
What shoulders, breast, what tender neck and eyes!
I rave, I die to touch her rosy arms,
Her round perfections and her secret charms.
How sweet her kisses after other lips,
How quick the movement of her swaying hips.
How soft her voice when at love's hour she cries:
"Oh let me die in these sweet ecstasies."
Her name is Flora—true: she knows no Greek,
Nor any language but her own to speak.
But what is that to me! Did Perseus fear
To wed Andromeda, his Indian dear?
With limbs like hers she needs not Sappho's wit—
No man will ever see she wanteth it.
    F. A. WRIGHT (*Pal. Anth.* 5.132)

Philaenion is dark and small,   **303**
But curlier than parsley;
Her skin's like down, more magical
Her voice than Venus' girdle. She
Provides for everything, what's more,
And often seems unwilling to
Ask for a thing. Philaenion, for
Such traits I'll be content with you,
At least, O golden Cypris, 'til
I find a girl more perfect still.
        ELSIE SPOERL (*Pal. Anth.* 5.121)

304   Shine, twy-horned Lady of the Night, shine on!
            Grace with thy light the fair Callistion,
            Pour down thy silvery moonbeams from above,
            And shed thy glory on our mutual love.
            Immortal, thou mayest gaze and feel no shame,
            Endymion set thine own fair soul aflame.
                EARL OF CROMER (*Pal. Anth.* 5.123)

305   I loved, I played, I drank my wine
                    In youth's brief blithesome hour of gladness.
                Who has not heard the voice divine
                    Inviting joy akin to madness?
                Alas, 'tis o'er! My wrinkled brow
                    Comes, like the warning of a sage,
                To say that pleasure's past, and now
                    My thoughts change to suit my age.
                EARL OF CROMER (*Pal. Anth.* 5.112)

ARCHIAS

*Cicero expected Archias to write a serious poem on himself;
what we have are pieces of the usual amatory and sepulchral
type:*

306   Empty all your quiver on me,
                            Every shaft employ,
                        Cruel hurt indeed you've done me,
                            Silly, silly boy.

                        But at least your chase is over,
                            All your arrows gone;
                        In my heart they've taken cover
                            And your sport is done.
                            F. A. WRIGHT (*Pal. Anth.* 5.58)

I, Theris, who lie buried on this shore,   **307**
    Tossed hither as a waif from out the deep,
Even in death must hearken to the roar
    Of the remorseless sea, that knows not sleep.
The stranger laid me in my narrow grave
    By the surf-beaten reef, and midst the dead,
Ever I hear the cruel, ceaseless wave
    Rumbling its hated thunder o'er my head.
      EARL OF CROMER (*Pal. Anth.* 7.278)

CRINAGORAS

Crinagoras, who lived in Rome in the time of Augustus, provides a specimen of Greek flattery of Roman patrons:

A parrot, bird that can   **308**
Talk with the voice of man,
Leaving his wicker cage
Spread out towards the woods his gay plumage.

And as he'd always been
Assiduously keen
To greet great Caesar's name,
Upon the hills he did it just the same.

The birds, anxious to learn,
With rivalry then burn,
Striving who first should be
To cry "Hail" unto the deity.

Orpheus on the mountain wild
The animals made mild,
But now, unbidden, all
The birds on thee, Caesar, melodious call.
      NORMAN DOUGLAS (*Pal. Anth.* 9.562)

Other pieces of Crinagoras deal with a lonely bed, a gift of a pen to a schoolboy, and the poet's remorse for disloyalty to his Muse:

309

Now to the right, now to the left I turn
Her place is empty—and I burn.
I twist and toss, and turn again
Rest brings no respite to my pain.
And restless still I shall abide
Until I have Gemella by my side.

    F. A. WRIGHT (*Pal. Anth.* 5.119)

310

Proclos, a silvern gift I send
To mark thy year that comes to end:
A reed-pen, with a cleft horn-tip
That swift across the page will slip.
A trifle—but with all my heart,
To aid thee in thy new-learn'd art.

    W. C. LAWTON (*Pal. Anth.* 6.227)

311

How long, upon vain hopes intent,
Wilt thou, O soul, on riches bent,
Toward chilly cloudlands fluttering still,
With dreams of wealth thy fancy fill?
No boon untoiled for comes to men.
Nay, turn thou to the Muse again.
For triflers leave thou far behind
The empty phantoms of the mind.

    W. C. LAWTON (*Pal. Anth.* 9.234)

AUTOMEDON

This first century B.C. epigrammatist ridicules the ease with which Athenians granted citizenship:

Charcoal in sacks if you bring ten   **312**
They'll make you straight a citizen,
But if a pig, one so magnanimous
Will then even be dubbed Triptolemus.
Also your backer Heraclides
With quite a small bribe satisfied is,
      Be it some cabbage kails,
      Lentils, or little snails.
Furnished with some such bakshish small,
Yourself Erechtheus, Cecrops, call,
Or Codrus p'rhaps—that's your affair—
No one an obol's damn will care.
    NORMAN DOUGLAS (*Pal. Anth.* 11.319)

But he likes specially gifted arrivals:

There's a girl just come to town   **313**
   Not a week ago;
Every trick in love that's known
   To you she will show;
Every mood of wantonness
In the dance she can confess
   Swaying to and fro,
Passion in her finger tips
Pliant arms and bending hips.
Better still she does not scorn
   With disdainful head
Suitors just a trifle worn
   Given up for dead;
Flattering caresses tries
Till they from the tomb arise
   Back to vigour led;
And returned to life once more
Voyage to Cythera's shore.
    F. A. WRIGHT (*Pal. Anth.* 5.129)

MARCUS ARGENTARIUS

*A favorite type of epigram is a description of a work of art.
The following by Marcus Argentarius (first century B.C.)
describes the device on a ring:*

314   Upon this seal Love whom none e'er withstands
          I see, guiding strong lions with his hands;
          One flaunts o'er them a whip, the other holds
          The reins; and grace abundant him enfolds.
          I fear this bane of men; he who wild beast
          Can tame won't pity mortals in the least.
                NORMAN DOUGLAS (*Pal. Anth.* 9.221)

But Marcus preferred live models, of whatever figure:

315   Thin Diocleia I would see, for though
          She is a fleshless Aphrodite, I
          Delight in her sweet ways; and if I lean
          Upon her delicate slight breasts I know
          That all the closer to her soul I lie,
          Because there's so little in between.
                ELSIE SPOERL (*Pal. Anth.* 5.102)

316   Yesterday my pretty Nell
             Left Mamma at home,
          Ran across and rang the bell,
             Slipped into my room;
          Came and sat upon my knee,
          Where I love her most to be.
          Both our hearts went pit-a-pat,
             For we feared that some
          Busybody rat-a-tat
             To my door would come.

"If they do"—dear Nellie sighed—
"There is nowhere here to hide."

She was right. A portly dame
    Just then forced the door,
Swiftly to my darling came
    Thrust her to the floor—
"You have got a treasure there;
Mother wants to have her share."
    F. A. WRIGHT (*Pal. Anth.* 5.127)

ANTIPATER OF
THESSALONICA

*From Antipater of Thessalonica, who lived at the end of the
first century B.C., we have a moral sea story and one on a
latter-day Europa:*

Two sailors, when the vessel sank,   **317**
    Clung to one plank their lives to save.
Tom foully struck Jack off the plank,
    And doomed him to a watery grave.
Avenging Justice eyed the strife,
    And punished quick. The sequel mark.
Jack swam ashore and saved his life,
    Whilst Tom was swallowed by a shark.
    EARL OF CROMER (*Pal. Anth.* 9.269)

A drachma and Europa's yours: **318**
    You run no risk, and she'll agree;
She has a bed as clean as can be,
    And coal when it is cold outdoors.
There really wasn't any use
    For you to be a bull, dear Zeus.
    ELSIE SPOERL (*Pal. Anth.* 5.109)

EVENUS

The date of Evenus is not known, but he may well belong with the present group. Here are poems of his on a bookworm and on a swallow eating a cicada:

319   Page-eater thou, the Muses' bitterest foe,
           Hidden destroyer, feeding constantly
           On stolen wisdom, why, black worm, lurk low
           In holy works, emblem of jealousy?
           Far from the Muses fly! And do not show
           The envious tip of thy sharp probe to me.
               NORMAN DOUGLAS (*Pal. Anth.* 9.251)

320 Child of Athens, honey nurtured, wouldst thou for thy feath-
             ered brood
       A prattling cicada capture, feasting them upon such food?
       Shall garrulous on garrulous, winged on the winged prey,
       And shall the guest of summer-time be summer-guest's pur-
             vey?
       Wil'st thou not drop it instantly? Neither just nor meet this
             wrong
       That singer's mouth should swallow up another skilled in
             song.
               NORMAN DOUGLAS (*Pal. Anth.* 9.122)

PHILIP OF THESSALONICA

Philip lived in Rome, and in about A.D. 40 made an anthology of poems written since Meleager. Here is one of his own on the Spartan Leonidas:

Seeing the martyred corpse of Sparta's king   **321**
    Cast 'mid the dead
Xerxes round the mighty limbs did fling
    His mantle red.
Then from the shades the glorious hero cried:
"Not mine a traitor's guerdon. 'Tis my pride
This shield upon my grave to wear.
    Forbear
Your Persian gifts; a Spartan I will go
    To Death below."
    JOHN ADDINGTON SYMONDS
    (*Pal. Anth.* 9.293)

LUCILIUS

Lucilius, whose patron was Nero, is an innovator in the type of epigram favored by Martial—that is, keeping the sting in the last line. The following specimens illustrate this touch:

A miser, traversing his house,   **322**
Espied, unusual there, a mouse,
And thus his uninvited guest
Briskly inquisitive addressed:
"Tell me, my dear, to what cause is it
I owe this unexpected visit?"
The mouse her host obliquely eyed,
And, smiling, pleasantly replied:
"Fear not, good fellow, for your hoard!
I come to lodge, and not to board."
    WILLIAM COWPER (*Pal. Anth.* 11.391)

They call thee rich; I deem thee poor;   **323**
Since, if thou darest not use thy store,
But savest only for thine heirs,
The treasure is not thine, but theirs.
    WILLIAM COWPER (*Pal. Anth.* 11.166)

324   The atoms are small things,
            the basis of all things.
            So said Epicurus;
            of this he'd assure us.
            But now Diophantus
            can atoms supplant thus:
            the genuine article
            he's duodecimal,
            infinitesimal,
            portion vigesimal,
            atomized particle.
                        RALPH GLADSTONE
                        (*Pal. Anth.* 11.103)

325   Nycilla dyes her locks, 'tis said,
                But 'tis a foul aspersion.
            She buys them black; they therefore need
                No subsequent immersion.
                        WILLIAM COWPER (*Pal. Anth.* 11.68)

ANTIPHILUS

*This Byzantine poet of the first century A.D. has some breezy
lines on sea-faring:*

326 On a ship's poop I'd like to lie, if I could have my way,
        With over it the weather-cloths, thumped loudly by the spray;
        A sputtering fire between two stones, edging it like a mound,
        A pot perched on them, boiling brisk, with bubbling empty
                sound;
        An unwashed cabin-boy to serve; for table I would make
        Use of some handy plank; maybe a game of give-and-take
        With sailors gossiping around. . . . Lately this chanced to
                me,
        Who always find myself at home in simple company.
                        NORMAN DOUGLAS (*Pal. Anth.* 9.546)

LUCIAN

*In epigram the famous satirist of the second century A.D.
sounds rather like Poor Richard:*

> Enjoy your goods as if your death were near: **327**
> Save them as if 'twere distant many a year.
> Sparing or spending, be thy wisdom seen
> In keeping ever to the golden mean.
>   WILLIAM HAY (*Pal. Anth.* 10.26)

> Things owned by mortals needs must mortal be.   **328**
> Away our best possessions from us flee;
> And if at times they seem disposed to stay,
> Then *we* from *them* too quickly flee away.
>   LORD NEAVES (*Pal. Anth.* 10.28)

Committing wrong the chance may be that you elude men's **329**
eyes;
You never can elude the gods, when wrong you e'en devise.
    LORD NEAVES (*Pal. Anth.* 10.27)

And here is Lucian in a lighter vein:

> A philosopher called Stesichore   **330**
> Was bitten by fleas till he swore.
>   So he put out the light,
>   And said: "Now you won't bite,
> Because you can't see me no more."
>   NORMAN DOUGLAS (*Pal. Anth.* 11.432)

His epigram on a dead child is touching:

> The frowning fates have taken hence   **331**
>   Callimachus, a childe

Five years of age: ah well is he
From cruell care exilde.
What though he lived but little tyme,
Waile nought for that at all:
For as his yeres not many were,
So were his troubles small.
TIMOTHE KENDALL (*Pal. Anth.* 7.308)

AMMIANUS

Beards were de rigeur for philosophers; here is a comment from a second century epigrammatist:

932   Thou thinkest that beard of thine brains can create,
And so that fly-flapper dost cultivate.
Shave it off quick, dear man, is my advice;
A beard like that creates not brains but lice.
NORMAN DOUGLAS (*Pal. Anth.* 11.156)

And here is Ammianus in elegiac mood:

333   Morn follows morn, and day succeeds to day,
We heed not what the fleeting hours forbode,
Sudden the Dark One seizes on his prey,
All reach the common goal, whate'er the road.
EARL OF CROMER (*Pal. Anth.* 11.13)

BABRIUS

The fullest collection of Aesopic fables in Greek is that of Babrius (second century A.D.), in the choliambic meter used by Hipponax and Herondas. Here are "The Carter and Hercules" and "The Ass's Shadow."

A carter from the village drove his wain: **334**
And when it fell into a rugged lane,
Inactive stood, nor lent a helping hand;
But to that God, whom of the heavenly band
He really honour'd most, Alcides, pray'd:
"Push at your wheels," the God appearing said,
"And goad your team; but, when you pray again,
Help yourself likewise, or you'll pray in vain."
    JAMES DAVIES

A man of Athens on a summer's day   **335**
To Megara was fain to make his way
On a pack-ass, he hired for a fixt sum.
So as he journey'd, when midday was come,
What time the sun pours down his beaming heat,
Under the ass's shade he sought retreat,
To shelter from the sun's excessive rays.
But the ass-driver now his right gainsays;
"Th' agreement was for seat, and not for shade."
To which the other said, "that he had paid
For the whole ass, and so its shadow bought."
So strifes about a shadow come to nought.
    JAMES DAVIES

OPPIAN

In the late second century A.D. one or several poets named Oppian wrote works on fishing, hunting, and fowling. The best, as science and as poetry, is the work on fishing called Halieutica. Where the subjoined selection commences the author had been discussing sex as a fisherman's lure.

As when abroad some celebrated Fair   **336**
Well-drest appears, and walks the publick Care,
The Youth of gayer Souls the Nymph pursue.

And hast too curious to the nearer View;
Indiff'rent gaze at first, but soon they find
An infant Passion struggling in their Mind:
Dull and insipid now no more invite
Their late pursuits of Glory or Delight:
Lost to themselves they seek a charming Dame,
Forget their Int'rest and indulge their Flame.

Thus equal Pangs of furious Passion bear
The sea-born Lovers to the scaly Fair.
Swung from the Shoulder of the vig'rous Swain
The Casting-Net involves th' unhappy Train.
The poor Galants with late Repentance blame
Their wayward Fates, and indiscreeter Flame.

But inky *Cuttles* further still improve
In bold pursuit, and Death-defying Love.
No Weels for them sea-lab'ring Swains prepare,
Nor hurl the spreading Lead-surrounded Snare.
A cord displays the female Captive's Charms,
Easie the Sport, and artless the Arms.
Bent on the Joy the swift Galants repair,
And cling encircled round th' unconscious Fair.

Thus when at length propitious Heav'n restores
A Brother long detain'd on forreign Shores,
His little Sisters rush with pious Hast,
Hang on his neck, and clasp around his Wast.

So the new Bride around her blooming Spouse
Her lovely Arms all wild with Pleasure throws,
In those dear Chains the willing Youth confines,
Nor in her Sleep the grateful Load resigns:
But in fond Slumbers knits the firm Embrace,
Catches his Breath, and hugs him to her Face.

Dragg'd to the Boat the close-compacted Train
Indissoluble Bands of Joy retain,
Neglect their Dangers, and their Fates approve,
False to their Nature, Constant to their Love.

When soft'ning Earth unfolds the blooming Year,
Diff'rent the Sport, nor useless the Snare.
On sandy Shores the Weel reclines, array'd

With Tamarisk, or Olive's balmy Shade.
Th' impatient Lovers seek the mimick Grove,
And court the flatt'ring scene of promis'd Love.
Too soon the rude intruding Swains annoy
Their softer Hours, and quell th' unheightened Joy.

With all th' Extravagance of wild Desire
The sable *Wrass* his speckled Females fire.
The still impatient Wish, and jealous Care
Torments the Lover, and confines the Fair.
A roving Choice th' imperious *Wrass* allows,
Nor knows th' Endearments of a single Spouse.
Immur'd beneath some spacious mossy Cell
In Rooms distinct the num'rous Females dwell;
In dull Retirement draw th' unactive Day,
Forego their Freedom, and their Lord obey.

Thus the new marri'd bashful Bride, at Home
Confin'd all Day within the nuptial Room,
The gay Impertinence of Visits flies,
While o'er her Cheeks the tell-tale Blushes rise.

The Husband *Wrass* with tender jealous Care
Maintains the Passage, and protects the Fair,
With instant Eye observes the dear Retreats,
And unfatigu'd the circling Bliss repeats.
Short Time for Food uxorious Care allows
The jealous Keeper and the vig'rous Spouse.
At Night's meridian Hour abroad he steals,
Short in his Stay, and hasty in his Meals.
But when the cloister'd Tribe of Females breed,
And racking Throes confess the ripen'd Seed,
With wild Concern the busy Parent flies,
Hast in his Fins and distraction in his Eyes;
Around the Cells with fond Impatience rolls,
Assists their Labours, in their Pain condoles.
His Wives and future Race divide his Cares,
The Father much, and much the Husband fears.

As when the Time-compleating Bride sustains
With unexperienced Womb *Lucina's* Pains,
An equal torrent of tempestuous Woes

Her Mother's sympathizing Heart overflows;
All pale without she sighs, th' immortal Pow'rs
With all the violence of Pray'r implores,
Till the decisive Shrieks within declare
The new Inhabitant of vital Air:
No less around the scaly Parent's Soul
Painful Suspense and wild Distraction roll.

    In *Asian* climes where rapid *Tigris* laves
His lofty banks, and bends the growling Waves,
Custom thus partial to the Sex allows
The *Bactrian* Archer and *Assyrian* spouse
Their num'rous Wives; in Rooms distinct they lie,
Succeed alternate to the nuptial Joy,
Impatient wait the slow returning Night,
And share the short Division of Delight.
The jealous Envy of superior Charms
Each Woman's soul with furious Rage alarms;
Domestic hate provokes th' incessant Jarr,
And Marriage is the Female State of War.

    Sharp-sighted *Jealousie!* tormenting Fiend!
Whom raving Griefs and wakeful Cares attend,
Distorted Frenzy's always at thy Side,
Thy wayward Sister and thy fruitful Bride;
Hence all the melancholly Train of Woes,
Revengeful Hate, and pale Destruction rose.

    Such broils the *Wrasses* Family molest,
Hard is his Duty, and disturb'd his Rest.
With curious View the prying Swain descries,
While round his Cells the pious Husband flies,
Above his Hook he strings the Cubic Weight;
A wriggling Shrimp supplies the living Bait.
With slow Descent the nodding Captive slides,
And fronts th' Apartment of the cloister'd Brides.
To swift Revenge the jealous Guardian moves,
Nor brooks the bold Intruder on his Loves.
With open Mouth assaults the shelly Foe,
Nor sees the pointed Fate that lurks below.
With well-tim'd Jerk the skilful Fisher draws,

And strikes the barbed Weapon thro' his Jaws.
He mounts reluctant to the sickly Air,
And gasps forgetful of his nuptial Care.
While thus the Swain with proud Success elate
In merry mood insults th' Unfortunate.
"Now, Wretch, your fond uxorious Cares employ,
And revel with your Wives in vary'd Joy:
Sole Lord below mov'd with haughty Air
Amidst a circle of obedient Fair;
Ne'er at your Change repine, on Earth you claim
One gayer Mistress, and a brighter Flame.
Your Nuptials here terrestrial Fire shall grace,
And rise to meet, and curl in your Embrace."

JOHN JONES (*Halieutica* 4.136-238)

QUINTUS OF SMYRNA

The events which fell between the stories of Iliad and Odyssey were told in the poems of the so-called epic cycle, from which the tragedians and Vergil may have drawn. These stories of the Trojan War which are not in Homer were worked into a 14-book hexameter poem called Posthomerica *by Quintus, of whom we surmise that his home was Smyrna and that he lived about the fourth century A.D. Quintus' language and style are quite Homeric, but a sentimentality, illustrated in the following selections, betrays a later date. First to help the Trojans after the death of Hector was the Amazon Penthesilea, who, after achieving marvels of heroism, encounters Achilles.*

He spake; he swung up in his mighty hand
And sped the long spear warrior-slaying, wrought
By Chiron, and above the right breast pierced
The battle-eager maid. The red blood leapt
Forth, as a fountain wells, and all at once

337

Fainted the strength of Penthesileia's limbs;
Dropped the great battle-axe from her nerveless hand;
A mist of darkness overveiled her eyes,
And anguish thrilled her soul. Yet even so
Still drew she difficult breath, still dimly saw
The hero, even now in act to drag
Her from the swift steed's back. Confusedly
She thought: "Or shall I draw my mighty sword,
And bide Achilles' fiery onrush, or
Hastily cast me from my fleet horse down
To earth, and kneel unto this godlike man,
And with wild breath promise for ransoming
Great heaps of brass and gold, which pacify
The hearts of victors never so athirst
For blood, if haply so the murderous might
Of Aeacus' son may hearken and may spare,
Or peradventure may compassionate
My youth, and so vouchsafe me to behold
Mine home again?—for O, I long to live!"
    So surged the wild thoughts in her; but the Gods
Ordained it otherwise. Even now rushed on
In terrible anger Peleus' son: he thrust
With sudden spear, and on its shaft impaled
The body of her tempest-footed steed,
Even as a man in haste to sup might pierce
Flesh with the spit, above the glowing hearth
To roast it, or as in a mountain-glade
A hunter sends the shaft of death clear through
The body of a stag with such winged speed
That the fierce dart leaps forth beyond, to plunge
Into the tall stem of an oak or pine.
So that death-ravening spear of Peleus' son
Clear through the goodly steed rushed on, and pierced
Penthesileia. Straightway fell she down
Into the dust of earth, the arms of death,
In grace and comeliness fell, for naught of shame
Dishonoured her fair form. Face down she lay
On the long spear outgasping her last breath,
Stretched upon that fleet horse as on a couch;

Like some tall pine snapped by the icy mace
Of Boreas, earth's forest-fosterling
Reared by a spring to stately height, amidst
Long mountain-glens, a glory of mother earth;
So from the once fleet steed low fallen lay
Penthesileia, all her shattered strength
Brought down to this, and all her loveliness.

Now when the Trojans saw the Warrior-queen
Struck down in battle, ran through all their lines
A shiver of panic. Straightway to their walls
Turned they in flight, heart-agonized with grief.
As when on the wide sea, 'neath buffetings
Of storm-blasts, castaways whose ship is wrecked
Escape, a remnant of a crew, forspent
With desperate conflict with the cruel sea:
Late and at last appears the land hard by,
Appears a city: faint and weary-limbed
With that grim struggle, through the surf they strain
To land, sore grieving for the good ship lost,
And shipmates whom the terrible surge dragged down
To nether gloom; so, Troyward as they fled
From battle, all those Trojans wept for her,
The Child of the resistless War-god, wept
For friends who died in groan-resounding fight.

Then over her with scornful laugh the son
Of Peleus vaunted: "In the dust lie there
A prey to teeth of dogs, to ravens' beaks,
Thou wretched thing! Who cozened thee to come
Forth against me? And thoughtest thou to fare
Home from the war alive, to bear with thee
Right royal gifts from Priam the old king,
Thy guerdon for slain Argives? Ha, 'twas not
The Immortals who inspired thee with this thought,
Who know that I of heroes mightiest am,
The Danaans' light of safety, but a woe
To Trojans and to thee, O evil-starred!
Nay, but it was the darkness-shrouded Fates
And thine own folly of soul that pricked thee on
To leave the works of women, and to fare

To war, from which strong men shrink shuddering back."
    So spake he, and his ashen spear the son
Of Peleus drew from that swift horse, and from
Penthesileia in death's agony.
Then steed and rider gasped their lives away
Slain by one spear. Now from her head he plucked
The helmet splendour-flashing like the beams
Of the great sun, or Zeus' own glory-light.
Then, there as fallen in dust and blood she lay,
Rose, like the breaking of the dawn, to view
'Neath dainty-pencilled brows a lovely face,
Lovely in death. The Argives thronged around,
And all they saw and marvelled, for she seemed
Like an Immortal. In her armour there
Upon the earth she lay, and seemed the child
Of Zeus, the tireless Huntress Artemis
Sleeping, what time her feet forwearied are
With following lions with her flying shafts
Over the hills far-stretching. She was made
A wonder of beauty even in her death
By Aphrodite glorious-crowned, the Bride
Of the strong War-god, to the end that he,
The son of noble Peleus, might be pierced
With the sharp arrow of repentant love.
The warriors gazed, and in their hearts they prayed
That fair and sweet like her their wives might seem,
Laid on the bed of love, when home they won.
Yea, and Achilles' very heart was wrung
With love's remorse to have slain a thing so sweet,
Who might have borne her home, his queenly bride,
To chariot-glorious Phthia; for she was
Flawless, a very daughter of the Gods,
Divinely tall, and most divinely fair.

        .   .   .   .   .

    Then did the warrior sons of Argos strip
With eager haste from corpses strown all round
The blood-stained spoils. But ever Peleus' son
Gazed, wild with all regret, still gazed on her,

The strong, the beautiful, laid in the dust;
And all his heart was wrung, was broken down
With sorrowing love, deep, strong as he had known
When that beloved friend Patroclus died.
    A. S. WAY (1.592-674, 716-721)

Paris has been wounded, and none but his deserted wife
Oenone might heal his hurt.

But through the livelong night no sleep laid hold   **338**
On Paris: for his help no leech availed,
Though ne'er so willing, with his salves. His weird
Was only by Oenone's hands to escape
Death's doom, if so she willed. Now he obeyed
The prophecy, and he went—exceeding loth,
But grim necessity forced him thence, to face
The wife forsaken. Evil-boding fowl
Shrieked o'er his head, or darted past to left,
Still as he went. Now, as he looked at them,
His heart sank; now hope whispered, "Haply vain
Their bodings are!"—but on their wings were borne
Visions of doom that blended with his pain.
Into Oenone's presence thus he came.
Amazed her thronging handmaids looked on him
As at the Nymph's feet that pale suppliant fell
Faint with the anguish of his wound, whose pangs
Stabbed him through brain and heart, yea, quivered through
His very bones, for that fierce venom crawled
Through all his inwards with corrupting fangs;
And his life fainted in him agony-thrilled.
As one with sickness and tormenting thirst
Consumed, lies parched, with heart quick-shuddering,
With liver seething as in flame, the soul,
Scarce conscious, fluttering at his burning lips,
Longing for life, for water longing sore;
So was his breast one fire of torturing pain.
Then in exceeding feebleness he spake:
"O reverenced wife, turn not from me in hate
For that I left thee widowed long ago!

Not of my will I did it: the strong Fates
Dragged me to Helen—oh that I had died
Ere I embraced her—in thine arms had died!
Ah, by the Gods I pray, the Lords of Heaven,
By all the memories of our wedded love.
Be merciful! Banish my bitter pain:
Lay on my deadly wound those healing salves
Which only can, by Fate's decree, remove
This torment, if thou wilt. Thine heart must speak
My sentence, to be saved from death or no.
Pity me—oh, make haste to pity me!
This venom's might is swiftly bringing death!
Heal me, while life yet lingers in my limbs!
Remember not those pangs of jealousy,
Nor leave me by a cruel doom to die
Low fallen at thy feet! This should offend
The Prayers, the Daughters of the Thunderer Zeus,
Whose anger followeth unrelenting pride
With vengeance, and the Erinnys execute
Their wrath. My queen, I sinned, in folly sinned;
Yet from death save me—oh, make haste to save!"
    So prayed he; but her darkly-brooding heart
Was steeled, and her words mocked his agony:
"Thou comest unto me!—thou, who didst leave
Erewhile a wailing wife in a desolate home!—
Didst leave her for thy Tyndarid darling! Go,
Lie laughing in her arms for bliss! She is better
Than thy true wife—is, rumor saith, immortal!
Make haste to kneel to her—but not to me!
Weep not to me, nor whimper pitiful prayers!
Oh that mine heart beat with a tigress' strength,
That I might tear thy flesh and lap thy blood
For all the pain thy folly brought on me!
Vile wretch! where now is Love's Queen glory-crowned?
Hath Zeus forgotten his daughter's paramour?
Have them for thy deliverers! Get thee hence
Far from my dwelling, curse of Gods and men!
Yea, for through thee, thou miscreant, sorrow came

On deathless Gods, for sons and sons' sons slain.
Hence from my threshold!—to thine Helen go!
Agonize day and night beside her bed:
There whimper, pierced to the heart with cruel pangs,
Until she heal thee of thy grievous pain."
 So from her doors she drave that groaning man—
Ah fool! not knowing her own doom, whose weird
Was straightway after him to tread the path
Of death! So Fate had spun her destiny thread.
 A. S. WAY (10.259-331)

*Paris can only stumble down the mountain to his death, and
Helen bewails him in a long speech.*

So cried she: but for him far less she mourned   **339**
Than for herself, remembering her own sin.
Yea, and Troy's daughters but in semblance wailed
For him: of other woes their hearts were full.
Some thought on parents, some on husbands slain,
These on their sons, on honoured kinsmen those.
 One only heart was pierced with grief unfeigned,
Oenone. Not with them of Troy she wailed,
But far away within that desolate home
Moaning she lay on her lost husband's bed.
As when the copses on high mountains stand
White-veiled with frozen snow, which o'er the glens
The west-wind blasts have strown, but now the sun
And east-wind melt it fast, and the long heights
With water-courses stream, and down the glades
Slide, as they thaw, the heavy sheets, to swell
The rushing waters of an ice-cold spring,
So melted she in tears of anguished pain,
And for her own, her husband, agonised,
And cried to her heart with miserable moans:
"Woe for my wickedness! O hateful life!
I loved mine hapless husband—dreamed with him
To pace to eld's bright threshold hand in hand,
And heart in heart! The gods ordained not so.

Oh had the black Fates snatched me from the earth
Ere I from Paris turned away in hate!
My living love hath left me!—yet will I
Dare to die with him, for I loathe the light."
    A. S. WAY (10.406-431)

Wildly Oenone flies down the rugged mountain side.

340 Through mountain gorges so she won to where
Wailed other Nymphs round Alexander's corpse.
Roared up about him a great wall of fire:
For from the mountain far and near had come
Shepherds, and heaped the death-bale broad and high
For love's and sorrow's latest service done
To one of old their comrade and their king.
Sore weeping stood they round. She raised no wail,
The broken-hearted, when she saw him there,
But, in her mantle muffling up her face,
Leapt on the pyre.
    A. S. WAY (10.448-468)

PALLADAS

*Palladas, who was a schoolmaster at Alexandria about 400
A.D., is one of the best poets in the* Anthology. *He was em-
bittered by his calling and by a shrewish wife, but his wit
though wry is not merely cynical.*

341   This life a theatre we well may call,
      Where every actor must perform with art;
    Or laugh it thro' and make a farce of all,
      Or learn to bear with grace his tragic part.
      ROBERT BLAND (*Pal. Anth.* 12.44)

342   Life is but a flying slave,
      Now escaped and now imprisoned.

Fortune tossed by every wave,
    Like some harlot gay bedizened.
Jest at both, nor grieve to see
The unrighteous in prosperity.
    F. A. WRIGHT (*Pal. Anth.* 10.87)

The stream that carries you doth carry all;   **343**
    Bear and forbear however fortune fall.
'Tis vain to strive and cry, whate'er you do;
    The stream that carries all will carry you!
    J. A. POTT (*Pal. Anth.* 10.73)

Life is a perilous voyage. The seas o'erwhelm   **344**
Full oft our bark without a hand to save,
And with the steersman Chance still at the helm
We can but doubting sail, to safety some,
To ruin others; all must cross the wave,
All to one port beneath the earth must come.
    L. P. CHAMBERLAYNE (*Pal. Anth.* 10.65)

Night passes. We are born day after day.   **345**
In what is past we have no more a part.
The hours of yesterday—mere aliens they,
Today our future life afresh we start.
Old age, say not that many years thou hast—
Today thou ownest nothing of the past.
    L. P. CHAMBERLAYNE (*Pal. Anth.* 10.79)

In place of fire God a woman gave;   **346**
Well will it be when neither gift we have.
But she is worse: we can put out our fires;
Woman's a blaze that burns and ne'er expires.
    F. A. WRIGHT (*Pal. Anth.* 9.167)

Wives are a curse,   **347**
Some bad, some worse:
Vexation beyond measure.
When they're in bed,

And when they're dead,
Our only hours of pleasure.
      F. A. WRIGHT (*Pal. Anth.* 11.381)

348   Tell me, and wouldst thou span the ends of earth,
Thou tiny body brought from clay to birth?
Nay, know thyself, and thine own limits see
Before thou dealest with immensity.
Count first the dust that does thy body make
Ere of the measureless thou measure take.
      F. A. WRIGHT (*Pal. Anth.* 11.349)

AESOP

The present bearer of the famous name lived about A.D. 400.

349   O Life, what refuge have we fleeing thee,
Save in Death only? Infinite, in truth,
Thy sorrows are, and unendurable
As unavoidable. Doubtless there are
Some beauties and some charms in Nature's gift—
The earth, the stars, the sea, the moon, the sun,
But all the rest is only grief and fear.
And if perchance some happiness be there,
There too is Nemesis, who takes revenge.
      LILLA CABOT PERRY (*Pal. Anth.* 10.123)

GLYCO

This "Vanity of Vanities" dates from about the same period:

350   All is dust, and all is laughter,
Think not of the dark hereafter.

Here on earth be gay and jolly,
Man's a fool and all is folly.

EARL OF CROMER (*Pal. Anth.* 10.124)

NONNOS

*The Dionysiaca of Nonnos, a fifth century Egyptian, in 48
books of hexameters, narrates all the myths connected with
Dionysus. The work is utterly decadent, and yet shows a new
strength growing out of decadence. The following passage is
Dionysus' prayer to the Moon when he is threatened by
Pentheus, and the Moon's reply.*

"O daughter of Helios, Moon of many turnings, nurse of **351**
all! O Selene, driver of the silver car! If thou art Hecate of
many names, if in the night thou doest shake thy mystic
torch in brandcarrying hand, come nightwanderer, nurse of
puppies because the nightly sound of the hurrying dogs is thy
delight with their mournful whimpering. If thou art stag-
hunter Artemis, if on the hills thou dost eagerly hunt with
fawnkilling Dionysos, be thy brother's helper now! For I have
in me the blood of ancient Cadmos, and I am being chased
out of Thebes, out of my mother Semele's home. A mortal
man, a creature quickly perishing, an enemy of god, persecutes
me. As a being of the night, help Dionysos of the night, when
they pursue me! If thou art Persephoneia, whipperin of the
dead, and yours are the ghosts which are subservient to the
throne of Tartaros, let me see Pentheus a dead man, and let
Hermes thy musterer of ghosts lull to sleep the tears of
Dionysos in his grief. With the Tartarean whip of thy Tisi-
phone, or furious Megaira, stop the foolish threats of Pen-
theus, this son of earth, since implacable Hera has armed a
lateborn Titan against Lyaios. I pray thee, master this im-
pious creature, to honour the Dionysos who revived the name
of primeval Zagreus. Lord Zeus, do thou also look upon the
threat of this madman. Hear me, father and mother! Lyaios

is contemned: let thy marriage lightning be the avenger of
Semele!"

To this appeal bullface Mene answered on high:

"Night-illuminating Dionysos, friend of plants, comrade of
Mene, look to your grapes; my concern is the mystic rites of
Bacchos, for the earth ripens the offspring of your plants when
it receives the dewy sparkles of unresting Selene. Then do
you, dancing Bacchos, stretch out your thyrsus and look to
your offspring; and you need not fear a race of puny men,
whose mind is light, whose threats the whips of the furies re-
press perforce. With you I will attack your enemies. Equally
with Bacchos I rule distracted madness. I am the Bacchic
Mene, not alone because in heaven I turn the months, but
because I command madness and excite lunacy. I will not
leave unpunished earthly violence against you. For already
Lycurgos who threatened Dionysos, so quick of knee once,
who sharply harried the Mainads, is a blind vagabond who
needs a guide. Already over the stretches of Erythraian reed-
beds a crowd of Indians lie dead here and there, dumb
witnesses to your valour, and foolish Deriades has been
swallowed up in the unwilling stream of his father Hydaspes,
pierced with an ivy spear—yes, he fled and fell into the sad
stream of his despondent father. The Tyrsenians learnt your
strength, when the standing mast of their ship was changed,
and turned into a vinestock of itself, the sail spread into a
shady canopy of leaves of gardenvine and rich bunches of
grapes, the forestays whistled with clumps of serpents hissing
poison, your enemies threw off their human shape and intelli-
gent mind and changed their looks to senseless dolphins wal-
lowing in the sea—still they make revel for Dionysos even in
the surge, skipping like tumblers in the calm water. Indian
Orontes also is dead, struck by your sharp thyrsus, and
drowned in the Assyrian floods, still fearing the name of
Bacchos even under the waters."

W. H. D. ROUSE (44.191-251)

TRYPHIODORUS

*Like Quintus of Smyrna, Tryphiodorus (fifth century A.D.)
wrote supplements to Homer. The following from* The Taking
of Troy *describes the emergence of the Greek warriors from
the wooden horse inside Troy.*

Meanwhile the Steed's deep caverns, op'ning wide,   **352**
Pour forth th' imprison'd Warriors from its side.
As when within some Oak the Bees have stor'd
In artful cavities their luscious hoard,
Forth issuing from their cells the swarms appear,
And spring t' assault the weary Traveller,
In scatter'd Legions fill th' extended shore,
And sip the dew from ev'ry fragant flow'r,
So from the teeming Monster's fatal sides
The *Greeks* forth rushing in 'tumultuous tides,
Pour through the streets, and send the sleeping Foe,
In Dreams of Terrour, to the Shades below.
The pavements float with gore; the mingled cries
Of flying *Trojans* echoing to the skies,
Shake the surrounding tow'rs: Old *Ilion* stands
Just nodding to her fall; the Victor bands
Traverse her paths, like Lyons bath'd in blood,
And bridge with slaughter'd heaps th' incumber'd road.
The *Trojan* matrons hear, alarm'd from far,
The clashing falchions, and the shouts of war:
Still fond of Liberty their necks they bow,
And bid the trembling Husband strike the blow.
The helpless Mother here, with plaintive tongue,
As the fond Swallow mourns her absent Young,
Wails o'er her slaughter'd Child: The youthful Bride
Sees her loved Consort falling by her side;
Struck at the sight, and scorning to sustain

The hated bondage of a Captive's chain,
With dauntless pride she braves the hostile sword,
Nor falls in death divided from her Lord.
The teeming Matron on the sanguine earth
Expires, and dying drops th' unfinish'd birth.
Bellona, thirsting for the blood of Men,
While the gor'd Battel streams in ev'ry vein,
Swells the full tide; and, issuing on her Car,
Wrap'd in a Whirlwind guides the tumult of the war.
Fell *Discord* animates the growing Fight,
And adds new horrours to the deathful night:
High as the Heav'ns her tow'ring head she bore,
And bade the thunder of the Battel roar.
Mars now unsheaths his sword; where-e'er he trod,
Destruction marched, and bath'd his steps in blood.

JAMES MERRICK (533-565)

COLLUTHUS

*Like Tryphiodorus, with whom he was probably contem-
porary, Colluthus, in his* Rape of Helen, *dealt with Homeric
material. In the passage below Hermione awakens to find her
mother Helen gone.*

353   At morning's dawn Hermione appears,
With tresses discompos'd and bathed in tears.
She roused her menial train; and thus express'd
The boding sorrows of her troubled breast:
     "Where, fair attendants, is my mother fled,
Who left me sleeping in her lonely bed?
For yesternight she took her trusty key,
Turn'd the strong bolt, and slept secure with me."
Her hapless fate the pensive train deplore
And in thick circles gather round the door;
Here all contend to moderate her grief,

And by their kind condolence give relief:
   "Unhappy princess, check the rising tear;
Thy mother, absent now, will soon appear.
Soon as thy sorrow's bitter source she knows,
Her speedy presence will dispel thy woes.
The virgin cheek with sorrow's weight o'ercome,
Sinks languid down and loses half its bloom.
Deep in the head the tearful eye retires,
There sullen sits nor darts its wonted fires.
Eager perchance the band of nymphs to meet,
She saunters devious from her favorite seat,
And of some flowery mead at length possess'd,
Sinks on the dew-bespangled lawn to rest.
Or to some kindred stream perchance she strays,
Bathes in Eurotas' stream, and round its margin plays."
   "Why talk ye thus" (the pensive maid replies
The tears of anguish trickling from her eyes)
"She knows each roseate bower, each vale and hill,
She knows the course of every winding rill.
The stars are set; on rugged rocks she lies:
The stars are up; nor does my mother rise.
What hills, what dales, thy devious steps detain?
Hath some relentless beast my mother slain?
But beasts, which lawless round the forest rove,
Revere the sacred progeny of Jove.
Or art thou fallen from some steep mountain's brow,
Thy corse conceal'd in dreary dells below?
But through the groves, with thickest foliage crown'd,
Beneath each shrivel'd leaf that strews the ground,
Assiduous have I sought thy corse in vain:
Why should we the guiltless grove arraign?
But have Eurotas' streams, which rapid flow,
O'erwhelmed thee bathing in its deeps below?
Yet in the deeps the Naiads live
And they to womankind protection give."
   Thus spoke she sorrowing, and reclined her head;
And sleeping seem'd to mingle with the dead.
     H. MEEN (328-366)

RUFINUS

The verses of Rufinus, possibly fifth or sixth century, all deal, and in a light mood, with love.

354

> Do not embrace a girl too thin,
> Nor one that is too fat;
> But rather choose the mean of such,
> For this one is deficient in
> The flesh superfluous in that:
> Want not too little or too much.
>
> ELSIE SPOERL (*Pal. Anth.* 5.37)

355

> A very natural girl I hate,
> Also a girl too temperate.
> As one is much too eager, so
> The other, likewise, is too slow.
>
> ELSIE SPOERL (*Pal. Anth.* 5.42)

356

> By all the gods I did not know
> How Cytherea takes a bath,
> Her own hands loosening her hair
> About her neck.—Sweet mistress, Oh
> Be kindly: visit not thy wrath
> Upon my eyes that saw thy fair
> Immortal form.—But can it be
> This isn't Cypris that I see?
> It's Rhodoclea! Where'd you get
> Beauty like that? I'd like to bet
> You stripped the goddess unaware.
>
> ELSIE SPOERL (*Pal. Anth.* 5.73)

357

> This wreath, O Rhodocleia, to thee I send,
> Which with my hands I've woven, dear, for thee.

Here lilies, rose-buds, damp narcissus blend,
Dark violets, and the moist anemone.
  My garland don, and put thy pride away:
  Thy flowers, and thou, shall bloom but for a day.
    W. C. Lawton (*Pal. Anth.* 5.74)

MACEDONIUS

*Macedonius, called "the Consul," has a number of pieces in
the* Anthology; *here are two:*

Earth, that gave body! Birth-Goddess, shelter in womb!   **358**
  My course between is run; now, Both, Farewell!
I depart hence; but whither? Whose being? from whom
  Crossed I to whom? and what then?—who can tell?
    William Stebbing (*Pal. Anth.* 7.566)

From loftiest turret to foundation-stone   **359**
This house was raised by righteousness alone:
For Macedonius with despoiling sword
Reft not from other men their toil-won hoard.
    W. C. Lawton (*Pal. Anth.* 9.649)

JOANNES BARBOCOLLAS

*This Spanish poet (A.D. 551) has some fine lines spoken by
a dying wife:*

As I looked on my Husband, and felt my last thread was spun,   **360**
  I praised God Death and God Hymen, the pair;
Hymen, that he had coupled us, Death, that he took the one,
  Leaves our offspring in such a father's care!
    William Stebbing (*Pal. Anth.* 7.555)

PAUL THE SILENTIARY

*Paul was a high official at the court of Justinian (ca. 560)
and a close friend of Agathias. About 80 of his epigrams sur-
vive, many on works of art.*

361   "Farewell!" I murmur, and then hold my breath,
            Whilst, fondly lingering, by thy side I stay,
        I shrink from parting as from cruel Death,
            Thy light is glorious as the summer's day.
        But day, though glorious, cannot tune a voice
            To sooth my troubles or enchant my ear,
        Whilst thy sweet siren notes my soul rejoice
            With music such as lovers yearn to hear.
              EARL OF CROMER (*Pal. Anth.* 5.241)

362   My name, my country—what are they to thee?
        What, whether base or proud my pedigree?
        Perhaps I far surpassed all other men;
        Perhaps I fell below them all; what then?
        Suffice it, stranger! that thou seest a tomb;
        Thou know'st its use; it hides—no matter whom.
              WILLIAM COWPER (*Pal. Anth.* 7.307)

363   Fair girl, I swore to stay apart from you
        Until the early light of the twelfth day.
        But oh, poor me, I was unable to
        Endure it, rather more twelve months away
        That morning seemed, I swear it, for us both.
        Implore the gods not to inscribe that oath
        On their avenging records, love, and by
        Your charms enchant my heart. Beneath the lash

Neither of you nor of the gods would I
Slow-burning, mistress, be consumed to ash.
ELSIE SPOERL (*Pal. Anth.* 5.254)

Here are lines on a mosquito net:

Soft Venus do I serve, and round the bed   **364**
Of happy brides my canopy is spread.
No hunter's net am I, but 'neath my mesh
Love takes new vigour from the breezes fresh.
F. A. WRIGHT (*Pal. Anth.* 9.765)

AGATHIAS

*Agathias (536-582) was a lawyer and historian, and made
a "Circle" of epigrams which was later worked into the
Anthology. The Anthology contains about a hundred of
Agathias' own pieces, of which the following are representative.*

I love not wine, but shouldst thou wish   **365**
That I its slave might be,
Thou needest but to taste the cup,
    Then hand it back to me.

For unto me that cup would bring
From thy dear lips a kiss,
And while I drank would softly tell
    How it received such bliss.
LILLA CABOT PERRY (*Pal. Anth.* 5.261)

Chaeronean Plutarch, to thy deathless praise   **366**
Does martial Rome this grateful statue raise;
Because both Greece and she thy fame have shared,
(Their heroes written and their lives compared;)

But thou thyself couldst never write thine own;
Their lives have parallels, but thine has none.
    JOHN DRYDEN (*Pal. Anth.* 16.331)

367   Not such your burden, happy youths, as ours—
      Poor women children nurtured daintily—
For ye have comrades when ill-fortune lours,
      To hearten you with talk and company;
And ye have games for solace, and may roam
      Along the streets and see the painters' shows.
But woe betide us if we stir from home—
      And there our thoughts are dull enough, God knows!
    W. M. HARDINGE (*Pal. Anth.* 5.297)

368]   Weeping and wakeful all the night I lie,
And with the dawn the grace of sleep is near,
But swallows flit about me with their cry,
And banish drowsihead and bring the tear.
Mine eyes must still be weeping for the dear
Thought of Rhodanthe stirs in memory:
Ye chattering foes, have done! it was not I
Who silenced Philomel: go, seek the sheer
Clefts of hills, and wail for Itylus
Or clamor from the hoopoe's craggy nest,
But let sweet sleep an hour abide with us,
Perchance a dream may come, and we be blest.
A dream may take Rhodanthe piteous,
And bring us to that haven of her breast.
    ANDREW LANG (*Pal. Anth.* 5.237)

MUSAEUS

*The story of Hero and Leander has been known and loved,
through Marlowe's version completed by Chapman, through
Schiller and through Grillparzer, by generations of readers
who valued it above all other classical myths. In the Renais-*

*sance it was believed that the Musaeus who wrote it was the
legendary bard who antedated Homer; modern criticism
recognizes in him a romantic note which is alien to the
classics and calls him the last full-blown bloom in the garden
of Greek poesy. Here is the opening:*

Sing, Muse, the beacon gleaming bright above,   **369**
That lit the nightly swimmer to his love;
The hidden meeting and the midnight tide
Which bore the bridegroom to his watchful bride;
The marriage robes sea-soaked, the moist embrace,
Abydos' town and Sestos—Hero's place;
Longing Leander on the salt-waves crest,
The lamp that led him to sweet Hero's breast;
Kind lamp—love's jewel—which the mighty Jove
Might well have taken to the orbs above,
And set it shining in the spangled sky
To be Love's star of all Heaven's company,
Seeing it was the planet of their bliss,
The glittering summons to the sleepless kiss,
Till the hard waves made end of him and this:
But help, high Muse! and teach me how to sing
Leander's death and lamp's extinguishing.

Sestos and white Abydos, cities twain,
Fronted each other upon Helle's main,
God Eros there, setting his shaft to string,
Wounded two bosoms with one shaft-shooting;
A maiden's and a youth's—Leander he,
And lovely Hero, Sestos' sweetest, she:
Each of each town the very best and boast,
A noble pair. If ever to that coast
Thou goest, inquire for Hero's tower, and roam
Where she Love's light-house nightly did illume.
Inquire for white Abydos, too, and muse
Where young Leander life and love did lose;
But now to tell how he fair Hero loved,
And how the maid to dote on him was moved.

Honey-sweet Hero, of a god-like race,

Was priestess to Queen Venus in that place;
And in her father's house by the sea set
Herself a Queen of Love, though virgin yet,
Dwelt; yet for modesty and beauty's shame
She never to the city markets came,
Nor mingled with the feast-days or the dance,
Lest envious eyes upon her eyes should glance;
For those ill-favoured flout at fairer faces;
But ever in the holy temple-places
She worshipped rose-lipped Venus, queen above,
And Eros eke, the tiny God of Love,
Beseeching that she might unscathed go,
Yet not the more escaped she delicious woe.
    EDWIN ARNOLD (1-41)

*All the folk of Sestos and Abydus foregathered for a festival
of Aphrodite. The fairest of the fair was Hero:*

370 And now the maiden Hero walked to Aphrodite's temple,
And as the radiance of the moon that floods the evening skies,
So the splendor of her beauty flowed from Hero's tranquil
    eyes.
The color of her perfect cheeks had just the tender glow
That mingles in the opening rose the blushes and the snow.
Yea, thou hadst said in Hero's limbs not one rose, but a field
Of roses, tinting all her skin with blushes, was revealed.
And neath the white skirts of the girl her rosy ankles gleamed.
Thus graces flowed from every limb. The men of old time
    deemed
The Graces to be three alone, and thus they wove their lies.
A hundred graces bloomed in each of Hero's laughing eyes!
    L. P. CHAMBERLAYNE (55-65)

*All are filled with admiration, and Leander with instant love.
Her timid eyes return his ardent glances, and after the festival
he steals up behind her:*

371 Lightly he touched her soft and rosy hand,
Heaving a deep sigh, plain to understand;

And she, as one an angered, drew it in,
But so that he might see 'twas no great sin.
Then bolder, by her stole he took the maid,
And prayed her turn one minute to the shade;
Whereat with pretty frown and faltering feet
She turned and stayed, and said with chiding sweet—
"Sir! Are you mad? How dare you hold me so?
Leave plucking of my gown and let me go."
    EDWIN ARNOLD (112-124)

Hero yields to Leander's eloquence. They introduce them-
selves to one another more fully, and Hero is in despair when
she finds that she will be separated from her lover by the
Hellespont. Leander passionately assures her that the Helles-
pont cannot obstruct his love:

For thy love's sake, O maiden, I will cross the tumbling sea   **372**
Regardless though its waves were fire, how wild so e'er they
    be.
I should not shudder at the roar nor the boom of the heavy
    billow,
For hope and love would buoy me up to swim toward thy
    pillow.
But every night will see me swim, thy husband, o'er the tide
Of surging Hellespont. Not far upon the other side
I dwell in old Abydos. Do thou only show a lamp
Forth from thy tower's high battlement, that through the
    murky damp
Its light may shine on me, and I, beholding it afar,
Shall be the bark of Eros, and thy lamp shall be my star,
And I shall never see nor care whether Bootes set,
Nor the belt of great Orion, nor the track of the Wain unwet,
For from my home across the strait I swim to a haven sweet.
But, darling, guard against the storm and gusts of driving
    sleet,
Lest they blow out the lamp, and straightway bear my soul
    afar,
Quenching my being's beacon, and my passion's morning star.
    L. P. CHAMBERLAYNE (203-218)

Hero confirms the arrangement and the lovers part. Leander
watches for the light, which Hero shields with the folds of her
dress, and when he sees it prays to the gods of love and the
sea and leaps into the waves. Finally he touches land and is
welcomed by Hero:

373   In gladness past all words her white arms flung
Round him, and on his panting bosom hung,
And led him from the cold and foamy beach
Up to her tower; and when her room they reach,
She wiped his pearly body clean of brine,
And took the salt smell off with unguents fine,
In rose-leaves dyed and scented rich and rare;
And then she clothed him with her own deep hair,
Yet panting from his voyage—while in his ear
She poured these tender accents:

                                    "Husband dear!
Sore hast thou toiled, as never one save thee,
Battling the horrid deep to come to me:
Forget upon my lips the waves' harsh taste,
The fierce sea-monsters and the roaring waste.
The port is reached: anchor, dear ship, and have
The goods you sailed for in your Hero's love."
                    EDWIN ARNOLD (260-272)

Many succeeding voyages are crowned with similar delight,
until winter brings rough weather. Leander is persistent, and
Hero cannot refuse. The closing episode begins with Leander
struggling in the wintry sea.

374   Tir'd with vain Toil, scar'd with each dreadful blast,
Leander's Strength, and Courage fail'd at last:
Long bravely obstinate for Love, and Life,
Long the brave Youth maintain'd the doubtful strife
With Winds, and Waves; 'til prest by mighty Odds,
A Mortal's Strength yields to the Pow'r of Gods.
To Beauty's Queen, descended from the Main,
Panting he prays, but panting prays in Vain!

Next, as he cleaves the Surge with fainter strokes,
With fainter Voice great *Neptune's* Aid invokes!
And, but hardly now supply'd with Breath,
While ev'ry Gasp imbibes the watry Death,
To *Boreas*, once a Lover, sighs his Pray'r,
To help a Lover in the last Despair!
Conjures Him by *Atthis*' sacred Name,
By the dear Mem'ry of th' *Athenian* Dame,
Conjures th' enamour'd *Wind* a Wretch to save,
Now, now, just sinking in th' ingulphing Wave!

   But, Ah! No God his supplication heard,
Thus in the Anguish of his Soul prefer'd!
Not youth's beseeching Groans; nor Cries of Love,
No Pray'rs th' *inexorable sisters* move!

   His feeble Limbs no more direct his Course;
The Billows rage with unresisted Force;
His slacken'd Nerves their wonted Aid deny;
In vain he rolls a deprecating Eye;
For now the rushing Wind the *Torch* assails,
Not pious *Hero's* watchful care avails;
Nor *Torch*, nor Lover the dire Blast evade!
Both sink at once in Night's eternal Shade!

   Mean time, aloft, the discontented Fair,
Ill-fated *Hero*, stands with anxious Care;
Computes the tedious Minutes from the Tow'r
And finds he stay'd beyond th' appointed Hour;
(The Light extinguisht) 'midst foreboding Fears,
She swels the Winds with Sighs, the Waves with Tears,
Vainly and oft she calls her much-lov'd Lord,
Beyond the Goddess, whom she serv'd, ador'd;
(Full on her Face rude Winds return her Moans—
Alas! unhear'd 'midst Nature's louder Groans!)
Now with herself expostulates in Grief;
And hopes she knows not whence, or why, Relief!
"Perhaps, arriv'd on th' unknown Shore he strays,
Perhaps, securely at *Abydos* stays!
Deter'd by Winds and a tempestuous Night!
Perhaps!—ah No! he saw the treach'rous Light!

Saw! and wou'd venture—why did I accurst?"
—Sudden she stops, and dares not think the *worst!*
   At length she sees, with restless sorrows torn,
Rising in Clouds, she sees th' ill-omen'd Morn!
Now roll'd around, her eager Eyes explore
The Rocks, the Beach, and distant-mazy Shore:
—Fruitless her search!—Now, now she looks (in vain!)
Yet, yet to find him struggling on the Main!
   But, O! too soon, as Chance directs her Eyes,
The lovely, naked, breathless Corse she spies!
Close at the *Basis* of the Tow'r he lay,
Dash'd on the Rocks, and beaten by the Spray;
Tost by the Buffets of the Waves to Shore;
—Now seen too soon, and overlook'd before!
Grief, Rage, Distraction, Fury, and Despair
With Soul-afflicting Horror seize the Fair!
Like the Prophetick *Pythian*, God-possest,
She bounds, she raves, she smites her groaning Breast;
No soft asswaging Vent her sorrows find,
Her red Eyes glare, expressive of her Mind!
Madness congeals the Fountain of her Tears,
And Fate in her determin'd Looks appears!
No Woman-Drops with mean complaining flow;
Ignoble Refuge of a vulgar Woe!
Oft as the dear pale Features struck her View,
To cruel Heav'n upbraiding Looks she threw;
With wishful Eyes ran o'er the well-known Face,
And meditates in Death a last Embrace;
Then smiles severe—in scorn of Future Fate,
And bids a while the mighty Spirit wait!
"Ye Gods! she cries, nor yet *Leander's* lost!
Thus, thus I catch my Husband's hov'ring Ghost!"
Straight rising with extatick Force to throw
Her darting Body, aim'd at His, below;
Headlong she sprang from the Tow'rs fearful Height!
And wing'd precipitate her downward Flight!
   For lost *Leander* thus his *Hero* fell!
None dy'd so greatly! None e'er lov'd so well!

She for the Youth, he perish'd for the Fair!
Not Death divides the *Lovely Loving Pair!*
    J. STERLING (310-340)

SYNESIUS

*Synesius (370-412 A.D.), whose family claimed descent from
the Heraclids and who himself became Bishop of Cyrene, is
the best example of the fusion of the Hellenic and Christian
strains in poetry, and hence a proper figure with which to
close one age and begin another. His ninth hymn, on the
Descent into Hell, like his others puts Christian doctrine in
Greek poetic form.*

Beloved, glorious, blest,   **375**
Seed of the Virgin of Solyma,
Thy praise I sing,
Who didst from the garden of Thy Father drive
The fount of guile,
The mighty serpent of earth,
Which gave the offspring of that earliest birth
The fruit abjured, the nurse that made death thrive.

Thine, O Father, diademed and glorious,
Child of the Virgin of Solyma,
Thy praise I sing.

Thou didst descend even unto the earth,
And, clad in semblance mortal,
Didst dwell with us,
The creatures of a day,
A little while;
Thou didst descend below the lowest portal
Of Tartarus,
Where Death
The myriad hosts of spirits shepherdeth.

Upon that day
Ancient Hades, child of Eld,
Shuddered when he beheld
Thy face, and Cerberus,
The folk-devouring hound,
From Hell's threshold slunk away.

Then didst Thou from their pain
Wherein they bound
So long had lain
The souls of all Thy holy ones redeeming,
Lead them in mystic revel without stain,
Dancing to their Father's house again.

Thee, O Father, diademed and glorious,
Child of the Virgin of Solyma.
Thee I sing.

O Lord,
When Thou ascendedst gleaming,
Victorious from Thy wars,
Before Thee trembled
All the hosts assembled
In tribes innumerous
Of Daemons which beneath the air be ever flying,
And Thy wonder passed through the stainless stars
In their dance undying.

Then Aether
With laughter rang—
Harmonia's sage sire—
And to his seven-stringed lyre
The song of triumph for Thy victory sang.
And Phosphor smiled,
Day's harbinger,
And golden Vesper,
Cytherea's starry child.
But Selene, filling

Her horned splendor from the stream of fire,
Led forth the heavenly quire
Which are her starry flocks.

Then the giant Sun outspread
Beneath Thy footsteps, far beyond all telling,
The tresses of his head,
In far-flung locks
Of radiant flame—
He knew the Son of God, the Master Artist Mind,
The day-spring whence his own fire came.

Then striding
With lightest tread
O'er the blue vaulting of the heavenly dome,
Thou camest to Thy home—
The spheres of Mind
Stainless abiding,
Whence pours
Of Good the very fount and source.
There didst Thou stand,
Round Thee on either hand
The heaven of heavens that can no utterance find.
There Time is not, whose feet do weary never,
Who sweeps the sons of men down his deep river;
Nor are the shameless spirits of mischief there,
Which make their lair
In the murky caves
'Neath Matter's heavy plunging waves.

But there Eternity,
Eld's ageless child,
Youth and age in unity,
Unresting, unhasting,
Steward divine,
Poureth the wine
In the mansion everlasting.
            L. P. CHAMBERLAYNE

INDEX
of Authors and Translators

Numbers refer to pages, not selections. Dates of Greek authors are frequently only approximations; Roman numerals indicate centuries. In the case of translators, single dates indicate the year of publication; double dates the life span. Where no date is given data may be found in the list of acknowledgements in the Preface.

Adam, James (1891), 288-90
Addaeus (320 B.C.), 301
Addison, Joseph (1735), 189
Aeschylus (525-456 B.C.), 216-225
Aesop (400 A.D.), 402
Agathias (VI A.D.), 411-12
Alcaeus (b. 620 B.C.), 186-88
Alcaeus of Messene (200 B.C.), 365
Alcman (VII B.C.), 195-97
Alexandrian Erotic Fragment (II B.C.), 363-4
Alexis (372-270 B.C.), 279
Allinson, F. G., 280-82
Ammianus (II A.D.), 388
Anacreon (b. 570 B.C.), 188-189
Anacreontics, 189-95
Anaxandrides (IV B.C.), 279
Anonymous, 161-4, *Fraser's Magazine*, July 1835; 302, *Spectator*, 1712; 334-7, Oxford, 1588; 363-4, 1928
Antipater of Sidon (130 B.C.), 367-9

Antipater of Thessalonica (I B.C.), 383
Antiphanes (388-311 B.C.), 277-8
Antiphilus (I A.D.), 386
Anyte (300 B.C.), 301-302
Apollonius of Rhodes (b. 295 B.C.), 310-24
Appleton, W. H. (1814-99), 185-6
Aratus (315-240 B.C.), 290-92
Archias (60 B.C.), 378
Archilochus (late VIII B.C.), 175-8
Arion (VII B.C.), 197
Aristophanes (450-385 B.C.), 259-70
Aristotle (384-322 B.C.), 274
Arnold, Edwin (1832-1904), 109, 185, 195, 197-8, 413-14, 415, 416
Asclepiades (270 B.C.), 303-304
Automedon (I B.C.), 380

Babrius (II A.D.), 388-9
Bacchylides (V B.C.), 208-12

422

Batrachomyomachia (VI B.C.), 145

Beaumont, John (1582-1627), 305-306

Bevan, Edwyn, 308

Bion (100 B.C.), 369-72

Blackie, J. S. (1809-95), 218-21, 222-3

Bland, Robert (1806), 368-9, 400

Bowles, William L. (1762-1850), 199

Brown, Norman O., 130-1, 134-5

Browning, Elizabeth Barrett (1806-61), 221-2, 369-72

Browning, Robert (1812-89), 236-8, 243-6

Bryant, William Cullen (1794-1878), 17-20, 34, 46, 50-1, 53, 62-4, 68-71, 96-105

Bulwer-Lytton, Edward (1831-1891), 225, 228-9

Butler, Samuel (1835-1902), 9

Callimachus (305-240 B.C.), 292-301

Callinus (VII B.C.), 160

Callistratus (?), 214

Calverley, C. S. (1831-84), 325-334

Campbell, Thomas (1774-1844), 214

Chamberlayne, Lewis P., 83-5, 311-14, 357-63, 374, 401, 414, 415, 419-21

Chamberlin, H. H., 352-57

Chapman, George (1559-1634), 71-4

Clark, Frank L., 15-17

Cleanthes (331-232 B.C.), 288-290

Coleridge, Henry N. (1800-1834), 160-1

Collins, W. L. (1817-1887), 267

Colluthus (V A.D.), 406-407

Congreve, William (1670-1729), 135-44

Conington, John (1825-69), 214

Cope, A. D. (1911), 268-9

Cory, William (1823-1892), 300

Cotterill, H. B., 62, 74-83, 90-3

Couch, H. N., 11, 233-4, 373

Cowley, Abraham (1618-77), 194, 195

Cowper, William (1731-1800), 26, 51-2, 60-1, 87-8, 385, 386, 410

Crinagoras (25 B.C.), 379-80

Cromer, Earl of (1903), 301-2, 307, 309, 368, 378, 379, 383, 388, 402, 410

Davies, James (1820-83), 388-9

Davies, J. F. (1885), 224-5

Delphian Oracle (early V), 212-213

Derby, Edward Earl of (1799-1869), 7, 27-33, 35, 41, 47, 53-6, 59-60

Dionysius (200 B.C.), 366

Dioscorides (200 B.C.), 366-7

Diphilus (late IV B.C.), 285

Dole, N. H. (1897), 165, 166-7, 175-6

Douglas, Norman (1868-1952), 379, 381, 382, 384, 386, 387, 388

Dryden, John (1631-1700), 8, 411-12

Edmonds, J. M., 196-7

Elton, C. A. (1812), 110-116, 165, 177, 185, 277

Empedocles (493-433 B.C.), 158-60

Epicharmus (V B.C.), 271

Epitaph for Chaeroneia (336 B.C.), 275

Erinna (330 B.C.), 277

Ernle, George, 3-7, 22-26, 42-45

Eupolis (late V B.C.), 270

Euripides (485-406 B.C.), 236-258

Evenus (?), 384

Fawkes, Francis (1780), 314, 324

Frere, John Hookham (1769-1843), 169-75, 259-61, 264-7

Garrett, F. E. (1865-1907), 273

Gladstone, Ralph, 273, 386

Glyco (400 A.D.), 402

Grene, David, 239-41

Grube, G. M. A., 247, 255

Grundy, G. B., 199

Hadas, Moses, 106-7, 216-17, 234-5, 257-8, 272

Hadas, Moses, and McLean, J. H., 238-9, 241, 246-7

Hardinge, W. M. (1878), 300, 412

Hay, William (1695-1755), 176, 387

Headlam, Walter (1866-1908), 375-6

Hedylus (270 B.C.), 307

Herodas (III B.C.), 343-51

Herrick, Robert (1591-1674), 193-4, 374

Hesiod (IX B.C.), 106-116

Hole, Richard (1746-1803), 116-128

Homer (X B.C.), *Iliad*, 3-61; *Odyssey*, 62-105

Homeric Hymns (VII-VI B.C.), 116-145

Hunt, Leigh (1784-1859), 66, 337-43

Hybrias (?), 214

Ibycus (VI B.C.), 198

Jebb, R. C. (1841-1905), 232-3, 259

Joannes Barbocollas (VI A.D.), 409

Jones, John, (1722), 389-93

Kahn, Charles H., 155-8, 271, 278

Kendall, Timothe (1577), 387-8

Kennedy, C. R. (1841), 275

Kennedy, W. R., 269-70

Lang, Andrew (1892), 368, 412

Lang, Andrew; Leaf, Walter; and Myers, Ernest (1883), 21, 37-39, 48

Lattimore, Richmond, 3, 8, 56-9, 178-83, 184, 186-7, 188, 201-208

Lawton, W. C. (1895 and 1923), 107-9, 309, 366, 380, 408, 409

Leaf, Walter, 272, 302, 308, 365-366, 375

Leonard, W. E., 158-60

Leonidas of Tarentum (280 B.C.), 307-308

Lucian (120-190 A.D.), 387-8

Lucilius (60 A.D.), 385-6

Lycophron (b. 320 B.C.), 285-288

Macedonius Consul (VI A.D.), 409

MacGregor, R. G. (1864), 300, 365

Macnaghten, Hugh (1924), 225

Marcus Argentarius (I B.C.), 382-3

Meen, H. (1780), 406-407

Meleager (75 B.C.), 373-76

Menander (324-290 B.C.), 280-284

Merivale, Charles (1833), 273-4

Merivale, J. H. (1779-1844), 177, 178, 187, 198, 200, 365

Merrick, James (1739), 405-406

Metagenes (410 B.C.), 270

Metrodorus (270 B.C.), 306

Mimnermus (VII B.C.), 164-5

Moero (300 B.C.), 309

Moore, Thomas (1779-1852), 185, 188, 192-3, 367

Morris, William (1834-96), 65-66, 88-90

Moschus (II B.C.), 352-63

Musaeus (VI A.D.), 412-19

Neaves, Lord (1800-76), 300, 304, 387

Nonnos (V A.D.), 403-404

Nossis (290 B.C.), 309

Oppian (II A.D.), 389-93

Ostwald, Martin, 167-8

Paley, F. A. (1815-88), 258, 270-271, 278-80, 283-5

Palladas (400 A.D.), 400-402

Palmer, G. H. (1842-1933), 93-94

Parmenides (early V B.C.), 155-8

Parnell, Thomas (1717), 145-53

Parrhasius (400 B.C.), 272

Paton, W. R. (1857-1921), 305

Paul the Silentiary (VI A.D.), 410-11

Perry, Lilla C. (1891), 402, 411

Philemon (361-262 B.C.), 284

Philip of Thessalonica (40 A.D.), 384-5

Philodemus (60 B.C.), 376-8

Pindar (518-438 B.C.), 201-208

Plato (429-337 B.C.), 273-4

Plumptre, E. H. (1865), 226-8

Pope, Alexander (1715), 13, 36, 40, 49, 67, 94-6

Posidippus (270 B.C.), 305-306

Poste, E. (1823-1902), 290-92

Pott, J. A., 305, 307, 401

Potter, Robert (1777), 217

Praxilla (450 B.C.), 272

Prior, Matthew (1664-1721), 292-5

Processional for Demetrius Poliorcetes (290 B.C.), 276

Quintus of Smyrna (IV A.D.), 393-400

Rawlinson, George (1812-1902), 212-13

Rogers, B. B. (1828-1919), 263-4

Rossetti, D. G. (1779-1852), 184-5

Rouse, W. H. D., 403-404

Royston, Lord (1832), 285-88

Rufinus (V A.D.), 408

Sappho (b. 612 B.C.), 182-6

Semonides (VII B.C.), 178-82

Shakespeare, William (1564-1616), 300

Sharpley, Hugo, 343-51

Shelley, Percy Bysshe (1792-1822), 128-30, 131-34, 144-5, 256-7, 273

Shorey, Paul (1857-1934), 175

Simmias (300 B.C.), 302

Simonides (556-468 B.C.), 199-201

Smith, Goldwin (1823-1910), 373

Solon (640-560 B.C.), 166-8

Sophocles (496-406 B.C.), 225-236

Spoerl, Elsie, 377, 382, 383, 408, 410-11

Stanley, Thomas (1651), 189-92

Stebbing, William, 366, 409

Stedman, Edmund C. (1833-1908), 85-7

Sterling, John (1728), 199, 416-419

Swallow Song (?), 215

Symonds, John Addington (1807-71 and 1840-93), 168, 183, 185, 200, 212, 215, 235-236, 242-3, 251-4, 274, 276-7, 283, 384-5

Synesius (370-412 A.D.), 419-21

Tennyson, Alfred (1809-1892), 21, 45-6

Theocritus (early III B.C.), 325-43

Theognis (540 B.C.), 168-75

Thucydides (471-401 B.C.), 258

Timotheus (450-360 B.C.), 258

Tryphiodorus (V A.D.), 405-406

Tyrtaeus (VII B.C.), 161-4

Tytler, H. W. (1752-1808), 295-300, 301

Verrall, A. W. (1851-1912), 230-32, 250-51

Wallace, William and Mary, 303-304

Walsh, Benjamin D. (1837), 262-3

Way, Arthur S., 208-12, 310-11, 393-400

Wilde, Oscar (1854-1900), 261-262

Wolff, Emily Ann, 154-5

Wordsworth, J. C., 223, 248-50, 254, 315-23

Wright, F. A., 307, 376-7, 378, 380, 381, 382-3, 400, 401-402, 411

Xenophanes (VI B.C.), 154-5